ENGINEERING PROBLEM SOLVING WITH C++

An Object Based Approach

Jeanine A. Ingber
Department of Computer Science
University of New Mexico

Delores M. Etter
U.S. Naval Academy

An Alan R. Apt Book

Prentice
Hall

Pearson Education, Inc.

Library of Congress Cataloging-in-Publication Data

CIP data on file

Vice President and Editorial Director, ECS: Marcia Horton
Publisher: Alan R. Apt
Associate Editor: Toni D. Holm
Editorial Assistant: Patrick Lindner
Vice President and Director of Production and Manufacturing, ESM: David W. Riccardi
Executive Managing Editor: Vince O'Brien
Assistant Managing Editor: Camille Trentacoste
Production Editor: Lakshmi Balasubramanian
Creative Director: Carole Anson
Art Director: Heather Scott
Art Editor: Xiaohong Zhu
Manufacturing Manager: Trudy Pisciotti
Manufacturing Buyer: Lisa McDowell
Marketing Manager: Pamela Shaffer
Marketing Assistant: Barrie Reinhold

©2003 Pearson Education, Inc.
Pearson Education, Inc.
Upper Saddle River, NJ 07458

All rights reserved. No part of this book may be reproduced, in any form
or by any other means, without permission in writing from the publisher.

The author and publisher of this book have used their best efforts in preparing this book. These efforts include
the development, research, and testing of the theories and programs to determine their effectiveness. The
author and publisher make no warranty of any kind, expressed or implied, with regard to these programs or the
documentation contained in this book. The author and publisher shall not be liable in any event for incidental
or consequential damages in connection with, or arising out of, the furnishing, performance, or use of these
programs.

The following chapter openers are courtesy of:
Chapter 2: National Aeronautics and Space Administration
Chapter 3: National Center for Atmospheric Research/University Corporation for Atmospheric Research,
National Science Foundation
Chapter 4: Texas Instruments Inc.
Chapter 5: Chevron Corporation
Chapter 6: United Airlines
Chapter 8: Professor M. Ingber, University of New Mexico
Chapter 9: Rainbow
Chapter 10: Professor George Luger

Printed in the United States of America

10 9 8 7 6 5 4 3 2 1

ISBN 0-13-091266-2

Pearson Education Ltd., London
Pearson Education Australia Pty. Ltd., Sydney
Pearson Education Singapore, Pte. Ltd.
Pearson Education North Asia Ltd., Hong Kong
Pearson Education Canada, Inc., Toronto
Pearson Educacìon de Mexico, S.A. de C.V.
Pearson Education—Japan, Tokyo
Pearson Education Malaysia, Pte. Ltd.
Pearson Education, Inc., Upper Saddle River, New Jersey

Preface

Object-based programming is used in many fields of engineering and science and is likely to be seen in the workplace. C++ is an object-based programming language derived from the C programming language, which makes it a good choice for an introduction to computing course for engineers and scientists. Using C++, object-based design and programming can be introduced early while focusing on the basic control structures, data structures, and functions necessary for scientific programming. The features of the C programming language that make it attractive for system-level operations are supported by C++, making the latter one of the most powerful and versatile programming languages available. This text was written to introduce engineering problem solving with an object-based programming approach. Our objectives are the following:

- to develop a consistent **methodology for solving engineering problems,**

- to present the **object-based features of C++** while focusing on the **fundamentals of programming,**

- to illustrate the problem-solving process with C++ through a variety of **engineering examples and applications,**

- to provide an easy-to-understand, **integrated introduction to function templates and classes defind in the Standard C++ Library.**

To accomplish these objectives, Chapter 1 presents a **five-step process** that is used consistently in the rest of the text for solving engineering problems. Chapter 2 introduces the use of **predefined objects and member functions** in the discussion of **data types** and **standard input and output.** Chapters 3–5 present the fundamental capabilities of C++ for solving engineering problems, **including control structures, data files, and functions.** Chapters 6 and 7 present **arrays** and introduce the reader to **function templates** and the **vector class.** Chapter 8 is an introduction to **programmer-defined classes.** Chapter 9 introduces the use of **pointers, dynamic memory allocation, and classes defined in the Standard C++ library to implement dynamic data structures.** Chapter 10 provides a more in-depth look at classes, including **overloading operators, inheritance, and virtual functions.** Throughout all these chapters, we present a large number of examples from many different engineering, science, and computer science disciplines. The solutions to these examples are developed using the five-step process and Standard C++.

Prerequisites

No prior experience with the computer is assumed. The mathematical prerequisites are **college algebra and trigonometry.** Of course, the initial material can be covered much faster if the student has used other computer languages or software tools.

In loving memory of our fathers:

Robert William Huckell,
a generous and thoughtful man
—Jeanine

Murvin Lee Van Camp,
a loving and supportive father
—Delores

Course Structure

The material in these chapters was selected to provide the basis for a one-term course in engineering and scientific computing. These chapters contain the essential topics of mathematical computations, character data, control structures, functions, arrays, classes, and pointers. Students with background in another computer language should be able to complete this material in one semester. A minimal course that provides only an introduction to C++ can be designed using the nonoptional sections of the text. (Optional sections are indicated in the Contents with an *.) Three ways to use the text, along with the recommended chapter sections, are

- **Introduction to C++** Many freshman introductory courses introduce the student to several computer tools in addition to an introduction to a language. For these courses, we recommend covering the nonoptional sections of Chapters 1–7. This material introduces students to the fundamental capabilities of C++, and they will be able to write substantial programs using mathematical computations, character data, control structures, functions, and arrays.

- **Problem Solving with C++** In a semester course devoted specifically to teaching students to master the C++ language, we recommend covering all nonoptional sections of Chapters 1–10. This material covers all the fundamental concepts of the C++ language, including mathematical computations, character data, control structures, functions, arrays, classes, and pointers.

- **Problem Solving with C++ and Numerical Techniques** Upper-level students or students who are already familiar with other high-level languages will be able to cover the material in this text very quickly. In addition, they will be able to apply the numerical technique material to their other courses. Therefore, we recommend that these students cover all sections of Chapters 1–10, including the optional material.

The chapters in this text were designed to give the instructor flexibility in the ordering of topics, especially regarding the decision of when to cover classes: before or after arrays. The introductory chapter on classes does not depend on the chapters on arrays, and the chapters on arrays do not depend on the introductory chapter on classes. The dependency chart on the next page illustrates the dependency of chapters.

Problem-Solving Methodology

The **emphasis on engineering and scientific problem solving** is an integral part of the text. Chapter 1 introduces a five-step process for solving engineering problems using the computer:

1. State the problem clearly.

2. Describe the input and output information, and determine required data types.

3. Work a simple example by hand.

4. Develop an algorithm and convert it to a computer program.

5. Test the solution with a variety of data.

Dependency Chart

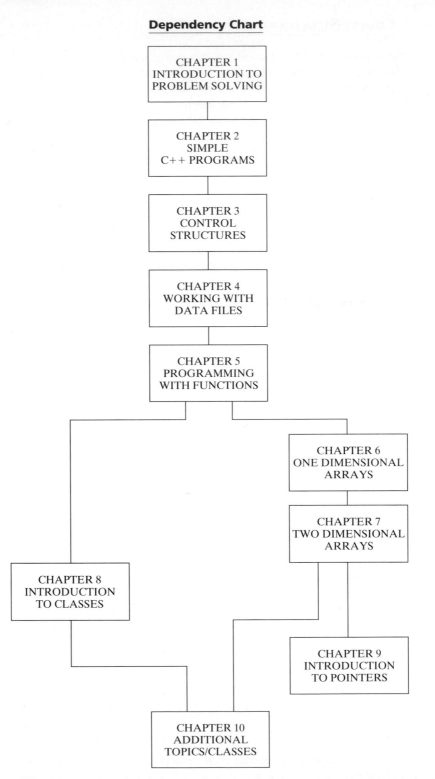

To reinforce the development of problem-solving skills, each of these five steps is clearly identified each time that a complete engineering problem is solved. In addition, **top-down design** and **stepwise refinement** are presented with the use of **decomposition outlines, pseudocode,** and **flowcharts.**

Engineering and Scientific Applications

Throughout the text, emphasis is placed on incorporating real-world engineering and scientific examples and problems. This emphasis is centered around a theme of grand challenges, which include

- prediction of weather, climate, and global change
- computerized speech understanding
- mapping of the human genome
- improvements in vehicle performance
- enhanced oil and gas recovery
- simulation

Each chapter begins with a photograph and a discussion of some aspect of one of these grand challenges that provides a glimpse of some of the exciting and interesting areas in which engineers might work. Later in the chapter, we solve a problem that not only relates to the introductory problem, but also has applications in other problem solutions. The grand challenges are also referenced in many of the other examples and problems.

Standard C++

The statements presented and all programs developed use C++ standards developed by the International Standards Organization and American National Standards Institute (ISO/ANSI) C++ Standards committee. ISO and ANSI together have published the first international standard for the C++ programming language. By using Standard C++, students learn to write **portable** code that can be transferred from one computer platform to another. Many of the standard capabilities of the C++ programming language are discussed in the text. Additional components of the C++ standard library are discussed in Appendix A.

Software Engineering Concepts

Engineers and scientists are expected to develop and implement user-friendly and **reusable** computer solutions. Learning software engineering techniques is therefore crucial to successfully developing these computer solutions. **Readability** and **documentation** are stressed in the development of programs. Additional topics that relate to software engineering issues are discussed throughout the text and include issues such as **software life cycle, portability, maintenance, modularity, recursion, abstraction, reusability, structured programming, validation,** and **verification.**

Four Types of Problems

Learning any new skill requires practice at a number of different levels of difficulty. We have developed four types of exercises that are used throughout the text to develop problem-solving skills. The first set of exercises is **Practice!** problems. These are short-answer questions that relate to the section of material just presented. Most sections are immediately followed by a set of **Practice!** problems so that students can determine if they are ready to continue to the next section. Complete solutions to all the **Practice!** problems are included at the end of the text.

The **Modify!** problems are designed to provide hands-on experiences with the programs developed in the **Problem-Solving Applied** sections. In these sections, we develop a complete C++ program using the five-step process. The **Modify!** problems ask students to run the program (which is available on our Instructor's Resource CD) with different sets of data to test their understanding of how the program works and of the relationships among the engineering variables. These exercises also ask the students to make simple modifications to the program and then run the program to test their changes.

Most chapters end with a set of **Exam Practice!** problems, and every chapter includes a set of **Programming Problems.** The **Exam Practice!** problems are short-answer questions that relate to the material covered in the chapter. These problems help students determine how well they understand the features of C++ presented in the chapter. The **Programming Problems** are new problems that relate to a variety of engineering applications, and the level of difficulty ranges from very straightforward to longer project assignments. Each programming problem requires that the student develop a complete C++ program or function. Engineering data sets for many of the problems are included on our Instructor's Resource CD to use in testing. Solutions to all of the Exam Practice! and some of the **Programming Problems** are included at the end of the text.

Study and Programming Aids

Margin notes are used to help the reader not only identify the important concepts, but also easily locate specific topics. In addition, margin notes are used to identify programming style guidelines and debugging information. **Style guidelines** show students how to write C++ programs that incorporate good software discipline; **debugging** sections help students recognize common errors so that they can avoid them. The programming style notes are indicated with the margin note **Style,** and the debugging notes are indicated with a **bug icon.** Object oriented features of C++ are indicated with an OOP icon to help student recognize these features early in the text. Each Chapter Summary contains a **summary of the style notes** and **debugging notes,** plus a list of the **Key Terms** from the chapter and a **C++ Statement Reference** of the new statements, to make the book easy to use as a reference.

Optional Numerical Techniques

Numerical techniques that are commonly used in solving engineering problems are also discussed in optional sections in the chapters, and include **interpolation, linear modeling (regression), root finding, numerical integration,** and the **solution to simultaneous equations.** The concept of a **matrix** is also introduced and then illustrated using a number of exam-

ples. All of these topics are presented assuming only a trigonometry and college algebra background.

Appendices

To further enhance reference use, the appendices include a number of important topics. Appendix A contains a discussion components in the C++ standard library. Appendix B presents the ASCII character codes. Appendix D contains a list of references used throughout the text. MATLAB Appendix also included as Appendix C.

Instructor's Resource CD

An **Instructor's Resource CD** is available for instructors who adopt this text. The CD contains all of the **example programs used in the text, complete solutions to most of the Programming Problems found at the end of each chapter,** as well as **data files to use with application problems** and a **complete set of PowerPoint slides** to assist the instructor in preparing lecture notes.

Acknowledgments

We would like to acknowledge the publishing team at Prentice Hall, including Patrick Lindner, Jake Warde, Lakshmi Balasubramanian, Heather Scott, and Xiaohong Zhu; special thanks go to Toni Holm and Alan Apt for their continued support and understanding. We would like to thank our reviewers, Kris Kempa, Boston College; William Retert, University of Wisconsin–Milwaukee; Phillip Barry, University of Minnesota; W. Douglas Maurer, George Washington University; Bahram Zartoshty, California State at Northridge; Marshall Bowen, Western Illinois; Anand Cousins, Seattle University; and Norbert Oppenheim, City College of New York, for their detailed comments and valuable insights. We also thank Prof. George Luger for contributing to the artwork. Jeanine Ingber thanks her family—Hillary, Allison, and Marc—for their extraordinary patience and support, especially Hillary, who was the motivating force behind this text. Delores Etter gratefully acknowledges the support from her husband Richard, an aerospace/mechanical engineer, who helped develop some of the engineering application problems and who enthusiastically encouraged the completion of this text.

Jeanine Ingber
Department of Computer Science
University of New Mexico

Delores Etter
U.S. Naval Academy

Contents

3 Control Structures   **79**

GRAND CHALLENGE: Global Change

4 Working with Data Files   **120**

GRAND CHALLENGE: Weather Prediction

5 Modular Programming with Functions   159

GRAND CHALLENGE: Enhanced Oil and Gas Recovery

8   An Introduction to Classes   325

GRAND CHALLENGE: Simulation Design of Advanced Composite Materials

9   An Introduction to Pointers   359

GRAND CHALLENGE: Oil and Gas Exploration

ENGINEERING PROBLEM SOLVING WITH C++

An Object Based Approach

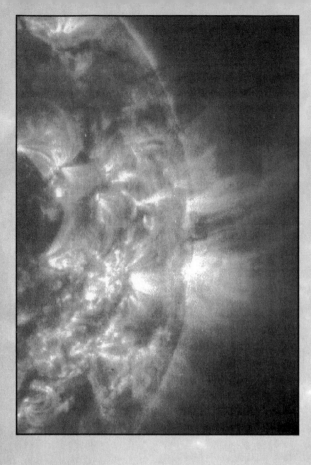

CHAPTER 1

An Introduction to Engineering Problem Solving

Chapter Outline

Objectives

1.1 Grand Challenges
1.2 Computing Systems
1.3 An Engineering Problem-Solving Methodology

Summary, Key Terms, Problems

OBJECTIVES Although most of this text is focused on teaching you to use the C++ language, we begin by describing some of the recent outstanding engineering achievements, and then we introduce a group of grand challenges—problems yet to be solved that will require technological breakthroughs in both engineering and science. One of the grand challenges includes the prediction of weather, which we used in the chapter-opening discussion. We also discuss some of the specific skills and nontechnical capabilities that are needed by engineers, such as communication skills, the ability to work in interdisciplinary teams, and the need for a societal responsibility in the development of problem solutions. Because most solutions to engineering problems use computers, we next describe computer systems with a discussion of both computer hardware and computer software and a discussion of the importance of learning the terminology associated with computer systems. Solving engineering problems effectively with the computer also requires a design plan or procedure, and in this chapter we define a problem-solving methodology with five steps for describing a problem and then developing a solution. Finally, after discussing computing and the problem-solving methodology, we return to the problem of weather prediction and discuss some of the different types of weather data that are currently being collected. These data are critical for developing the understanding and intuition needed to create a mathematical model to predict weather. The data are also important because they can be used to test hypothetical models as they are developed. Data analysis helps engineers and scientists better understand complex physical phenomena so that they can then apply that knowledge to developing solutions to new problems.

3

1.1   Grand Challenges

Engineers solve real-world problems using scientific principles from disciplines that include computer science, mathematics, physics, biology, and chemistry. It is this variety of subjects, as well as the challenge of real problems, that makes engineering so interesting and so rewarding. In this section, we present some of the outstanding engineering achievements of recent years, followed by a discussion of some of the important engineering challenges we face as we go into the next century. Finally, we consider some of the nontechnical skills and capabilities needed by the engineers of the 21st century.

Recent Engineering Achievements

Since the development of the computer in the late 1950s, a number of very significant engineering achievements[1,2][1] have occurred. In 1989, the National Academy of Engineering selected the **10 engineering achievements** that it considered to be the most important accomplishments during the previous 25 years. These achievements illustrate the multidisciplinary nature of engineering, and demonstrate how engineering has improved our lives and expanded the possibilities for the future while providing a wide variety of interesting and challenging careers. We now briefly discuss these 10 achievements; a set of suggested readings at the end of the chapter includes more detailed information on these topics.

10 engineering achievements

The development of the **microprocessor,** a tiny computer smaller than a postage stamp, is one of the top engineering achievements of the last 25 years. Microprocessors are used in electronic equipment, household appliances, toys, and games, as well as in automobiles, aircraft, and space shuttles, because they provide powerful yet inexpensive computing capabilities. Microprocessors also provide the computing power inside calculators and personal computers.

moon landing

Several of the top 10 achievements relate to the exploration of space. The **moon landing** was probably the most complex and ambitious engineering project ever attempted. Major breakthroughs were required in the design of the Apollo spacecraft, the lunar lander, and the three-stage Saturn V rocket. Even the design of the spacesuit was a major engineering project that resulted in a system that included a three-piece suit and backpack, which together weighed 190 pounds. The computer played a key role not only in the designs of the various systems, but it also played a critical role in the communications required during an individual moon flight; a single flight required the coordination of over 450 people in the launch control center and over 7,000 others on nine ships, in 54 aircraft, and at stations located around the earth.

application satellites

The space program also provided much of the impetus for the development of **application satellites** that are used to provide weather information, relay communication signals, map uncharted terrain, and provide environmental updates on the composition of the atmosphere. The global positioning system (GPS) is a constellation of 24 satellites that broadcasts position, velocity, and time information worldwide. GPS receivers measure the time it takes for signals to travel from the GPS satellite to the receiver. Using information received from 4 satellites, a microprocessor in the receiver can then determine very precise measurements of the receiver's location; the accuracy varies from a few meters to centimeters, depending on the computation techniques used.

---

[1]The references in the text material are summarized in Appendix D.

computer-aided
design and
manufacturing

Another of the top engineering achievements recognizes the contributions of **computer-aided design and manufacturing** (CAD/CAM). CAD/CAM has generated a new industrial revolution by increasing the speed and efficiency of many types of manufacturing processes. CAD allows the design to be done using the computer, which then produces the final schematics, parts lists, and computer simulation results. CAM uses design results to control machinery or industrial robots to manufacture, assemble, and move components.

The origins of the **jumbo jet** came from the U.S. Air Force C-5A cargo plane that began operational flights in 1969. Much of the success of the jumbo jets can be attributed to the high bypass fanjet that allows them to fly farther with less fuel and with less noise than previous jet engines. The core of the engine operates like a pure turbojet, in which compressor blades pull air into the engine's combustion chamber. The hot expanding gas thrusts the engine forward and at the same time spins a turbine that in turn drives the compressor and the large fan on the front of the engine. The spinning fan provides the bulk of the engine's thrust.

advanced
composite materials

The aircraft industry was also the first industry to develop and use **advanced composite materials** that consist of materials that can be bonded together in such a way that one material reinforces the fibers of the other material. Advanced composite materials were developed to provide lighter, stronger, and more temperature-resistant materials for aircraft and spacecraft. New markets for composites now exist in sporting goods. For example, downhill snow skis use layers of woven Kevlar fibers to increase their strength and reduce weight, and golf club shafts of graphite/epoxy are stronger and lighter than the steel in conventional shafts. Composite materials are also used in the design of prosthetics for artificial limbs.

computerized axial
tomography

The areas of medicine, bioengineering, and computer science were teamed for the development of the **computerized axial tomography** (CAT) scanner machine. This instrument can generate three-dimensional images or two-dimensional slices of an object using X-rays that are generated from different angles around the object. Each X ray measures a density from its angle, and very complicated computer algorithms combine the information from all the X-rays to reconstruct a clear image of the inside of the object. CAT scans are routinely used to identify tumors, blood clots, and brain abnormalities. The U.S. Army is developing a rugged, lightweight CAT scanner that can be transported to medical stations in combat zones.

genetic engineering

The work of geneticists and engineers has resulted in many new products as a result of **genetic engineering.** These products range from insulin to growth hormones to infection-resistant vegetables. A genetically engineered product is produced by splicing a gene that produces a valuable substance from one organism into another organism that will multiply itself and the foreign gene along with it. The first commercial genetically engineered product was human insulin, which appeared under the trade name Humulin. Current work is investigating the use of genetically altered microbes to clean up toxic waste and to degrade pesticides.

Lasers are light waves that have the same frequency and travel in a narrow beam that can be directed and focused. CO_2 lasers are used to drill holes in materials that range from ceramics to composite materials. Lasers are also used in medical procedures to weld detached retinas, seal leaky blood vessels, vaporize brain tumors, and perform delicate inner-ear surgery. Three-dimensional pictures called holograms are also generated with lasers.

Fiber-optic communications use **optical fiber,** a transparent glass thread that is thinner than a human hair. This optical fiber can carry more information than either radio waves or electric waves in copper telephone wires, and it does not produce electromagnetic waves that can cause interference on communication lines. Transoceanic fiber-optic cables provide communication channels between continents. Fiber optics is also used in medical instrumentation to allow surgeons to thread light into the human body for examination and laser surgery.

Grand Challenges for the Future

Although the recent achievements of engineers have produced dramatic results, there are still many important problems to be solved. In this section, we present a group of **grand challenges**—fundamental problems in science and engineering with broad potential impact. The grand challenges were identified by the Office of Science and Technology Policy in Washington, DC, as part of a research and development strategy [3] for high-performance computing. The paragraphs that follow briefly present a few of these grand challenges and outline the types of benefits that will come with their solutions. Just as the computer played an important part in the top 10 engineering achievements of the last 25 years, the computer will play an even greater role in solving problems related to these grand challenges.

prediction of
weather

The **prediction of weather, climate, and global change** requires that we understand the coupled atmosphere and ocean biosphere system. This includes understanding CO_2 dynamics in the atmosphere and ocean, ozone depletion, and climatological changes due to the releases of chemicals or energy. This complex interaction also includes solar interactions. A major eruption from a solar storm near a "coronal hole" (a venting point for the solar wind) can eject vast amounts of hot gases from the sun's surface toward the earth's surface at speeds over a million miles per hour. This ejection of hot gases bombards the earth with X rays, and can interfere with communication and cause power fluctuations in power lines. Learning to predict changes in weather, climate, and global change involves collecting large amounts of data for study and developing new mathematical models that can represent the interdependency of many variables. We will analyze the weather patterns at Denver International Airport over a one-year period in later chapters. We will also develop a model for predicting ozone-mixing ratios in the middle atmosphere using satellite data, and we analyze the altitude and velocity information for a helium-filled weather balloon.

Computerized
speech
understanding

Computerized speech understanding could revolutionize our communication systems, but many problems are involved. Teaching a computer to understand words from a small vocabulary spoken by a single person is currently possible. However, to develop systems that are speaker-independent and that understand words from large vocabularies and from different languages is very difficult. Subtle changes in one's voice, such as those caused by a cold or stress, can affect the performance of speech-recognition systems. Even assuming that the computer can recognize the words, we find that it is not simple to determine their meaning. Many words are context-dependent and thus cannot be analyzed separately. Intonation such as raising one's voice can change a statement into a question. Although there are still many difficult problems left to address in automatic speech recognition and understanding, exciting applications are everywhere. Imagine a telephone system that determines the languages being spoken and translates the speech signals so that each person hears the conversation in his or her native language. We will analyze actual speech data to demonstrate some of the techniques used in word recognition.

Human Genome
Project

The goal of the **Human Genome Project** is to locate, identify, and determine the function of each of the 50,000 to 100,000 genes that are contained in human DNA (deoxyribonucleic acid), which is the genetic material found in cells. At a historic White House event on June 26, 2000, the Human Genome Project and Celera Genomics Corporation announced that they have both completed an initial sequencing of the human genome. The sequence represents only the first step in the full decoding of the genome, because most of the individual genes and their specific functions must still be deciphered and understood. The deciphering of the human genetic code will lead to many technical advances, including the ability to detect most, if not all, of the over 4,000 known human genetic diseases such as sickle-cell anemia and cystic fibrosis.

However, deciphering the code is complicated by the nature of genetic information. Each gene is a double-helix strand composed of base pairs (adenine bonded with thymine or cytosine bonded with guanine) arranged in a steplike manner with phosphate groups along the side. These base pairs can occur in any sequential order, and represent the hereditary information in the gene. The number of base pairs in human DNA has been estimated to be around 3 billion. DNA directs the production of proteins for all metabolic needs, so the proteins produced by a cell may provide a key to the sequence of base pairs in the DNA. We will write programs to compute the molecular weights of amino acids, the building blocks of proteins, and to compute the molecular weights of general molecular formulas.

Exploration of space has resulted in many exciting events in the past 5 years. On December 7, 1995, the Galileo spacecraft arrived at Jupiter. The Galileo Solid State Imaging Team began studying Jupiter and its moons and returning a steady steam of images and scientific data. In June of 2000, NASA announced that images from the Mars Global Surveyor, the satellite currently in orbit around Mars, suggest that liquid water has seeped onto the surface in the geologically recent past. Images have been made available to the public on an ongoing basis during these journeys in order to share with the public the excitement of exploration and new discoveries being made. We will use one of these images (an image of water channels on Mars), as input to a program that performs a simple digital image modification, called smoothing.

The design of **advanced composite materials** to provide lighter, stronger, and more temperature resistant materials is an example of an engineering challenge aided by the use of **Computer Simulation.** Encapsulating materials are now being engineered to insulate critical components in electronic assemblies from thermal and mechanical shock. It may be important for an encapsulating material to be tough against penetration on the outside while providing damping from vibration on the inside near the electronic assemble. Simulation of advanced composite materials allows for experimentation that may not be possible, due to size, speed, dangers to health and safety, or the economics of conducting the experiment. In simulations, mathematical models of physical phenomena are translated into computer software that specifies how calculations are performed. By repeatedly running the software using different data, an understanding of the phenomenon of interest emerges. We will write a program to simulate the design of a molten plastic material.

These grand challenges are only a few of the many interesting problems waiting to be solved by engineers and scientists. The solutions to problems of this magnitude will be the result of organized approaches that combine ideas and technologies. The use of computers and engineering problem-solving techniques will be a key element in the solution process.

Computer
Simulation

Changing Engineering Environment

The engineer of the 21st century will work in an environment that requires many nontechnical skills and capabilities [4]. Although the computer will be the primary computational tool of most engineers, the computer will also be useful in developing additional nontechnical abilities.

Engineers need strong **communication skills** for both oral presentations and for preparing written materials. Computers provide the software to assist in writing outlines and developing materials and graphs for presentations and technical reports. The problems at the end of this chapter include written and oral presentations to provide practice of these important skills.

The **design, process,** and **manufacture** path, which consists of taking an idea from a concept to a product, is one that engineers must understand firsthand. Every step of this process uses computers in areas from design analysis, machine control, robotic assembly, quality assurance, and market analysis. Several problems in the text relate to these topics. For example, in Chapter 4, programs are developed to simulate the reliability of systems that use multiple components.

Engineering teams of the future will be **interdisciplinary teams,** just as the engineering teams of today are interdisciplinary teams. The discussions of the top 10 engineering achievements of the last 25 years clearly show the interdisciplinary nature of those achievements. The teams that address, and will eventually solve, the grand challenges will also be interdisciplinary teams. Learning to interact in teams and to develop organizational structures for effective team communication is an important skill for engineers. A good way to begin developing engineering team skills is to organize teams to study for exams. Assign specific topics to members of the team with the assignment that they then review these topics for the team, with examples and potential test questions.

The engineers of the 21st century need to understand the **world marketplace.** This involves understanding different cultures, political systems, and business environments. Courses in these topics and in foreign languages help provide some understanding, but exchange programs with international experiences provide invaluable knowledge in developing a broader world understanding.

Engineers are problem solvers, but problems are not always formulated carefully. An engineer must be able to extract a problem statement from a problem discussion and then determine the important issues related to the problem. This involves not only developing order, but also learning to correlate chaos. It means not only **analyzing** the data, but also **synthesizing** a solution using many pieces of information. The integration of ideas can be as important as the decomposition of the problem into manageable pieces. A problem solution may involve not only abstract thinking about the problem, but also experimental learning from the problem environment.

Problem solutions must also be considered in their **societal context.** Environmental concerns should be addressed as alternative solutions to problems are being considered. Engineers must also be conscious of ethical issues in providing test results, quality verifications, and design limitations. It is unfortunate that tragedies like the Challenger explosion are sometimes the impetus for bringing issues of responsibility and accountability into the forefront. Ethical issues are never easy to resolve, and some of the exciting new technological achievements will bring more ethical issues with them. For example, the mapping of the genome will potentially provide ethical, legal, and social implications. Should the gene therapy that allows doctors to combat diabetes also be used to enhance athletic ability? Should prospective parents be given detailed information related to the physical and mental characteristics of an unborn child? What kind of privacy should an individual have over his or her genetic code? Very complicated issues arise with any technological advancement because the same capabilities that can do a great deal of good can often be applied in ways that are harmful.

The material presented in this text is only one step in building the knowledge, confidence, and understanding needed by engineers of the 21st century. However, we enthusiastically begin the process with an introduction to the range of computing systems available to engineers and an introduction to a problem-solving methodology that will be used throughout this text as we use C++ to solve engineering problems.

1.2 Computing Systems

Before we begin our presentation of object-based programming with C++, a brief discussion of computing will be useful, especially for those who have not had prior experience with computer   computers. A **computer** is a machine that is designed to perform operations that are specified program

with a set of instructions called a **program.** Computer **hardware** refers to the computer equipment, such as the keyboard, the mouse, the terminal, the hard disk, and the printer. Computer **software** refers to the programs that describe the steps that we want the computer to perform.

Computer Hardware

processor

All computers have a common internal organization, as shown in Figure 1.1. The **processor** is the part of the computer that controls all the other parts. It accepts input values (from a device such as a keyboard) and stores them in the **memory.** It also interprets the instructions in a computer program. If we want to add two values, the processor will retrieve the values from memory, and send them to the **arithmetic logic unit** (ALU). The ALU performs the

arithmetic logic unit

read-only memory random-access memory

addition and the processor then stores the result in memory. The **processing unit** and the ALU use internal memory composed of **read-only memory** (ROM) and **random-access memory** (RAM) in their processing; most data are stored in external memory, or secondary memory, using disk drives that are attached to the processor. The processor and ALU together are called the **central processing unit** (CPU). A **microprocessor** is a CPU that is contained in a single integrated-circuit (IC) chip, which contains millions of components in an area smaller than a postage stamp.

We usually instruct the computer to write the values that it has computed to a data file or to print the values on the terminal screen or on paper using a printer. The computer can also write information to diskettes, which store the information magnetically or to a writable **compact disk** (CD) which stores digital information using a process similar to the process used to stamp out LP records. A printed copy of information is called hard copy, and information stored on a disk or CD is called an **electronic copy** or a soft copy.

Computers come in all sizes, shapes, and forms. Personal computers (PCs) laptops and hand held computers range from inexpensive models that are commonly used in homes and offices, to very expensive models. A **workstation** is a computer that is also small enough to fit on a desktop, but in most cases is more powerful and also more expensive than a PC.

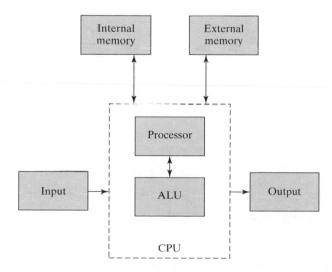

Figure 1.1 Internal organization of a computer.

Supercomputers are the fastest of all computers, and can process billions of instructions per second. As a result of their speed, supercomputers are capable of solving very complex problems that cannot be feasibly solved on other computers. High-speed computer **networks** allow computers to communicate with each other so that they can share resources and information.

Computer Software

Computer software contains the instructions or commands that we want the computer to perform. There are several important categories of software, which include operating systems, software tools, and language compilers. Figure 1.2 illustrates the interaction between these categories of software and the computer hardware. We now discuss each of these software categories in more detail.

Operating Systems.   Some software, such as the operating system, typically comes with the computer hardware when it is purchased. The operating system provides an interface between you (the user) and the hardware by providing a convenient and efficient environment in which you can select and execute the software on your system.

Operating systems also contain a group of programs called utilities that allow you to perform functions such as printing files, copying files, and listing the files that you have saved on file system. Whereas these utilities are common to most operating systems, the

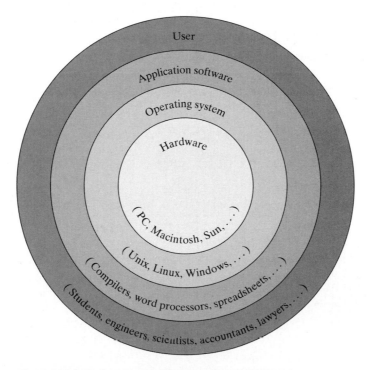

Figure 1.2 Software interface to the computer.

commands themselves vary from operating system to operating system. For example, to list your files with UNIX (a powerful operating system frequently used with workstations), or Linux (UNIX for PCs), the command is **ls**. Some operating systems simplify the interface with the operating system by using icons and menus; examples of user-friendly **graphical user interface** (GUI) systems, are the Macintosh environment and the Windows environment.

> graphical user
> interface

Because C++ programs can be run on many different platforms or hardware systems and because a specific computer can use different operating systems, it is not feasible to discuss the wide variety of operating systems that you might use while taking this course. We assume that your professor will provide the specific operating system information that you need to know to use the computers available at your university; this information is also contained in the operating system manuals.

Application software.   Numerous application programs are available to perform common operations. For example, **word processors,** such as Microsoft Word and WordPerfect, are application programs that have been written to help you enter and format text. Word processors allow you to move sentences and paragraphs and often have capabilities that allow you to enter mathematical equations and to check your spelling and grammar. Word processors are also used to enter computer programs and store them in files. Very sophisticated word processors allow you to produce well-designed pages that combine elaborate charts and graphics with text and headlines; these word processors use a technology called desktop publishing that combines a very powerful word processor with a high-quality printer to produce professional-looking documents.

Spreadsheet programs are software tools that allow you to easily work with data that can be displayed in a grid of rows and columns. Spreadsheets were initially used for financial and accounting applications, but many science and engineering problems can be easily solved using spreadsheets. Most spreadsheet packages include plotting capabilities, so they can be especially useful in analyzing and displaying information. Lotus 1-2-3, Quattro, and Excel are popular spreadsheet packages.

Another popular group of software tools are **database management programs,** such as dBASE IV, Microsoft Access, and Paradox. These programs allow you to store a large amount of data, and then easily retrieve pieces of the data, and format them into reports. Databases are used by large organizations such as banks, hospitals, hotels, and airlines. Scientific databases are also used to analyze large amounts of data. Meteorology data is an example of scientific data that require large databases for storage and analysis.

> Computer-aided
> design

Computer-aided design (CAD) packages, such as AutoCAD, AutoSketch, and CADKEY, allow you to define objects and then manipulate them graphically. For example, you can define an object and then view it from different angles or observe a rotation of the object from one position to another.

There are also some very powerful **mathematical computation tools,** such as MATLAB, Mathematica, MATHCAD, and Maple. Not only do these tools have very powerful mathematical commands, but they are also **graphics tools** that provide extensive capabilities for generating graphs. This combination of computational power and visualization power make them particularly useful tools for engineers. Appendix C contains a discussion on using MATLAB to plot data from a data file generated by a C++ program.

If an engineering problem can be solved using a software tool, it is usually more efficient to use the software tool than to write a program in a computer language to solve the problem.

However, many problems cannot be solved using software tools, or a software tool may not be available on the computer system that must be used for solving the problem; thus, we also need to know how to write programs using computer languages. The distinction between a software tool and a computer language is becoming less clear as some of the more powerful tools such as MATLAB and Mathematica include their own language in additional to specialized operations.

Computer Languages.   Computer languages can be described in terms of levels. Low-level languages or **machine languages** are the most primitive languages. Machine language is tied closely to the design of the computer hardware. Because computer designs are based on two-state technology (devices with two states such as open or closed circuits, on or off switches, positive or negative charges), machine language is written using two symbols, which are usually represented using the digits 0 and 1. Therefore, machine language is also a **binary** language, and the instructions are written as sequences of 0's and 1's called binary strings. Since machine language is closely tied to the design of the computer hardware, the machine language for a Sun computer for example is different from the machine language for a Hewlett Packard (HP) computer.

machine languages

An **assembly language** is also unique to a specific computer design, but its instructions are written in symbolic statements instead of binary. Assembly languages usually do not have very many statements, and thus writing programs in assembly language can be tedious. In addition, to use an assembly language you must also know information that relates to the specific computer hardware. Instrumentation that contains microprocessors often requires that the programs operate very fast, and thus the programs are called real-time programs. These **real-time programs** are often written in assembly language to take advantage of the specific computer hardware in order to perform the steps faster.

assembly language

High-level languages are computer languages that have English-like commands and instructions and include languages such as C++, C, Fortran, Ada, Java, and Basic. Writing programs in high-level languages is certainly easier than writing programs in machine language or in assembly language. However, a high-level language contains a large number of commands and an extensive set of **syntax** (or grammar) rules for using the commands. To illustrate the syntax and punctuation required by both software tools and high-level languages, we compute the area of a circle with a specified diameter in Table 1.1 using several different languages and tools. Notice both the similarities and the differences in this simple computation.

High-level
languages

syntax

TABLE 1.1 Comparison of Software Statements

Software	Example Statement
C++	area = 3.141595*(diameter/2)*(diameter/2);
C	area = 3.141595*(diameter/2)*(diameter/2);
MATLAB	area = pi*((diameter/2)∧ 2);
Fortran	area = 3.141595*(diameter/2.0)**2
Ada	area := 3.141595*(diameter/2)**2;
Java	area = 3.141595*(diameter/2)*(diameter/2);
Basic	let a = 3.141595*(d/2)*(d/2)

Executing a Computer Program.   A program written in a high-level language such as C++ must be translated into machine language before the instructions can be executed by

compiler

the computer. A special program called a **compiler** is used to perform this translation. Thus, in order to be able to write and execute C++ programs on a computer, the computer's software must include a C++ compiler. C++ compilers are available for the entire range of computer hardware, from supercomputers to personal computers.

If any errors are detected by the compiler during compilation, corresponding error messages are printed. We must correct our program statements and then perform the compilation step again. The errors identified during this stage are called **parse errors,** or **syntax errors.** For example, if we want to divide the value stored in a variable called sum by 3, the correct expression in C++ is sum/3; if we incorrectly write the expression using the backslash, as in sum\3, we have a syntax error and an error message will be reported by the compiler when we attempt to compile our program. The process of compiling, correcting statements that have syntax errors, and recompiling must often be repeated several times before the program compiles without error. When there are no syntax errors, the compiler can successfully translate the program and generate a program in machine language that performs the steps specified by

source program
object program

the original C++ program. The original C++ program is referred to as the **source program,** and the machine language version is called an **object program.** Thus, the source program and the object program specify the same steps, but the source program is specified in a high-level language and the object program is specified in machine language.

Once the program has compiled correctly, additional steps are necessary to prepare the object program for **execution.** This preparation involves **linking** other machine language statements to the object program and then **loading** the program into memory. After this linking and loading, the program steps are then executed by the computer. New errors called **execution errors, run-time errors,** or **logic errors** may be identified in this stage; these errors are also called **program bugs.** Execution errors often cause termination of a program. For example, the program statements may attempt to reference an invalid memory location, which may generate an execution error. Some execution errors do not stop the program from executing, but they cause incorrect results to be computed. These types of errors can be caused by programmer errors in determining the correct steps in the solutions and by errors in the data processed by the program. When execution errors occur due to errors in the program statements, we must correct the errors in the source program and then begin again with the compilation step. This process is called **debugging** and can be quite time consuming. Even when a program appears to execute properly, we must check the answers carefully to be sure that they are correct. The computer will perform the steps precisely as we specify, and if we specify the wrong steps, the computer will execute these wrong (but syntactically legal) steps and thus present us with an answer that is incorrect.

The processes of compilation, linking and loading, and execution are outlined in Figure 1.3.

A C++ compiler often has additional capabilities that provide a user-friendly environment for implementing and testing C++ programs. For example, some C++ environments such as Microsoft Visual C++ contain text processors so that program files can be generated, compiled, and executed in the same software package, as opposed to using a separate word processor that requires the use of operating system commands to transfer back and forth between the word processor and the compiler. Many C++ programming environments include debugger programs, which are useful in identifying errors in a program. Debugger programs allow us to see values stored in variables at different points in a program and to step through the program line by line.

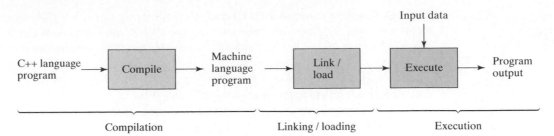

Figure 1.3 Program compilation, linking, and execution.

As we present new statements in C++, we will also point out common errors associated with the statements or useful techniques for locating errors associated with the statements. The debugging aids will be summarized at the end of each chapter.

Terminology

In this section of this text, we presented an introduction to computing systems. We introduced many new terms to describe hardware and software and the process of compiling, linking, executing, and debugging code. In subsequent chapters, we will begin discussing the C++ programming language and we will introduce additional terminology necessary to describe the features and the syntax of the language. The terminology may seem overwhelming at first, but if you take the time to learn this new vocabulary, it will greatly improve your ability to understand the material and communicate effectively when asking or answering questions. To help you identify and learn the important terminology, we have included margin notes and a list of key terms at the end of each chapter to identify the introduction of key terms.

1.3 An Engineering Problem-Solving Methodology

Problem solving is a key part of not only engineering courses, but also of courses in computer science, mathematics, physics, and chemistry. Therefore, it is important to have a consistent approach to solving problems. It is also helpful if the approach is general enough to work for all these different areas, so that we do not have to learn one technique for mathematics problems, a different technique for physics problems, and so on. The problem-solving process that we present works for engineering problems and can be tailored to solve problems in other areas as well; however, it does assume that we are using the computer to help solve the problem.

The process or methodology for problem solving that we will use throughout this text has five steps:

1. State the problem clearly.

2. Describe the input and output information of the problem.

3. Work the problem by hand (or with a calculator) for a simple set of data.

4. Develop a solution and convert it to a computer program.

5. Test the solution with a variety of data.

Engineering Grand Challenges

Prediction of Weather, Climate, and Global Change

To predict weather, climate, and global change, we must understand the complex interactions of the atmosphere and the oceans. These interactions are influenced by many things, including temperature, winds, ocean currents, precipitation, soil moisture, snow cover, glaciers, polar sea ice, and the absorption of ultraviolet radiation by ozone in the earth's atmosphere. As a result of concern over the ozone depletion in the atmosphere, the SCISAT-1 satellite, **Photo 1**, is scheduled for launch in June of 2002 from Vandenburg Air Force Base in California. The satellite will monitor the absorption of atmospheric molecules such as ozone to improve our understanding of the chemical processes involved in the depletion of the ozone layer, with particular emphasis on the processes occurring over Canada and the Arctic The mission is being headed by ACE Science Data Centre at the University of Waterloo.

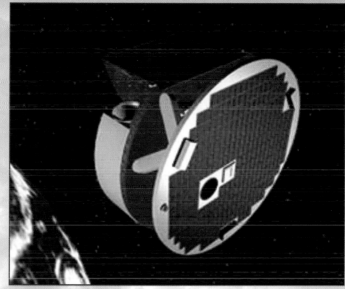

Photo 1   *SCISAT-1 Satellite*

Photo 2 illustrates the total atmospheric ozone concentration in the southern hemisphere. This data comes from a spectrometer on the Russian Meteor-3 satellite.

Photo 3 shows equipment designed to generate miniature tornadoes. Results from experiments like this give us insight to better predict weather phenomena.

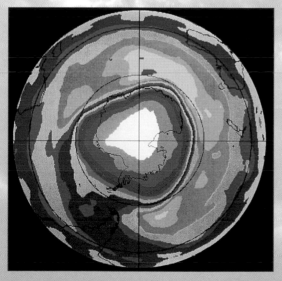

Photo 2   *Ozone Model*

Photo 3   *Tornado Machine*

Improvements in Vehicle Performance

Significant improvements in vehicle performance will not only affect the modes of transportation available to us, but can also improve the environment by reducing pollution and by providing more efficient energy consumption.Computer-aided design techniques allow us to analyze the three-dimensional fluid flow around a vehicle, **Photo 4**. We can also analyze new designs using wind tunnels, which can generate various wind speeds to test the performance of new structures, **Photo 5**. Improvements in transportation have taken advantage of engineering breakthroughs in other areas, such as satellite navigation. The Global Positioning System (GPS) satellites are used to determine the exact location of a GPS receiver. A computer within the receiver then uses that information to direct a driver to a desired location, as shown in **Photo 6**.

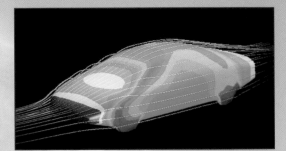

Photo 4   *Car Aerodynamics*

Photo 6   *Computer-navigated car*

Photo 5   *Wind Tunnel*

Computerized Speech Understanding

Computerized speech understanding could revolutionize our communication systems. We still cannot converse normally with computers, but there are applications that use some forms of speech understanding Educational games such as the one illustrated in **Photo 7** use speech input to teach skills such as language and mathematics; these programs understand words from limited vocabularies. Other computer programs can be designed to respond to verbal commands, or computers can take their input from verbal instructions instead of through a keyboard, **Photo 8**.

Photo 7   *Educational Game*

Photo 8   *Speech Input to Computer*

Enhanced Oil and Gas Recovery

Economical and ecologically sound techniques are needed for the identification and recovery of oil and gas reserves. Sonar signal processing techniques are being developed to identify potential reserves under the ocean, which are then recovered by oil platforms **Photo 10.** Underground reserves can be located by techniques that map the geological structure, as shown in the computer model in **Photo 11** that was developed using seismic signal processing. This information can be used to determine the materials in the various layers, and thus to indicate areas that are likely to contain oil or gas. Understanding the geological structure and relationships of different regions, such as the Mauna Loa volcano rift shown in **Photo 12**, gives engineers and scientists new information in understanding the earth's structure and the materials of which it is composed.

Photo 10   *Oil Platform*

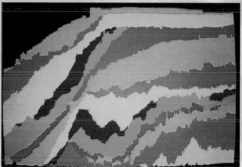

Photo 11   *Computerized Model of Earth Layers*

Photo 12   *Geological Experiments in a Volcano*

Researchers are currently exploring the use of speech to simplify access to the information contained in hundreds of gauges and instruments in an airline cockpit, **Photo 9**. For instance, in a future airliner, the pilot may be able to verbally ask for information, such as fuel status, and a computer will respond in synthesized speech with the amount of fuel remaining.

Photo 9   *Airline Cockpit*

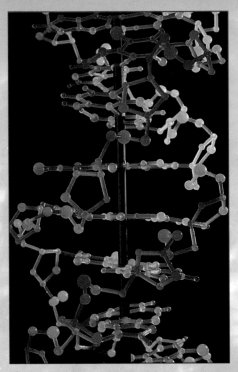

Photo 13 *DNA molecule model*

Photo 14 *Equipment for DNA sequencing*

Human Genome Project

Photo 15 *Bands of DNA*

The goal of the Human Genome Project is to locate, identify, and determine the function of each of the 50,000 to 100,000 genes contained in human DNA (deoxyribonucleic acid). A model of the double-helix DNA molecule is shown in **Photo 13**. Each gene is composed of base pairs arranged in a step-like manner, and it is the identification of the order of these base pairs that provides the key to the human genome. The structure of genes can be studied using equipment such as the electrophoresis machine in **Photo 14**. This machine contains a gel that can separate radioactively tagged DNA fragments using an electric field. **Photo 15** shows an engineer separating bands of DNA for a gene-splicing experiment.

Photo Credits: 1 Courtesy of Canadian Space Agency 2 Courtesy of Photo Researchers, Inc. 3 Courtesy of Rainbow. 4 Courtesy of Photo Researchers, Inc. 5 Courtesy of National Aeronautics and Space Administration. 6 Courtesy of Photo Researchers, Inc. 7 Courtesy of FPG International.l 8 Courtesy of Rainbow. 9 Courtesy of FPG International. 10 Courtesy of Amoco Corporation. 11 Courtesy of Rainbow. 12 Courtesy of The Image Works. 13 Courtesy of FPG International. 14 Courtesy of Photo Researchers, Inc.15 Courtesy of Rainbow.

We now discuss each of these steps using an example of computing the distance between two points in a plane.

1. PROBLEM STATEMENT

The first step is to state the problem clearly. It is extremely important to give a clear, concise problem statement to avoid any misunderstandings. For this example, the problem statement is the following:

Compute the straight-line distance between two points in a plane.

2. INPUT/OUTPUT DESCRIPTION

The second step is to describe the information, or data values, that are required to solve the problem and then identify the values that need to be computed for the final solution. Each of these values will be represented by an object in a C++ program. These objects represent the input and the output for the problem, and collectively can be called input/output (I/O). For many problems, a diagram that shows the input and output is useful. At this point, the program is an "abstraction," because we are not defining the steps to determine the output; instead, we are only showing the information that is required in order to compute the desired output. The **I/O diagram** for this example is as follows:

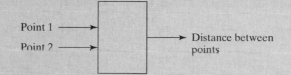

3. HAND EXAMPLE

The third step is to work the problem by hand or with a calculator, using a simple set of data. This is a very important step, and should not be skipped even for simple problems. This is the step in which you work out the details of the problem solution. If you cannot take a simple set of numbers and compute the output (either by hand or with a calculator), then you are not ready to move on to the next step; you should reread the problem, and perhaps consult reference material. The solution by hand for this specific example follows:

Let the points p1 and p2 have the following coordinates:

$$p1 = (1, 5); \; p2 = (4, 7).$$

We want to compute the distance between the two points, which is the hypotenuse of a right triangle, as shown in Figure 1.4. Using the Pythagorean theorem, we can compute the distance with the following equation:

$$\text{distance} = \sqrt{(\text{side}_1)^2 + (\text{side}_2)^2}$$
$$= \sqrt{(4-1)^2 + (7-5)^2}$$
$$= \sqrt{13}$$
$$= 3.61.$$

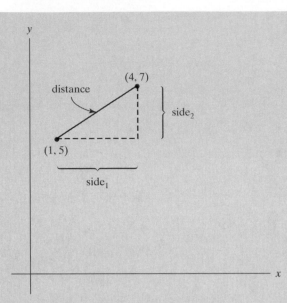

Figure 1.4 Straight-line distance between two points.

4. ALGORITHM DEVELOPMENT

Once you can work the problem for a simple set of data, you are then ready to develop an **algorithm,** or a step-by-step outline, of the problem solution. For simple problems such as this one, the algorithm can be listed as operations that are performed one after another. This outline of steps decomposes the problem into simpler steps, as shown by the following outline of the steps required to compute and print the distance between two points:

Decomposition Outline

1. Give values to the two points.

2. Compute the lengths of the two sides of the right triangle generated by the two points.

3. Compute the distance between the two points, which is equal to the length of the hypotenuse of the triangle.

4. Print the distance between the two points.

This **decomposition outline** is then converted to C++ commands so that we can use the computer to perform the computations. From the solution shown next, you can see that the commands are very similar to the steps used in the hand example. The details of these commands are explained in Chapter 2.

```
/*-------------------------------------------------------*/
/*   Program chapter1_1                                  */
/*                                                       */
/*   This program computes the                           */
/*   distance between two points.                        */
```

```
#include <iostream>
#include <cmath>

using namespace std;

int main()
{
    // Declare and initialize objects.
    double x1(1), y1(5), x2(4), y2(7),
           side_1, side_2, distance;

    // Compute sides of a right triangle.
    side_1 = x2 - x1;
    side_2 = y2 - y1;
    distance = sqrt(side_1*side_1 + side_2*side_2);

    // Print distance.
    cout << "The distance between the two points is "
         << distance << endl;

    // Exit program.
    return 0;
}
/*-------------------------------------------------------*/
```

5. TESTING

The final step in our problem-solving process is testing the solution. We should first test the solution with the data from the hand example because we have already computed the solution. When the C++ statements in this solution are executed, the computer displays the following output:

The distance between}whe points is 3.60555.

This output matches the value that we calculated by hand. If the C++ solution did not match the hand solution, then we should review both solutions to find the error. Once the solution works for the hand example, we should also test it with additional sets of data to be sure that the solution works for other valid sets of data.

The set of steps demonstrated in this example are used in developing the programs in the Problem Solving Applied sections in the chapters that follow.

SUMMARY

A group of outstanding recent engineering achievements was presented to demonstrate the diversity of engineering applications. A set of grand challenges was then presented to illustrate some of the exciting and difficult problems that currently face engineers and scientists. We also discussed some of the nontechnical skills required to be a successful engineer. Because the solutions to most engineering problems, including the grand challenges, will be by computer, we presented a summary of the components of a computer system, from computer hardware to computer software and the importance of learning the new terminology. We also introduced a five-step problem-solving methodology that we will use to develop a computer solution to a problem. These five steps are as follows:

1. State the problem clearly.

2. Describe the input and output information for the problem.

3. Work the problem by hand (or with a calculator) for a simple set of data.

4. Develop an algorithm and convert it to a computer program.

5. Test the solution with a variety of data.

This process will be used throughout the text as we develop solutions to problems.

Key Terms

algorithm
arithmetic logic unit (ALU)
assembler
assembly language
binary
bug
central processing unit (CPU)
compiler
computer
database management
debug
debugger
decomposition outline
desktop publishing
electronic copy
execution
grand challenges
graphics tool
hardware
high-level language
I/O diagram
linking/loading
logic error

machine language
mathematical computation tool
memory
microprocessor
network
object program
objects
operating system
parse error
personal computer (PC)
problem-solving process
processor
program
real-time program
software
source program
spreadsheet
supercomputer
syntax
utility
word processor
workstation

Problems

Exam Practice!

True/False

Indicate whether the following statements are true or false:

1. A CPU consists of an ALU, memory, and a processor.
2. Linking and loading is the step that prepares the object program for execution.

3. An algorithm describes the problem solution step by step, while a computer program solves the problem in one step.
4. A computer program is the implementation of an algorithm.

Multiple Choice

Circle the letter for the best answer to complete each statement.

5. Instructions and data are stored in
   (a) the arithmetic logic unit (ALU).
   (b) the control unit (processor).
   (c) the central processing unit (CPU).
   (d) the memory.
   (e) the keyboard.
6. An operating system is
   (a) the software that is designed by users.
   (b) a convenient and efficient interface between the user and the hardware.
   (c) the set of utilities that allow us to perform common operations.
   (d) a set of software tools.
7. Source code is
   (a) the result of compiler operations.
   (b) the process of getting information from the processor.
   (c) the set of instructions in a computer language that solve a specific problem.
   (d) the data stored in the computer memory.
   (e) the values entered through the keyboard
8. An algorithm refers to
   (a) a step-by-step solution to solve a specific problem.
   (b) a collection of instructions that the computer can understand.
   (c) a code that allows us to type in text materials.
   (d) stepwise refinement.
   (e) a set of math equations to derive the problem solution.
9. Object code is
   (a) the result of compiler operations on the source code.
   (b) the process of obtaining information from the processor.
   (c) a computer program.
   (d) a process involving the listing of commands required to solve a specific problem.
   (e) the result of the linking and loading process.

Additional Problems

The following problems combine an assignment in which you will learn more about one of the topics in this chapter with an opportunity to improve your written communication skills. (Perhaps your professor will even select some of the written reports for oral presentation in class.) Each report should include at least two references, so you will want to learn how to use library computers to locate reference information. Prepare your report using word-processor software. If you do not already know how to use a word processor, ask your professor for guidance on locating manuals or seminars to help you learn to use one of the word processors available on your university's computer systems.

10. Write a short report on one of these outstanding engineering achievements:

   Moon landing
   Composite materials
   Application satellites
   Jumbo jets
   Microprocessors
   Lasers
   CAD/CAM
   Fiber optics
   CAT scans
   Genetically engineered products

   A good starting point for finding references is the set of suggested readings at the end of this chapter.

11. Write a short report on one of these grand challenges:

   Predication of weather, climate, and global change
   Computerized speech understanding
   Mapping of the human genome
   Improved vehicle performance
   Enhanced oil and gas recovery

   A good starting point for finding references is the set of suggested readings at the end of this chapter.

12. Write a short report on an outstanding engineering achievement that is not included in the list given in this chapter. Past issues of *Scientific American* and the Web would provide some good ideas of recent achievements.

13. Write a short report on a topic that you think is a grand engineering challenge that was not included in the list given in this chapter. Recent issues of *Scientific American* and the Web would provide some results in topics of current research that could be a potential grand challenge.

Suggested Readings

For further reading on the top 10 achievements or on the grand challenges, we recommend the following articles from *Scientific American:* Barton, John H. "Patenting Life." *Scientific American,* March 1991, pp. 40–46. Berns, Michael W. "Laser Surgery." *Scientific American,* June 1991, pp. 84–90. Biship, David J., Peter L. Gammel, and David A. Huse. "Resistance in High-Temperature Superconductors." *Scientific American,* Feb. 1993, pp. 48–55. Brown, Barbara E. and John C. Ogden. "Coral Bleaching." *Scientific American,* Jan. 1993, pp. 64–71. Bugg, Charles E., William M. Carson, and John A. Montgomery. "Drugs by Design." *Scientific American,* December 1993, pp. 92–101. Capecchi, Mario R. "Targeted Gene Replacement." *Scientific American,* Mar. 1994, pp. 52–61. Cava, Robert J. "Superconductors beyond 1-2-3." *Scientific American,* August 1990, pp. 42–49. Charlson, Robert J. and Tom M. L. Wigley. "Sulfate Aerosol and Climatic Change." *Scientific American,* Feb. 1994, pp. 48 57. Chou, Tsu-Wei, Roy L. McCullough, and R. Byron Pipes. "Composites." *Scientific American,* October 1986, pp. 192–203. Coffin, Millard F., and Olav Eldholm. "Large Igneous Provinces."

Scientific American, October 1993, pp. 42–49. Conn, Robert W., et al. "The International Thermonuclear Experimental Reactor." *Scientific American,* April 1992, pp. 103–110. Corcoran, Elizabeth. "Calculating Reality." *Scientific American,* January 1991, pp. 100–109. Curl, Robert F., and Richard E. Smalley. "Fullerenes." *Scientific American,* October 1991, pp. 54–63. Depp, Steven W. and Webster E. Howard. "Flat-Panel Displays." *Scientific American,* Mar. 1993, pp. 90–99. Desurvire, Emmanuelf. "Lightwave Communications: The Fifth Generation." *Scientific American,* January 1992, pp. 114–121. Ditto, William L., and Louis M. Pecora. "Mastering Chaos." *Scientific American,* August 1993, pp. 78–85. Doolittle, Russell F., and Peer Bork. "Evolutionarily Mobile Modules in Proteins." *Scientific American,* October 1993, pp. 50–57. Drexhage, Martin G., and Cornelius T. Moynihan. "Infrared Optical Fibers." *Scientific American,* November 1988, pp. 110–116. Dunker, Kenneth F. and Basile G. Rabbat. "Why America's Bridges are Crumbling." *Scientific American,* Mar. 1993, pp. 66–73. Gasser, Charles S., and Robert T. Fraley. "Transgenic Crops." *Scientific American,* June 1992, pp. 62–69. Goulding, Michael. "Flooded Forests of the Amazon." *Scientific American,* April 1993, pp. 114–121. Greenberg, Donald P. "Computers and Architecture." *Scientific American,* February 1991, pp. 104–109. Halsey, Thomas C., and James E. Martin. "Electroheological Fluids." *Scientific American,* October 1993, pp. 58–67. Hess, Wilmot, et al. "The Exploration of the Moon." *Scientific American,* October 1969, pp. 55–72. Holloway, Marguerite. "Sustaining the Amazon." *Scientific American,* June 1992, pp. 90–100. Holloway, Marguerite. "Nurturing Nature." *Scientific American,* Apr. 1994, pp. 98–109. Homer-Dixon, Thomas F., Jeffrey H. Boutwell, and George W. Rathjens. "Environmental Change and Violent Conflict." *Scientific American,* Feb. 1993, pp. 38–47. Jewell, Jack L., James P. Harbison, and Axel Scherer. "Microlasers." *Scientific American,* November 1991, pp. 86–94. Johnston, Arch C., and Lisa R. Kanter. "Earthquakes in Stable Continental Crust." *Scientific American,* March 1990, pp. 68–75. Keyes, Robert W. "The Future of the Transistor." *Scientific American,* June 1993, pp. 70–99. Kusler, Jon A., William J. Mitsch, and Joseph S. Larson. "Wetlands." *Scientific American,* January 1994, pp. 16–72. Lents, James M., and William J. Kelly. "Clearing the Air in Los Angeles." *Scientific American,* October 1993, pp. 32–41. Likharev, Konstantin K. and Tord Claeson. "Single Electronics." *Scientific American,* June 1992, pp. 80–86. Luhmann, Janet G., James B. Pollack and Lawrence Colin. "The Pioneer Mission to Venus." *Scientific American,* Apr. 1994, pp. 90–97. Mahowald, Misha A., and Carver Mead. "The Silicon Retina." *Scientific American,* May 1991, pp. 76–82. Matthews, Dennis L., and Mordecai D. Rosen. "Soft-X-Ray Lasers." *Scientific American,* December 1988, pp. 86–91. Osada, Yoshihito and Simon B. Ross-Murphy. "Intelligent Gels." *Scientific American,* May 1993, pp. 82–87. Paabo, Svante. "Ancient DNA." *Scientific American,* November 1993, pp. 86–93. Pollack, Henry N. and David S. Chapman. "Underground Records of Changing Climate." *Scientific American,* June 1993, pp. 44–53. Rennie, John. "DNA's New Twists." *Scientific American,* April 1993, pp. 122–133. Repetto, Robert. "Accounting for Environmental Assets." *Scientific American,* June 1992, pp. 94–101. Rhodes, Daniela and Aaron Klug. "Zinc Fingers." *Scientific American,* Feb. 1993, pp. 56–65. Richelson, Jeffrey T. "The Future of Space Reconnaissance." *Scientific American,* January 1991, pp. 38–44. Ross, Philip E. "Eloquent Remains." *Scientific American,* May 1992, pp. 114–125. Steinberg, Morris A. "Materials for Aerospace." *Scientific American,* October 1986, pp. 67–72. Swade, Doron D. "Redeeming Charles Babbage's Mechanical Computer." *Scientific American,* Mar. 1993, pp. 86–91. Veldkamp, Wilfrid B., and Thomas J. McHugh. "Binary Optics." *Scientific American,* May 1992, pp. 92–97. Wallich, Paul. "Silicon Babies." *Scientific American,* December 1991, pp. 124–134.

CHAPTER 2

GRAND CHALLENGE:
Vehicle Performance

Wind tunnels are test chambers built to generate precise wind speeds. Accurate scale models of new aircraft can be mounted on force-measuring supports in the test chamber, and measurements of the forces on the model can be made at many different wind speeds and angles. Some wind tunnels can operate at hypersonic velocities, generating wind speeds of thousands of miles per hour. The size of wind-tunnel test sections vary from a few inches across to sizes large enough to accommodate a jet fighter. At the completion of a wind-tunnel test series, many sets of data have been collected that can be used to determine lift, drag, and other aerodynamic performance characteristics of a new aircraft at its various operating speeds and positions.

Simple C++ Programs

Chapter Outline

Objectives

Summary, Key Terms, C++ Statement Summary, Style Notes, Debugging Notes, Problems

OBJECTIVES

In this chapter, we present an **introduction to object-based programming** and outline the **structure of a simple C++ program** that defines objects, performs computations, and then prints the results. We then present the **syntax and the semantics for the C++ statements** that define and initialize constants and variable objects, that compute new values using **simple arithmetic operations,** that **read user-supplied information** from the keyboard during the execution of a program, and that **print information** on the screen. Additional functions are presented for most of the computations commonly used to solve engineering problems. With these C++ statements and functions, we then have the capability to **write complete programs.** We also graphically explain **linear interpolation,** which is then used to solve a problem that analyzes wind-tunnel data. An additional problem is solved that analyzes the velocity and acceleration values of an advanced turboprop engine. Finally, a C++ program is presented that allows you to check the specific **limitations of data types** for your system.

OOP | **2.1** Introduction to Object-Based Programming

Bjarne Stroustrup of AT&T Bell Laboratories developed C++ in the early 1980s. C++ supports all of the C programming language operators and control structures, as well as the definition and use of functions. The C++ language is a superset of C, so most C programs can be compiled

23

object-oriented
programming
language

using a C++ compiler. Although C++ is derived from C, it is best to think of C++ as a new, **object-oriented programming language.**

When designing an object-based program to solve a problem, we begin by identifying the data requirements of the problem and how the data will be used within the program. If, for example, we want to write a program to determine the straight-line distance between two points in a plane, the data requirements include points in a plane and a distance. A point in a plane is defined by an *x*- and a *y*-coordinate, and the distance can be calculated using a mathematical formula that includes addition, subtraction and the square root function. The values that will be assigned to *x* and *y* will most likely be floating-point values (as opposed to integer values) so we can represent them in a C++ program using the predefined data type known as `double`. We can define an object of type `double` to represent the *x*-coordinate and another object of type `double` to define the *y*-coordinate. A square-root function and operators for addition and subtraction are defined in C++ for objects of type `double`; thus, we can calculate the distance between two points with the following statement:

```
dist = sqrt((x2 - x1)*(x2 - x1) + (y2 - y1)*(y2 - y1));
```

If calculating distance between two points in a plane is our only requirement, then the preceding approach is reasonable. However, if our application required manipulating points and using points to define more complex geometric objects, it would be convenient to have operators and functions that operated on points directly. This would enable us to find the distance between two points with the following simplified statement:

```
dist = point1 - point2;
```

abstract data types

where the operator − is defined as the distance formula. Object-oriented programming languages support the definition of **abstract data types** for representing data objects required in real world applications.

object-oriented
design

Through careful **object-oriented design,** new data types can be used as building blocks for additional, more complex data types. Suppose an application requires us to track the movement of particles suspended in a fluid. A particle can be defined as a *point,* a *radius,* a *magnitude,* and a *density.* In this application, a *point* is used as part of the definition of a more complex object. However, if we have defined a data type that can represent a point, and a particle is a point with added properties, an object-based approach to the problem suggests that we use the *point* data type to derive a new data type to represent a *particle.* A *particle* object will have the ability to use the functions and operators defined for *point* objects, and additional functions and operators can be defined if needed to work with particles.

As problems become larger and more complex, it is very common to work with data that are not easily represented and manipulated using only objects of predefined data types. It is also common to have multiple programmers working on large, complex problems. In these situations, an object-based approach to the design and implementation of a solution is desirable. Well-designed data types can be reused, increasing productivity. A well-designed, object-based solution allows for easy, consistent manipulation of data objects, reducing the chance for errors and the amount of time spent debugging and rewriting broken programs.

inheritance

Using C++, programmers can define new data types using a mechanism called a `class`. New data types can be derived from existing data types through **inheritance.** Designing and implementing new data types requires a significant amount of time and effort, as you will see when you read Chapters 8 and 10. To prepare you for these chapters, we will begin by presenting the basics of programming using objects of the predefined data types provided in C++.

2.2 Program Structure

In this section, we analyze the structure of a specific C++ program, and then we present the general structure of a C++ program. The program that follows was first introduced in Chapter 1; it computes and prints the distance between two points.

```
/*------------------------------------------          -------*/
/*   Program chapter1_1                                      */
/*                                                           */
/*   This program computes the                              */
/*   distance between two points.                           */

#include <iostream>
#include <cmath>

using namespace std;

int main()
{
   //  Declare and initialize objects.
   double x1(1), y1(5), x2(4), y2(7),
          side_1, side_2, distance;

   //  Compute sides of a right triangle.
   side_1 = x2 - x1;
   side_2 = y2 - y1;
   distance = sqrt(side_1*side_1 + side_2*side_2);

   //  Print distance.
   cout << "The distance between the two points is "
        << distance << endl;

   //  Exit program.
   return 0;
}
/*------------------------------------------          ----*/
```

We now briefly discuss the statements in this specific example; each of the statements is discussed in detail in later sections of this chapter.

comments

The first five lines of this program contain **comments** that give the program a name (chapter1_1) and that document its purpose:

```
/*-------------------------------------------------------------*/
/*       Program chapter1_1                                    */
/*                                                             */
/*       This program computes the                            */
/*       distance between two points.                         */
```

Comments may begin with the characters / * and end with the characters * / or, for single-line comments, may begin with the characters / /. Comments beginning with the characters / / will terminate at the end of the current line. A comment can be on a line by itself, or it can be on the same line as a command; a comment beginning with the characters / * can also extend over several lines.

Each of the comment lines here is a separate comment because each line begins with / * and ends with * /. Although comments are optional, good style requires that comments be used throughout a program to improve its readability and to document the computations. In the text programs, we always use initial comments to give a name to the program and to describe the general purpose of the program; additional explanation comments are also included throughout the program. C++ allows comments and statements to begin anywhere on a line.

preprocessor directives

Preprocessor directives give instructions to the compiler that are preformed before the program is compiled. The most common directive inserts additional statements in the program; it contains the characters *#include* followed by the name of the file containing the additional statements. This program contains the following two preprocessor directives:

```
#include <iostream>
#include <cmath>
```

These directives specify that statements in the files *iostream* and *cmath* should be included in place of these two statements before the program is compiled. The < and > characters around the file names indicate that the files are included with the Standard C++ library; this library is contained in the files that accompany an ANSI C++ compiler. The file *iostream* contains information related to the output statement used in this program, and the file *cmath* contains information related to the function used in this program to compute the square root of a value. Preprocessor directives are generally included after the initial comments describing the program's purpose. The next statement

```
using namespace std;
```

using directive

is called a **using directive.** The using directive tells the compiler to use the library filecoames declared in namespace *std*. Namespaces are part of the new ANSI Standard C++. Some older compilers do not support namespaces. If your compiler does not accept the using namespace statement then you will need to omit the using namespace std; statement and change the name of the files used in the preprocessor directives to the following:

```
#include<iostream.h>
#include<math.h>
```

Older compiles use a *.h* extention for most of their header file names. You will see the file *math.h* included in C programs, as well as C++ programs because *math.h* is the C name of the C library header file. New compilers differentiate between C and C++ header file names. The C++ name for the *math.h* header file is *cmath.* In general, the C++ name for a C library header file is the same as the C name with the following changes: the *.h* is dropped and the letter itbf c is added to the beginning of the file name. We will use the new ANSI Standard C++ names in this text.

Every C++ program contains exactly one set of statements called a main function. The keyword int indicates that the function returns an integer value to the operating system. The parentheses following main are required because main is a function. The body of the function is enclosed by braces, { }. In order to easily identify the body of the function, we place these braces on lines by themselves. Thus, the two lines following the preprocessor directives specify the beginning of the main function:

```
int main()
{
```

declarations
statements

The main function contains two types of commands: **declarations** and **statements.** The declarations define the memory locations that will be used by the statements and therefore must precede any statements that reference these memory locations. The declarations may or may not give initial values to be stored in the memory locations. A comment precedes the declaration statement in the following program:

```
// Declare and initialize objects.
double x1(1), y1(5), x2(4), y2(7),
       side_1, side_2, distance;
```

These declarations specify that the program will use seven objects named *x1*, *y1*, *x2*, *y2*, *side_1*, *side_2*, and *distance*. The term double indicates that the objects are of type double, one of the built-in C++ data types. Each object will store a double-precision floating-point value; these objects can store noninteger values such as 12.5 and −0.0005 with many digits of precision. In addition, this statement specifies that *x1* should be **initialized** (given an initial value) to the value 1, *y1* should be initialized to the value 5, *x2* should be initialized to the value 4, and *y2* should be initialized the value 7. The initial values of *side_1*, *side_2*, and *distance* are not specified and should not be assumed to be initialized to zero. Because the declaration was too long for one line, we split it over two lines; the indenting of the second line indicates that it is a continuation of the previous line. *The indenting is a matter of style and readability; it is not required.* The semicolon ends the declaration statement.

initialized

Style

The statements that specify the operations to be performed in the example program are the following:

```
// Compute sides of a right triangle
side_1 = x2 - x1;
side_2 = y2 - y1;
distance = sqrt(side_1*side_1 + side2*side_2);

//  Print distance
cout << "The distance between the two points is "
     << distance << endl;
```

These statements compute the lengths of the two sides of the right triangle formed by two points (see Figure 1.4, page 16) and then compute the length of the hypotenuse of the right triangle. The details of the syntax of these assignment statements are discussed later in the chapter. After the distance is computed, it is printed with the *cout* statement. This output statement is too long for a single line, so we separate the statement into two lines; the indenting of the second line again indicates that it is a continuation of the previous line. A semicolon ends the output statement. Additional comments were used to explain the computations and the output statement. Note that all C++ statements are required to end with a semicolon.

To end execution of the program and return control to the operating system, we use a `return(0);` statement.

```
//  Exit program
return (0);
```

This statement returns a value of 0 to the operating system. A value of zero indicates a successful end of execution.

The body of the main function then ends with the right brace on a line by itself, and another comment line to delineate the end of the main function.

```
}
/*-------------------------------------------------------------------------*/
```

Style

Note that we have included blank lines (also called whitespace) in the program to separate different components. These blank lines make a program more readable and easier to modify. The statements within the main function were indented in order to show the structure of the program. This spacing provides a consistent style, and makes our programs easier to read.

Now that we have closely examined the C++ program from Chapter 1, we can compare its structure to the general form of a C++ program:

```
preprocessing directives
int main()
{
declarations;
statements;
}
```

This structure is evident in the programs developed in this chapter and in the chapters that follow.

Modify!

1. Create a file containing the sample program discussed in this section using either an editor that is part of your C++ compiler or using a word processor. Then compile and execute the program. You should get this output:

```
The distance between the two points is  3.61
```

2. Change the values given to the two points to the coordinates $(-1, 6)$ and $(2, 4)$. Run the program with these new values. Did the distance change? Explain.

3. Change the values given to the two points so that they represent the coordinates $(1, 0)$ and $(5, 7)$. Check the program's answer with your calculator.

4. Change the values given to the two points so that they represent the same coordinates $(2, 4)$ and $(2, 4)$. Does the program give the correct answer?

2.3   Constants and Variables

constants

variables
identifier

Constants and variables represent objects that we use in our programs. **Constants** are specific values such as 2, 3.1416, −1.5, 'a', or "hello" that we include in the C++ statements. The value of these objects cannot be changed. **Variables** are memory locations that are assigned a name or **identifier.** The identifier is used to reference the value stored in the memory location. A useful analogy for a memory location and its corresponding identifier is a mailbox that is associated with the name of an individual; the memory location (or mailbox) then contains an object. The following shows the objects, their identifiers, and their initial values after the following declaration statement from program Chapter1_1:

```
double x1(1), y1(5), x2(4), y2(7),
       side_1, side_2, distance;
```

x1 [1]   y1 [5]

x2 [4]   y2 [7]

side_1 [?]   side_2 [?]   distance [?]

garbage

memory snapshot

The values of objects that were not given initial values are unspecified and thus are indicated with a question mark; sometimes these values are called **garbage** values because their values are unpredictable. A diagram such as this that shows an object along with its identifier, and its value is called a **memory snapshot.** A memory snapshot shows the contents of a memory location at a specified point in the execution of the program. The preceding memory snapshot shows the objects and their contents after execution of the declaration statement. We frequently use memory snapshots to show the contents of objects both before and after a statement is executed in order to show its effect. The rules for selecting a valid identifier are as follows:

- An identifier must begin with an alphabetic character or the underscore character.

- Alphabetic characters in an identifier can be lowercase or uppercase letters.

- An identifier can contain digits, but not as the first character.

case sensitive

C++ is **case sensitive,** which means uppercase letters are distinguished from lowercase letters; thus *Total, TOTAL,* and *total* represent three different objects. C++ also includes keywords with special meaning to the C++ compiler that cannot be used for identifiers; a complete list of keywords is given in Table 2.1.

Examples of valid identifiers are *distance, x_1, X_sum, average_measurement,* and *initial_time.* Examples of invalid identifiers are 1x (begins with a digit), switch (a keyword), $sum (contains an invalid character $), and rate% (contains an invalid character %).

Style

An identifier name should be carefully selected so that it reflects the contents of the objects. If possible, the name should also indicate the units of measurement. For example, if an object represents a temperature measurement in degrees Fahrenheit, use an identifier such as *temp_F* or *degrees_F.* If an object represents an angle, name it *theta_rad* to indicate that the angle is measured in radians or *theta_deg* to indicate that the angle is measured in degrees.

TABLE 2.1   Keywords

asm	auto	bool	break
case	catch	char	class
const	const_cast	continue	default
delete	do	double	dynamic_cast
else	enum	explicit	export
extern	false	float	for
friend	goto	if	inline
int	long	mutable	namespace
new	operator	private	protected
public	register	reinterpret_cast	return
short	signed	sizeof	static
static_cast	struct	switch	template
this	throw	true	try
typedef	typeid	typename	union
unsigned	using	virtual	void
volatile	wchar_t	while	

Declarations statments included in a main function (and other C++ functions that we write) must include not only the identifiers of the objects that we plan to use in our program, but they must also specify the data type of the object. These data types are presented after a discussion on scientific notation.

Practice!

Determine which of the following names are valid identifiers. If a name is not a valid identifier, give the reason that it is not acceptable, and suggest a valid replacement.

1. density
2. area
3. Time
4. xsum
5. x_sum
6. tax-rate
7. perimeter
8. sec**2
9. degrees_C
10. break
11. #123
12. x$y
13. count
14. void
15. f(x)
16. f2
17. Final_Value
18. w1.1
19. reference1
20. reference_1
21. m/s

Scientific Notation

floating-point
scientific notation

A **floating-point** value is one that can represent both integer and non-integer values, such as 2.5, −0.004, and 15.0. A floating-point value expressed in **scientific notation** is rewritten as a **mantissa** times a power of 10, where the mantissa has an absolute value greater than or equal to 1.0 and less than 10.0. For example, in scientific notation, 25.6 is written as 2.56×10^1, −0.004 is written as $-4.0 \times 10^{(-3)}$, and 1.5 is written as 1.5×10^0. In **exponential notation**, the letter e is used to separate the mantissa from the exponent of the power of 10. Thus, in exponential notation, 25.6 is written as 2.56e1, −0.004 is written as −4.0e-3, and 1.5 is written as 1.5e0.

exponential
notation

precision

range

The number of digits allowed by the computer for the decimal portion of the mantissa determines the **precision,** and the number of digits allowed for the exponent determines the **range.** Thus, values with two digits of precision and an exponent range of -8 to 7 could include values such as 2.3×10^5 (230,000) and $5.9 \times 10^{(-8)}$ (0.000000059). This precision and exponent range would not be sufficient for many of the types of values that we use in engineering problem solutions. For example, the distance in mile from Mars to the Sun, with seven digits of precision, is 141,517,510, or 1.4151751×10^8; to represent this value, we would need at least seven digits of precision and an exponent range that included the integer 8.

Practice!

In problems 1 through 6, express the value in scientific notation. Specify the number of digits of precision needed to represent each value.

1. 35.004.
2. 0.00042.
3. $-50,000$.
4. 3.15723.
5. -0.09997.
6. 10, 000,028.

In problems 7 through 12, express the value in floating-point notation.

7. 1.03e-5.
8. -1.05e5.
9. -3.552e6.
10. 6.67e-4.
11. 9.0e-2.
12. -2.2e-2.

Numeric Data Types

Numeric data types are used to specify the types of numbers that will be contained in objects. In C++, the built-in numeric types are either integers or floating-point values. The following diagram shows the built-in numeric data types and their specifiers that are discussed in the next few paragraphs:

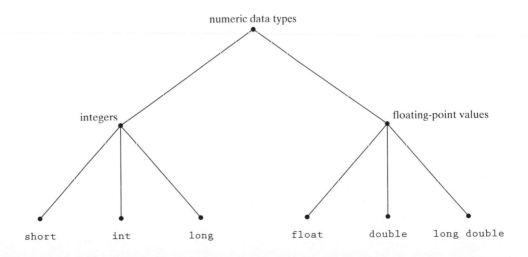

The **type specifiers** for signed integers are `short`, `int`, and `long`, for short integer, integer, and long integer, respectively. The specific ranges of values are **system dependent,** which means that the ranges can vary from one system to another. In the last section of this chapter, we present a program that you can use to determine the ranges of the numeric data types on your system. On many systems, the short integer data type range from −32,768 to 32,767, and the integer and long integer type often represents values from −2,147,483,648 to 2,147,483,647. (The unusual limits such as 32,767 and 2,147,483,647 relate to conversions of binary values to decimal values.) C++ also allows an `unsigned` qualifier to be added to integer specifiers. An `unsigned` integer can represent only positive values. Signed and `unsigned` integers can represent the same number of values, but the ranges are different. For example, if an `unsigned short` has the range of values from 0 to 65,535, then a `short` integer has the range of values from −32,768 to 32,767; both data types can represent a total of 65,536 values.

The type specifiers for floating-point values are `float` (single precision), `double` (double precision), and `long double` (extended precision). The following statement from program chapter1_1 thus defines seven objects that all contain double-precision floating-point values:

```
double x1(1), y1(5), x2(4), y2(7),
       side_1, side_2, distance;
```

The difference between the `float`, `double`, and `long double` types relates to the precision (or accuracy) and the range of the values represented. The precision and range are system dependent. Table 2.2 contains precision and range information for integers and floating-point values used by the Visual C++ compiler. A program given in Section 2.11 allows you to obtain this information for your computer system. On most systems, a `double` data type stores about twice as many decimal digits of precision as are stored with a `float` data type.

TABLE 2.2   Example Data-Type Limits*

Integers

short	Maximum = 32,767
int	Maximum = 2,147,483,647
long	Maximum = 2,147,483,647

Floating Point

float	6 digits of precision
	Maximum exponent = 38
	Maximum value = $3.402823e + 38$
double	15 digits of precision
	Maximum exponent = 308
	Maximum value = $1.797693e + 308$
long double	15 digits of precision
	Maximum exponent = 308
	Maximum value = $1.797693e + 308$

*Microsoft Visual C++ 6.0 compiler.

In addition, a `double` value will have a wider range of exponent values than a `float` value. The `long double` value may have more precision and a still wider exponent range, but this is again system dependent. A floating-point constant such as 2.3 is assumed to be a `double` constant. To specify a `float` constant or a `long double` constant, the letter (or suffix) F or L must be appended to the constant. Thus, 2.3F and 2.3L represent a `float` constant and a `long double` constant, respectively.

Boolean Data Type

boolean data type

The **boolean data type,** named after the mathematician George Boole, can specify only two values: true and false. In C++, the value zero is interpreted as false and any nonzero value is considered to be true. There are two predefined boolean constants, *true* and *false,* that can also be used. Boolean objects can be defined using the type specifier `bool`. The following example illustrates the use of boolean objects and constants:

```
bool error(false), status(true);
cout << error << endl << status;
```

The output from this program is

```
0
1
```

Boolean objects are very useful in controlling the flow of a program and flagging error conditions.

Character Data Type

Character data

Character data is easy to work with in C++, but to work with characters effectively, we need to understand more about their representation in the computer's memory. Recall that all information stored in a computer is represented internally as sequences of binary digits (0 and 1). Each character corresponds to a binary code value. The most commonly used binary codes are American Standard Code for Information Interchange (ASCII) and Extended Binary Coded Decimal Interchange Code (EBCDIC). In the discussions that follow, we assume that ASCII code is used to represent characters. Table 2.3 contains a few characters, their binary

TABLE 2.3   Examples of ASCII Codes

Character	ASCII Code	Integer Equivalent
newline, \n	0001010	10
%	0100101	37
3	0110011	51
A	1000001	65
a	1100001	97
b	1100010	98
c	1100011	99

form in ASCII, and the integer values that correspond to the binary values. The character 'a' is represented by the binary value 1100001, which is equivalent to the integer value of 97. A total of 128 characters can be represented in the ASCII code. A complete ASCII code table is given in Appendix B.

A character constant is enclosed in single quotes, as in 'A', 'b', and '3'. The type specifier for character objects is char. Once a character is stored in memory as a binary value, the binary value can be interpreted as a character or as an integer, as illustrated in Table 2.3. However, it is important to note that the binary ASCII representation for a character digit is not equal to the binary representation for an integer digit.

From Table 2.3, we see that the ASCII binary representation for the character digit 3 is 0110011, which is equivalent to the binary representation of the integer value 51. Thus, performing a computation with the character representation of a digit does not yield the same result as performing the computation with the integer representation of the digit. The following program illustrates this feature of character data:

```
/*-----------------------------------------------------------*/
/* Program chapter2_1                                         */
/*                                                            */
/* This program prints a char and an int                     */

#include <iostream>
using namespace std;

int main()
{
// Declare and initialize objects.
char ch ('3');
int i(3);

// Print both values.
cout << "value of ch: " << ch << " value of i: " << i << endl;

// Assign character to integer
i = ch;

// Print both values.
cout << "value of ch: " << ch << " value of i: " << i << endl;

// Exit program
return( 0);
}
/*-----------------------------------------------------------*/
```

The output from this program is

```
value of ch: 3; value of i: 3
value of ch: 3; value of i: 51
```

string
C style strings
string objects

String Data

A **string** constant is a sequence of characters enclosed within double quotes, as in "sensor", "F18", or "Jane Doe". String objects can be represented as **C style strings** using arrays of type char, or as **string objects** using the *string* class. Both representations will be discussed in detail in Chapter 6. In this section, we give a brief introduction to the *string* class.

The C++ compiler does not have a built-in data type named *string*, but a *string* class definition is provided in the standard C++ library file *string*. To use the *string* class, a program must include the following preprocessor directive:

```
#include <string>
```

The following program illustrates the use of the *string* class:

```
/*-------------------------------------------------*/
/* Program chapter2_2                              */
/*                                                 */
/* This program prints a greeting                  */
/* using the string class.                         */

#include <iostream>
#include <string>     // Required for string class
using namespace std;

int main()
{
// Declare and initialize two string objects.
string salutation("Hello"), name("Jane Doe");

// Output greeting.
cout << salutation << ' ' << name << '!' << endl;

// Exit program.
return(0);
}
```

The output from this program is

```
Hello Jane Doe!
```

Symbolic Constants

symbolic constant

A **symbolic constant** is defined using the const modifier. Engineering constants such as π or the acceleration of gravity are good candidates for symbolic constants. For example, consider the following declaration statement to assign a value to the symbolic constant *PI*:

```
const double PI = acos(-1.0);
```

The *acos* function, when evaluated at -1, will return an approximation for π that includes 15 digits of precision. Statements that need to use the value of π would then use the symbolic constant *PI* as illustrated in this statement:

```
area = PI*radius*radius;
```

which computes the area of a circle.

Symbolic constants are usually defined with uppercase identifiers (as in PI instead of pi) to indicate that they are symbolic constants, and, of course, the identifiers should be selected so that they are easy to remember. Once an identifier has been declared and initialized using the `const` modifier, its value cannot be changed within the program.

Practice!

Give the declaration statements required to define symbolic constants for these constants:

1. Speed of light, $c = 2.99792 \times 10^8$ m/s

2. Charge of an electron, $e = 1.602177 \times 10^{-19}$ C

3. Avogadro's number, $N_A = 6.022 \times 10^{23}$ mol^{-1}

4. Acceleration of gravity, $g = 9.8$ m/s^2

5. Acceleration of gravity, $g = 32$ ft/s^2

6. Mass of the Earth, $M_E = 5.98 \times 10^{24}$ kg

7. Radius of the Moon, $r = 1.74 \times 10^6$ m

8. Unit of length, UnitLength = 'm'

9. Unit of time, UnitTime = 's'

2.4 C++ Operators

operators

To perform operations in a program, such as addition, multiplication, and comparison of objects, we use special **operators** that are defined for the built in data types supported by C++. In this section, we will look at several of these operators.

Assignment Operator

assignment
statement

An **assignment statement** uses the **assignment operator,** = to assign a value to an identifier. The general form of the assignment statement is

assignment
operator

```
identifier = expression;
```

where an expression can be a constant, another object, or the result of an operation. Consider the following two sets of statements that declare and give values to the objects *sum, x1,* and *ch*:

```
//Set One                   //Set Two
double sum(10.5);           double sum;
int x1(3);                  int x1;
char ch('a');               char ch;

                            sum = 10.5;
                            x1 = 3;
                            ch = 'a';
```

After either set of statements is executed, the value of *sum* is 10.5, the value of *x1* is 3 and the value of *ch* is 'a', as shown in the following memory snapshot:

sum | 10.5 | x1 | 3 | ch | 'a' |

The statements in Set One declare and initialize the objects at the same time in the type declaration statement; the assignment statements in Set Two could be used at any point in the program and thus may be used to change (as opposed to initialize) the values of objects that have already been declared.

Multiple assignments are also allowed in C++, as in the following statement, which assigns a value of zero to each of the objects *x, y,* and *z*:

```
x = y = z = 0;
```

Multiple assignments are discussed further at the end of this section.

We can also assign a value from one object to another with an assignment statement:

```
rate = state_tax;
```

The assignment operator should not be confused with equality. Assignment statements should be read as *is assigned the value of;* thus, the foregoing statement is *rate is assigned the value of state_tax.* If *state_tax* contains the value 0.06, then *rate* also contains the value 0.06 after the statement is executed; the value in *state_tax* is not changed. The memory snapshots before and after this statement is executed are the following:

Before: rate | ? | state_tax | 0.06 |

After: rate | 0.06 | state_tax | 0.06 |

If we assign a value to an object that has a different data type, then a conversion must occur during the execution of the statement. Sometimes the conversion can result in information being lost. For example, consider the following declaration and assignment statement:

```
int a;
  ...
a = 12.8;
```

Because *a* is defined to be an integer, it cannot store a value with a nonzero decimal portion. Therefore, in this case, the memory snapshot after executing the assignment statement is the following:

a   12

To determine whether a numeric conversion will work properly, we use the following order, which is from high to low:

```
high:    long double
         double
         float
         long integer
         integer
low:     short integer
```

If a value is moved to a data type that is higher in order, no information will be lost; if a value is moved to a data type that is lower in order, information may be lost. Thus, moving an integer to a double will work properly, but moving a float to an integer may result in the loss of some information or in an incorrect result. In general, use only assignments that do not cause potential conversion problems. Unsigned integers were not included in the list because errors can occur in both directions.

Arithmetic Operators

arithmetic
operation

An assignment statement can be used to assign the result of an **arithmetic operation** to an object, as shown in this statement that computes the area of a square:

```
area_square = side*side;
```

Here the operator * is used to indicate multiplication. The operators **+** and **-** are used to indicate addition and subtraction, and the operator **/** is used for division. Thus, each of the following statements is a valid computation for the area of a triangle:

```
area_triangle = 0.5*base*height;
```

```
area_triangle = (base*height)/2;
```

The use of parentheses in the second statement is not required, but is used for readability.
        Consider this assignment statement:

```
x = x + 1;
```

In algebra, this statement is invalid because a value cannot be equal to itself plus 1. However, this assignment statement should not be read as an equality; instead, it should be read as *x is assigned the value of x plus 1.* With this interpretation, the statement indicates that the value stored in the object *x* is incremented by 1. Thus, if the value of *x* is 5 before this statement is executed, then the value of *x* will be 6 after the statement is executed.

modulus operator

C++ also includes a **modulus operator %** that is used to compute the remainder in a division between two integers. For example, 5%2 is equal to 1, 6%3 is equal to 0, and 2%7 is equal to 2. (The quotient of 2/7 is zero with a remainder of 2.) If a and b are integers, then the expression a/b computes the integer quotient, whereas the expression $a\%b$ computes the integer remainder. Thus, if a is equal to 9 and b is equal to 4, the value of a/b is 2 and the value of $a\%b$ is 1. An illegal instruction occurs if the value of b is equal to zero in either a/b or $a\%b$ because the computer cannot perform division by zero. If either of the integer values in a and b is negative, the result of $a\%b$ is system dependent.

The modulus operator is useful in determining whether an integer is a multiple of another number. For example, if $a\%2$ is equal to zero, then a is even; otherwise, a is odd. If $a\%5$ is equal to zero, then a is a multiple of 5. We will use the modulus operator frequently in the development of engineering solutions.

binary operators

unary operators

The five operators (+, −, *, /, %) discussed in the previous paragraphs are **binary operators**—operators that operate on two values. C++ also includes **unary operators** — operators that operate on a single value. For example, plus and minus signs can be unary operators when they are used in an expression such as $-x$.

truncated result

The result of a binary operation with values of the same type is another value of the same type. For example, if a and b are `double` values, then the result of a/b is also a `double` value. Similarly, if a and b are integers, then the result of a/b is also an integer; however, an integer division can sometimes produce unexpected results because any decimal portion of the integer division is dropped; the result is a **truncated result,** not a rounded result. Thus, 5/3 is equal to 1, and 3/6 is equal to 0.

mixed operation

An operation between values with different types is a **mixed operation.** Before the operation is performed, the value with the lower type is converted or promoted to the higher type (as discussed in conversions within assignment statements), and thus the operation is performed with values of the same type. For example, if an operation is specified between an integer and a floating point, the integer will be promoted to a floating point before the operation is performed; the result will be a floating point.

Suppose that we want to compute the average of a set of integers. If the sum and the count of the integers have been stored in the integer objects *sum* and *count,* it would seem that the following statements should correctly compute the average:

```
int sum, count;
double average;
...
average = sum/count;
```

cast operator

However, the division between two integers gives an integer result that is then promoted to a double value. Thus, if *sum* is 18, and *count* is 5, then the value of *average* is 3.0, not 3.6. To compute this average correctly, we use a **cast operator**—a unary operator that allows us to specify a type change in the value before the next computation. In this example, the cast (`double`) is applied to *sum*:

```
average = (double)sum/count;
```

The value of *sum* is promoted to a `double` value before the division is performed. The division is then a mixed operation between a `double` value and an integer, so the value of *count* is promoted to a `double` value; the result of the division is then a `double` value that is assigned to *average*. If the value of *sum* is 18, and the value of *count* is 5, the value of *average* is now correctly computed to be 3.6. The cast operator affects only the value used in the computation; it does not change the value stored in the object *sum*.

Practice!

Give the value computed by each of the following sets of statements.

```
1. int a(27), b(6), c;
   ...
   c = b%a;
```

```
2. int a(27), b(6);
   double c;
   ...
   c = a/(double)b;
```

```
3. int a;
   double b(6), c(18.6);
   ...
   a = c/b;
```

```
4. int b(6);
   double a, c(18.6);
   ...
   a = (int) c/b;
```

Precedence of Operators

precedence of arithmetic operators

In an expression that contains more than one arithmetic operator, we need to be concerned about the order in which the operations are performed. Table 2.4 contains the **precedence of the arithmetic operators,** which matches the standard algebraic precedence. Operations within parentheses are always evaluated first; if the parentheses are nested, the operations within the innermost parentheses are evaluated first. Unary operators are evaluated before the binary operations *, /, and %; binary addition and subtraction are evaluated last. If there are several operators of the same precedence level in an expression, the objects or constants are grouped (or associated) with the operators in a specific order, as specified in Table 2.4. For example, consider the following expression:

```
a*b + b/c*d
```

Because multiplication and division have the same precedence level, and because the associativity (the order for grouping the operations) is from left to right, this expression will be

TABLE 2.4   Precedence of Arithmetic Operators

Precedence	Operator	Associativity
1	Parentheses: ( )	Innermost first
2	Unary operators: + − (type)	Right to left
3	Binary operators: * / %	Left to right
4	Binary operators: + −	Left to right

evaluated as if it contained the following:

```
(a*b) + ((b/c)*d)
```

The precedence order does not specify whether *a*b* is evaluated before *(b/c)*d*; the order of evaluation of these terms is system dependent.

The spacing within an arithmetic expression is a style issue. Some people prefer to put spaces around each operator. We prefer to put spaces only around binary addition and subtraction, because they are evaluated last. *Choose the spacing style that you prefer, but then use it consistently.*

Style

Assume that we want to compute the area of a trapezoid and that we have declared four objects of type `double`: *base, height_1, height_2,* and *area*. Assume further that the objects *base, height_1,* and *height_2* already have values. A statement to correctly compute the area of the trapezoid is

```
area = 0.5*base*(height_1 + height_2);
```

Suppose that we omitted the parentheses in the expression

```
area = 0.5*base*height_1 + height_2;
```

The statement would be executed as if it were this statement:

```
area = ((0.5*base)*height_1) + height_2;
```

Although an incorrect answer has been computed, there is no error message to alert us to the error. Therefore, it is important to be very careful when converting arithmetic expressions into C++. In general, use parentheses to indicate the order of operations in a complicated expression to avoid confusion and to be sure that the expression is evaluated in the manner desired.

You may have noticed that there is no operator for exponentiation to compute values such as x^4. A special mathematical function to perform exponentiation will be discussed in the section on elementary math functions. Of course, exponentiations with integer exponents such as a^2 can be computed with repeated multiplications, as in a*a.

The evaluation of long expressions should be broken into several statements. For example, consider the following equation:

$$f = \frac{x^3 - 2x^2 + x - 6.3}{x^2 + 0.05005x - 3.14}.$$

If we try to evaluate the expression in one statement, it becomes too long to be read easily:

```
f = (x*x*x - 2*x*x + x - 6.3)/(x*x + 0.05005*x - 3.14);
```

We could break the statement into two lines:

```
f = (x*x*x - 2*x*x + x - 6.3)/
    (x*x + 0.05005*x - 3.14);
```

Another solution is to compute the numerator and denominator separately:

```
numerator = x*x*x - 2*x*x + x - 6.3;
denominator = x*x + 0.05005*x - 3.14;
f = numerator/denominator;
```

The objects *x, numerator, denominator,* and *f* must be floating-point objects in order to compute the correct value of *f.*

Practice!

In problems 1 through 3, give C++ statements to compute the indicated values. Assume that the identifiers in the expressions have been defined as objects of type `double` and have also been assigned appropriate values. Use the following constant:

Acceleration of gravity: $g = 9.80665$ m/s^2

1. Distance traveled:

$$\text{Distance} = x_0 + v_0 t + at^2.$$

2. Tension in a cord:

$$\text{Tension} = \frac{2m_1 m_2}{m_1 + m_2} * g.$$

3. Fluid pressure at the end of a pipe:

$$P_2 = P_1 + \frac{pv\left(A_2^2 - A_1^2\right)}{2A_1^2}.$$

In problems 4 through 6, give the mathematical equations computed by the C++ statements. Assume that the following symbolic constants have been defined, where the units of G are m^3/(kg $*$ s^2):

```
const double PI = acos(-1.0);
const double G = 6.67259e-11;
```

4. Centripetal acceleration:

```
centripetal = 4*PI*PI*r/(T*T);
```

5. Potential energy:

```
potential_energy = -G*M_E*m/r;
```

6. Change in potential energy:

```
change = G*M_E*m*(1/R_E - 1/(R_E + h));
```

Overflow and Underflow

The values stored in a computer have a wide range of allowed values. However, if the result of a computation exceeds the range of allowed values, an error occurs. For example, assume that the exponent range of a floating-point value is from -38 to 38. This range should accommodate most computations, but it is possible for the results of an expression to be outside of this range. For example, suppose that we execute the following commands:

```
x = 2.5e30;
y = 1.0e30;
z = x*y;
```

overflow

The values of x and y are within the allowable range. However, the value of z should be 2.5e60, but this value exceeds the range. This error is called exponent **overflow** because the exponent of the result of an arithmetic operation is too large to store in the memory assigned to the object. The action generated by an exponent overflow is system dependent.

underflow

Exponent **underflow** is a similar error caused by the exponent of the result of an arithmetic operation being too small to store in the memory assigned to the object. Using the same allowable range as in the previous example, we obtain an exponent underflow with the following commands:

```
x = 2.5e-30;
y = 1.0e30;
z = x/y;
```

Again, the values of x and y are within the allowable range, but the value of z should be 2.5e-60. Because the exponent is less than the minimum value allowed, we have caused an exponent underflow. Again, the action generated by an exponent underflow is system dependent; on some systems, the result of an operation with exponent underflow is set to zero.

Increment and Decement Operators

increment operator
decrement operator

prefix
postfix

The C++ language contains unary operators for incrementing and decrementing objects; these operators cannot be used with constants or expressions. The **increment operator** $++$ and the **decrement operator** $--$ can be applied either in a **prefix** position (before the identifier), as in $++count$, or in a **postfix** position (after the identifier), as in $count++$. If an increment or decrement operator is used in a statement by itself, it is equivalent to an assignment statement that increments or decrements the object. Thus, the statement

```
y--;
```

is equivalent to the statement

```
y = y - 1;
```

If the increment or decrement operator is used in an expression, then the expression must be evaluated carefully. If the increment or decrement operator is in a prefix position, the identifier is modified, and then the new value is used in evaluating the rest of the expression. If the increment or decrement operator is in a postfix position, the old value of the identifier is used to evaluate the rest of the expression, and then the identifier is modified. Thus, the execution of

```
w = ++x - y;
```
                                                                                   (2.1)

is equivalent to the execution of this pair of statements:

$x = x + 1;$

$w = x - y;$

Similarly, the statement

```
w = x++ - y;
```
                                                                                   (2.2)

is equivalent to the pair of statements

$w = x - y;$

$x = x + 1;$

When executing either Equation (2.1) or Equation (2.2), if we assume that the value of x is equal to 5 and the value of y is equal to 3, then the value of x increases to 6. However, after executing Equation (2.1), the value of w is 3, but after executing Equation (2.2), the value of w is 2.

The increment and decrement operators have the same precedence as the other unary operators. If several unary operators are in an expression, they are associated from right to left. When using postfix notation, the value of the object will be incremented by the time the end of the statement is reached. Exactly when the increment occurs is system dependent. For this reason, the value of the object being modified is not definite from the point at which the postfix operator is applied to the end of the statement.

Abbreviated Assignment Operators

C++ allows simple assignment statements to be abbreviated. For example, each of the following pair of statements contains equivalent statements:

$x = x + 3;$
$x += 3;$

$sum = sum + x;$
$sum += x;$

$d = d/4.5;$
$d /= 4.5;$

$r = r\%2;$
$r \%= 2;$

In fact, any statement of the form

```
identifier = identifier operator expression;
```

can be written in the form

```
identifier operator = expression;
```

Earlier in this section, we used the following **multiple-assignment** statement:

```
x = y = z = 0;
```

The interpretation of this statement is clear, but the interpretation of the following statement is not as evident:

```
a = b += c + d;
```

To evaluate this properly, we use Table 2.5, which indicates that the assignment operators are evaluated last, and their associativity is right to left. Thus, the statement is equivalent to the following:

```
a = (b += (c + d));
```

If we replace the abbreviated forms with the longer forms of the operations, we have

```
a = (b = b + (c + d));
```

or

```
b = b + (c + d);
a = b;
```

Evaluating this statement was good practice with the precedence and associativity table, but, in general, statements used in a program should be more readable. Therefore, using abbreviated assignment statements in a multiple-assignment statement is not recommended. Also, note that the spacing convention that we use inserts spaces around abbreviated operators and multiple-assignment operators because these operators are evaluated after the arithmetic operators.

TABLE 2.5   Precedence of Arithmetic and Assignment Operators

Precedence	Operator	Associativity
1	Parentheses: ( )	Innermost first
2	Unary operators: +- ++ - (type)	Right to left
3	Binary operators: * / %	Left to right
4	Binary operators: + -	Left to right
5	Assignment operators: = += -= *= /= %=	Right to left

Practice!

Give a memory snapshot after each statement is executed, assuming that *x* is equal to 2 and that *y* is equal to 4 before the statement is executed. Also, assume that all the objects are integers.

1. `z = x++ * y;`   2. `z = ++x * y;`
3. `x += y;`   4. `y %= x;`

2.5 Standard Input and Output

cin
cout

C++ uses the object **cin** (pronounced "see in") to perform standard input and the object **cout** (pronounced "see out") to perform standard output. These objects are defined in the Standard C++ library file *iostream*. To use either of these objects in a program, we must include the following preprocessor directive:

```
#include <iostream>
```

The cout Object

stream

output buffer

The *cout* object is defined to **stream** output to the standard output device. The word stream suggests a continual stream of characters that is generated by the program and sent to an **output buffer.** When the output buffer is filled, the contents are displayed on the standard output device. For our examples, we will assume that the standard output device is the screen.

The operator ≪ is used with *cout* to output a value to the screen. The following statement outputs three values to the screen:

```
cout << "The radius of the circle is "
     << radius << " centimeters\n";
```

newline

Each value to be output must be preceded by the ≪ operator. In the foregoing example, the first value to be output is the string "The radius of the circle is", the second value to be output is the value of the object *radius*, the third value to be output is the string "centimeters \n". The characters (\n) represent the **newline** character; the newline character causes an advance to a new line on the screen when printed. The following example illustrates the use of *cout:*

```
double radius(10), area;
const double PI=acos(-1.0);
cout << "The radius of the circle is: " << radius
     << " centimeters\n"
     << "The area is " << PI*radius*radius
     << " square centimeters\n";
```

The output from these statements is

```
The radius of the circle is: 10 centimeters
The area is 314.158 square centimeters
```

Notice that no decimal point is displayed in the value of *radius*, even though *radius* is declared to be of type `double`. Although this is the default formatting in C++, we can override this format using **stream functions** and **manipulators**.

stream functions
manipulators

ostream

Stream Functions and Manipulators

member functions
dot operator (.)

The object *cout* is an object of type *ostream*. The *ostream* class defintion, and the definition of *cout* are included in the Standard C++ Library. The *ostream* `class` includes stream functions that are **member functions** of the *ostream* class and can be called by *ostream* objects. A special operator called the **dot operator** (.) is used when an object calls one of its member functions. The following program uses member functions of the *ostream* class to format output:

```
/*-----------------------------------------------------------*/
/* Program chapter2_3                                        */
/*                                                           */
/*     This program computes area of a circle.              */
/*     Results are displayed with two digits                */
/*     to the right of the decimal point.                   */

#include <iostream>
#include <cmath>
using namespace std;

const double PI=acos(-1.0);

int main()
{
     // Declare and initialize objects.
     double radius(10), area;
     area = PI*radius*radius;

     // Call the setf member function to set format flags
     cout.setf(ios::fixed);
     cout.setf(ios::showpoint);

     // Call the precision member function to set the
     // precision for output
     cout.precision(2);
     cout << "The radius of the circle is: " << radius
          << " centimeters" << endl << "The area is "
          << area << " square centimeters" << endl;

     // exit program
     return 0;
}
/*-----------------------------------------------------------*/
```

The output from this program is

```
The radius of the circle is: 10.00 centimeters
The area is 314.16 square centimeters
```

TABLE 2.6   Common Format Flags

Flag	Meaning
ios::showpoint	display the decimal point
ios::fixed	decimal notation
ios::scientific	scientific notation
ios::right	print right justified
ios::left	print left justified

The *setf( )* function is used to set *format flags* that control the formatting of output. These flags remain set until they changed by another call to the *setf( )* function or they are unset by a call to the function *unsetf( )*. Table 2.6 lists several of the more commonly used format flags.

The *precision( )* function specifies the number of significant digits to be displayed for floating-point values. When used with *ios::fixed,* it specifies how many digits to print to the right of the decimal point. This is illustrated in program chapter2_4.

endl

The manipulator **endl** was used in this example to advance to a new line on the screen. The *endl* manipulator sends a newline character to the output device and it prints the contents of the output buffer immediately, rather than waiting until the buffer is full. When *cout* statements are used to print memory snapshots of a program for debugging, the *endl* manipulator should be used in place of (\n) to ensure that you see your output before the next statement is executed.

Manipulators could have been used in program chapter2_3 instead of the *setf( )* function to format the output. The Standard C++ library file *iostream* includes a set of predefined manipulators such as *endl*. Another Standard C++ library file named *iomanip* includes additional manipulators that are useful for formatting output. Two of these manipulators are **setw()** and

setw
setprecision

setprecision(). The *setw( )* manipulator specifies a width, or number of columns, to be used for printing a value and is useful when output needs to be presented in a table format. The *setprecision( )* manipulator works the same as the function *precision( )*. To use the manipulators in *iomanip,* we must include the following preprocessor directive:

```
#include <iomanip>
```

The following program illustrates the use of manipulators:

```
/*-----------------------------------------------------------*/
/* Program chapter2_4                                        */
/*                                                           */
/*    This program computes area of a circle.               */
/*    Results are displayed with two significant digits     */
```

```
#include <iostream>
#include <iomanip>
#include <cmath>
using namespace std;

const double PI=acos(-1.0);

int main()
{
    // Declare and initialize objects.
    double radius(4.6777), area;
    area = PI*radius*radius;

    cout << setprecision(4)
         << "The radius of the circle is: "
         << setw(10) << radius << " centimeters" << endl;
    cout.setf(ios::scientific);
    cout << "The area of the circle is: " << setw(12) << area \\
         << " square centimeters" << endl;

    // exit program
    return 0;
}
/*----------------------------------------------------------------*/
```

The output from this program is

```
The radius of the circle is:       4.678 centimeters
The area of the circle is:    6.8743e+02 square centimeters
```

The *setw()* manipulator is included in the *iomanip* library file. When the *setw()* manipulator precedes an object in an output statement, the value of the following object is printed **right justified** in a field width specified by the integer argument of the *setw()* manipulator. A list of predefined manipulators is included in Appendix A.

Practice!

Assume that the integer object *sum* contains the value 150 and that the `double` object *average* contains the value 12.368 and that the header files *iomanip* and *iostream* have been included. Show the output generated by the following code segments. Assume each is an independent code segment.

1. `cout << sum << " " << average;`

2. `cout << sum;`
   `cout << average;`

3. `cout << sum << endl << average;`

Practice!

```
4. cout.precision(2);
   cout << sum << endl << average;

5. cout.setf(ios::showpoint);
   cout. precision(3);
   cout << sum << ',' << average;

6. cout.setf(ios::fixed);
   cout.setf(ios::showpoint);
   cout.precision(3);
   cout << sum << ',' << average;

7. cout << setprecision(2) << sum << endl << average;

8. cout << fixed << setprecision(3)
        << setw(10) << average << endl << setw(10)
        << sum << endl;
```

The cin Object

cin
istream

The object **cin** is an object of type *istream*. The *istream* class defintion, and the definition of *cin* are included in the Standard C++ Library file named iostream. The *cin* object is defined to stream input from the standard input device. For our examples, we will assume that the standard input device is the keyboard. The input operator ≫ is used with *cin* to input a value from the keyboard and assign the value to an object. The ≫ operator uses whitespace (blanks, tabs, newlines) as delimiters, or separates, for values on the input stream and so the ≫ operator discards all whitespace. The following statement inputs three values from the keyboard:

```
cin >> var1 >> var2 >> var3;
```

In the preceding example, the first value entered from the keyboard will be assigned to the object *var1,* the second value to *var2,* and the third value to *var3*. When a *cin* statement is executed, the program waits for input. A *cout* statement usually precedes a *cin* statement to user prompt *prompt* the user to enter data. This prompt should describe the order and data type of the values that are to be entered from the keyboard. The data typed at the keyboard is not actually sent to the program until the <Enter> key is hit. This allows the user to backspace and make corrections while entering data.

Data values entered from the keyboard must be separated by whitespace, but it does not matter how many whitespace characters are used. The *cin* statement will continue to discard whitespace until it receives values for each of the objects in the statement. The values entered must be compatible with the data type of the objects in the cin statement. Potential input errors will be discussed in Chapter 5.

The following example illustrates the use of *cin*:

```
double rate, hours;
int id;
```

```
char code;
cout << "Enter the floating point rate of pay "
        << "and hours worked;";
cin >> rate >> hours;
cout << "Enter the employee's integer id: ";
cin >> id;
cout << "Enter the tax code (h,r,l): "
cin >> code;
cout << rate << endl << hours << endl
        << id << endl << code << endl;
```

If the input stream from the keyboard contained the three lines of input

```
10.5  40
556
r
```

the objects in the input statement would be assigned values as shown in figure 0.0:

rate	10.5	hours	40
id	556	code	'r'

The *cout* statement would print the following output to the screen:

```
10.5
40
556
r
```

The ≫ operator interprets the input value according to the data type of the object that follows. The ≫ operator also discards all whitespace. For some applications requiring character data, it may not be desirable to discard whitespace. The function **get()** is a member function of the *istream* class and can be called by *cin* to get a single character from the input stream. The statements

get()

```
char ch;
cin.get(ch);
```

will read the next character from the keyboard and assign the character to the object *ch*. The *get()* function does not discard whitespace, but rather treats whitespace as valid character data, as illustrated in the following example:

```
char ch1, ch2, ch3;
cout << "Enter three characters: ";
cin.get(ch1);
cin.get(ch2);
cin.get(ch3);
cout << ch1 << ch2 << ch3;
```

If the input stream from the keyboard contained the two lines

```
a
1
```

the objects ch1, ch2, and ch3 would be assigned values as shown in figure 0.0:

ch1 `'a'`   ch2 `'\n'`   ch3 `1`

The output would be

```
a
1
```

The *get()* function treats whitespace as valid character data; thus, the newline character was input from the keyboard and stored in the object *ch2*.

2.6 Numerical Technique: Linear Interpolation

The collection of data from an experiment or from observing a physical phenomenon is an important step in developing a problem solution. These data points can generally be considered to be coordinates of points of a function $f(x)$. We would often like to use these data points to determine estimates of the function $f(x)$ for values of x that were not part of the original set of data. For example, suppose that we have data points $(a, f(a))$ and $(c, f(c))$. If we want to estimate the value of $f(b)$, where $a < b < c$, we could assume that a straight line joined $f(a)$ and $f(c)$ and then use linear interpolation to obtain the value of $f(b)$. If we assume that the points $f(a)$ and $f(c)$ are joined by a cubic (third-degree) polynomial, we could use a cubic-spline interpolation method to obtain the value of $f(b)$. Most interpolation problems can be solved using one of these two methods [6, 9]. Figure 2.1 contains a set of six data points that have been connected with straight-line segments and that have been connected with cubic degree polynomial segments. It should be clear that the values determined for the function between sample points depend on the type of interpolation that we select. In this section, we discuss linear interpolation.

A graph with two arbitrary data points $f(a)$ and $f(c)$ is shown in Figure 2.2. If we assume that the function between the two points can be estimated by a straight line, we can then compute the function value at any point $f(b)$ using an equation derived from similar triangles:

$$f(b) = f(a) + \frac{b-a}{c-a}[f(c) - f(a)].$$

Recall that we are also assuming that $a < b < c$.

To illustrate using this interpolation equation, assume that we have a set of temperature measurements taken from the cylinder head in a new engine that is being tested for possible use in a race car. These data are plotted with straight lines connecting the points in Figure 2.3,

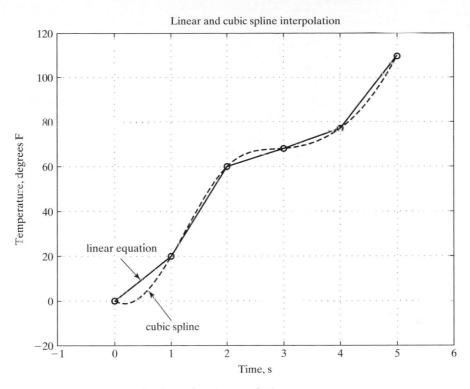

Linear and cubic spline interpolation

Figure 2.1 Linear and cubic spline interpolation.

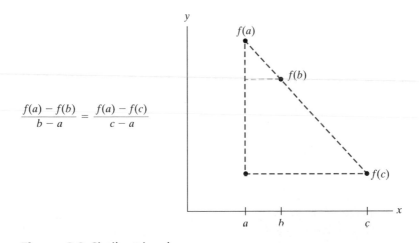

$$\frac{f(a) - f(b)}{b - a} = \frac{f(a) - f(c)}{c - a}$$

Figure 2.2 Similar triangles.

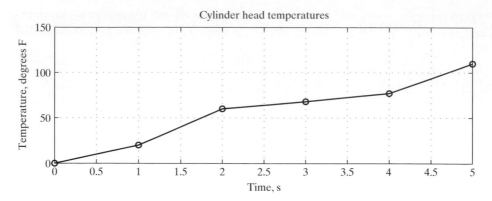

Figure 2.3 Cylinder head temperatures.

and they are also listed here:

Time, s	Temperature, degrees F
0.0	0.0
1.0	20.0
2.0	60.0
3.0	68.0
4.0	77.0
5.0	110.0

Assume that we want to interpolate a temperature to correspond to the value 2.6 seconds. We then have the following situation:

a	2.0	f(a)	60.0
b	2.6	f(b)	?
c	3.0	f(c)	68.0

Using the interpolation formula, we have

$$f(b) = f(a) + \frac{b - a}{c - a}[f(c) - f(a)]$$

$$= 60.0 + \frac{0.6}{1.0}$$

$$= 64.8.$$

In this example, we used linear interpolation to find the temperature that corresponds to a specified time. We could also interchange the roles of temperature and time, so that we plot temperature on the x-axis and time on the y-axis. In this case, we can use the same process to compute the time that a specified temperature occurred, assuming that we have a pair of data points with temperatures below and above the specified temperature.

Practice!

Assume that we have the following set of data points, which is also plotted in Figure 2.4:

Time (s)	Temperature (degrees F)
0.0	72.5
0.5	78.1
1.0	86.4
1.5	92.3
2.0	110.6
2.5	111.5
3.0	109.3
3.5	110.2
4.0	110.5
4.5	109.9
5.0	110.2

1. Use your calculator to compute temperatures at the following times using linear interpolation:

   0.3, 1.25, 2.36, 4.48

2. Use your calculator to compute time values that correspond to the following temperatures using linear interpolation:

   81, 96, 100, 106

3. Suppose Problem 2 asked you to compute the time value that corresponds to the temperature 110 degrees Fahrenheit. What complicates this problem? How many time values correspond to the temperature 110 degrees Fahrenheit? Find each of the corresponding time values using linear interpolation. (You may want to refer to Figure 2.5, which contains a plot of these data with the temperature data on the x-axis and the time values on the y-axis.)

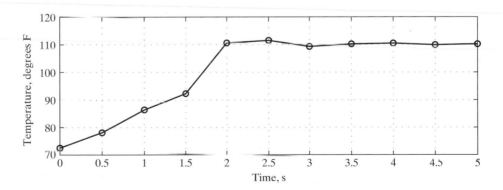

Figure 2.4 Temperature values.

Practice!

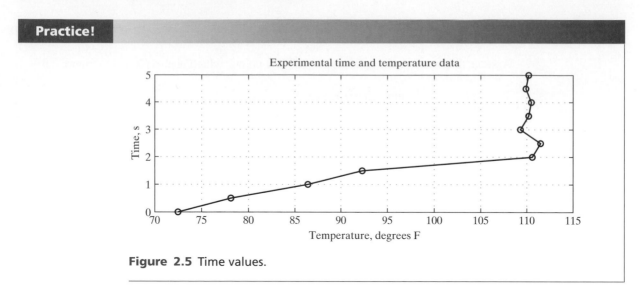

Figure 2.5 Time values.

2.7 Problem Solving Applied: Wind-Tunnel Data Analysis

In this section, we use the new statements presented in this chapter along with linear inter-polation to solve a problem related to the grand challenge discussed in the chapter-opening section.

wind tunnel   A **wind tunnel** is a test chamber built to generate different wind speeds, or Mach numbers (which is the wind speed divided by the speed of sound). Accurate scale models of aircraft can be mounted on force-measuring supports in the test chamber, and then measurements of the forces on the model can be made at many different wind speeds and angles. At the end of an extended wind-tunnel test, many sets of data have been collected and can be used to determine the coefficient of lift, drag, and other aerodynamic performance characteristics of the new aircraft at its various operating speeds and positions [2, 6]. Data collected from a wind-tunnel

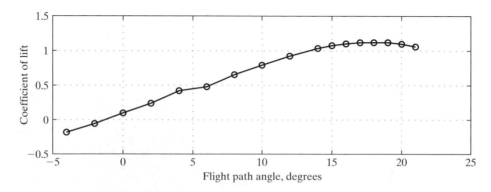

Figure 2.6 Coefficients of lift.

test are plotted in Figure 2.6 and are as follows:

Flight-Path Angle (degrees)	Coefficient of Lift
24	20.182
22	20.056
0	0.097
2	0.238
4	0.421
6	0.479
8	0.654
10	0.792
12	0.924
14	1.035
15	1.076
16	1.103
17	1.120
18	1.121
19	1.121
20	1.099
21	1.059

Assume that we would like to use linear interpolation to determine the coefficient of lift for additional flight-path angles that are between 24 degrees and 21 degrees. Write a program that allows the user to enter the data for two points and a flight-path angle between those points. The program should then compute the corresponding coefficient of lift.

1. PROBLEM STATEMENT

Use linear interpolation to compute a new coefficient of lift for a specified flight-path angle.

2. INPUT/OUTPUT DESCRIPTION

The following diagram shows that the input to the program includes two consecutive points $(a, f(a))$ and $(c, f(c))$ and new flight-path angle b. The output is the new coefficient of lift, $f(b)$. Objects of type `double` will be used to represent the data.

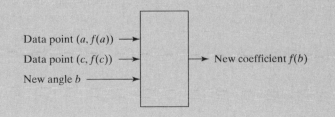

3. HAND EXAMPLE

Suppose that we want to determine the coefficient of lift for a flight-path angle of 8.7 degrees. From the data, we see that this point falls between 8 and 10 degrees:

```
a    8.0     f(a)    0.654
b    8.7     f(b)    ?
c   10.0     f(c)    0.792
```

Using the linear equation formula, we can compute $f(b)$:

$$f(b) = f(a) + \frac{b - a}{c - a}[f(c) - f(a)]$$

$$= 0.654 + \frac{0.7}{2.0}(0.792 - 0.654)$$

$$= 0.702.$$

As expected, this value of $f(b)$ falls between $f(a)$ and $f(c)$.

4. ALGORITHM DEVELOPMENT

The first step in the development of an algorithm is the decomposition of the problem solution into a set of sequentially executed steps:

Decomposition Outline

1. Read the coordinates of the adjacent points and the new flight-path angle.

2. Compute the new coefficient of lift.

3. Print the new coefficient of lift.

This program has a simple structure, so we can convert the decomposition directly into C++:

```
/*-----------------------------------------------------------*/
/*  Program chapter2                                         */
/*                                                           */
/*  This program uses linear interpolation to                */
/*  compute the coefficient of lift for an angle.            */

#include <iostream>
#include <iomanip>
#include <cmath>
using namespace std;
```

```
int main()
{
    //  Declare objects

    double a, f_a, b, f_b, c, f_c;
    // Get user input from the keyboard.
    cout << "Use degrees for all angle measurements. \n";
    cout << "Enter first angle and lift coefficient: \n";
    cin >> a >> f_a;
    cout << "Enter second angle and lift coefficient: \n";
    cin >> c >> f_c;
    cout << "Enter new angle: \n";
    cin >> b;

    //  Use linear interpolation to compute new lift.
    f_b = f_a + (b-a)/(c-a)*(f_c - f_a);

    //  Print new lift value.
    cout << fixed << setprecision(3);
    cout << "New lift coefficient: " << f_b << endl;

    //  Exit program.
    return 0;
}
/*-----------------------------------------------------------*/
```

5. TESTING

We first test the program using the data from the hand example. This generates the following interaction:

```
Use degrees for all angle measurements.
Enter first angle and lift coefficient:
8 0.654
Enter second angle and lift coefficient:
10 0.792
Enter new angle
8.7
New lift coefficient: 0.702
```

The value computed matches the hand example, so we can then test the program with other time values. If the new coefficient value had not matched the result from the hand example, we would then need to determine if the error is in the hand example or in the C++ program. For the linear interpolation to work properly, the new angle must be between the first and second angle that we entered. For this program, we assume that this relationship is maintained. In the next chapter, we learn how to use new C++ commands to be sure that the new angle is between the first and second angles.

These problems relate to the program developed in this section for computing new data values with linear interpolation.

1. Use the program to determine the coefficients of lift to go with the following flight-path angles:

   $-3.2, -0.1, 5, 16.5, 19.5$

2. Modify the program so that it prints the new angle in radians. (Recall that 180 degrees $= \pi$ radians.)

3. Suppose that the data used with the program contained values with the angles in radians instead of degrees. Would the program need to be changed? Explain.

4. Modify the program so that it interpolates for a new angle, instead of a new coefficient. (You may want to refer to Figure 2.7, which contains a plot of this data with the coefficients of lift on the x-axis and the flight-path angle on the y-axis.)

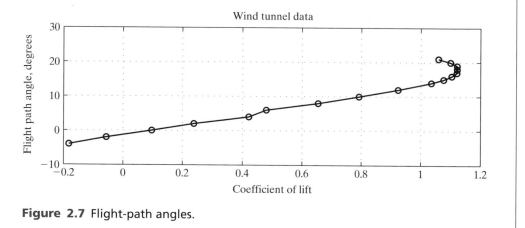

Figure 2.7 Flight-path angles.

2.8 Basic Functions

Arithmetic expressions that solve engineering problems often require computations other than addition, subtraction, multiplication, and division. For example, many expressions require the use of exponentiation, logarithms, exponentials, and trigonometric functions. In this section, we discuss mathematical functions and character functions that are available in the Standard C++ library. Before we discuss the rules relating to functions, we present a specific example. The following statement computes the sine of an angle *theta* and stores the result in the object *b*:

```
b = sin(theta);
```

The *sin()* function assumes that the argument is in radians. If the object *theta* contains a value in degrees, we can convert the degrees to radians with a separate statement. (Recall that 180 degrees $= \pi$ radians.)

```
const double PI = acos(-1.0);
...
theta_rad = theta*PI/180;
b = sin(theta_rad);
```

The conversion can also be specified within the function reference

```
b = sin(theta*PI/180);
```

function arguments

A function reference, such as *sin(theta)*, represents a single value. The parentheses following the function name contain the inputs to the function, which are called **function arguments.** A function may contain no arguments, one argument, or many arguments, depending on its definition. If a function contains more than one argument, it is very important to list the arguments in the correct order. Some functions also require that the arguments be in specific units. For example, the trigonometric functions assume that arguments are in radians. Most of the mathematical functions assume that the arguments are `double` values; if a different type argument is used, it is promoted to a `double` before the function is executed.

A function reference can also be part of the argument of another function reference. For example, the following statement computes the logarithm of the absolute value of x:

```
b = log(abs(x));
```

When one function is used to compute the argument of another function, be sure to enclose the argument of each function in its own set of parentheses. This nesting of functions is also called composition of functions.

We now discuss several categories of functions that are commonly used in engineering computations. Other functions will be presented throughout the remaining chapters as we discuss relevant subjects. Tables of common functions are included on the inside front cover. Appendix A also contains more information on the functions included in the Standard C++ library.

Elementary Math Functions

The elementary math functions include functions to perform a number of common computations such as computing the absolute value of a number and the square root of a number. In addition, they also include a group of functions used to perform rounding. These functions assume that the type of all arguments is `double`, and the functions all return a `double`; if an argument is not a `double`, a conversion will occur using the rules described in Section 2.3. The following preprocessor directive should be used in programs referencing the mathematical functions available in the Standard C++ library:

```
#include <cmath>
```

We now list these functions with a brief description:

abs(x)   This function computes the absolute value of x.

sqrt(x)   This function computes the square root of x, where $x >= 0$.

pow(x,y)   This function is used for exponentiation,
                and computes the value of x to the y power, or x^y.
                Errors occur if $x = 0$ and $y <= 0$, or if $x < 0$ and y is not an integer.

ceil(x)   This function rounds x to the nearest integer toward infinity.
                For example, ceil(2.01) is equal to 3.

floor(x)   This function rounds x to the nearest integer toward negative infinity.
                For example, floor(2.01) is equal to 2.

exp(x)   This function computes the value of e^x,
                where e is the base for natural logarithms, or approximately 2.718282.

log(x)   This function returns ln x, the natural logarithm of x to the base e.
                Errors occur if $x <= 0$.

log10(x)   This function returns $\log_{10} x$, the common logarithm of x to the base 10.
                Errors occur if $x <= 0$.

Remember that the logarithm of a negative value or zero does not exist, and thus an execution error occurs if you use a logarithm function with a negative value for its argument.

Practice!

Evaluate the following expressions:

1. `floor(-2.6)`   2. `ceil(-2.6)`
3. `pow(2,-3)`   4. `sqrt(floor(10.7))`
5. `abs(-10*2.5)`   6. `floor(ceil(10.8))`
7. `log10(100) + log10(0.001)`   8. `abs(pow(-2,5))`

Trigonometric Functions

trigonometric functions

The **trigonometric functions,** also included in file *cmath,* assume that all arguments are of type `double` and that each function returns a value of `double`. In addition, as previously stated, the trigonometric functions also assume that angles are represented in radians. To convert radians to degrees, or degrees to radians, use the following conversions:

```
const double PI = acos(-1.0);
...
angle_deg = angle_rad*(180/PI);
angle_rad = angle_deg*(PI/180);
```

sin(x)   This function computes the sine of x, where x is in radians.
cos(x)   This function computes the cosine of x, where x is in radians.

tan(x)	This function computes the tangent of x, where x is in radians.
asin(x)	This function computes the arcsine, or inverse sine, of x, where x must be in the range $[-1, 1]$. The function returns an angle in radians in the range $[-\pi/2, \pi/2]$.
acos(x)	This function computes the arccosine, or inverse cosine, of x, where x must be in the range $[-1, 1]$. The function returns an angle in radians in the range $[0, \pi]$.
atan(x)	This function computes the arctangent, or inverse tangent, of x. The function returns an angle in radians in the range $[-\pi/2, \pi/2]$.
atan2(y,x)	This function computes the arctangent or inverse tangent of the value y/x. The function returns an angle in radians in the range $[-\pi, \pi]$.

Note that the *atan* function always returns an angle in Quadrant I or IV, whereas the *atan2* function returns an angle that can be in any quadrant, depending on the signs of x and y. Thus, in many applications, the *atan2* function is preferred over the *atan* function.

The other trigonometric and inverse trigonometric functions can be computed using the following equations [10]:

$$\sec x = \frac{1}{\cos x} \qquad a \sec x = a \cos\left(\frac{1}{x}\right)$$

$$\csc x = \frac{1}{\sin x} \qquad a \csc x = a \sin\left(\frac{1}{x}\right)$$

$$\cot x = \frac{1}{\tan x} \qquad a \cot x = a \cos\left(\frac{x}{\sqrt{1+x^2}}\right)$$

 Using degrees instead of radians is a common error in programs with trigonometric functions.

Practice!

In problems 1 through 3, give assignment statements for computing the indicated values, assuming that the objects have been declared and given appropriate values. Also assume that the following declarations have been made:

```
const double g = 9.8:
const double PI = 3.141593;
```

1. Velocity computation:

$$\text{Velocity} = \sqrt{v_0^2 + 2a(x - x_0)}$$

2. Length contraction:

$$\text{Length} = \sqrt[k]{1 - \left(\frac{v}{c}\right)^2}$$

3. Distance of the center of gravity from a reference plane in a sector of a hollow cylinder:

$$\text{Center} = \frac{38.1972(r^3 - s^3)\sin a}{(r^2 - s^2)a}$$

In problems 4 through 6, give the equations that correspond to the assignment statement.

4. Electrical oscillation frequency:

```
frequency = 1/sqrt(2*pi*c/L);
```

5. Range for a projectile:

```
range = (v0*v0/g)*sin(2*theta);
```

6. Speed of a disk at the bottom of an incline:

```
v = sqrt(2*g*h/(1 + I/(m*pow(r,2))));
```

Hyperbolic Functions*

Hyperbolic functions

cmath

Hyperbolic functions are functions of the natural exponential function e^x; the inverse hyperbolic functions are functions of the natural logarithm function *ln x*. These functions are useful in specialized applications such as the design of some types of digital filters. The Standard C++ library includes several hyperbolic functions that are described next. The hyperbolic functions are included in the Standard C++ library, and a preprocessor directive including the information in **cmath** should be used with these functions.

sinh(x)   This function computes the hyperbolic sine of x, which is equal to

$$\frac{e^x + e^{-x}}{2}.$$

cosh(x)   This function computes the hyperbolic cosine of x, which is equal to

$$\frac{e^x - e^{-x}}{2}.$$

tanh(x)   This function computes the hyperbolic tangent of x, which is equal to

$$\frac{\sinh x}{\cosh x}.$$

Additional hyperbolic functions and the inverse hyperbolic functions can be computed using these relationships [10]:

$$\coth x = \frac{\cosh x}{\sinh x}.$$

$$\operatorname{sech} x = \frac{1}{\cosh x}.$$

$$\operatorname{csch} x = \frac{1}{\sinh x}.$$

$$\operatorname{asinh} x = \ln\left(x + \sqrt{x^2 + 1}\right).$$

$$\operatorname{acosh} x = \ln\left(x + \sqrt{x^2 - 1}\right) \quad (\text{for } |x| \geq 1).$$

$$\operatorname{atanh} x = \frac{1}{2}\ln\left(\frac{1 + x}{1 - x}\right) \quad (\text{for } |x| < 1).$$

$$\operatorname{atanh} x = \frac{1}{2}\ln\left(\frac{x + 1}{x - 1}\right) \quad (\text{for } |x| > 1).$$

$$\operatorname{asech} x = \ln\left(\frac{1 + \sqrt{1 - x^2}}{x}\right) \quad (\text{for } 0 < x \leq 1).$$

$$\operatorname{acsch} x = \ln\left(\frac{1}{x} + \frac{\sqrt{1 + x^2}}{|x|}\right) \quad (\text{for } x \neq 0).$$

 Many of the hyperbolic functions and inverse trigonometric functions have restrictions on the range of acceptable values for arguments. If the arguments are entered from the keyboard, remind the user of the range restrictions. In the next chapter, we introduce C++ statements that allow you to determine whether a value is in the proper range during program execution.

Practice!

Give assignment statements for calculating the following values, given the value of x (assume that the value of x is in the proper range of values for the calculations).

1. `coth x`   2. `sec x`
3. `csc x`   4. `acoth x`
5. `acosh x`   6. `acsc x`

Character Functions

The Standard C++ library contains many functions for use with character data. These functions fall into two categories: one set of functions is used to convert characters between uppercase and lowercase, and the other set is used to perform character comparisons. The following preprocessor directive should be used in programs referencing these character functions:

```
#include <cctype>
```

The following statement converts the lowercase letter stored in the object ch to an uppercase character and stores the result in the character object *ch_upper*:

```
ch_upper = toupper(ch);
```

If *ch* is a lowercase letter, the function *toupper* returns the corresponding uppercase letter; otherwise, the function returns *ch*. **Note that no change is made to the object *ch*.**

The character comparison functions return a nonzero value if the comparison is true; otherwise they return zero. The following statement calls the function *isdigit()*. *isdigit()* will return a nonzero value if *ch* is a digit (0–9) or the value 0 (false) if *ch* is not a digit:

```
digit = isdigit(ch);
```

A list of these functions along with a brief explanation is given in Appendix A.

2.9 Problem Solving Applied: Velocity Computation

In this section, we perform computations in another application related to the vehicle performance grand challenge. An advanced turboprop engine called the unducted fan (UDF) is one of the promising new propulsion technologies being developed for future transport aircraft [6]. Turboprop engines, which have been in use for decades, combine the power and reliability of jet engines with the efficiency of propellers. They are a significant improvement over earlier piston-powered propeller engines. Their application has been limited to smaller commuter-type aircraft, however, because they are not as fast or powerful as the fanjet engines used on larger airliners. The UDF engine employs significant advancements in propeller technology, which narrow the performance gap between turboprops and fanjets. New materials, blade shapes, and higher rotation speeds enable UDF-powered aircraft to fly almost as fast as fanjets, and with greater fuel efficiency. The UDF is also significantly quieter than the conventional turboprop.

During a test flight of a UDF-powered aircraft, the test pilot has set the engine power level at 40,000 N (newtons), which causes the 20,000-kg aircraft to attain a cruise speed of 180 m/s (meters/second). The engine throttles are then set to a power level of 60,000 N and the aircraft begins to accelerate. As the speed of the plane increases, the aerodynamic drag increases in proportion to the square of the airspeed. Eventually, the aircraft reaches a new cruise speed where the thrust from the UDF engines is just offset by the drag. The equations used to estimate the velocity and acceleration of the aircraft from the time that the throttle is reset until the plane reaches its new cruise speed (at approximately 120 s) are the following:

$$\text{Velocity} = 0.00001 * \text{time}^3 - 0.00488 * \text{time}^2 + 0.75795 * \text{time} + 181.3566;$$

$$\text{Acceleration} = 3 - 0.000062 * \text{velocity}^2.$$

Plots of these functions are shown in Figure 2.8. Note that the acceleration approaches zero as the velocity approaches its new cruise speed.

Write a program that asks the user to enter a time value that represents the time elapsed (in seconds) since the power level was increased. Compute and print the corresponding acceleration and velocity of the aircraft at the new time value.

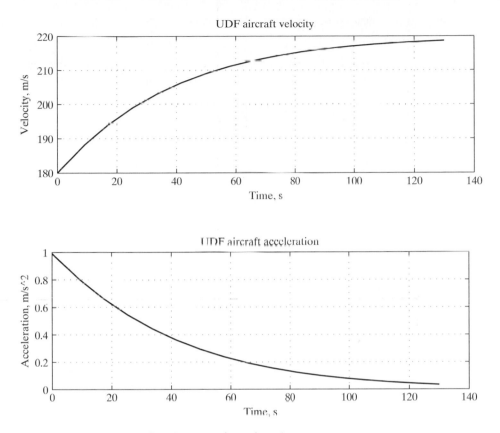

Figure 2.8 UDF aircraft velocity and acceleration.

1. PROBLEM STATEMENT

Compute the new velocity and acceleration of the aircraft after a change in power level.

2. INPUT/OUTPUT DESCRIPTION

The following diagram shows that the input to the program is a time value, and that the output of the program is the pair of new velocity and acceleration values. The built-in data type `double` can be used to represent these values.

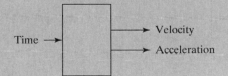

3. HAND EXAMPLE

Suppose that the new time value is 50 seconds. Using the equations given for the velocity and accelerations, we can compute these values:

Velocity = 208.3 m/s;
Acceleration = 0.31 m/s^2.

4. ALGORITHM DEVELOPMENT

The first step in the development of an algorithm is the decomposition of the problem solution into a set of sequentially executed steps:

Decomposition Outline

1. Read new time value.

2. Compute corresponding velocity and acceleration values.

3. Print new velocity and acceleration.

Because this program is a very simple program, we can convert the decomposition directly to C++.

```cpp
/*-------------------------------------------------------*/
/*  Program chapter2_6                                   */
/*                                                       */
/*  This program estimates new velocity and             */
/*  acceleration values for a specified time.           */

#include <iostream>
#include <iomanip>
#include <cmath>
using namespace std;

int main()
{
   //  Declare objects.
   double time, velocity, acceleration;

   //  Get time value from the keyboard.
   cout << "Enter new time value in seconds: \n";
   cin >> time;

   //  Compute velocity and acceleration.
   velocity = 0.00001*pow(time,3) - 0.00488*pow(time,2)
              + 0.75795*time + 181.3566;
   acceleration = 3 - 0.000062*velocity*velocity;
```

```
//  Print velocity and acceleration.
cout << fixed << setprecision(3);
cout << "Velocity = " << setw(10)
     << velocity << " m/s" << endl;
cout << "Acceleration = " << setw( 14)
     << acceleration << "m/s^2" << endl;

//  Exit program.
return 0;
}
/*-----------------------------------------------------------*/
```

5. TESTING

We first test the program using the data from the hand example. This generates the following interaction:

```
Enter new time value in seconds:
50
Velocity = 208.304 m/s
Acceleration =    0.310 m/s^2
```

Because the values computed match the hand example, we can then test the program with other time values. If the values had not matched the hand example, we would need to determine whether the error is in the hand example or in the program.

Modify!

These problems relate to the program developed in this section for computing velocity and acceleration values.

1. Use this program to find the time at which the velocity is equal to 210 m/s.

2. Use this program to find the time at which the acceleration is equal to 0.5 m/s^2.

3. Modify the program so that the input values are entered in minutes instead of seconds. Remember that the equations will still assume that the time values are in seconds.

4. Modify the program so that the output values are printed in feet per second and feet per second^2. (Recall that 1 meter = 39.37 inches.)

2.10 System Limitations

In Section 2.2, we presented a table that contained the maximum values for the various types of integers and floating-point values for the Visual C++ 6.0 compiler. To print a similar table for your system, use the program presented next. Note that the program includes three header files. The *iostream* header file is necessary because the program uses *cout;* the *climits* header file is necessary because it contains information relative to the ranges of integer types; and the *cfloat* header file is necessary because it contains information relative to the ranges of floating-point types. Appendix A contains more information on the constants and limits that are system dependent.

```
/*-----------------------------------------------------*/
/*   Program chapter2_7                                */
/*                                                     */
/*   This program prints the system limitations.       */

#include <iostream>
#include <climits>
#include <cfloat>
using namespace std;
int main()
{
   //  Print integer type maxima. /
   cout << "short maximum: " << SHRT_MAX << endl;
   cout << "int maximum: " << INT_MAX << endl;
   cout << "long maximum: " << LONG_MAX << endl << endl;

   // Print float precision, range, maximum. /
   cout << "float precision digits: " << FLTDIG << endl;
   cout << "float maximum exponent: "
        << FLT_MAX_10_EXP << endl;
   cout << "float maximum: " << FLT_MAX << endl << endl;

   //  Print double precision, range, maximum.  /
   cout << "double precision digits: " << DBL_DIG << endl;
   cout << "double maximum exponent: "
        << DBL_MAX_10_EXP << endl;
   cout << "double maximum: " << DBL_MAX << endl << endl;

   //  Print long precision, range, maximum.  /
   cout << "long double precision: " << LDBL_DIG << endl;
   cout << "long double maximum exponent: "
        << LDBL_MAX_10_EXP << endl;
   cout << "long double maximum: " << LDBL_MAX << endl;

   //  Exit program.
   return 0;
}
/*-----------------------------------------------------*/
```

SUMMARY

In this chapter, we presented the C++ statements necessary to write simple programs that compute and print new values. We also presented the statement that allows us to enter information through the keyboard when the program is executing. The computations that were presented included the standard arithmetic operations and a large number of functions that can be used to perform the types of computations needed for engineering solutions.

Key Terms

abbreviated assignment	mantissa
argument	math function
ASCII code	memory snapshot
assignment statement	modulus
associativity	multiple assignment
binary codes	object
binary operator	overflow
case sensitive	parameter
cast operator	postfix
character	precedence
comment	precision
composition	prefix
constant	preprocessor directive
declaration	prompt
EBCDIC code	range
exponential notation	scientific notation
expression	Standard C++ library
field width	statement
floating-point value	symbolic constant
garbage value	system dependent
hyperbolic function	trigonometric function
identifier	truncate
initial value	unary operator
keyword	underflow
linear interpolation	whitespace

C++ Statement Summary

Preprocessor directives to include information from the files in the Standard C++ library:

General Form:

```
#include<filename>
```

Example:

```
#include <iostream>
#include <cmath>
#include <string>
```

Type Declaration Statement

General Form:

```
datatype identifier [,identifier];
```

Examples: Declarations for integers:

```
short sum=(0);
int year_1, year_2;
long k;
```

Declarations for floating-point values:

```
float height_1, height_2;
double length=(10), side1, side2;
long double distance, velocity;
```

Declarations for characters and strings:

```
char ch;
string name;   //Requires #include<string>
```

Declarations for symbolic constants: General Form:

```
const datatype identifier = expression;
```

Example:

```
const double PI = acos(-1.0);
```

Assignment statement: General Form:

```
identifier = expression;
```

Example:

```
area = 0.5*base*(height_1 + height_2);
```

Keyboard input statement: General Form:

```
cin >> identifier [>> identifier];
```

Example:

```
cin >> hours;
cin >> minutes >> seconds;
```

Character input from keyboard: General Form:

```
cin.get(identifier);
```

Example:

```
cin.get(ch);
```

Screen output statement: General Form:

```
cout << expression [<< expression];
```

Example:

```
cout << "The area is " << area << " square feet. " << endl;
```

Program exit statement: General Form:

```
return integer;
```

Example:

```
return 0;
```

Style **Notes**

1. Use comments throughout a program to improve the readability and to document the steps in it.
2. Use blank lines and indenting to identify the structure of a program.
3. Use the units in an object name when possible.
4. Symbolic constants should be used for engineering constants such as π, and they should be uppercase so that they are easily identified.
5. Use consistent spacing around arithmetic and assignment operators.
6. Use parentheses in complicated expressions to improve readability.
7. The evaluation of long expressions should be broken into several statements.
8. Be sure to include units along with numerical values in the output of a program.
9. Use a prompt to the user to describe the information and units for values to be entered from the keyboard.

Debugging Notes

1. Remember that declarations and C++ statements must end with a semicolon.
2. Preprocessor directives do not end with a semicolon.
3. If possible, avoid mixed assignments that could potentially cause information to be lost.
4. Use parentheses in a long expression to be sure that it is evaluated as desired.
5. Use double precision or extended precision to avoid problems with exponent overflow or underflow.

6. Errors can occur if user input values do not match the data type of the variable used in the cin statement.
7. Be sure to use the operator ≫ with *cin* (not ≪).
8. Be sure to use the operator ≪) with *cout* (not ≫) .
9. In nested function references, each set of arguments must be in its own set of parentheses.
10. Remember that the logarithm functions cannot be used with negative values for arguments.
11. Be sure to use angles in radians with the trigonometric functions.
12. Remember that many of the inverse trigonometric functions and hyperbolic functions have restrictions on the ranges of allowable input values.
13. Remember that the integer representation for a character digit is not the same as the integer representation of the numerical digit.

Problems

Exam Practice!

Indicate whether the following statements are true (T) or false (F)

1. The execution of a program begins with the main function. T F
2. C++ is not case sensitive.   T F
3. Declarations can be placed anywhere in the program.   T F
4. Statement and declarations must end with a semicolon.   T F
5. The result of an integer division is a rounded result.   T F

Indicate if the following declaration statements are correct or not. If the statement is incorrect, modify it so that it is a correct statement.

9. `int i, j, k,`
10. `float f1(11), f2(202.00);`
11. `DOUBLE D1, D2, D3;`
12. `float a1(a2);`
13. `int n, m_m;`
14. Which of the following is NOT a C++ keyword?
    (a) `const`
    (b) `goto`
    (c) `static`
    (d) `when`
    (e) `unsigned`
15. In a declaration, the type specifier and the object name are separated by
    (a) a period.
    (b) a space.
    (c) an equal sign.
    (d) a semicolon.
    (e) none of the above.
16. Which of the following declarations would properly define x, y, and z as double objects?
    (a) `double x, y, z;`
    (b) `long double x,y,z`

(c) `double x=y=z;`
(d) `double X, Y, Z`

17. In C++, the binary operator % is applied to compute
 (a) integer division.
 (b) floating-point division.
 (c) the remainder of integer division.
 (d) the remainder of floating-point division.
 (e) none of the above.

18. Which of the following assignments produces a value of zero?
 (a) `result = 9%3 - 1;`
 (b) `result = 8%3 - 1;`
 (c) `result = 2 - 5%2;`
 (d) `result = 2 - 6%2;`
 (e) `result = 2 - 8%3;`

Give the corresponding snapshots of memory after each of the following set of statements has been executed.

19. `int x1;`

    `. . .`
    `x1 = 3 + 4%5 - 5;`
    `int x(1), z(5);`
    `. . .`
    `z = z/++x;`
20. `double a(3.8), z;`
    `int n(2), y;`
    `. . .`
    `x = (y=a/n)*2;`

Give the output generated by the sets of statements in Problems 21 through 23.

21. `float value_1(5.78263);`

    `. . .`
    `cout << "value_1 = " << value_1;`
22. `double value_4(66.45832);`

    `. . .`
    `cout << scientific << "value_4 = " << value_4`
23. `int value_5(7750);`

    `. . .`
    `cout << "value_5 = " << fixed << value_5 << endl;`

Programming Problems

Conversions. This set of problems involves conversions of a value in one unit to another unit. Each program should prompt the user for a value in the specified units and then print the converted value, along with the new units.

1. Write a program to convert miles to kilometers. (Recall that 1 mi = 1.6093440 km.)
2. Write a program to convert meters to miles. (Recall that 1 mi = 1.6093440 km.)

3. Write a program to convert pounds to kilograms. (Recall that 1 kg = 2.205 lb.)
4. Write a program to convert newtons to pounds. (Recall that 1 lb = 4.448 N.)
5. Write a program that converts degrees Fahrenheit (TF) to degrees Rankin (TR). (Recall that TF = TR − 459.67 degrees Rankin.)
6. Write a program that converts degrees Celsius (TC) to degrees Rankin (TR). (Recall that TF = TR − 459.67 degrees Rankin and that TF = (9/5) TC + 32 degrees Fahrenheit.)
7. Write a program that converts degrees Kelvin (TK) to degrees Fahrenheit (TF). (Recall that TR = (9/5) TK and that TF = TR − 459.67 degrees Rankin.)

Areas and Volumes.   These problems involve computing an area or a volume using input from the user. Each program should include a prompt to the user to enter the objects needed.

8. Write a program to compute the area A of a rectangle with sides a and b. (Recall that $A = a * b$.)
9. Write a program to compute the area A of a triangle with base b and height h. (Recall that $A = \frac{1}{2}(b * h)$.)
10. Write a program to compute the area A of a circle with radius r. (Recall that $A = \pi r^2$.)
11. Write a program to compute the area A of a sector of a circle when u is the angle in radians between the radii. (Recall that $A = r^2\theta/2$.)
12. Write a program to compute the area A of a sector of a circle when d is the angle in degrees between the radii. (Recall that $A = r^2\theta/2$, where θ is in radians.)
13. Write a program to compute the area A of an ellipse with semiaxes a and b. (Recall that $A = \pi a * b$.)
14. Write a program to compute the area A of the surface of a sphere of radius r. (Recall that $A = 4\pi r^2$.)
15. Write a program to compute the volume V of a sphere of radius r. (Recall that $V = (4/3)\pi r^3$.)
16. Write a program to compute the volume V of a cylinder of radius r and height h. (Recall that $V = \pi r^2 h$.)

Amino Acid Molecular Weights.   The amino acids in proteins are composed of atoms of oxygen, carbon, nitrogen, sulfur, and hydrogen, as shown in Table 2.7. The molecular weights of the individual elements are as follows:

Element	Atomic Weight
Oxygen	15.9994
Carbon	12.011
Nitrogen	14.00674
Sulfur	32.066
Hydrogen	1.00794

17. Write a program to compute and print the molecular weight of glycine.
18. Write a program to compute and print the molecular weights of glutamic and glutamine.

TABLE 2.7 Amino Acid Molecules

Amino Acid	O	C	N	S	H
Alanine	2	3	1	0	7
Arginine	2	6	4	0	15
Asparagine	3	4	2	0	8
Aspartic	4	4	1	0	6
Cysteine	2	3	1	1	7
Glutamic	4	5	1	0	8
Glutamine	3	5	2	0	10
Glycine	2	2	1	0	5
Histidine	2	6	3	0	10
Isoleucine	2	6	1	0	13
Leucine	2	6	1	0	13
Lysine	2	6	2	0	15
Methionine	2	5	1	1	11
Phenylanlanine	2	9	1	0	11
Proline	2	5	1	0	10
Serine	3	3	1	0	7
Threonine	3	4	1	0	9
Tryptophan	2	11	2	0	11
Tyrosine	3	9	1	0	11
Valine	2	5	1	0	11

19. Write a program that asks the user to enter the number of atoms of each of the five elements for an amino acid. Then compute and print the molecular weight for this amino acid.

20. Write a program that asks the user to enter the number of atoms of each of the five elements for an amino acid. Then compute and print the average weight of the atoms in the amino acid.

Logarithms to the base b. To compute the logarithm of x to base b, we can use the following relationship

$$\log_b x = \frac{\log_e x}{\text{lob}_e b}.$$

21. Write a program that reads a positive number and then computes and prints the logarithm of the value to base 2. For example, the logarithm of 8 to base 2 is 3 because $2^3 = 8$.

22. Write a program that reads a positive number and then computes and prints the logarithm of the value to base 8. For example, the logarithm of 64 to base 8 is 2 because $8^2 = 64$.

CHAPTER 3

GRAND CHALLENGE:
Global Change

Weather balloons are used to collect data from the upper atmosphere. The balloons are filled with helium and rise to an equilibrium point where the difference between the densities of the helium inside the balloon and the air outside the balloon is just enough to support the weight of the balloon. During the day, the sun warms the balloon, causing it to rise to a new equilibrium point; in the evening, the balloon cools, and it descends to a lower altitude. The balloon can be used to measure the temperature, pressure, humidity, chemical concentrations, or other properties of the air around the balloon. A weather balloon may stay aloft for only a few hours or as long as several years collecting environmental data. The balloon falls back to earth as the helium leaks out or is released.

Control Structures

Chapter Outline

Objectives

3.1 Algorithm Development
3.2 Conditional Expressions
3.3 Selection Statements
3.4 Loop Structures
3.5 Problem Solving Applied: Weather Balloons

Summary, Key Terms, C++ Statement Summary, Style Notes, Debugging Notes, Problems

OBJECTIVES

In this chapter, we present **structured programming** in terms of **sequence, selection,** and **repetition structures.** After defining these structures using **pseudocode** and **flowcharts,** we then discuss the C++ statements for implementing these structures. Sequence structure does not require new statements. Selection and repetition structures use **conditional statements** for control. The selection structure is implemented with two different structures: if statements and the switch statement. These structures provide alternative paths in a program. The repetition structure is implemented with three different loop structures: while **loops,** do while **loops,** and for **loops.** Examples of three common forms of input loops are given, including **counter-controlled loops, sentinel-controlled loops** and **end-of-data** loops. An example that applies to weather balloons is used to illustrate conditional statements and loops.

3.1 Algorithm Development

In Chapter 2, the C++ programs that we developed were very simple. The steps were sequential, and typically involved reading information from the keyboard, computing new information, and then printing the new information. In solving engineering problems, most of the solutions require more complicated steps, and thus we need to expand the algorithm development part of our problem-solving process.

Top-Down Design

Top-down design presents a "big picture" description of the problem solution in sequential steps. This overall description of the problem is then refined until the steps are detailed enough to translate to language statements. We used decomposition outlines in Chapters 1 and 2 to provide the first definition of a problem solution. This outline is written in sequential steps, and can be shown in a diagram or a step-by-step outline. For very simple problems, such as the one that follows, which was developed in Chapter 2, we can go from the decomposition outline directly to the C++ statements:

Decomposition Outline

1. Read the new time value.

2. Compute the corresponding velocity and acceleration values.

3. Print the new velocity and acceleration.

divide-and-conquer

pseudocode
flowchart

However, for most problem solutions, we need to refine the decomposition outline into a description with more detail. This process is often referred to as a **divide-and-conquer** strategy, because we keep breaking the problem solution into smaller and smaller portions. To describe this stepwise refinement, we use pseudocode or flowcharts.

The refinement of an outline into more detailed steps can be done with **pseudocode** or a **flowchart.** Pseudocode uses English-like statements to describe the steps in an algorithm, and a flowchart uses a diagram to describe the steps in an algorithm. The fundamental steps in most algorithms are shown in Figure 3.1, along with the corresponding notation in pseudocode and flowcharts.

Pseudocode and flowcharts are tools to help us determine the order of steps to solve a problem. Both tools are commonly used, although they are not generally both used with the same problem. In order to give examples of both tools, some problem solutions will use pseudocode and others will use flowcharts; the choice between pseudocode and flowcharts is usually a personal preference. Sometimes we need to go through several levels of pseudocode or flowcharts to develop complex problem solutions; this is the stepwise refinement that we mentioned previously in this section. Decomposition outlines, pseudocode, and flowcharts are working models of the solution, and thus are not unique. Each person working on a solution will have different decomposition outlines and pseudocode or flowchart descriptions, just like the C++ programs developed by different people will be somewhat different, although they solve the same problem.

Structured Programming

sequence
selection
repetition

A structured program is one written using simple control structures to organize the solution to a problem. A simple structure is usually defined to be a **sequence,** a **selection,** or a **repetition.** A sequence structure contains steps that are performed one after another; a selection structure contains one set of steps that is performed if a condition is true and another set of steps that is performed if the condition is false; a repetition structure contains a set of steps that is repeated as long as a condition is true. We now discuss each of these simple structures and use pseudocode and flowcharts to give specific examples.

A sequence contains steps that are performed one after another. All the programs developed in Chapter 2 have a sequence structure. For example, the pseudocode for the program that performed the linear interpolation follows, and the flowchart for the program that computed the velocity and acceleration of the aircraft with the unducted engine is shown in Figure 3.2.

Refinement in Pseudocode

```
main: read a,fₐ
read c,t_c
set f_b to fₐ + b-a/c-a * (f_c - fₐ)
print f_b
```

A selection structure contains a condition that can be evaluated as either true or false. If the condition is true, then one set of statements is executed; if the condition is false, then another set of statements is executed. For example, suppose that we have computed values for the numerator and denominator of a fraction. Before we compute the division, we want to be sure that the denominator is not close to zero. Therefore, the condition that we want to test is "denominator close to zero." If the condition is true, then we want to print a message indicating that we cannot compute the value. If the condition is false, which means that the denominator is

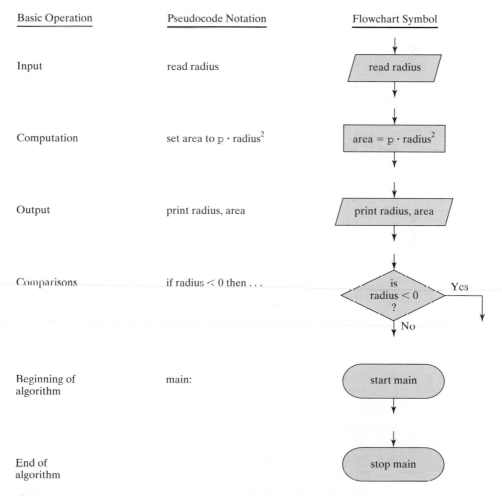

Figure 3.1 Pseudocode notation and flowchart symbols.

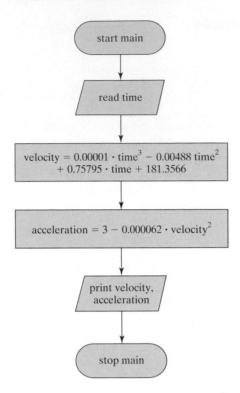

Figure 3.2 Flowchart for unducted fan problem solution from Section 2.9.

not close to zero, then we compute and print the value of the fraction. In defining this condition, we need to define "close to zero." For this example, we will assume that close to zero means that the absolute value is less than 0.0001. A pseudocode description follows, and a flowchart description of this structure is shown in Figure 3.3.

```
if |denominator| < 0.0001
        print "Denominator close to zero"
else
        set fraction to numerator/denominator
        print fraction
```

Note that this structure also contains a sequence structure (compute a fraction and then print the fraction) that is executed when the condition is false. We give more variations of the selection structure later in this chapter.

The repetition structure allows us to repeat (or loop through) a set of steps as long as a condition is true. For example, we might want to compute a set of velocity values that correspond to time values of 0, 1, 2, ..., 10 seconds. We do not want to develop a sequential structure that has a statement to compute the velocity for a time of 0, another statement to compute the velocity for a time of 1, and then another statement to compute the velocity for a time of 2, and so on. Although this structure would require only 11 statements in this case, it

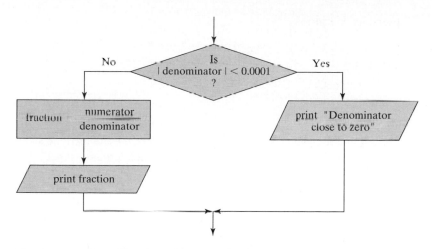

Figure 3.3 Flowchart for selection structure.

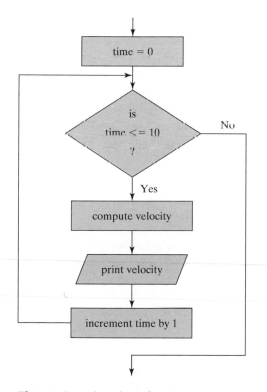

Figure 3.4 Flowchart for repetition structure.

could require hundreds of statements if we wanted to compute the velocity values over a long period. If we use the repetition structure, we can develop a solution in which we initialize the time to 0. Then, as long as the time value is less than or equal to 10, we compute and print a velocity value, and increment the time value by 1. When the time value is greater than 10, we exit the structure. Figure 3.4 contains the flowchart for this repetition structure, and the pseudocode follows:

```
set time to 0
while time <= 10
       compute velocity
       print velocity
       increment time by 1
```

In the remaining sections of this chapter, we present the C++ statements for performing selections and repetitions and then develop example programs that use these structures.

Evaluation of Alternative Solutions

There are usually many ways to solve the same problem. In most cases, there is not a single best solution, but some solutions are better than others. Selecting a good solution becomes easier with experience, and we will give examples of the elements that contribute to good solutions in this text. For example, a good solution is one that is readable; therefore, a good solution is not necessarily the shortest solution, because short solutions are often not very readable. We will strive to avoid subtle or clever steps that shorten a program, but are difficult to understand.

As you begin to develop a solution to a problem, it is a good idea to try to think of several ways to solve it. Sketch the decomposition outline and pseudocode or flowchart for several solutions. Then choose the solution that you think will be the easiest to translate into C++ statements. Some algorithms fit different languages better than others, so you also want to pick a solution that is a good fit to the C++ language. Occasionally, other aspects of a solution must also be considered, such as execution speed and memory requirements.

Error Conditions

As we develop an algorithm, we usually assume that the input data are correct. However, in real applications, there are often errors in the input data. Therefore, it may be important to test for errors in the input data that could occur and would cause the program to work incorrectly. Methods for testing for errors in input data will be discussed in Chapter 4. There may also be conditions that could arise as we compute new values that could cause problems. For example, suppose that we are performing a computation in which the denominator value for a division operation turns out to be zero. Or suppose that the result of an altitude computation is negative.

error conditions   These are examples of **error conditions** (which are separate from errors in the algorithm) that could occur when a program is executed.

Some error conditions can be checked within the program itself using statements that we present in this chapter, but if we check for every possible error condition, our programs become long, and a large percentage of the statements are checking for error conditions. Therefore, how do we decide which error conditions to check in our programs? Sometimes the problem statement will include information on error conditions that could occur, and the response to take if they are detected. Usually, though, error conditions are not mentioned. In these cases, we suggest that you develop an algorithm based on the problem statement, and then generate a list of potential error conditions that could arise. If possible, discuss these with the person or group that will be using the program. Otherwise, include error checks that seem to catch the most common types of errors, and then include written documentation to go with the program that describes the error conditions that your program will catch and the ones that your program does not catch.

Once you have decided which error conditions you will incorporate in your algorithm, you still need to decide what to do if one of the error conditions occurs. There are usually two possibilities: You can exit the program, or you can attempt to correct the error and continue with the program. In either case, you should probably print an error message that describes the error condition that occurred and the action that you are taking. Be sure that the error message gives as much information as possible. Instead of printing "Error occurred in input data," print messages such as "Temperature out of bounds," "Time value is negative," or "Pressure exceeds safety limits."

Generation of Test Data

The generation of test data is a very important part of developing problem solutions. Test data should include data to test each of the error conditions that is checked in our programs. Test data should also test each path through our program. As programs become longer, generating test data to completely test the program becomes very difficult. Entire courses and books are based on this validation and verification topic.

We now give some suggestions on generating test data sets. First, use the data from the hand example. If this does not work properly, we are not off to a good start! Once these data work correctly, begin using test data that are correct, but cover different ranges of values. Be sure to use test data that test the boundary conditions, or limits, if the data are supposed to be with in certain ranges. Once the program seems to work for valid data, begin including the error conditions to see whether the program handles them properly. In general, use many small sets of data instead of one large set of data to test the program.

If you find an error in testing the program, go back to the algorithm development step. Correct the error in the decomposition outline and the pseudocode or flowchart, and then correct the C++ program. When you make a major change in the program, you should completely retest the program. Sometimes changes affect parts of the program that we had not anticipated. This retesting is easier if we keep a log of the test sets used so that we can repeat them.

program walkthrough

Finally, we want to mention a technique called a **program walkthrough** that is commonly used in industry in the development of large programs. In a program walkthrough, the people who have developed an algorithm for a complicated problem present their solution to a small group of people who are knowledgeable about the problem, but did not take part in the algorithm development. The interaction between the people who developed the algorithm and the people who are analyzing it usually results in identifying potential problems with the algorithm and the generation of potential test data for the software after it is coded. The result is that the final program is completed sooner with more confidence in its accuracy. You might try simple program walkthroughs with other students in your class as you solve more complicated problems.

3.2 Conditional Expressions

conditions

relational operators

logical operators

Because both selection and repetition structures use **conditions,** we must discuss conditions before presenting the statements that implement selection and repetition structures. A condition is an expression that can be evaluated to be true or false, and it is composed of expressions combined with **relational operators;** a condition can also include **logical operators.** In this

evaluation order

section, we present relational operators and logical operators and discuss the **evaluation order** when they are combined in a single condition.

Relational Operators

The relational operators that can be used to compare two expressions in C++ are shown in the following list:

Relational Operator	Interpretation
<	is less than
<=	is less than or equal to
>	is greater than
>=	is greater than or equal to
==	is equal to
! =	is not equal to

Blanks can be used on either side of a relational operator, but blanks cannot be used to separate a two-character operator such as ==.

Sample conditions are the following:

```
a < b
x+y >= 10.5
fabs(denominator) < 0.0001
```

Given the values of the identifiers in these conditions, we can evaluate each one to be true or false. For example, if a is equal to 5 and b is equal to 8.4, then $a < b$ is a true condition. If x is equal to 2.3 and y is equal to 4.1, then $x + y >= 10.5$ is a false condition. If $denominator$ is equal to 20.0025, then $fabs(denominator) < 0.0001$ is a false condition.

Style

For readability, we use spaces around the relational operator in a logical expression, but not around the arithmetic operators in the conditions.

In C++, a true condition is assigned a value of 1 and a false condition is assigned a value of zero. Therefore, the following statement is valid:

```
d = b > c;
```

If $b > c$, then d is assigned a value of 1; otherwise, a value of zero is assigned to d. A single value can be used in place of a condition. For example, consider the following statement:

```
if (a)
    count++;
```

If the condition value is zero, then the condition is assumed to be false; if the value is nonzero, then the condition is assumed to be true. Therefore, in the previous statement, the value of *count* will be incremented if a is *nonzero*.

Logical Operators

logical operators

Logical operators can also be used within conditions. However, logical operators compare conditions, not expressions. C++ supports three **logical operators: and, or,** and **not.** These

TABLE 3.1   Logical Operators

A	B	A && B	A || B	!A	!B
False	False	False	False	True	True
False	True	False	True	True	False
True	False	False	True	False	True
True	True	True	True	False	False

logical operators are represented by the following symbols:

Logical Operation	Symbol
and	&&
or	||
not	!

For example, consider the following condition:

```
a<b && b<c
```

Style

The relational operators have higher precedence than the logical operator; therefore, this condition is read "a is less than b, and b is less than c." *In order to make a condition more readable, we insert spaces around the logical operator, but not around the relational operators.* Given values for a, b, and c, we can evaluate this condition as true or false. For example, if a is equal to 1, b is equal to 5, and c is equal to 8, then the condition is true. If a is equal to -2, b is equal to 9, and c is equal to 2, then the condition is false.

If A and B are conditions, then the logical operators can be used to generate new conditions $A \&\& B$, $A \| B$, $!A$, and $!B$. The condition $A \&\& B$ is true only if both A and B are true. The condition $A \| B$ is true if either or both A and B are true. The ! operator changes the value of the condition which it precedes. Thus, the condition $!A$ is true only if A is false, and the condition $!B$ is true only if B is false. These definitions are summarized in Table 3.1.

When expressions with logical operators are executed, C++ will only evaluate as much of the expression as necessary to evaluate it. This is known as short circuiting. For example, if A is false, then the expression $A \&\& B$ is also false, and there is no need to evaluate B. Similarly, if A is true, then the expression $A \| B$ is true, and there is no need to evaluate B.

Precedence and Associativity

A condition can contain several logical operators, as in the following:

```
!(b==c || b==5.5)
```

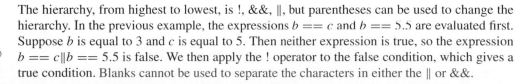

The hierarchy, from highest to lowest, is !, &&, \|\|, but parentheses can be used to change the hierarchy. In the previous example, the expressions $b == c$ and $b == 5.5$ are evaluated first. Suppose b is equal to 3 and c is equal to 5. Then neither expression is true, so the expression $b == c \| b == 5.5$ is false. We then apply the ! operator to the false condition, which gives a true condition. Blanks cannot be used to separate the characters in either the \|\| or &&.

TABLE 3.2   Operator Precedence for Arithmetic, Relational, and Logical Operators

Precedence	Operation	Associativity
1	( )	innermost first
2	++ -- + - ! (type)	right to left (unary)
3	* / %	left to right
4	+ -	left to right
5	< <= > >=	left to right
6	== !=	left to right
7	&&	left to right
8	||	left to right
9	= += -= *= /= %=	right to left

A common error is to use = instead of == in a logical expression.

A condition can contain both arithmetic operators and relational operators, as well as logical operators. Table 3.2 contains the precedence and the associativity order for the elements in a condition.

Practice!

Determine whether the following conditions in programs 1 through 8 are true or false. Assume that the following objects have been declared and initialized as shown:

$$a = 5.5 \quad b = 1.5 \quad k = 3$$

1. $a < 10.0 + k$
2. $a + b >= 6.5$
3. $k != a - b$
4. $b - k > a$
5. $!(a == 3 * b)$
6. $-k <= k + 6$
7. $a < 10\ \&\&\ a > 5$
8. $fabs(k) > 3\ \|\|\ k < b - a$

3.3   Selection Statements

The if statement allows us to test conditions and then perform statements based on whether the conditions are true or false. C++ contains two forms of if statements-the simple if statement and the **if/else** statement. C++ also contains a switch statement that allows us to test multiple conditions and then execute groups of statements based on whether the conditions are true or false.

Simple if Statements

The simplest form of an if statement has the following general form:

```
if (condition)
    statement 1;
```

If the condition is true, we execute statement 1; if the condition is false, we skip statement 1.

Style

The statement within the if statement is indented so that it is easier to visualize the structure of the program from the statements.

If we wish to execute several statements (or a sequence structure) when the condition is true, we use a **statement block** which is composed of a set of statements enclosed in braces. The location of the braces is a matter of style; two common styles are shown:

statement block

```
Style 1                    Style 2
if (condition)                 if (condition) {
{                                  statement 1;
    statement 1;                   statement 2;
    statement 2;                   ...
    ...                            statement n;
    statement n;               }
}
```

Style

In the text solutions, we use the first style convention; thus, both braces are on lines by themselves. *Although this makes the program a little longer, it also makes it easier to notice if a brace has been mistakenly omitted.* Figure 3.5 contains flowcharts of the control flow with simple if statements containing either one statement to execute, or several statements to execute, if the condition is true.

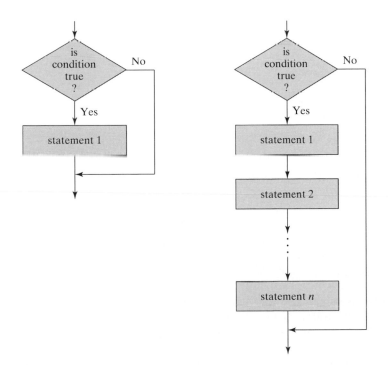

Figure 3.5 Flowcharts for selection statements.

A specific example of an `if` statement follows:

```
if (a < 50)
{
    ++count;
    sum += a;
}
```

If *a* is less than 50, then *count* is incremented by 1 and *a* is added to *sum;* otherwise, these two statements are skipped.

nesting of if statements

The statements inside an `if` statement block can be any C++ statement, including another `if` statement. This **nesting of if statements** is illustrated in the following example:

```
if(count < 50)
{
    count++;
    sum = sum + a;
    if(count < 40)
    {
        a++;
    }
}
```

If *count* is less than 50, we increment *count* by 1 and add *a* to *sum*. In addition, if *count* is less than 40, then we also increment *a*. If *count* is not less than 50, then we skip all of these statements. *For readability, indent the statements in each if statement block.*

Style

if/else Statement

An `if/else` statement allows us to execute one statement block if a condition is true and a different statement block if the condition is false. The simplest form of an `if/else` statement is the following:

```
if (condition)
    statement 1;
else
    statement 2;
```

empty statement

Statements 1 and 2 can be replaced by statement blocks. Statement 1 or statement 2 can also be an **empty statement,** which is just a semicolon. If statement 2 is an empty statement, then the `if/else` statement should probably be posed as a simple `if` statement. There are situations in which it is convenient to use an empty statement for statement 1; however, these statements can also be rewritten as simple `if` statements with the conditions reversed. For example, the following two statements are equivalent:

```
if (a < b)            if (a >= b)
    ;                     count++;
else
    count++;
```

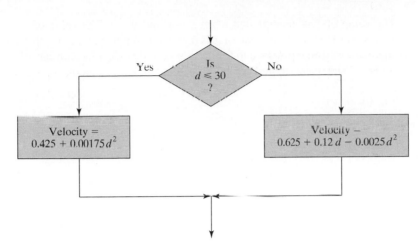

Figure 3.6 Flowchart for if/else statement.

Consider this if/else statement:

```
if (d <= 30)
    velocity = 0.425 + 0.00175*d*d;
else
    velocity = 0.625 + 0.12*d - 0.0025*d*d;
```

In this example, velocity is computed with the first assignment statement if the distance d is less than or equal to 30; otherwise, velocity is computed with the second assignment statement. A flowchart for this if/else statement is shown in Figure 3.6.

Another example of the if/else statement is

```
if (fabs(denominator) < 0.0001)
    cout << "Denominator close to zero" << endl;
else
{
    x = numerator/denominator;
    cout << "x = " << x << endl;
}
```

In this example, we examine the absolute value of the object *denominator*. If this value is close to zero, we print a message indicating that we cannot perform the division. If the value of *denominator* is not close to zero, we compute and print the value of x. The flowchart for this statement was shown in Figure 3.3.

Consider the following set of nested if/else statements:

```
if (x > y)
    if (y < z)
        k++;
    else
        m++;
else
    j++;
```

The value of k is incremented when $x > y$ and $y < z$. The value of m is incremented when $x > y$ and $y >= z$. The value of j is incremented when $x <= y$. With careful indenting, this statement is straightforward to follow. Suppose that we now eliminate the `else` portion of the inner `if` statement. If we keep the same indention, the statements become the following:

```
if (x > y)
   if (y < z)
      k++;
else
   j++;
```

It might appear that j is incremented when $x <= y$, but that is not correct. The C++ compiler will associate an `else` statement with the closest `if` statement within a block. Therefore, no matter what indenting is used, the previous statement is executed as if it were the following:

```
if (x > y)
   if (y < z)
      k++;
   else
      j++;
```

Thus, j is incremented when $x > y$ and $y >= z$. If we intended for j to be incremented when $x <= y$, then we would need to use braces to define the inner statement as a block:

```
if (x > y)
{
   if (y < z)
      k++;
}
else
   j++;
```

conditional operator

To avoid confusion and possible errors when using **if/else** statements, you should routinely use braces to clearly define the statement blocks.

C++ allows a **conditional operator** to be used in place of a simple `if/else` statement. This conditional operator is a ternary operator because it has three arguments: a condition, a statement to perform if the condition is true, and a statement to perform if the condition is false. The operation is indicated with a question mark following the condition and with a colon between the two statements. To illustrate, the following two statements are equivalent:

```
if (a<b)                          a<b ? count++ : c = a + b;
   count++;
else
   c = a + b;
```

The conditional operator (specified as ?:) is evaluated before assignment operators, and if there is more than one conditional operator in an expression, they are associated from right to left.

In this section, we have presented a number of ways to compare values in selection statements. A caution is necessary when comparing floating-point values. As we saw in Chapter 2, floating-point values can sometimes be slightly different than we expect them to be because of the conversions between binary and decimal values. For example, earlier in this section, we did not compare *denominator* with zero, but instead used a condition to see if the absolute value of *denominator* was less than a small value. Similarly, if we wanted to know whether y was close to the value 10.5, we should use a condition such as *fabs(y − 10.5) <= 0.0001* instead of *y == 10.5*. In general, do not use the equality operator with floating point values.

Practice!

In problems 1 through 7, draw a flowchart to perform the steps indicated. Then give the corresponding C++ statements. Assume that the objects have been declared and have reasonable values.

1. If time is greater than 15.0, increment time by 1.0.

2. When the square root of *poly* is less than 0.5, print the value of *poly*.

3. If the difference between *volt_1* and *volt_2* is larger than 10.0, print the values of *volt_1* and *volt_2*.

4. If the value of *den* is less than 0.05, set *result* to zero; otherwise, set *result* equal to *num* divided by *den*.

5. If the natural logarithm of *x* is greater than or equal to 3, set *time* equal to zero and decrement *count*.

6. If *dist* is less than 50.0 and *time* is greater than 10.0, increment *time* by 2; otherwise, increment *time* by 2.5.

7. If *dist* is greater than or equal to 100.0, increment *time* by 2.0. If *dist* is between 50 and 100, increment *time* by 1. Otherwise, increment *time* by 0.5.

switch Statement

The `switch` statement is used for multiple-selection decision making. In particular, it is often used to replace nested `if/else` statements. Before giving the general discussion of the `switch` statement, we present a simple example that uses nested `if/else` statements and then an equivalent solution that uses the `switch` statement.

Suppose that we have a temperature reading from a sensor inside a large piece of machinery. We want to print a message on the control screen to inform the operator of the temperature status. If the status code is 10, the temperature is too hot, and the equipment should be turned off; if the status code is 11, the operator should check the temperature every 5 minutes; if the status code is 13, the operator should turn on the circulating fan; for all other status codes, the equipment is operating in a normal mode. The correct message could be printed with the following set of nested `if/else` statements:

```
if (code == 10)
{
   cout << "Too hot - turn equipment off." << endl;
}
else
{
   if (code == 11)
   {
      cout << "Caution - recheck in 5 minutes." << endl;
   }
   else
   {
      if (code == 13)
      {
         cout << "Turn on circulating fan." << endl;
      }
      else
      {
         cout << "Normal mode of operation." << endl;
      }
   }
}
```

An equivalent statement is the following `switch` statement:

```
switch (code)
{
   case 10:
      cout << "Too hot - turn equipment off." << endl;
      break;
   case 11:
      cout << "Caution - recheck in 5 minutes." << endl;
      break;
   case 13:
      cout << "Turn on circulating fan." << endl;
      break;
   default:
      cout << "Normal temperature range." << endl;
      break;
}
statement 1;
```

The `break` statement causes execution of the program to continue with the statement following the `switch` statement (*statement* 1 in this example), thus skipping the rest of the statements in the braces.

Nested `if/else` statements do not always easily translate to a `switch` statement. However, when the conversion works, the `switch` statement is usually easier to read. It is also easier to determine the statement grouping needed for the `switch` statement.

controlling
expression

The `switch` statement selects the statements to perform based on a **controlling expression,** which must be an expression of type integer or character. In the general form given below, the `case` labels (*label_1, label_2, ...*) determine which statements are executed, and thus in some languages this structure is called a **case structure.** The statements executed are the ones that correspond to the `case` for which the label is equal to the controlling expression.

case labels
default label

The **case labels** must be unique constants; an error occurs if two or more of the case labels have the same value. The **default label** is used to give a statement to execute if none of the other statements is executed; the `default` label is optional.

```
switch (controlling expression)
{
    case label_1:
        statements;
    case label_2:
        statements;

    ...
    default:
        statements;
}
```

The statements in the `switch` structure usually contain the `break` statement. When the `break` statement is executed, the execution of the program breaks out of the `switch` structure and continues executing with the statement following the `switch` structure. Without the break statement, all statements will be executed that follow the ones selected with the case label.

Although the default clause in the `switch` statement is optional, we recommend that it be included so that the steps are clearly specified for the situation in which none of the case labels is equal to the controlling expression. We also use the `break` statement in the `default` clause to emphasize that the program continues with the statement following the `switch` statement.

It is valid to use several `case` labels with the same statement, as in

```
switch (op_code)
{
    case 'N':
    case 'R':
        cout << "Normal operating range." << endl;
        break;
    case 'M':
        cout << "Maintenance needed." << endl;
        break;
    default:
        cout << "Error in code value." << endl;
        break;
}
```

When more than one `case` label is used for the same statement, the evaluation is performed as if the logical **or** operator joined the cases. For this example, the first statement is executed if *op_code* is equal to 'N' **or** if *op_code* is equal to 'R'.

Practice!

Convert the following nested `if`/`else` statements to a `switch` statement:

```
if (rank==1 || rank==2)
{
    cout << "Lower division" << endl;
}
else
{
    if (rank==3 || rank==4)
    {
        cout << "Upper division" << endl;
    }
    else
    {
        if (rank==5)
        {
            cout << "Graduate student" << endl;
        }
        else
        {
            cout << "Invalid rank" << endl;
        }
    }
}
```

3.4 Loop Structures

Loops are used to implement repetitive structures. C++ contains three different loop structures-the `while` loop, the `do/while` loop, and the `for` loop. In addition, C++ allows us to use two additional statements with loops to modify their performance-the `break` statement (which we used with the `switch` statement) and the `continue` statement.

Before presenting these loop structures, we would like to present two debugging suggestions that are useful when trying to find errors in programs that contain loops. When compiling longer programs, it is not uncommon to have a large number of compiler errors. Rather than trying to find all errors after compiling, we suggest that you recompile your program after correcting one or two obvious syntax errors. One error will often generate several error messages. Some of these error messages may describe errors that are not in your program, but were printed because the original error confused the compiler.

The second debugging suggestion relates to errors inside a loop. When you want to determine whether the steps in a loop are working the way that you want, include *cout* statements in the loop to provide a memory snapshot of key objects each time the loop is executed. Then, if there is an error, you have much of the information that you need to determine what is causing the error. Remember to use the *endl* manipulator in your *cout* statements to be sure that the output buffer is printed to the screen after each debugging statement.

while Loop

The general form of a while loop follows:

```
while (condition)
    statement;
```

The condition is evaluated before the statements within the loop are executed. If the condition is false, the statement block is skipped, and execution continues with the statement following the while loop. If the condition is true, then the statement block is executed, and the condition is evaluated again. If it is still true, then the statement block is executed again, and the condition is evaluated again. This repetition continues until the condition is false.

infinite loop

The statements that form a loop must modify objects that are used in the condition; otherwise, the value of the condition will never change, and we will either never execute the statements in the loop or we will never be able to exit the loop. An **infinite loop** is generated if the condition in a while loop is always true.

Most systems have a defined limit on the amount of time that can be used by a program, and will generate an execution error when this limit is exceeded. Other systems require that the user enter a special sequence of characters, such as the control key followed by the character c (abbreviated as <cntrl> c) to stop or abort the execution of a program. Nearly everyone eventually writes a program that inadvertently contains an infinite loop, so be sure you know the special characters to abort the execution of a program for your system.

The following pseudocode and program use a while loop to generate a conversion table for converting degrees to radians. The degree values start at 0 degrees, increment by 10 degrees, and go through 360 degrees.

```
Refinement in Pseudocode
main:   set degrees to zero
        while degrees <= 360
                convert degrees to radians
                print degrees, radians
                add 10 to degrees
/*------------------------------------------------------*/
/*   Program chapter3_1                                 */
/*                                                      */
/*   This program prints a degree-to-radian table       */
/*   using a while loop structure.                       */

#include <iostream>
#include <iomanip>
using namespace std;

const double PI = 3.141593;

int main()
{
    //  Declare and initialize objects.
    int degrees(0);
    double radians;
```

```
//  Set formats.
cout.setf(ios::fixed);
cout.precision(6);

//  Print radians and degrees in a loop.
cout << "Degrees to Radians \n";
while (degrees <= 360)
{
   radians = degrees*PI/180;
   cout << setw(6) << degrees << setw(10) << radians << endl;
   degrees += 10;
}

//  Exit program.
return 0;
}
/*-------------------------------------------------------*/
```

The first few lines of output from the program follow:

```
Degrees to Radians
     0   0.000000
    10   0.174533
    20   0.349066
     .    ...
```

do/while Loop

The do/while loop is similar to the while loop, except that the condition is tested at the end of the loop instead of at the beginning of the loop. Testing the condition at the end of the loop ensures that the do/while loop is always executed at least once; a while loop will not be executed at all if the condition is initially false. The general form of the do/while loop is as follows:

```
do
{
   statements;
} while (condition);
```

The following pseudocode and program print the degree-to-radian conversion table using a do/while loop instead of a while loop:

```
Refinement in Pseudocode
main: set degrees to zero
        do
              convert degrees to radians
              print degrees, radians
              add 10 to degrees
        while degrees <= 360
```

```
/*-------------------------------------------------------*/
/*   Program chapter3_2                                  */
/*                                                       */
/*   This program prints a degree-to-radian table        */
/*   using a do-while loop structure.                    */

#include <iostream>
#include <iomanip>

const double PI = 3.141593;

int main()
{
    // Declare and initialize objects.
    int degrees(0);
    double radians;

    // Set formats.
    cout.setf(ios::fixed);
    cout.precision(6);

    // Print degrees and radians in a loop.
    cout << "Degrees to Radians \n";
    do
    {
        radians = degrees*PI/180;
        cout << setw(6) << degrees << setw(10) << radians << endl;
        degrees += 10;
    } while (degrees <= 360);

    // Exit program.
    return 0;
}
/*-------------------------------------------------------*/
```

for Loop

Many programs require loops that are based on the value of a object that increments (or decrements) by the same amount each time through the loop. When the object reaches a specified value, we then want to exit the loop. This type of loop can be implemented as a `while` loop, but it can also be easily implemented with the `for` loop. The general form of the `for` loop is as follows:

```
for (expression_1; expression_2; expression_3)
{
    statements;
}
```

loop-control object

The first expression is used to initialize the **loop-control object,** *expression_2* specifies the condition that must be true to continue the loop repetition, and *expression_3* specifies the modification to the loop-control object that follows the execution of the statement block.

For example, if we want to execute a loop 10 times, with the value of the object k going from 1 to 10 in increments of 1, we could use the following `for` loop structure:

```
for (int k=1; k<=10; k++)
{
    statements;
}
```

In this example, the object k is declared and initialized in the the first expression and can be referenced inside the braces of the `for` loop. The full scope of k is system dependent.

If we want to execute a loop with the value of the object n going from 20 to 0 in increments of -2, we could use this loop structure:

```
for (n=20; n>=0; n-=2)
{
    statements;
}
```

In this form, the object n is assigned an initial value in the first expression, but must be declared before the `for` statement. The `for` loop could also have been written in the form

```
for (n=20; n>=0; n=n - 2)
{
    statements;
}
```

Both forms are valid, but the abbreviated form for the third expression is commonly used because it is shorter.

The following expression computes the number of times that a `for` loop will be executed:

$$\text{floor}\left(\frac{\text{final value} - \text{initial value}}{\text{increment}}\right) + 1.$$

If this value is negative, the loop is not executed. Thus, if a `for` statement has the structure

```
for (int k=5; k<=83; k+=4)
{
    statements;
}
```

then it would be executed the following number of times:

$$\text{floor}\left(\frac{83 - 5}{4}\right) + 1 = \text{floor}\left(\frac{78}{4}\right) + 1 = 20.$$

The value of k would be 5, 9, 13, and so on, until the final value of 81. The loop would not be executed with the value of 85 because the loop condition is not true when k is equal to 85.

nested `for` statements

Consider the following set of **nested `for` statements:**

```
for(int k=1; k<=3; k++)
{
```

```
    for(int j=0; j<2; j++)
    {
      count++;
    }
}
```

The outer `for` loop will be executed three times. The inner `for` loop will be executed twice each time the outer `for` loop is executed. Thus, the object *count* will be incremented six times.

The following pseudocode and program print the degree-to-radian conversion table shown earlier with a `while` loop, now modified to use a `for` loop. Note that the pseudocode for the `while` loop solution to this problem and the pseudocode for the `for` loop solution to this problem are identical.

```
Refinement in Pseudocode
main:    set degrees to zero
         while degrees <= 360
                 convert degrees to radians
                 print degrees, radians
                 add 10 to degrees
```

```
/*-------------------------------------------------      */
/*   Program chapter3_3                                  */
/*                                                       */
/*   This program prints a degree-to-radian table        */
/*   using a for loop structure.                          */

#include <iostream>
#include <iomanip>
using namespace std;

const double PI = 3.141593;

int main()
{
   //  Declare the objects.
   double radians;

   //  Set formats.
   cout.setf(ios::fixed);
   cout.precision(6);

   //  Print degrees and radians in a loop.
   cout << "Degrees to Radians \n";
   for (int degrees=0; degrees<=360; degrees+=10)
   {
     radians = degrees*PI/180;
     cout << setw(6) << degrees << setw(10) << radians << endl;
   }

   //  Exit program.
   return 0;
}
/*-------------------------------------------------*/
```

Practice!

For problems 1 through 5, determine the number of times that the `for` loop is executed.

```
1. for (int k=3; k<=20; k++)
   {
   statements;
   }

2. for (int k=3; k<=20; ++k)
   {
   statements;
   }

3. for (int count=-2; count<=14; count++)
   {
   statements;
   }

4. for (int k=2; k>=10; k)
   {
   statements;
   }

5. for (int time=10; time>=5; time++)
   {
       statements;
   }
```

6. What is the value of *count* after the nested `for` loops are executed?

```
int count(0);
for(int k=-1; k<4; k++)
{
        for(int j=3; j>0; j--)
        {
                count++;
        }
}
```

The initialization and modification expressions in a `for` loop can contain more than one statement, as shown in this `for` statement that initializes and updates two objects in the loop:

```
for (int k=1, j=5; k<=10; k++, j++)
{
    sum_1 += k;
    sum_2 += j;
}
```

comma operator   When more than one statement is used, they are separated by commas, and are executed from left to right. This **comma operator** is executed last in operator precedence.

break and continue Statements

iteration

We used the `break` statement in a previous section with the `switch` statement. The `break` statement can also be used with any of the loop structures presented in this section to immediately exit from the loop in which it is contained. In contrast, the `continue` statement is used to skip the remaining statements in the current pass or **iteration** of the loop, and then continue with the next iteration of the loop. Thus, in a `while` loop or a `do/while` loop, the condition is evaluated after the `continue` statement is executed to determine if the statements in the loop are to be executed again. In a `for` loop, the loop-control object is modified, and the repetition–continuation condition is evaluated to determine whether the statements in the loop are to be executed again. Both the `break` and `continue` statements are useful in exiting either the current iteration or the entire loop, respectively, when error conditions are encountered.

To illustrate the difference between the `break` and the `continue` statements, consider the following loop that reads values from the keyboard:

```
sum = 0;
for (int k=1; k<=20; k++)
{
    cin >> x;
    if (x > 10.0)
       break;
    sum += x;
}
cout << "Sum = " << sum << endl;
```

This loop reads up to 20 values from the keyboard. If all 20 values are less than or equal to 10.0, then the statements compute the sum of the values and print the sum. But, if a value is read that is greater than 10.0, then the `break` statement causes control to break out of the loop, and execute the *cout* statement. Thus, the sum printed is only the sum of the values up to the value greater than 10.0.

Now, consider this variation of the previous loop:

```
sum = 0;
for (int k=1; k<=20; k++)
{
    cin >> x;
    if (x > 10.0)
       continue;
    sum += x;
}
cout << "Sum = " << sum << endl;
```

In this loop, the sum of all 20 values is printed if all values are less than or equal to 10.0. However, if a value is greater than 10.0, then the `continue` statement causes control to skip the rest of the statements in that iteration of the loop, and to continue with the next iteration of the loop, Hence, the sum printed is the sum of all values in the 20 values that are less than or equal to 10.

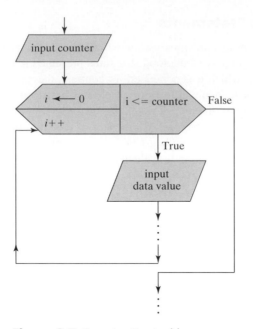

Figure 3.7 Counter Control loop.

Structuring Input Loops

Loops are often required for reading data from the keyboard or from a data file. Data files will be discussed in Chapter 4. In this section we introduce three common forms of input loops: the **counter-controlled loop,** the **sentinel-controlled loop,** and the **end-of-data loop.** We illustrate how each of these loops is implemented when reading data from standard input.

counter-controlled
loop

sentinel-controlled
loop

end-of-data loop

A **counter-controlled** loop can be used for reading input data if the number of data values is known before the data are entered. The number of data values to be input is read from the keyboard and stored in a counter. The counter is then used to control the number of iterations of the input loop. A flowchart of this looping structure is given in Figure 3.7.

This loop is easily implemented using a `while` loop or a `for` loop. We use a `for` loop in the following example to calculate the average of a set of exam scores entered from the keyboard:

```
/*-------------------------------------------------------------*/
/*  Program chapter3_4                                         */
/*  This programs finds the average of a set of exam scores.  */

#include<iostream>
using namespace std;

int main()
{
// Declare and initialize objects.
   double exam_score, sum(0), average;
   int counter;

// Prompt user for input.
   cout << "Enter the number of exam scores to be read ";
```

```
      cin >> counter;
      cout << "Enter " << counter << " exam scores separated "
                                  << " by whitespace ";

// Input exam scores using counter-controlled loop.
      for(int i=1; i<=counter; i++)
      {
         cin >> exam_score;
         sum = sum + exam_score;
      }

// Calculate average exam score.
      average = sum/counter;
      cout << counter << " students took the exam.\n";
      cout << "The exam average is " << average << endl;

// Exit program
      return 0;
}
/*------------------------------------------------------------*/
```

sentinel-controlled
loop

A **sentinel-controlled loop** can be used to input data if a special data value exists that can be used to indicate the end of data. This value must be a value that cannot occur naturally in the input data. A flowchart of this looping structure is given in Figure 3.8.

We will use a `while` loop to implement this structure. To calculate the average of a set of exam scores, we can use this loop structure, with a negative value as the sentinel value, as illustrated in the next example.

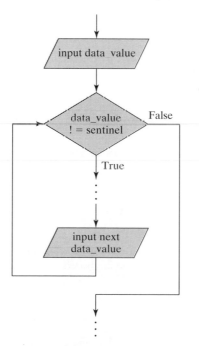

Figure 3.8 Sentinel-controlled loop

```
/*------------------------------------------------------------*/
/*   Program chapter3_5                                        */
/*   This programs finds the average of a set of exam scores. */

#include<iostream>
using namespace std;

int main()
{
// Declare and initialize objects.
   double exam_score, sum(0), average;
   int count(0);

// Prompt user for input.
   cout << "Enter exam scores separated by whitespace.\n";
   cout << "Enter a negative value to indicate the end of data. ";

// Input exam scores using sentinel-controlled loop.
   cin >> exam_score;
   while(exam_score >= 0)
   {
      sum = sum + exam_score;
      count++;
      cin >> exam_score;
   }

// Calculate average exam score.
   average = sum/count;
   cout << count << " students took the exam.\n";
   cout << "The exam average is " << average << endl;

// Exit program
   return 0;
}
/*------------------------------------------------------------*/
```

end-of-data loop

The **end-of-data loop** is the most flexible loop for reading input data. The loop is structured to continue executing the statements inside the loop while new data are available. No prior knowledge of the number of data values is required, and no sentinel value is required. Execution of the loop terminates when the end of data is encountered. The *eof( )* function can be used to determine whether the end of data has been encountered. The *eof( )* function is a member of the *istream* class, and it returns a value of true if the end of data has been reached. A flowchart of this looping structure is given in Figure 3.9. The end-of-data loop is easily implemented using a `while` loop, as illustrated in the following example, which calculates the average of a set of exam scores, entered from the keyboard:

```
/*------------------------------------------------------------*/
/*   Program chapter3_6                                        */
/*   This programs finds the average of a set of exam scores. */

#include<iostream>
using namespace std;
```

```cpp
int main()
{
// Declare and initialize objects.
double exam_score, sum(0), average;
int count(0);

// Prompt user for input.
cout << "Enter exam scores separated by whitespace. ";

// Input exam scores using end-of-data loop.
cin >> exam_score;
while(!cin.eof())
{
    sum = sum + exam_score;
    count++;
    cin >> exam_score;
}

// Calculate average exam score.
average = sum/count;
cout << count << " students took the exam.\n";
cout << "The exam average is " << average << endl;

// Exit program
return 0;
}
```

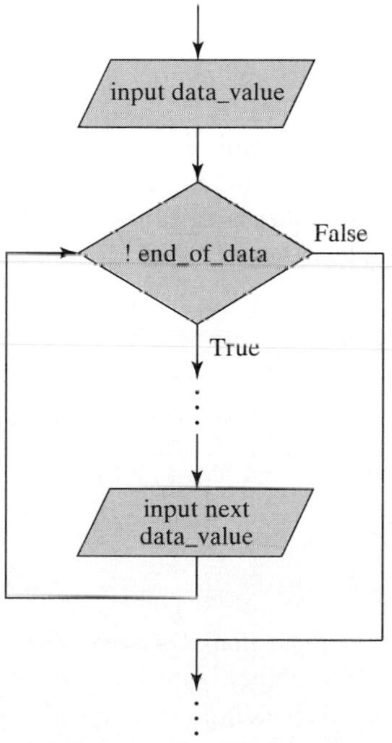

Figure 3.9 End-of-data loop

```
/* ----------------------------------------------------------------*/
```

In program *chapter3_5*, the first input statement attempts to read an exam score from the keyboard. If a data value is read, the *eof( )* function returns a value of false, and the statements within the body of the loop are executed. Notice the use of the ! operator in the expression controlling the `while` statement. The last statement in the `while` loop is another input statement that attempts to read the next exam score from the keyboard. This is the correct structure for an end-of-data loop. The `while` loop will continue to execute while the end of data has not been reached.

The eof() function will not return a value of true until after the end of data is encountered. For this reason it is common to be off by one when reading and counting data if the correct structure of the end-of-data loop is not used. When using the end-of-data loop with standard input you need to know what key sequence your system recognizes as the end of data indicator. Many Unix and Linux systems recognize the <cntrl> d key sequence as an end-of-data indicator.

3.5   Problem Solving Applied: Weather Balloons

Weather balloons are used to gather temperature and pressure data at various altitudes in the atmosphere. The balloon rises because the density of the helium in the balloon is less than the density of the surrounding air outside the balloon. As the balloon rises, the surrounding air becomes less dense, and thus the balloon's ascent slows until it reaches a point of equilibrium. During the day, sunlight warms the helium trapped inside the balloon, which causes the helium to expand and become less dense and the balloon to rise higher. During the night, however, the helium in the balloon cools and becomes more dense, causing the balloon to descend to a lower altitude. The next day, the sun heats the helium again and the balloon rises. Over time, this process generates a set of altitude measurements that can be approximated with a polynomial equation.

Assume that the polynomial $\text{alt}(t) = -0.12t^4 + 12t^3 - 380t^2 + 4100t + 220$, where the units of t are hours, represents the altitude or height in meters during the first 48 hours following the launch of a weather balloon. The corresponding polynomial model for the velocity in meters per hour of the weather balloon is $v(t) = -0.48t^3 + 36t^2 - 760t + 4100$.

Print a table of the altitude and the velocity for this weather balloon using units of meters and meters per second. Let the user enter the start time, increment in time between lines of the table, and ending time, where all the time values must be less than 48 hours. In addition to printing the table, also print the peak altitude and its corresponding time.

1. PROBLEM STATEMENT

Using the polynomials that represent the altitude and velocity for a weather balloon, print a table using units of meters and meters per second. Also find the maximum altitude (or height) and its corresponding time.

2. INPUT/OUTPUT DESCRIPTION

The following I/O diagram shows the user input that represents the starting time, time increment, and ending time for the table. The output is the table of altitude and velocity values and the maximum altitude and its corresponding time. We can use the built-in data type `double` for our input and output objects.

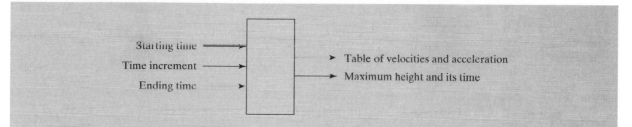

3. HAND EXAMPLE

Assume that the starting time is 0 hours, the time increment is 1 hour, and the ending time is 5 hours. To obtain the correct units, we need to divide the velocity value in meters per hour by 3600 in order to get meters per second. Using our calculator, we can then compute the following values:

Time	Altitude (m)	Velocity (m/s)
0	220.00	1.14
1	3,951.88	0.94
2	6,994.08	0.76
3	9,414.28	0.59
4	11,277.28	0.45
5	12,645.00	0.32

We can also determine the maximum altitude for this table, which is 12,645.00 meters; it occurred at 5 hours.

4. ALGORITHM DEVELOPMENT

We first develop the decomposition outline because it breaks the solution into a series of sequential steps.

Decomposition Outline

1. Get user input to specify times for the table.

2. Generate and print conversion table and find maximum height and corresponding time.

3. Print maximum height and corresponding time.

The second step in the decomposition outline represents a loop in which we generate the table and, at the same time, keep track of the maximum height. As we refine this outline, and particularly step 2 into more detail, we need to think carefully about finding the maximum height. Look back at the hand example. Once the table has been printed, it is easy to look at it and select the maximum height. However, when the computer is computing and printing the table, it does not have all the data at one time; it only has the information for the current line in the table. Therefore, to keep track of the maximum, we need to specify a separate object to store the maximum value. Each time that we compute a new height, we will compare that value to the maximum value. If the new value is larger, we replace the maximum with this new value. We will also need to keep track of the corresponding time. The following refinement in pseudocode outlines these new steps:

```
Refinement in Pseudocode
main: read initial, increment, final values from keyboard
      set max_height to zero
      set max_time to zero
      print table heading
      set time to initial
      while time <= final
              compute height and velocity
              print height and velocity
              if height > max_height
                     set max_height to height
                     set max_time to time
              add increment to time
      print max_time and max_height
```

The steps in the pseudocode are now detailed enough to convert into C++. Note that we convert the velocity from meters per hour to meters per second in the *cout* statement.

```
/*-----------------------------------------------------------*/
/*   Program chapter3_7                                      */
/*                                                           */
/*   This program prints a table of height and              */
/*   velocity values for a weather balloon.                 */

#include <iostream>
#include <iomanip>
#include <cmath>
using namespace std;

int main()
{
// Declare and initialize objects.
   double initial, increment, final, time, height,
          velocity, max_time(0), max_height(0);
   int loops;

// Get user input.
   cout << "Enter initial value for table (in hours) \n";
   cin >> initial;
   cout << "Enter increment between lines (in hours) \n";
   cin >> increment;
   cout << "Enter final value for table (in hours) \n";
   cin >> final;

   // Print report heading.
   cout << "\n\nWeather Balloon Information \n";
```

```
cout << "Time     Height      Velocity \n";
cout << "(hrs)    (meters)    (meters/s) \n";

// Set formats.
cout.setf(ios::fixed);
cout.precision(2);

//  Compute and print report information.
//  Determine number of iterations required.
//  Use integer index to avoid rounding error.
loops = (int)( (final - initial)/increment );

for (int count=0; count<=loops; count++)
{
   time = initial + count*increment;
   height = -0.12*pow(time,4) + 12*pow(time,3)
            - 380*time*time + 4100*time + 220;
   velocity = -0.48*pow(time,3) + 36*time*time
              - 760*time + 4100;
   cout << setw(6) << time << setw(10) << height
        << setw(10) << velocity/3600 << endl;
   if (height > max_height)
   {
      max_height = height;
      max_time = time;
   }
}
// Print maximum height and corresponding time.
cout << "\nMaximum balloon height was " << setw(8)
     << max_height << " meters \n";

cout << "and it occurred at " << setw(6) << max_time
     << " hours \n";

/* Exit program. */
return 0;
}
/*-------------------------------------------------------*/
```

5. TESTING

If we use the data from the hand example, we have the following interaction with the program:

```
Enter initial value for table (in hours)
0
Enter increment between lines (in hours)
1
Enter final value for table (in hours)
5
```

```
Weather  Balloon  Information
Time          Height          Velocity
(hrs)         (meters)        (meters/s)
0               220.00        1.14
1              3951.88        0.94
2              6994.08        0.76
3              9414.28        0.59
4             11277.28        0.45
5             12645.00        0.32
```

Maximum balloon height was 12645.00 meters and it occurred at 5.00 hours

Figure 3.10 contains a plot of the altitude and velocity of the balloon for a period of 48 hours. From the plots, we can see the periods during which the balloon rises or falls.

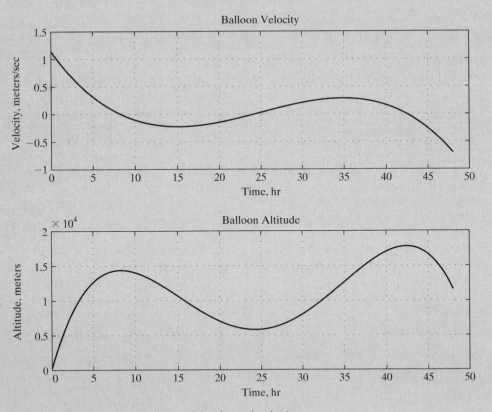

Figure 3.10 Weather balloon altitude and velocity.

Modify!

These problems relate to the program developed in this section that prints a table of weather balloon information.

1. Use this program to generate a table showing the weather balloon information for every 10 minutes for 2 hours, starting at 4 hours after the balloon was launched.

2. Modify the program to include a check to be sure that the final time is greater than the initial. If it is not, ask the user to reenter the complete set of report information.

3. The equations given in this section were developed to be accurate only for time from 0 to 48 hours, so modify the program to print a message to the user that specifies an upper bound of 48 hours. Also, check the user input to be sure that it stays within the proper bounds. If there are any errors, ask the user to reenter the complete set of report information.

4. If there are two times with the same maximum height, this program will print the first time that the maximum height occurred. Modify the program so that it will print the last time that the maximum height occurred.

SUMMARY

In this chapter, we covered the use of conditions and `if` statements and `switch` statements to select the proper statements to be executed. We also presented techniques for repeating sets of statements that used loops. These loops can be implemented as `while` loops or as `for` loops. These selection and repetition structures are used in most programs.

Key Terms

case label	loop
case structure	loop-control object
condition	program walkthrough
controlling expression	pseudocode
counter-controlled loop	relational operator
data file	repetition
decomposition outline	selection
default label	sentinel-controlled loop
divide and conquer	sequence
end-of-data loop	statement block
error condition	stepwise refinement
flowchart	test data
for loop	top-down design
iteration	validation and verification
logical operator	while loop

C++ Statement Summary

if statement:

```
if (temp > 100)
   cout << "Temperature exceeds limit" << endl;
```

if/else statement:

```
if (d <= 30)
   velocity = 4.25 + 0.00175*d*d;
else
   velocity = 0.65 + 0.12*d - 0.0025*d*d;
```

conditional statement:

```
temp>100 ? cout << "Caution \n" : cout << "Normal \n";
```

switch statement:

```
switch (op_code)
{
   case 'n':
   case 'r':
      cout << "Normal Operating range \n";
      break;
   case 'm':
      cout << "Maintenance needed \n";
      break;
   default:
      cout << "Error in code value \n";
      break;
}
```

while **loop:**

```
while (degrees <= 360)
{
   radians = degrees*PI/180;
   cout << degrees << '\t' << radians << endl;
   degrees += 10;
}
```

do/while loop:

```
do
{
   radians = degrees*PI/180;
   cout << degrees << '\t' << radians << endl;
   degrees += 10;
} while (degrees <= 360);
```

`for` loop:

```
for (int degrees=0; degrees<=360; degrees+=10)
{
    radians = degrees*PI/180;
    cout << degrees << '\t' << radians << endl;
}
```

`break` statement:

```
break;
```

`continue` statement;

```
continue;
```

Style **Notes**

1. Use spaces around the relational operator in a logical expression in a simple condition; use spaces around the logical operator and not around the relational operators in a complicated condition.
2. Indent the statements within a statement block or inside a loop. If loops or compound statements are nested, indent each nested set of statements from the previous statement.
3. Use braces even when they are not required to clearly identify the structure of a complicated statement.
4. Use the `default` case within the `switch` statement to emphasize the action to take when none of the case labels matches the controlling expression.
5. Use braces to identify the body of every loop; put each brace on a line by itself so that the body of the loop is easily identified.

Debugging Notes

1. When you discover and correct an error in a program, start the testing step over again. In particular, rerun the program with all the test data sets again.
2. Be sure to use the relational operator `==` instead of `=` in a condition for equality.
3. Put the braces surrounding a block of statements on lines by themselves; this will help you avoid omitting them.
4. Do not use the equality operator with floating-point values; instead, test for values "close to" a desired value.
5. Recompile your program frequently when correcting syntax errors; correcting one error may remove many error messages.
6. Use *cout* statements to give memory snapshots of the values of key objects when debugging loops. Remember to use the *endl* manipulator instead of '\n' to ensure that the values are printed immediately after the statement is executed.
7. It is easier than you think to generate an infinite loop; be sure you know the special characters needed to abort the execution of a program on your system if it goes into an infinite loop.

Problems

Exam Practice!

True/False Problems
Indicate whether the following statements are true (T) or false (F).

1. If a condition's value is zero, then the condition is evaluated as false. T F
2. If the condition's value is neither zero nor 1, then it is an invalid condition. T F
3. The expression $a == 2$ is used to determine whether the value of a is equal to 2, and the expression $a = 2$ assigns the value of 2 to the object a. T F
4. The logical operators && and || have the same level precedence. T F
5. The keyword `else` is always associated with the closest `if` statement unless braces are used to define blocks of statements. T F
6. To debug a loop, we can use *cout* statements in the loop to provide memory snapshots of objects. T F

Syntax Problems
Identify any syntax errors in the following statements. Assume that the objects have all been defined as integers.

```
7. for (b=1, b=<25, b++)
8. while (k =1)
9. switch (sqrt (x))
   {
        case 1:
           cout << "Too low. \n";
           break;
        case 2:
           cout << "Correct range. \n";
           break;
        case 3:
           cout << "Too high.\n";
           break
   }
```

Multiple-Choice Problems
Circle the letter for the best answer to complete each statement or for the correct answer to each question.

10. Consider the following statement:

    ```
    int i=100, j=0;
    ```

    Which of the following statements are true?
    (a) `i<3`
    (b) `!(j<1)`
    (c) `(i>0) || (j>50)`
    (d) `(j<i) && (i <= 10)`

11. If $a1$ is true and $a2$ is false, then which of the following expressions are true?
   (a) `a1 && a2`
   (b) `a1 || a2`
   (c) `!(a1 || a2)`
   (d) `!a1 && a2`
12. Which of the following are unary operators?
   (a) `!`
   (b) `||`
   (c) `&&`
13. The expression

   `(!((3-4%3) < 5 && (6/4 > 3)))` is

   (a) true.
   (b) false.
   (c) invalid.
   (d) none of the above.

Problems 14 through 16 refer to the following statements:

```
int sum(0), count;
for (count=0; count<=4; count++)
    sum += count;
cout << "sum = " << sum << endl;
```

14. What would you see on the screen if these statements are executed?
   (a) sum = 1
   (b) sum = 6
   (c) sum = 10
   (d) four lines of output
   (e) error message
15. What is the value of count after execution of the for loop?
   (a) 0
   (b) 4
   (c) 5
   (d) an unpredictable integer
16. How many times is the for loop executed?
   (a) 0
   (b) 4
   (c) 5
   (d) 6

Memory Snapshot Problems
Give the corresponding snapshots of memory after the following set of statements is executed:

17.
```
int a = 750;
if(a > 0)
    if(a >= 1000)
        a = 0;
```

```
        else
            a *= 2;
    else
        a *= 10;
18. char ch = '*';
    switch(ch)
    {
      case '+':
          cout << "addition\n";
          break;
      case '-':
          cout << "subtraction\n";
          break;
      case '*':
          cout << "multiplication\n";
          break;
      case '/':
          cout << "division\n";
          break;
      default:
          cout << "other\n";
    }
```

Programming Problems

Unit Conversions.   Problems 19 through 23 generate tables of unit conversions. Include a table heading and column headings for the tables. Choose the number of decimal places based on the values to be printed.

19. Generate a table of conversions from radians to degrees. Start the radian column at 0.0, and increment by $\pi/10$, until the radian amount is 2π.
20. Generate a table of conversions from degrees to radians. The first line should contain the value for 0 degrees and the last line should contain the value for 360 degrees. Allow the user to enter the increment to use between lines in the table.
21. Generate a table of conversions from inches to centimeters. Start the inches column at 0.0 and increment by 0.5 in. The last line should contain the value 20.0 in. (Recall that 1 in. $= 2.54$ cm.)
22. Generate a table of conversions from mph to ft/s. Start the mph column at 0, and increment by 5 mph. The last line should contain the value 65 mph. (Recall that 1 mi $= 5,280$ ft.)
23. Generate a table of conversions from ft/s to mph. Start the ft/s column at 0 and increment by 5 ft/s. The last line should contain the value 100 ft/s. (Recall that 1 mi $= 5,280$ ft.)

Currency Conversions.   Problems 24 through 27 generate tables of currency conversions. Use title and column headings. Assume the following conversion rates or check the Web for current rates:

```
1 dollar ($) = 9.02 Mexican Pesos
1 yen (Y) = $ 0.01 U.S. Dollars
1 dollar ($) = 11.30 South African Rand
```

24. Generate a table of conversions from pesos to dollars. Start the pesos column at 5 pesos and increment by 5 pesos. Print 25 lines in the table.
25. Generate a table of conversions from yen to pesos. Start the yen column at 1 Y and increment by 2 Y. Print 30 lines in the table.
26. Generate a table of conversions from yen to South African rand. Start the yen column at 100 Y and print 25 lines, with the final line containing the value 10,000 Y.
27. Generate a table of conversions from dollars to pesos, South African rand, and yen. Start the column with $1 and increment by $1. Print 50 lines in the table.

Temperature Conversions.   Problems 28 through 30 generate temperature-conversion tables. Use the following equations that give relationships between temperatures in degrees Fahrenheit (TF), degrees Celsius (TC), degrees Kelvin (TK), and degrees Rankin (TR):

```
TF = TR - 459.67 degrees R
TF = (9/5)TC + 32 degrees F
TR = (9/5)TK
```

28. Write a program to generate a table of conversions from Fahrenheit to Celsius for values from 0 degrees F to 100 degrees F. Print a line in the table for each 5-degree change. Use a while loop in your solution.
29. Write a program to generate a table of conversions from Fahrenheit to Kelvin for values from 0 degrees F to 200 degrees F. Allow the user to enter the increment in degrees Fahrenheit between lines. Use a do while loop in your solution.
30. Write a program to generate a table of conversions from Celcius to Rankin. Allow the user to enter the starting temperature and increment between lines. Print 25 lines in the table. Use a for loop in your solution.

Timber Regrowth.   A problem in timber management is to determine how much of an area to leave uncut so that the harvested area is reforested in a certain period. It is assumed that reforestation takes place at a known rate per year, depending on climate and soil conditions. A reforestation equation expresses this growth as a function of the amount of timber standing and the reforestation rate. For example, if 100 acres are left standing after harvesting and the reforestation rate is 0.05, then $100 + 0.05 * 100$, or 105 acres, are forested at the end of the first year. At the end of the second year, the number of acres forested is $105 + 0.05 * 105$, or 110.25 acres.

31. Assume that there are 14,000 acres total with 2,500 acres uncut, and that the reforestation rate is 0.02. Print a table showing the number of acres forested at the end of each year, for a total of 20 years.
32. Modify the program developed in Problem 31 so that the user can enter the number of years to be used for the table.
33. Modify the program developed in Problem 31 so that the user can enter a number of acres and the program will determine how many years are required for the number of acres to be completely reforested.

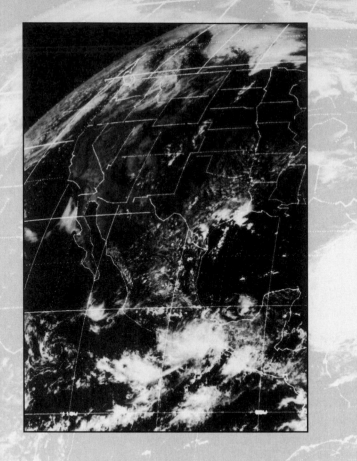

CHAPTER 4

GRAND CHALLENGE:
Weather Prediction

Weather satellites provide a great deal of information to meteorologists who attempt to predict the weather. Large volumes of historical weather data can also be analyzed and used to test models for predicting weather. In general, we can do a reasonably good job of predicting the overall weather patterns; however, local weather phenomena such as tornadoes, water spouts, and microbursts are still very difficult to predict. Even predicting heavy rainfall or large hail from thunderstorms is often difficult. Although Doppler radar is useful in locating regions within storms that could contain tornadoes or microbursts, the radar detects the events as they occur and thus gives little time for issuing appropriate warnings to populated areas or aircraft. Accurate and timely prediction of weather and associated weather phenomena is still an elusive goal.

Working with Data Files

Chapter Outline

Objectives

4.1 Defining File Streams
4.2 Reading Data Files
4.3 Generating a Data File
4.4 Problem Solving Applied: Data Filters—Modifying an HTML File
4.5 Error Checking
4.6 Numerical Technique: Linear Modeling*
4.7 Problem Solving Applied: Ozone Measurements*

Summary, Style Notes, Debugging Notes

OBJECTIVES   In this chapter, we introduce **data files.** After discussing **stream class inheritance** and the definition of **file stream objects** we discuss several common methods for reading data files. An example that applies to data filtering is used to illustrate opening and reading data files, and creating new data files. We also discuss errors that can be encountered when reading data files and how these errors can be handled. The numerical technique of **linear modeling** (or linear regression) with both equations and graphs, and a specific example is presented that uses a linear model for predicting ozone mixing ratios in the middle atmosphere.

4.1   Defining File Streams

Engineering problem solutions often involve large amounts of data. These data can be generated by the program as output, or they can be input data that are used by the program. It is not generally feasible either to print large amounts of data to the screen or to read large amounts of data from the keyboard. In these cases, we usually use data files to store the data. These data files are similar to the program files that we create to store our C++ program. In fact, a C++ program file is an input data file to the C++ compiler and the object program is an output file from the C++ compiler. In this section, we discuss the C++ statements for interacting with data files and give examples that generate and read information from data files.

Stream Class Inheritance

An important object-oriented feature of the C++ language is **inheritance.** Inheritance allows a class to inherit the functionality of an existing class. In Chapter 2, we introduced the stream objects *cin* and *cout* that are defined for standard input and output (input from the keyboard and output to the screen). Recall that *cin* is an object of type *istream* and can call member functions of the *istream* class, including the function *get( )*. *cout* is an object of type *ostream* and can call member functions of the *ostream* class, including the functions *setf( )* and *precision( )*. When working with data files, we need to define **file stream objects** with similar functionality, but that have the ability to stream data to and from data files. C++ provides **file stream classes** to support file input and file output. The **ifstream class** is used to define file stream objects that stream input from a file, and the **ofstream class** is used to define file stream objects that stream output to a file.

file stream objects
file stream classes
ifstream class
ofstream class

  The *ifstream* class is derived from the *istream* class, and thus it inherits all of the functionality of the *istream* class. An object of type *ifstream* can call any of the member functions of the *istream* class and can be used in the same way that *cin* can be used. The *ifstream* class also includes additional member functions required to work with data files that are not included in the *istream* class.

  The *ofstream* class is derived from the *ostream* class and inherits all of the functionality of the *ostream* class. Additional member functions required to work with data files are also included in the *istream* class. An object of type *ofstream* can be used in the same way that *cout* can be used.

  The *ifstream* class and the *ofstream* class are defined in the header file **fstream.** This file must be included in any program that uses *ifstream* or *ofstream*.

ifstream Class

ifstream object

Each data file used for input in a program must have an **ifstream object** associated with it. A type declaration statement is used to define an object of type *ifstream,* as in

```
ifstream sensor1;
```

After an *ifstream* object is defined, it must then be associated with a specific file. The *ifstream* class includes a member function named *open( )*. This function is called by the *ifstream* object and a file name is passed as an argument to this function. The file name needs to be a string constant or a C-style string object. Thus, the following statement specifies that the *ifstream* object *sensor1* is going to be used with a file named *sensor1.dat* from which we will read information:

```
sensor1.open("sensor1.dat");
```

It is also possible to initialize a *ifstream* object at the time it is defined:

```
ifstream sensor1("sensor1.dat");
```

Here the *open* function is called automatically when the *ifstream* object *sensor1* is created.

  When a data file is being used for input, the file must exist and contain data values to be used by the program. If the file cannot be opened, an error flag is set. No error message will be generated, and your program will continue to execute, but all attempts to read from the data file will be ignored. Thus, when opening a file for input, it is always good practice to check the status of the file stream object to insure that the file open was successful. One method of checking the status of the file stream object is to have the object call the **member function fail()**. The *fail()* function is a member of the *ifstream* class, and it returns a value of true if the data file failed to open, as shown in the following example:

member function fail()

```
ifstream sensor1;
sensor1.open("sensor1.dat");
if( sensor1.fail() ) //open failed
{
    cout << "File sensor1.dat could not be opened";
    exit(1); //end execution of the program
}
```

The status of a file stream object can also be checked directly:

```
ifstream sensor1("sensor1.dat);
if( !sensor1 ) //open failed
{
    cout << "File sensor1.dat could not be opened";
    exit(1); //end execution of the program
}
```

For clarity, we will usually use the first method for opening a data file and checking the status of the file stream.

Once an input file stream has been defined and successfully associated with a data file, it can be used in the same way that *cin* is used. If each line in the *sensor1.dat* file contains a time and sensor reading, we can read one line of this information and store the values in the objects *t* and *motion* with this statement:

```
sensor1 >> t >> motion;
```

Note that we used the input operator with *sensor1* to input numeric values from the *sensor1.dat* file. If the data file held character data, the *get()* function could also be used with *sensor1*.

When reading information from a data file, print a few lines of the information to be sure that the data are being read correctly.

ofstream Class

A type declaration statement is used to define an object of type *ofstream*, as in

```
ofstream balloon;
```

ofstream object

After an **ofstream object** is defined, it must be associated with a specific file. The *ofstream* `class` also includes a member function named *open()*. This function is called by the *ofstream* object and a file name is passed as an argument to this function. Thus, the following statement specifies that the *ofstream* object *balloon* will write data to a file named *balloon.dat:*

```
balloon.open("balloon.dat");
```

It is also possible to initialize an *ofstream* object at the time it is defined, as in

```
ofstream balloon("balloon.dat");
```

When an *ofstream* object calls the *open()* function, a file with the specified name is created if a file by that name does not already exist. If the file already exists, it is opened and the old contents of the file are overwritten by the new data. It is possible to open an existing file for output and append new data to the end of the existing data by adding a second argument to the open function, as in

```
balloon.open("balloon.data", ios::app);
```

Once an *ofstream* object has been defined and associated with a data file, the *ofstream* object can be used in the same way that *cout* is used. As an example, consider the program developed in Chapter 3 that computed and printed a table of time, altitude, and velocity data. If we wanted to modify this program so that it generated a data file containing this set of data, we could use the *ofstream* object *balloon* that has been associated with an output file named *balloon.dat* using these statements:

```
balloon << time << ' ' << height << ' '
        << velocity/3600 << endl;
```

A blank space is used to separate the values, and the *endl* manipulator causes a skip to a new line after each group of three values is written to the file.

close() function
The **close() function** is used to close a file after we are finished with it; the function is called by a file stream object. To close the two files used in these example statements, we use the following statements:

```
sensor1.close();
balloon.close();
```

If a file has not been closed when the `return 0` statement is executed, it will be closed automatically.

A *string* object is often used to specify the name of a data file because we frequently use the same program with different data files. It is often desirable to prompt the user to enter the name of a data file at run time and store the name of the file as a *string* object. This string can then be used by the *open()* function as illustrated in the following code segment:

```
...
string filename;
cout << "enter the name of the output file";
cin >> filename;
balloon.open(filename.c_str());
...
```

We declared filename to be a *string* object, since these are easy to work with. However, the *open()* function expects a C-style string as an argument, so *filename* must call the function *c_str()*. The function *c_str()* is a member of the *string* class, and it returns a C-style string that is equivalent to the *string* object *filename*. We will use this combination of statements in all the sample programs that use files in this and the chapters that follow.

4.2   Reading Data Files

To read information from a data file, we must first know some details about the file. Obviously, we must know the file name so that we can open the file. We must also know the order and data type of the values stored in the file so that we can declare corresponding identifiers correctly. Finally, we need to know if there is any special information in the file to help us determine how much information is in the file. If we attempt to execute an input statement after we have read all the data in the file, the value of the input object will remain unchanged. This may cause unexpected results in our program. To avoid this situation, we need to know when we have read all the data.

Data files generally have one of three common structures. Some files have been generated such that the first line in the file contains the number of lines (also called records) with information that follow. For example, suppose that a file containing sensor data has 150 sets of time and sensor information. The data file could be constructed such that the first line contains only the value 150, and that line would then be followed by 150 lines containing the sensor data. To read the data from this file, we use a counter-controlled loop, as discussed in Chapter 3.

trailer signal
Another form of file structure uses a **trailer signal** or sentinel signal. These signals are special data values that are used to indicate or signal the last record of a file. For example, the sensor data file constructed with a sentinel signal would contain the 150 lines of information followed by a line with special values, such as −999.0 for the time and sensor value. These sentinel signals must be values that could not appear as regular data in order to avoid confusion. To read data from this type of file, we use a sentinel-controlled loop, as discussed in Chapter 3.

The third data file structure does not contain an initial line with the number of valid data records that follow, and it does not contain a trailer or sentinel signal. For this type of data file, we use the value returned by the file stream object to help us determine when we have reached the end of the file. To read data from this type of file, we use and **end-of-file loop,** as discussed in Chapter 3.

end-of-file loop

We now present programs for reading sensor information and printing a summary report that contains the number of sensor readings, the average value, the maximum value, and the minimum value. Each of the three common file formats discussed will be used in the following programs.

Specified Number of Records

Assume that the first record in the sensor data file contains an integer that specifies the number of records of sensor information that follow. Each of the following lines contains a time and sensor reading:

```
sensor1.dat
```

```
10
0.0   132.5
0.1   147.2
0.2   148.3
0.3   157.3
0.4   163.2
0.5   158.2
0.6   169.3
0.7   148.2
0.8   137.6
0.9   135.9
```

The process of first reading the number of data points and then using that to specify the number of times to read data and accumulate information is easily described using a variable-controlled loop. In the pseudocode and program shown next, the first actual data value is used to initialize the *max* and *min* values. If we set the *min* value initially to zero and all the sensor values were greater than zero, the program would print the erroneous value of zero for the minimum sensor reading. The pseudocode and program for this solution are as follows:

```
Refinement in Pseudocode
main:   set sum to zero
        read number of data points
        set k to 1
        while k<= number of data points
                read time, motion
                if k=1
                        set max to motion
                        set min to motion
                add motion to sum
                if motion>max
                        set max to motion
                if motion<min
                        set min to motion
                increment k by 1
        set average to sum/number of data points
        print average, max, min


/*-------------------------------------------------------*/
/*  Program chapter4_1                                   */
/*                                                       */
/*  This program generates a summary report from        */
/*  a data file that has the number of data points      */
/*  in the first record.                                 */

#include <fstream>
#include <string>
using namespace std;
```

```cpp
int main()
{
   //  Declare and initialize objects.
   int num_data_pts, k;
   double time, motion, sum(0), max, min;
   string filename;
   ifstream sensor1;

   //  Prompt user for name of input file.
   cout << "enter the name of the input file";
   cin >> filename;

   //  Open file and read the number of data points.
   sensor1.open(filename.c_str());
   if( sensor1.fail() )
   {
       cout << "Error opening input file\n";
   }
   else
   {
       sensor1 >> num_data_pts;

   //  Read data and compute summary information.
       for (k=1; k<=num_data_pts; k++)
       {
           sensor1 >> time >> motion;
           if (k == 1)
           {
              max = min = motion;
           }
           sum += motion;
           if (motion > max)
           {
              max = motion;
           }
           if (motion < min)
           {
              min = motion;
           }
       }

   //  Set format flags.
       sensor1.setf(ios::fixed);
       sensor1.setf(ios::showpoint);
       sensor1.precision(2);

   //  Print summary information.
       cout << "Number of sensor readings: "
            << num_data_pts << endl;
       cout << "Average reading:           "
            << sum/num_data_pts << endl;
```

```
            cout << "Maximum reading:         "
                 << max << endl;
            cout << "Minimum reading:         "
                 << min << endl;

    //   Close file and exit program.
        sensor1.close();
    }   //end else
    return 0;
}   //end main
/*--------------------------------------------------------*/
```

The report printed by this program using the sensor1.dat file is as follows:

```
Number of sensor readings: 10
Average reading:          149.77
Maximum reading:          169.30
Minimum reading:          132.50
```

Trailer or Sentinel Signals

Assume that the data file *sensor2.dat* contains the same information as the *sensor1.dat* file, but instead of giving the number of valid data records at the beginning of the file, a final record contains a trailer signal. The time value on the last line in the file will contain a negative value so that we know that it is not a valid line of information. The contents of the data file are as follows:

```
sensor2.dat
0.0   132.5
0.1   147.2
0.2   148.3
0.3   157.3
0.4   163.2
0.5   158.2
0.6   169.3
0.7   148.2
0.8   137.6
0.9   135.9
-99   -99
```

The process of reading and accumulating information until we read the trailer signal is easily described using a do/while loop structure, as shown in the following pseudocode and program:

```
Refinement in Pseudocode
main:    set sum to zero
         set number of points to 0
         read time, motion
         set max to motion
         set min to motion
         do
```

```
                     add motion to sum
                     if motion > max
                             set max to motion
                     if motion < min
                             set min to motion
                     increment number of points by 1
                     read time, motion
                while time >= 0
                set average to sum/number of data points
                print average, max, min


/*------------------------------------------------------*/
/*   Program chapter4_2                                 */
/*                                                      */
/*   This program generates a summary report from       */
/*   a data file that has a trailer record with         */
/*   negative values.                                   */

#include <fstream>
#include <string>
using namespace std;

int main()
{
   //   Declare and initialize objects.
   int num_data_pts(0), k;
   double time, motion, sum(0), max, min;
   string filename;
   ifstream sensor2;

   //   Prompt user for name of input file.
   cout << "enter the name of the input file";
   cin >> filename;

   //   Open file and read the first data point.
   sensor2.open(filename.c_str());
   if(sensor2.fail())
   {
        cout << "Error opening input file\n";
   }
   else
   {
        sensor2 >> time >> motion;

   //   Initialize objects using first data point.
        max = min = motion;

   //   Update summary data until trailer record read.
        do
        {
           sum += motion;
           if (motion > max)
```

```
                 {
                    max = motion;
                 }
                 if (motion < min)
                 {
                    min = motion;
                 }
                 num_data_pts++;
                 sensor2 >> time >> motion;
            } while (time >= 0);

   //  Set format flags.
            sensor2.setf(ios::fixed);
            sensor2.setf(ios::showpoint);
            sensor2.precision(2);

   //  Print summary information.
            cout << "Number of sensor readings:   "
                 << num_data_pts << endl
                 << "Average reading:             "
                 << sum/num_data_pts << endl
                 << "Maximum reading:             "
                 << max << endl
                 << "Minimum reading:             "
                 << min << endl;

   //  Close file and exit program.
            sensor2.close();
      }  //end else
      return 0;
}  //end main
/*- - - - - - - - - - - - - - - - - - - - - - - - - - - - - - - - - - - - - - - - - - - - - -*/
```

The report printed by this program using the *sensor2.dat* file is exactly the same as the report printed using the *sensor1.dat* file.

End-of-File

A special end-of-file indicator is inserted at the end of every data file; the *eof()* function, can be used to detect when this indicator has been reached in a data file. The function is a member of the *ifstream* class, and it returns a value of true if the end-of-file indicator has been read in the data file associated with the file stream object. Consider the following statements:

```
data1 >> x;
while ( !data1.eof() )
{
   count++;
   sum += x;
   data1 >> x;
}
ave = sum/count;
```

The first input statement attempts to read a value for x from the data file associated with the input file stream object *data1*. If a data value is read, the *eof()* function returns a value of 0, and the statements within the loop are executed. The last statement inside the while loop is an input statement that attempts to read the next value of x from the data file. The while loop will continue to execute while the end of the data file has not been reached. When there is no more data in the file and the end-of-file indicator is read, the next call to the *eof()* function will return a value of 1, and control will pass to the statement following the while loop. loop. This is the correct structure for and end-of-file loop. The eof() function will not return a value of true until after the end of file indicator has been read. For this reason it is important to test for the end of file immediately after an input statement.

You can also use the value returned by the input file stream object to detect when and end-of-file has been reached, as illustrated in the following statements:

```
while ( data1 >> x )
{
    count++;
    sum += x;
}
```

The while loop uses the value returned by the *data1 fstream* object to control execution. The input request will return a value of *true* if a data value is read from the *data1* file stream and a value of *false* if a data value cannot be read from the file stream. In our examples, we will use the *eof()* function for clarity.

We now assume that the data file *sensor3.dat* contains the same information as the *sensor2.dat* file, except that it does not include the trailer signal. In the following pseudocode and program, we read and accumulate information until we reach the end of the data file:

```
Refinement in Pseudocode
main:   set sum to zero
        set number of points to 0
        Proper while look structure
        read time, motion
        while not at the end of the file
                add 1 to the number of points
                if number of points is 1
                        set max to motion
                        set min to motion
                add motion to sum
                if motion > max
                        set max to motion
                if motion < min
                        set min to motion
                read time, motion
        set average to sum/number of data points
        print average, max, min


/*-------------------------------------------------------*/
/*  Program chapter4_3                                   */
/*                                                       */
/*  This program generates a summary report from        */
```

```
/*  a data file that does not have a header record    */
/*  or a trailer record.                              */

#include <fstream>
#include <string>
using namespace std;

int main()
{
   //  Declare and initialize objects.
   int num_data_pts(0), k;
   double time, motion, sum(0), max, min;
   string filename;
   ifstream sensor3;

   //  Prompt user for name of input file.
   cout << "enter the name of the input file";
   cin >> filename;

   //  Open file and read the first data point.
   sensor3.open(filename.c_str());

   if(sensor3.fail())
   {
      cout << "Error opening input file\n";
   }
   else
   {
   //  While not at the end of the file,
   //  read and accumulate information
      sensor3 >> time >> motion;  // initial input
      while ( !sensor3.eof() )
      {
         num_data_pts++;
         if (num_data_pts == 1)
         {
            max = min = motion;
         }
         sum += motion;
         if (motion > max)
         {
            max = motion;
         }
         if (motion < min)
         {
            min = motion;
         }
         sensor3 >> time >> motion;  // input next
      }

   //  Set format flags.
      sensor3.setf(ios::fixed);
```

```
      sensor3.setf(ios::showpoint);
      sensor3.precision(2);
//   Print summary information
      cout << "Number of sensor readings: "
           << num_data_pts << endl
           << "Average reading:           "
           << sum/num_data_pts << endl
           << "Maximum reading:           "
           << max << endl
           << "Minimum reading:           "
           << min << endl;

//   Close file and exit program.
      sensor3.close();
   } //end else
   return 0;
} //end main
/*-------------------------------------------------------*/
```

The report printed using the *sensor3.dat* file is exactly the same as the report printed using *sensor1.dat* or *sensor2.dat*.

   The programs in this section work properly if the data files exist and contain the information expected. If this program is going to be used routinely with sensor data, statements should be included to be sure that the file structure is the one expected. Also, a division-by-zero error would occur if the number of points were zero. The division-by-zero error could be avoided by comparing the number of points to zero before printing the report.

   All three file structures are commonly used in engineering and scientific applications. Therefore, it is important to know which type of structure is used when you work with a data file. If you make the wrong assumption, you may get incorrect answers instead of an error message. Sometimes the only way to be sure of the file structure is to print the first few lines and the last few lines of the file.

Modify!

In two of the programs developed in this chapter, the loop contained a condition that tested for the first time that the loop was executed. When the condition was true, the *max* and *min* values were initialized to the first motion value. If the data files used with these programs were very long, the time required to execute this selection statement could begin to be substantial. One way to avoid this test is to read the first set of data and initialize the objects before entering the loop. This change may also require other changes in the program.

1. Modify program chapter4_1 so that the condition is removed that tests for the first time that the loop is executed.

2. Modify program chapter4_3 so that the condition is removed that tests for the first time that the loop is executed.

4.3 Generating a Data File

Generating a data file is similar to printing a report; instead of writing the line to the terminal screen, we write it to a data file. Before we generate the data file, though, we must decide what file structure we want to use. In the previous discussion, we presented the three most common file structures-files with an initial record giving the number of valid records that follow, files with a trailer or sentinel record to indicate the end of the valid data, and files with only valid data records and no special beginning or ending records.

There are advantages and disadvantages to each of the three file structures discussed. A file with a trailer signal is simple to use, but choosing a value for the trailer signal must be done carefully so that it does not contain values that could occur in the valid data. If the first record in the data file will contain the number of lines of actual data, we must know how many lines of data will be in the file before we begin to generate the file. It may not always be easy to determine the number of lines before executing the program that generates the file. The simplest file to generate is the one that contains only the valid information, with no special information at the beginning or end of the file. If the information in the file is going to used with a plotting package, it is usually best to use this third file structure which includes only valid information.

We now present a program that is a modification of the program presented in Chapter 3 that printed a table of time, height, and velocity values for a weather balloon. In addition to generating a table of information that is displayed on the screen, we also write the time, height, and velocity information to a data file. Compare this program with the one in Section 3.5 on page 108:

```
/*-------------------------------------------------------------*/
/*  Program chapter4_4                                         */
/*                                                             */
/*  This program generates a file of height and               */
/*  velocity values for a weather balloon. The                */
/*  information is also printed in a report.                   */

#include <fstream>
#include <iomanip>
#include <cmath>
#include <string>
using namespace std;

int main()
{
   //  Declare and initialize objects.
   double initial, increment, final, time, height,
         velocity, max_time(0), max_height(0);
   int loops, itime;
   string filename;
   ofstream balloon;

   //  Prompt user for name of output file.
   cout << "enter the name of the output file";
   cin >> filename;
```

```
//  Open output file
balloon.open(filename.c_str());

//  Get user input.
cout << "Enter initial value for table (in hours) \n";
cin >> initial;
cout << "Enter increment between lines (in hours) \n";
cin >> increment;
cout << "Enter final value for table (in hours) \n";
cin >> final;

//  Set format flags for standard output.
cout.setf(ios::fixed);
cout.precision(2);

//  Set format flags for file output.
balloon.setf(ios::fixed);
balloon.precision(2);

//  Print report heading.
cout << "\n\nWeather Balloon Information \n";
cout << "Time     Height    Velocity \n";
cout << "(hrs)    (meters)  (meters/s) \n";

//  Determine number of iterations required.
//  Use integer index to avoid rounding error.
loops = (int)((final - initial)/increment);
for (itime=0; itime<=loops; itime++)
{
   time = initial + itime*increment;

   height = -0.12*pow(time,4) + 12*pow(time,3)
            - 380*time*time + 4100*time + 220;
   velocity = -0.48*pow(time,3) + 36*time*time
              - 760*time + 4100;

//  Print report information.
   cout << setw(6) << time << setw(10) << height
        << setw(10) << velocity/3600 << endl;

//  Write data to file.
   balloon << setw(6) << time << setw(10) << height
           << setw(10) << velocity/3600 << endl;

   if (height > max_height)
   {
      max_height = height;
      max_time = itime;
   }
}
```

```
    //  Report maximum height and corresponding time.
    cout << "\nMaximum balloon height was "
        << setw(8) << max_height
        << " meters\nand it occurred at "
        << setw(6) << max_time << endl;

    //  Close file and exit program.
    balloon.close();
    return 0;
}
/*------------------------------------------------------*/
```

The first few lines of a data file generated by this program, using an initial time of 0 hours, an increment of 0.5 hours, and a final time of 48 hours, are as follows:

```
    0.00     220.00      1.14
    0.50    2176.49      1.04
    1.00    3951.88      0.94
    ...
```

This file is in a form to be easily plotted using a package such as Matlab, as discussed in Appendix C; a plot of this specific file was shown in Figure 3.7 in Chapter 3.

Modify!

1. Modify program chapter4_4 so that it generates a file in which the last line of the data file contains negative values for the time, height, and velocity.

2. Modify program chapter4_4 so that it generates a file in which the first line contains a number that specifies the number of valid lines of data that follow in the data file.

4.4 Problem Solving Applied: Data Filters—Modifying an HTML File

Programs called **data filters** are often used to read the information in a data file, modify the contents of the file, and write the modified data to a new file. Suppose we have found an html document on the Web with important information that we would like save as plain text with all of the hypertext markup language (html) commands removed. An html command, also called a tag, has the following general form:

```
<html command>
```

We can write a C++ program that reads an html file and filters out all of the tags. The text from the file, minus the tags, is output to a new file.

1. PROBLEM STATEMENT

Write a program to remove the tags from an html file and save the text to a new file.

2. INPUT/OUTPUT DESCRIPTION

The following diagram shows that the input to the program is an html file. The output of the program is the text from the html file with the tags removed.

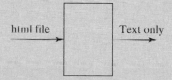

3. HAND EXAMPLE

For the hand example, we will use a very small html file that just has a few lines. Here is the sample html file:

```
<HTML>
<HEAD>
<META HTTP-EQUIV="Content-Type" CONTENT="text/html;
  charset=ISO-8859-1">
<TITLE>HomePage</TITLE>

<META NAME="GENERATOR" CONTENT="Internet Assistant for
  Microsoft Word 2.04z">
</HEAD>
<BODY BGCOLOR = "#118187" >
<HR>
<b><font size=4>
<p>
J. Ingber
<br>
Department of Computer Science
<br>
University of New Mexico
</b></font>
</BODY>
</HTML>
```

The text without tags should be

```
HomePage
J. Ingber
Department of Computer Science
University of New Mexico
```

4. ALGORITHM DEVELOPMENT

We first develop the decomposition outline because it breaks the solution into a series of sequential steps.

Decomposition Outline

1. Read a character from the file.

2. Determine if character is part of an html tag.

3. Print all characters that are not part of an html tag.

The first step in the decomposition outline involves a loop in which we read each character from the file. The condition to exit the loop will be a test for the end of the file. Our program will have two distinct states. In one state, we will be reading the text of the file (not a tag), so we will output each character as we read it. In the other state, we will be reading a tag, so the character will not be printed. We will use an object of type bool to keep track of which state we are in. If we are in the text state, the character '<' will mark the beginning of a tag. If we are in the tag state, the character '>' will mark the end of a tag. The refinement in pseudocode is as follows:

```
Refinement in Pseudocode
main:   set text_state to true
        read character
        while not end-of-file
        if text_state is true
           if character = '<'
              set text_state to false
           else
              print character to file
        else
           if character = '>'
              set text_state to true
        read next character
```

The steps in the pseudocode are now detailed enough to convert into C++:

```
/*-------------------------------------------------------------------*/
/* Program chapter4_4                                                */
/* This program reads an html file, and writes the text             */
/* without the tags to a new file.                                  */

#include<iostream>
#include<fstream>
using namespace std;

int main()
{
   // Declare objects.
   char character;
```

```
bool text_state(TRUE);
string infile, outfile;
ifstream html;
ofstream htmltext;

// Prompt user for name of input file.
cout << "enter the name of the input file";
cin >> infile;

// Prompt user for name of output file.
cout << "enter the name of the output file";
cin >> outfile;

// Open files
html.open(infile.c_str());
if(html.fail())
{
    cout << "Error opening input file\n";
    return 0;
}
htmltext.open(outfile.c_str());

// Read first character from html file.
html.get(character);

while(!html.eof())
{
// Check state.
    if(text_state)
    {
        if(character == '<')        // Beginning of a tag.
            text_state=FALSE;       // Change States.
        else
            htmltext << character;  // Still text, write to
                                    //    the file.

    }
    else
    {

// Command state, no output required.
        if(character == '>')        // End of tag.
            text_state = TRUE;      // Change States.
    }

// Read next character from html file.
    html.get(character);
}
return 0;
}
```

5. TESTING

Using the html file from the hand example, we get the following output:

```
HomePage
J. Ingber
Department of Computer Science
University of New Mexico
```

This matches the output from the hand example.

4.5 Error Checking

Input from a file or from standard input can result in an error if the input data are not what the program is expecting. The following statement reads two values from standard input:

```
cin >> ivar1, ivar2;
```

If *ivar1* and *ivar2* are integer objects, then the data entered from the keyboard must be two integer numbers, separated by whitespace. If any other type of data is encountered, an error occurs, and the *cin* object is placed in an error state. When an *istream* object is placed in an error state, all subsequent statements using the *istream* object are ignored, as illustrated in the following example:

```
int ivar1, ivar2;
cin >> ivar1 >> ivar2;
while(!cin.eof())
{
    cout << ivar1 << ' ' << ivar2 << endl;
    cin >> ivar1 >> ivar2;
}
```

Suppose the following two lines of data were entered from the keyboard:

```
1 40
2,30
```

The first line of data is read, and the value 1 is assigned to *ivar1* and the value 40 to *ivar2*. The *eof()* function returns a value of false, since an end-of-file was not encountered, and the statements inside the while loop are executed. The first statement inside the while loop prints the values of *ivar1* and *ivar2* to the screen as follows:

```
1 40
```

The second statement attempts to reads the next two integer values from the keyboard. The value 2 is read and assigned to the object *ivar1*. The comma is the next character on the input stream. Since the comma is not valid data for an integer object, it cannot be assigned to the object *ivar2*. As a result, the *cin* object is placed in an error state. The value of *ivar2* in unchanged, and all future references to the *cin* object are ignored, resulting in an infinite loop. The program continues to execute and the values of *ivar1* and *ivar2* are again printed to the screen as follows:

```
2  40
```

Since the *cin* object is in an error state, the *cin* statement inside the while loop is ignored; thus, an end-of-file is never encountered. This results in an infinite loop, with the values

```
2  40
```

being continually printed to the screen.

When an *istream* object is in an error state, the value of the *istream* object will be false when tested. Thus, we can check for an error state by adding the following test:

```cpp
int ivar1, ivar2;
cin >> ivar1 >> ivar2;
while(!cin.eof())
{
    //Test error state of cin
    if( !cin )
    {
        cerr << "Error encountered while reading from standard input ";
        exit(1);
    }
    else  //no error, proceed normally
    {
        cout << ivar1 << ' ' << ivar2 << endl;
        cin >> ivar1 >> ivar2;
    }
}
```

standard error

Testing for the error state will eliminate the infinite loop. The *cerr* object is used to output the message that alerts the user that there is a problem with the input data. The *cerr* object, also referred to **standard error,** is defined in the standard *iostream* library. Output streamed to *cerr* will appear on the screen immediately following execution of the statement.

Recovering from an Input Error

When an input error is encountered, we may want to continue with our program, rather than exit the program. To do this, we need to reset the error state of the *istream* object. One method for resetting the error state of an istream object after an error has occurred is to have the istream object call the member function *clear()*. This will restore the *istream* object to a good state, and input can resume.

However, we must be careful to remove the bad data from the input stream or our next input will result in the same input error.

We will now add a few statements to our previous example to reset the error state of the *cin* object and remove the bad data from the input stream:

```
int ivar1, ivar2;
cin >> ivar1 >> ivar2;
while(!cin.eof())
{
      //Test error state of cin
      if( !cin )
      {
            cerr << "Error encountered while reading from standard
                   input" << endl;

            //Clear the error state to enable input
            cin.clear();

            //Remove all characters to the end of the line.
            char bad_ch;
            cin.get(bad_ch);
            while(bad_ch != '\n')
            {
                cin.get(bad_ch);
            }

            //Prompt the user to reenter input data
            cout << "Enter new data, two integer values separated
                   by white space ";
            cin >> ivar1 >> ivar2;
      }
      else  //no error, proceed normally
      {
            cout << ivar1 << ' ' << ivar2 << endl;
            cin >> ivar1 >> ivar2;
      }
}
```

Practice!

Assume the following line of data is entered at the keyboard:

```
1,2.3
```

Give the corresponding snapshots of memory after each of the following sets of statements are executed:

1. `int i(0), j(0);`
   `cin >> i >> j;`

2. `double x(0), y(0);`
   `cin >> x >> y;`

3. `char ch1, ch2;`
   `cin >> ch1 >> ch2;`

4. `char ch;`
   `double x, y;`
   `cin >> x >> ch >> y;`

4.6 Numerical Technique: Linear Modeling*

Linear modeling is the name given to the process that determines the linear equation that is the best fit to a set of data points in terms of minimizing the sum of the squared distances between the line and the data points. (This process is also called **linear regression.**) To understand the process, we first consider the set of temperature values presented in Section 2.5 that were collected from the cylinder head of a new engine.

linear regression

Time, s	Temperature, Degrees F
0	0
1	20
2	60
3	68
4	77
5	110

If we plot these data points, we find that they appear to be close to a straight line. In fact, we could determine a good estimate of a straight line through these points by drawing it on a graph and then computing the slope and y-intercept. Figure 4.1 contains a plot of the points (with

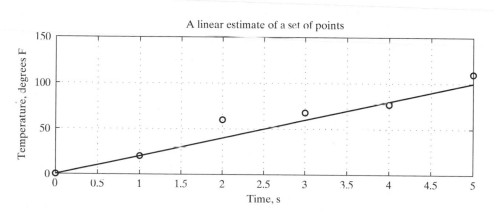

Figure 4.1 A linear estimate to model a set of points.

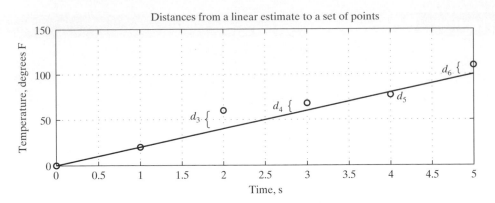

Figure 4.2 Distances between points and linear estimates.

time on the x-axis and temperature on the y-axis), along with the straight line with the equation

$$y = 20x.$$

To measure the quality of the fit of this linear estimate to the data, we first determine the vertical distance from each point to the linear estimate; these distances are shown in Figure 4.2. The first two points fall exactly on the line, so d_1 and d_2 are zero. The value of d_3 is equal to $60 - 40$, or 20; the rest of the distances can be computed in a similar way. If we compute the sum of the distances, some of the positive and negative values would cancel each other and give a sum that is smaller than it should be. To avoid this problem, we could add absolute values or squared values; linear regression uses squared values. Therefore, the measure of the quality of the fit of this linear estimate is the sum of the squared distances between the points and the linear estimates. This sum can be easily computed and is 573.

If we drew another line through the points, we could compute the sum of squares that corresponds to this new line. Of the two lines, the best fit is provided by the line with the smaller least-squares   sum of squared distances, or the **least-squares** distance. To find the line with the smallest sum of squared distances, we begin with a general linear equation:

$$y = mx + b$$

We then write an equation that computes the sum of the squared distances between the given data points and this general equation. Using techniques from calculus, we can then compute the derivatives of the equation with respect to m and b, and set the derivatives equal to zero. The values of m and b that are determined in this way represent the straight line with the minimum summation notation   sum of squared distances. Before giving these equations for m and b, we define **summation notation.**

The set of data points given at the beginning of this section can be represented by the points $(x_1, y_1), (x_2, y_2), \ldots, (x_6, y_6)$. The symbol $\sum$ represents a summation, and thus the sum of the x-coordinates can be expressed in the following notation:

$$\sum_{k=1}^{6} x_k$$

This summation is read as "the sum of x_k as k goes from 1 to 6." The value of this summation for the example data points is $(0+1+2+3+4+5)$, or 15. Other sums that could be computed using the example data points are as follows:

$$\sum_{k=1}^{6} y_k = 0 + 20 + 60 + 68 + 77 + 110 = 335,$$

$$\sum_{k=1}^{6} y_k^2 = 0^2 + 20^2 + 60^2 + 68^2 + 77^2 + 110^2 = 26{,}653,$$

$$\sum_{k=1}^{6} x_k y_k = 0 \times 0 + 1 \times 20 + 2 \times 60 + 3 \times 68 + 4 \times 77 + 5 \times 110 = 1{,}202.$$

We now return to the problem of finding the best linear fit to a set of points. Using the procedure described before that is based on results from calculus, we find that the slope and y-intercept for the best linear fit to a set of n data points, in a least-squares sense, are the following:

$$m = \frac{\sum_{k=1}^{n} x_k \cdot \sum_{k=1}^{n} y_k - n \cdot \sum_{k=1}^{n} x_k y_k}{\left(\sum_{k=1}^{n} x_k\right)^2 - n \cdot \sum_{k=1}^{n} x_k^2}, \tag{4.1}$$

$$b = \frac{\sum_{k=1}^{n} x_k \cdot \sum_{k=1}^{n} x_k y_k - \sum_{k=1}^{n} x_k^2 \cdot \sum_{k=1}^{n} y_k}{\left(\sum_{k=1}^{n} x_k\right)^2 - n \cdot \sum_{k=1}^{n} x_k^2}. \tag{4.2}$$

For the sample set of data, the optimum value for m is 20.83, and the optimum value for b is 3.76. The set of data points and this best-fit linear equation are shown in Figure 4.3. The sum of squares for this best fit is 356.82, compared with 573 for the straight line in Figure 4.2.

One of the advantages of performing a linear regression for a set of data points that is nearly linear in nature is that we can then estimate or predict points for which we had no data. For example, in the cylinder-head temperature example, suppose that we want to estimate the temperature for the cylinder head at 3.3 seconds. By using the equation computed with linear

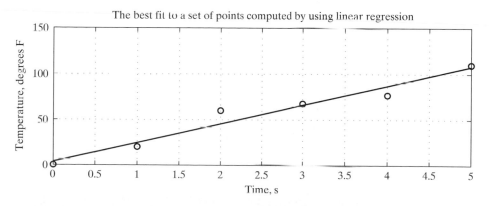

Figure 4.3 Least-squares linear regression model.

regression, we find that the estimated temperature is

$$y = mx + b$$

$$= (20.83)(3.3) + 3.76$$

$$= 72.5.$$

With an equation model, we can compute estimates that we could not compute with linear interpolation. For example, using the linear model, we can compute an estimate of the temperature for 8 seconds, but we could not compute an estimate at 8 seconds using linear interpolation, because we do not have a point with a time greater than 8 seconds. (This would be extrapolation, not interpolation.)

It is also important to remember that linear models do not provide a good fit to all sets of data. Therefore, it is important to first determine whether a linear model is a good model for the data before using it to predict new data points. A technique for measuring the quality of a linear model for a set of data is presented in the problem set at the end of Chapter 5.

In the next section, we develop a problem solution that determines the best fit for a set of sensor data collected from a satellite, and then we use that model to estimate or predict other sensor values.

4.7   Problem Solving Applied: Ozone Measurements*

Satellite sensors can be used to measure many different pieces of information that help us understand more about the atmosphere, which is composed of a number of layers around the earth [12]. Starting at the earth's surface, we know that the layers are the troposphere, stratosphere, mesosphere, thermosphere, and exosphere, as shown in Figure 4.4. Each layer of the

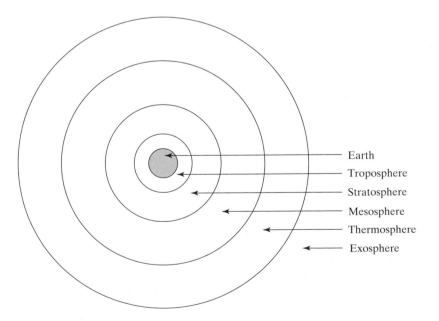

Earth
Troposphere
Stratosphere
Mesosphere
Thermosphere
Exosphere

Figure 4.4 Atmospheric layers around the earth.

atmosphere can be characterized by its temperature profile. The troposphere is the inner layer of the atmosphere, varying in height from around 5 km at the poles to 18 km at the equator. Most cloud formations occur in the troposphere, and there is a steady fall of temperature with increasing altitude. The stratosphere is characterized by relatively uniform temperatures over considerable differences in altitude. It extends from the troposphere to about 50 km (about 31 miles) above the earth. Pollutants that drift into the stratosphere may remain there for many years before they drift back to the troposphere, where they can be diluted and removed by the weather. The mesosphere extends from 50 to approximately 85 km (about 53 miles) above the earth's surface. In this layer, the air mixes fairly readily. Above the mesosphere is the thermosphere, which extends from 85 to about 140 km (about 87 miles) above the earth. In this region, the heating is due to the absorption of solar energy by atomic oxygen. The ionosphere is a relatively dense band of charged particles within the thermosphere. Some types of communications use the reflection of radio waves off the ionosphere. Finally, the exosphere is the highest region of the atmosphere. In the exosphere, the air density is so low that an air molecule moving upward is more likely to escape the atmosphere than it is to hit another molecule.

A satellite experiment was launched on the NIMBUS 7 spacecraft in 1978 to collect data on the composition and structure of the middle atmosphere [13]. The instrumentation and sensors collected data from October 25, 1978, to May 28, 1979, returning more than 7,000 sets of data to the earth each day. These data were used to determine temperature, ozone, water vapor, nitric acid, and nitrogen dioxide distributions in the stratosphere and mesosphere.

Consider a problem in which we have collected a set of data measuring the ozone mixing ratio in parts per million volume (ppmv). Over small regions, these data are nearly linear, and thus we can use a linear model to estimate the ozone at altitudes other than ones for which we have specific data. Write a program that reads a data file named *zone1.dat* containing the altitude in km and the corresponding ozone mixing ratios in ppmv for a region over which we want to determine a linear model. The data file contains only valid data and thus does not have a special header line or trailer line. Use the least-squares technique presented in the previous section to determine and print the model. Also, print the beginning and ending altitudes to indicate the region over which the model is accurate.

1. PROBLEM STATEMENT

Use the least-squares technique to determine a linear model for estimating the ozone mixing ratio at a specified altitude.

2. INPUT/OUTPUT DESCRIPTION

The following I/O diagram shows that the data file *zone1.dat* is the input and that the output is the range of altitudes and the linear model:

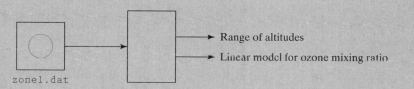

3. HAND EXAMPLE

Assume that the data consist of the following four data points:

Altitude (km)	Ozone Mixing Ratio (ppmv)
20	3
24	4
26	5
28	6

We now need to evaluate Equations (4.1) and (4.2), which are repeated here for convenience:

$$m = \frac{\sum\limits_{k=1}^{n} x_k \cdot \sum\limits_{k=1}^{n} y_k - n \cdot \sum\limits_{k=1}^{n} x_k y_k}{\left(\sum\limits_{k=1}^{n} x_k\right)^2 - n \cdot \sum\limits_{k=1}^{n} x_k^2}, \tag{4.1}$$

$$b = \frac{\sum\limits_{k=1}^{n} x_k \cdot \sum\limits_{k=1}^{n} x_k y_k - \sum\limits_{k=1}^{n} x_k^2 \cdot \sum\limits_{k=1}^{n} y_k}{\left(\sum\limits_{k=1}^{n} x_k\right)^2 - n \cdot \sum\limits_{k=1}^{n} x_k^2}. \tag{4.2}$$

To evaluate these equations using the hand example data, we need to compute the following group of sums:

$$\sum_{k=1}^{4} x_k = 20 + 24 + 26 + 28 = 98,$$

$$\sum_{k=1}^{4} y_k = 3 + 4 + 5 + 6 = 18,$$

$$\sum_{k=1}^{4} x_k y_k = 20 \cdot 3 + 24 \cdot 4 + 26 \cdot 5 + 28 \cdot 6 = 454,$$

$$\sum_{k=1}^{4} x_k^2 = (20)^2 + (24)^2 + (26)^2 + (28)^2 = 2436.$$

Using these sums, we can now compute the values of m and b:

$m = 0.37$;

$b = -4.6$.

4. ALGORITHM DEVELOPMENT

We first develop the decomposition outline because it divides the solution into a series of sequential steps.

Decomposition Outline

1. Read data file values and compute corresponding sums and ranges.

2. Compute slope and *y*-intercept.

3. Print range of altitudes and linear model.

The first step in the decomposition outline involves a loop in which we read the data from the file and at the same time add the corresponding values to the sums needed for computing the linear model. We will also need to determine the number of data points as we read the file. The condition to exit the loop will be a test for the end-of-file, because there is no header or trailer information. Because we want to keep track of the altitude ranges, we also need to save the first and last altitude values. Steps 2 and 3 of the decomposition outline are sequential steps involving computations and printing. Therefore, the refinement in pseudocode is as follows:

```
Refinement in Pseudocode
main:    set count to zero
         set sumx, sumy, sumxy, sumx2 to zero
         while not at end-of-file
                read x, y
                increment count by 1
                if count = 1
                        set first to x
                add x to sumx
                add y to sumy
                add x2 to sumx2
                add xy to sumxy
         set last to x
         compute slope and y intercept
         print first, last, slope, y intercept
```

The steps in the pseudocode are now detailed enough to convert into C++:

```
/*-------------------------------------------------------------*/
/*  Program chapter4_5                                         */
/*                                                            */
/*  This program computes a linear model for a set           */
/*  of altitude and ozone mixing ratio values.               */

#include <fstream>
#include <string>
using namespace std;

int main()
{
   // Declare and initialize objects.
   int count(0);
   double x, y, first, last, sumx(0), sumy(0), sumx2(0),
          sumxy(0), denominator, m, b;
```

```
      string filename;
      ifstream zone1;

      //  Open input file.
      zone1.open(filename.c_str());
      if(zone1.fail())
      {
        cout << "Error opening input file\n";
      }
      else
      {

      //  While not at the end of the file,
      //  read and accumulate information.
        zone1 >> x >> y;
        while ( !zone1.eof() )
        {
          ++count;
          if (count == 1)
            first = x;
          sumx += x;
          sumy += y;
          sumx2 += x*x;
          sumxy += x*y;
          zone1 >> x >> y;
        }
        last = x;

      //  Compute slope and y-intercept.
        denominator = sumx*sumx - count*sumx2;
        m = (sumx*sumy - count*sumxy)/denominator;
        b = (sumx*sumxy - sumx2*sumy)/denominator;

      //  Set format flags
        cout.setf(ios::fixed);
        cout.precision(2);

      //  Print summary information.
        cout << "Range of altitudes in km: \n";
        cout << first << " to " << last << endl << endl;
        cout << "Linear model: \n";
        cout << "ozone-mix-ratio = " << m << "  altitude + "
             << b << endl;

      //  Close file and exit program.
        zone1.close();
      }
      return 0;
}
/*------------------------------------------------------------*/
```

5. TESTING

Using the data from the hand example as the contents of the data file *zone1.dat,* we get the following program output:

```
Range of altitudes in km:
20.00 to 28.00

Linear model:
ozone-mix-ratio = 0.37 altitude + -4.60
```

This matches the values computed from the hand example.

Modify!

These problems relate to the program developed in this section. You may need to use the following relationship in some of the problems:

$$1 \text{ km} = 0.621 \text{ mi}$$

1. Add statements to the program so that it allows you to enter an altitude in km, and then uses the model to estimate a corresponding ozone mix ratio.

2. Modify your program in Problem 1 so that it checks that the altitude that you enter is within the range that is appropriate for this model.

3. Modify the program in Problem 2 so that it allows you to enter the altitude in miles. (The program should convert miles to kilometers.)

4. Modify the original program so that it also prints a linear model so that it can be used with altitudes that are in miles instead of kilometers. Assume that the data file still contains altitudes in kilometers.

SUMMARY

In this chapter, we covered the statements necessary to read information from a data file so that we could use the information in a program. We also presented the statements to generate a data file from a program. Data files are commonly used in solving engineering problems; therefore, this concept was presented early in the text so that we could use it in many of the later problem solutions. We introduced a technique for handling errors that may occur when inputting data. Finally, we covered the concept of generating a linear model for a set of data points and included the equations for determining the best fit in terms of least squares.

Key Terms

data file
data filters
file close function
file fail function
file open function
end-of-file indicator
error condition
file stream object
file stream class
ifstream class
ifstream object
input file stream

least squares
linear modeling
linear regression
ofstream class
ofstream object
output file stream
sentinel signal
standard error
stream class inheritances
summation notation
trailer signal

C++ Statement Summary

Declaration for file stream objects:

```
ifstream sensor1;
ofstream balloon;
```

File open function:

```
//filename is a string object
sensor1.open(filename.c_str());
balloon.open(filename.c_str());
```

File fail function:

```
if (sensor1.fail())
```

File input:

```
sensor1 >> t >> motion;
```

File output:

```
balloon << setw(8) << time << setw(8) << height << setw(8) << velocity;
```

Output to standard error:

```
cerr << "Error encountered on input";
```

File close function:

```
sensor1.close();
```

Style **Notes**

1. Prompt the user to enter filenames so that they can be determined at run time.

Debugging Notes

1. When debugging a program that reads data from a data file, print the values as soon as they are read to check for errors in reading the information.
2. When debugging a program that reads a data file, be sure that your program checks for successful opening of the file.
3. To avoid infinite loops when inputting data, check the error status of the istream object before each iteration of the loop.
4. To avoid problems with operating systems that are case sensitive, use filenames with lowercase letters.

Problems

Data Filters.   Programs called data filters are often used to read the information in a data file and then analyze the contents. In many cases, this data filter program is designed to remove any data errors that would cause problems with other programs that read the information from the data file. The next set of programs is designed to perform error checking and data analysis on information in a data file. Generate data files to test all features of the programs.

1. Write a program that reads a data file that should contain only integer values and thus should contain only digits, plus or minus signs, and whitespace. The program should print any invalid characters located in the file, and at the end it should print a count of the invalid characters located.
2. Write a program that analyzes a data file that has been determined to contain only integer values and whitespace. The program should print the number of lines in the file and the number of integer values (not integer digits).
3. Write a program that reads a file that contains only integers, but some of the integers have embedded commas, as in 145,020. The program should copy the information to a new file, removing any commas from the information. Do not change the number of values per line in the file.
4. Write a program that reads a file containing integer and floating-point values separated by commas, which may or may not be followed by additional whitespace. Generate a new file that contains the integers and floating-point values separated only by spaces; remove all whitespace characters between the values, and insert a single space between the values. Do not change the number of values per line in the file.
5. Write a program that reads a file containing data values computed by an accounting software package. While the file contains only numerical information, the values may contain embedded commas and dollar signs, as in $3,200, and negative values are enclosed in parentheses, as in (200.56). Write a program to generate a new file that contains the values with the commas and dollar signs removed, and with a leading minus sign instead of the parentheses. Do not change the number of values per line in the file.

6. A very useful program is one that compares two files, character by character, to determine whether they are exactly the same. Write a program to compare two files. The program should print a message indicating that the files are exactly the same or that there are differences. If the files are different, the program should print the line numbers for lines that are not the same.

7. Developing secret codes has interested people for centuries. A simple coding scheme can be developed by replacing each character in a text file by another character that is a fixed number of positions away in the collating sequence. For example, if each character is replaced by the character that is two characters to its right in the alphabet, then the letter 'a' is replaced by the letter 'c', the letter 'b' is replaced by the letter 'd' and so on. Write a program that reads the text in a file and then generates a new file that contains the coded text using this scheme. Change only the alphanumeric characters.

8. Write a program to decode the scheme presented in Problem 7. Test the program by using files generated by Problem 7.

Sounding Rocket Trajectory. Sounding rockets are used to probe different levels of the atmosphere to collect information such as that used to monitor the levels of ozone in the atmosphere. In addition to carrying the scientific package for collecting data in the upper atmosphere, the rocket carries a telemetry system in its nose to transmit data to a receiver at the launch site. Besides the scientific data, performance measurements on the rocket itself are transmitted to be monitored by range safety personnel and to be later analyzed by engineers. These performance data include altitude, velocity, and acceleration data. Assume that this information is stored in a file and that each line contains contains four values: time, altitude, velocity, and acceleration. Assume that the units are s, m, m/s, and m/s^2, respectively.

9. Assume that the file rocket1.dat contains an initial line that specifies the number of actual data lines that follows. Write a program that reads these data and determines the time at which the rocket begins falling back to earth. (*Hint:* Determine the time at which the altitude begins to decrease.)

10. The number of stages in the rocket can be determined by the number of times that the velocity increases to some peak and then begins decreasing. Write a program that reads these data and determines the number of stages on the rocket. Use the data file rocket2.dat. It contains a trailer line with the value -99 for all four values.

11. Modify the program in Problem 10 so that it prints the times that correspond to the firing of each stage. Assume that the firing corresponds to the point at which the velocity begins to increase.

12. After each stage of the rocket is fired, the acceleration will initially increase and then decrease to -9.8 m/s^2, which is the downward acceleration due to gravity. Find the periods of the rocket flight during which the acceleration is due only to gravity. Allow the acceleration to range within 65% of theoretical value for these periods. Use the data file rocket3.dat, which does not contain a header line or a trailer line.

Suture Packaging. Sutures are strands or fibers used to sew living tissue together after an injury or an operation. Packages of sutures must be sealed carefully before they are shipped to hospitals so that contaminants cannot enter the packages. The object that seals the package is referred to as a *sealing die*. Generally, sealing dies are heated with an electric heater. For the sealing process to be a success, the sealing die is maintained at an established temperature and must contact the package with a predetermined pressure for an established time period. The period in which the sealing die contacts the package is called the dwell time. Assume that the acceptable range of parameters for an acceptable seal are the following:

```
Temperature:       150-170 degrees C
Pressure:          60-70 psi
Dwell time:        2-2.5 s
```

13. A data file named suture.dat contains information on batches of sutures that have been rejected during a one-week period. Each line in the data file contains the batch number, temperature, pressure, and dwell time for a rejected batch. The quality control engineer would like to analyze this information and needs a report that computes the percent of the batches rejected due to temperature, the percent rejected due to pressure, and the percent rejected due to dwell time. It is possible that a specific batch may have been rejected for more than one reason, and it should be counted in all applicable totals. Write a program to compute and print these three percentages.

14. Modify the program developed in Problem 13 so that it also prints the number of batches in each rejection category and the total number of batches rejected. (Remember that a rejected batch should appear only once in the total, but could appear in more that one rejection category.)

15. Write a program to read the data file suture.dat and make sure that the information relates only to batches that should have been rejected. If any batch should not be in the data file, print an appropriate message with the batch information.

Timber Regrowth.   A problem in timber management is to determine how much of an area to leave uncut so that the harvested area is reforested in a certain period. It is assumed that reforestation takes place at a known rate per year, depending on climate and soil conditions. A reforestation equation expresses this growth as a function of the amount of timber standing and the reforestation rate. For example, if 100 acres are left standing after harvesting and the reforestation rate is 0.05, then $100 + 0.05 * 100$, or 105 acres, are forested at the end of the first year. At the end of the second year, the number of acres forested is $105 + 0.05 * 105$, or 110.25 acres.

16. Assume that there are 14,000 acres total with 2,500 acres uncut and that the reforestation rate is 0.02. Print a table showing the number of acres forested at the end of each year for a total of 20 years.

17. Modify the program developed in Problem 16 so that the user can enter the number of years to be used for the table.

18. Modify the program developed in Problem 16 so that the user can enter a number of acres and the program will determine how many years are required for the number of acres to be completely reforested.

Weather Patterns.   In Chapter 1, we discussed the types of information that are collected by the National Weather Bureau. Figure 1.5 contained a sample of the reports that are available with weather information. A group of data files included in the instructors CD that accompanies this text contains weather information for Stapleton International Airport for the period January–December 1991. Each file contains data from 1 month; each line in the file contains 32 pieces of information, in the order shown in Figure 1.5. The data have been edited so that they are totally numeric. If a field of information contained T, for a trace amount, the corresponding value in the data file contains 0.001. There are nine possible weather types, and because several weather types can occur during a single day, nine fields are used to store this information. For example, if weather type 1 occurred, the first of the nine fields will contain a 1; otherwise, it will contain a 0. If weather type 2 occurred, the second of the nine fields will contain a 1; otherwise, it will contain a 0. The peak wind-gust direction has been converted to an integer using the following:

```
N  1
NE 2
E  3
SE 4
S  5
SW 6
W  7
NW 8
```

The values on each line in the data file are separated by blanks, and the data files are named jan91.dat, feb91.dat, and so on.

19. Write a program to determine the number of days that had temperatures in the following categories for January 1991:
    a. Below 0
    b. 0–32
    c. 33–50
    d. 51–60
    e. 61–70
    f. Over 70
    Note that the range of temperatures in one day may fall in several of the categories.
20. Modify the program developed in Problem 19 so that it prints percentages instead of the number of days.
21. Modify the program developed in Problem 19 so that it uses the period May–August 1991.
22. Write a program that computes the average temperature for days with fog in November 1991.
23. Write a program that determines the date in December 1991 with the largest difference between the maximum temperature and the minimum temperature. Print the date, both temperatures, and the difference.

Critical-Path Analysis.   A critical-path analysis is a technique used to determine the schedule for a project. This information is important in the planning stages before a project is begun, and it is also useful to evaluate the progress of a project that is partially completed. One method for this analysis starts by dividing a project into sequential events and then dividing each event into various tasks. Although one event must be completed before the next one is started, various tasks within an event can occur simultaneously. The time it takes to complete an event, therefore, depends on the number of days required to finish its longest task. Similarly, the total time it takes to finish a project is the sum of time it takes to finish each event. Assume that the critical path information for a major construction project has been stored in a data file. Each line of the data file contains an event number, a task number, and the number of days required to complete the task. The data have been stored such that all the task data for event 1 are followed by all the task data for event 2, and so on. Thus, a typical set of data might be as follows:

Event	Task	Number of Days
1	15	3
1	27	6
1	36	4
2	15	5
3	18	4
3	26	1
4	15	2
4	26	7
4	27	7
5	16	4

24. Write a program to read the critical-path information and print a project completion timetable that lists each event number, the maximum number of days for a task within the event, and the total number of days for the project completion.
25. Write a program to read the critical-path information and print a report that lists the event number and task number for all tasks requiring more than five days.
26. Write a program to read the critical path information and print a report that lists the number of each event and a count of the number of tasks within the event.

CHAPTER 5

GRAND CHALLENGE:
Enhanced Oil and Gas Recovery

The design and construction of the Alaskan pipeline presented numerous engineering challenges. One of the important problems that had to be addressed was protecting the permafrost (i.e., the permanently frozen subsoil in arctic or subarctic regions) from the heat of the pipeline itself. The oil flowing in the pipeline is warmed by pumping stations and by friction from the walls of the pipe, so the supports holding the pipeline must be insulated or even cooled to keep them from melting the permafrost at their bases. In addition, the components of the pipeline had to be very reliable because of the inaccessibility of some locations. More importantly, component failure could cause damage to human life, animal life, and the environment around the pipeline. Therefore, the analysis of the reliability of equipment in applications such as this one is an important topic in engineering.

Modular Programming with Functions

Chapter Outline

Objectives

OBJECTIVES

In this chapter, we discuss the importance of dividing programs into functions (or modules) that perform specific operations. In C++, modules are available from libraries such as the Standard C++ library; modules also can be written specifically to accompany a main function. This chapter presents several examples of additional library functions from the Standard C++ library and of **programmer-defined functions.** The library function for generating a **random number** is used in an application that discusses instrumentation reliability and presents a computer simulation to estimate reliability. Numerical techniques for finding **real roots of polynomials** and **numerical integration** are discussed. The incremental search technique and Newton–Raphson method are implemented in C++ using programmer-defined modules. **Numerical integration** using the trapezoidal rule is also implemented in C++, and **recursive functions** that can reference themselves are introduced.

5.1 Modularity

modules

The execution of a C++ program begins with the statements in the `main` function. A program may also contain other functions, and it may refer to functions in another file or in a library. These functions, or **modules,** are sets of statements that typically perform an operation or that compute a value. For example, the *cout* object prints a line of information on the terminal screen, and the *sqrt* function computes the square root of a value.

To maintain simplicity and readability in longer and more complex problem solutions, we develop programs that use a `main` function and additional functions, instead of using one long `main` function. By separating a solution into a group of modules, we make each module simpler and easier to understand, thus adhering to the basic guidelines of structured programming presented in Chapter 3.

The process of developing a problem solution is often one of "divide and conquer," as was discussed in Chapter 2 when we first discussed the decomposition outline. The decomposition outline is a set of sequentially executed steps that solves the problem, so it provides a good starting point for selecting potential functions. In fact, it is not uncommon for each step in the decomposition outline to correspond to one or more function references in the `main` function.

Breaking a problem solution into a set of modules has many advantages. Because a module has a specific purpose, it can be written and tested separately from the rest of the problem solution. An individual module is smaller than the complete solution, so testing it is easier. Also, once a module has been carefully tested, it can be used in new problem solutions without being retested. For example, suppose that a module is developed to find the average of a group of values. Once this module is written and tested, it can be used in other programs that need to compute an average. This reusability is a very important issue in the development of large software systems because it can save development time. In fact, libraries of commonly used modules (such as the Standard C++ library) are often available on computer systems.

modularity

The use of modules (called **modularity**) often reduces the overall length of a program because many problem solutions include steps that are repeated several places in the program. By incorporating these steps that are repeated in a function, the steps can be referenced with a single statement each time that they are needed.

Several programmers can work on the same project if it is separated into modules because the individual modules can be developed and tested independently of each other. This allows the development schedule to be accelerated because some of the work can be done in parallel.

abstraction

The use of modules that have been written to accomplish specific tasks supports the concept of **abstraction.** The modules contain the details of the tasks, and the programmer can reference the modules without worrying about these details. The I/O diagrams that we use in developing a problem solution are an example of abstraction: We specify the input information and the output information without giving the details of how the output information is determined. In a similar way, we can think of modules as "black boxes" that have a specified input and that compute specified information; we can use these modules to help develop a solution. Thus, we are able to operate at a higher level of abstraction to solve problems. For example, the Standard C++ library contains functions that compute the logarithms of values.

We can reference these functions without being concerned about the specific details, such as whether the functions are using infinite-series approximations or lookup tables to compute the specified logarithms. By using abstraction, we can reduce the development time of software at the same time that we increase its quality.

To summarize, some of the advantages of using modules in a problem solution are the following:

- A module can be written and tested separately from other parts of the solution, and thus module development can be done in parallel for large projects.

- A module is a small part of the solution, and thus testing it separately is easier.

- Once a module is tested carefully, it does not need to be retested before it can be used in new problem solutions.

- The use of modules usually reduces the length of a program, making it more readable.

- The use of modules promotes the concept of abstraction that allows the programmer to "hide" the details in modules; this allows us to use modules in a functional sense without being concerned about the specific details.

Additional benefits of modules will be pointed out as we progress through this chapter.

Structure charts
module charts

Structure charts, or **module charts,** show the module structure of a program. The `main` function references additional functions, which may also reference other functions themselves. Figure 5.1 contains structure charts for the programs developed in the Problem Solving Applied sections in this chapter and in the next two chapters. Note that a structure chart does not indicate the sequence of steps that are contained in the decomposition outline. The structure chart shows the separation of the program tasks into modules and indicates which modules reference other modules. Therefore, both the decomposition outline and the structure chart provide different but useful views of a problem solution. Also, note that the structure chart does not contain the modules referenced from the Standard C++ library, because they are used so frequently and because they are an integral part of the C++ environment.

As we begin to develop solutions to more complicated problems, the programs become longer. Therefore, we include here three suggestions for debugging longer programs. First, it is sometimes helpful to run a program using a different compiler because different compilers have different error messages; in fact, some compilers have extensive error messages, whereas others give very little information about some errors. Another useful step in debugging a long program is to add comment indicators (/* and */) around some sections of the code so that you can focus on other parts of the program. Of course, you must be careful that you do not comment out statements that affect objects needed for the parts of the program that you want to test. Finally, test complicated functions by themselves. This is usually done with a

driver

special program called a **driver,** whose purpose is to provide a simple interface between you and the function that you are testing. Typically, this program asks you to enter the parameters that you want passed to the function, and it then prints the value returned by the function. The usefulness of a driver program will become more apparent as we cover the next few sections.

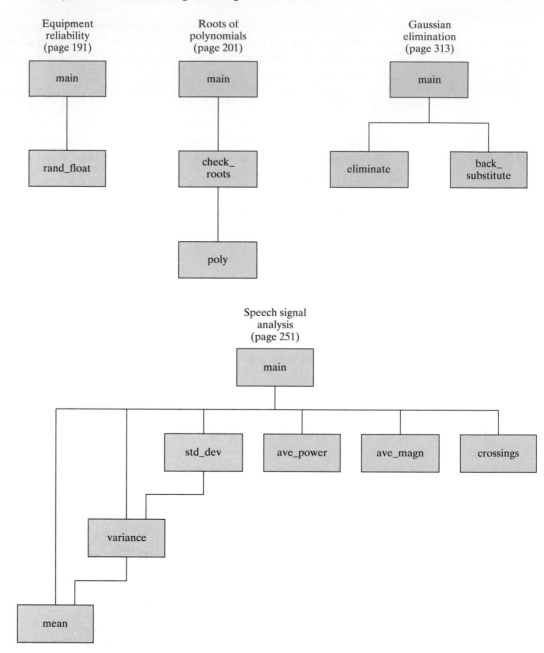

Figure 5.1 Example structure chart.

5.2 Programmer-Defined Functions

The execution of a program always begins with the main function. Additional functions are called, or invoked, when the program encounters function names. These additional functions must be defined in the file containing the main function or in another available file or library of files. (If the function is included in a system library file, such as the *sqrt* function, it is often called a **library function;** other functions are usually called **programmer-written,** or **programmer-defined, functions.**) After executing the statements in a function, the program execution continues with the statement that called the function.

library function
*programmer-
defined
functions*

Function Definition

Suppose we need to perform the simple task of converting from degrees Celsius to degrees Fahrenheit. We can write a programmer-defined function to perform this task. Our function will have one parameter, a temperature in degrees Celsius, and will return the temperature in degrees Fahrenheit. We can write the function as follows:

```
/*-------------------------------------------------------*/
/*  This function converts from degrees Celsius         */
/*  to degrees Fahrenheit.                              */

double Celsius_to_Fahr(double Celsius)
{
// Declare objects.
  double temp;

// Convert from degrees Celsius to degrees Fahrenheit.
  temp = (9.0/5.0)*Celsius + 32;

  return temp;
}
/*      -------------------------------------------------*/
```

function header

A function definition consists of a **function header** followed by declarations and statements. The function header defines the type of value that is returned by the function (double in our example); if the function does not return a value, the type is void. The function name and parameter list follow the return_type. Thus, the general form of a function definition is

```
return_type function_name(parameter declarations)
{
   declarations;
   statements;
}
```

*parameter
declarations*

function body

Style

The **parameter declarations** represent the information passed to the function; if there are no input parameters the parameter list can be omitted. However, the function name must always be followed by a set of parentheses, as we do when defining int main(). Additional objects used by a function are defined in the declarations. The declarations and the statements within a function form the **function body** and are enclosed in braces. The function name should be selected to help document the purpose of the function. Comments should also be included within the function to further describe the purpose of the function and to document the steps. *We also use a comment line with dashes to separate a programmer-defined function from the main function and from other programmer-defined functions.*

All functions that return a value must include a return **statement.** The general form of the return statement is

```
return expression;
```

The expression specifies the value to be returned to the statement that referenced the function.

The expression type used in the `return` statement should match the return_type indicated in the function definition to avoid potential errors.

The cast operator (discussed in Chapter 2) can be used to explicitly specify the type of the expression if necessary. A `void` function does not return a value, and thus has this general function header:

```
void function_name(parameter declarations)
```

The `return` statement in a `void` function is optional, and it does not contain an expression. The general form is

```
return;
```

Style

Functions can be defined before or after the main function. Remember that a right brace specifies the end of the main function. However, one function must be completely defined before another function begins; function definitions cannot be nested within each other. *In our programs, we include the main function first, and then additional functions are included in the order in which they are referenced in the program.*

We will now present an example of a program that uses a programmer-defined function. The *sinc(x)* function, plotted in Figure 5.2, is commonly used in many engineering applications. The most common definition for *sinc(x)* is the following:

$$f(x) = \text{sinc}(x)$$
$$= \frac{\sin(x)}{x}.$$

(The *sinc(x)* function is also occasionally defined to be *sin((πx)/(πx).)* The values of this function can be easily computed, except for *sinc(0),* which gives an indeterminant form of 0/0. In this case, l'Hopital's theorem from calculus can be used to prove that *sinc(0) = 1.*

Assume that we want to develop a program that allows the user to enter interval limits, *a* and *b.* The program should then compute and print 21 values of *sinc(x)* for values of *x* evenly spaced between *a* and *b,* inclusively. Thus, the first value of *x* should be *a.* An increment should then be added to obtain the next value of *x,* and so on, until the 21st value, which should be *b.*

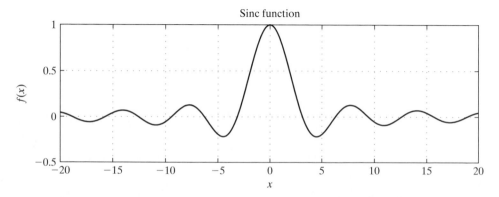

Figure 5.2 Sinc function in [-20, 20].

Therefore, the increment in x is

$$x\_increment = \frac{interval\_width}{20} = \frac{b - a}{20}.$$

Select values for a and b, and convince yourself that, with this increment, and with a as the first value, the 21st value will be b.

Because $sinc(x)$ is not part of the mathematical functions provided by the Standard C++ library, we implement this problem solution two ways. In one solution, we include the statements to perform the computations of $sinc(x)$ in the main function; in the other solution, we write a programmer-defined function to compute $sinc(x)$, and then reference the programmer-defined function each time that the computations are needed. Both solutions are now presented so that you can compare them:

Solution 1

```
/*-------------------------------------------------------------*/
/*  Program chapter5_1                                         */
/*                                                            */
/*  This program prints 21 values of the sinc                */
/*  function in the interval [a,b] using                     */
/*  computations within the main function.                   */

#include <iostream>
#include <cmath>
using namespace std;

int main()
{
   // Declare objects.
   double a, b, x_incr, new_x, sinc_x;

   // Get interval endpoints from the user.
   cout << "Enter end points a and b (a<b): \n";
   cin >> a >> b;
   x_incr = (b - a)/20;

   // Set Formats
   cout.setf(ios::fixed);
   cout.precision(6);

   // Compute and print table of sinc(x) values.
   cout << "x and sinc(x) \n";
   for (int k=0; k<=20; k++)
   {
      new_x = a + k*x_incr;
      if (fabs(new_x) < 0.0001)
      {
         sinc_x = 1.0;
      }
      else
      {
         sinc_x = sin(new_x)/new_x;
```

```
      }
      cout << new_x << " " << sinc_x << endl;
   }

   //  Exit program.
   return 0;
}
/*----------------------------------------------------------*/
```

Solution 2

```
/*----------------------------------------------------------*/
/*  Program chapter5_2                                      */
/*                                                          */
/*  This program prints 21 values of the sinc               */
/*  function in the interval [a,b] using a                  */
/*  programmer-defined function.                            */
/*                                                          */

#include <iostream>
#include <cmath>
using namespace std;

//Function Prototype
double sinc(double x);

int main()
{
   //  Declare objects
   double a, b, x_incr, new_x;

   //  Get interval endpoints from the user.
   cout << "Enter endpoints a and b (a<b): \n";
   cin >> a >> b;
   x_incr = (b- a)/20;

   //  Set Formats
   cout.setf(ios::fixed);
   cout.precision(6);

   //  Compute and print table of sinc(x) values.
   cout << "x and sinc(x) \n";
   for (int k=0; k<=20; k++)
   {
      new_x = a + k*x_incr;
      cout << new_x << " " << sinc(new_x) << endl;
   }

   //  Exit program.
   return 0;
}
```

```
/*------------------------------------------------------------*/
/*   This function evaluates the sinc function.         */

double sinc(double x)
{
   if (fabs(x) < 0.0001)
   {
     return 1.0;
   }
   else
   {
     return sin(x)/x;
   }
 }
/*------------------------------------------------------------*/
```

The following output represents a sample interaction that could occur with either program:

```
Enter endpoints a and b (a<b):
-5 5
x and sinc(x)
-5.000000 -0.191785
-4.500000 -0.217229
-4.000000 -0.189201
-3.500000 -0.100224
-3.000000 0.047040
-2.500000 0.239389
-2.000000 0.454649
-1.500000 0.664997
-1.000000 0.841471
-0.500000 0.958851
0.000000 1.000000
0.500000 0.958851
1.000000 0.841471
1.500000 0.664997
2.000000 0.454649
2.500000 0.239389
3.000000 0.047040
3.500000 -0.100224
4.000000 -0.189201
4.500000 -0.217229
5.000000 -0.191785
```

Figure 5.3 contains plots of the 21 values computed for four different intervals $[a, b]$. The program computes only 21 values, so the resolution in the plots is affected by the size of the interval: A smaller interval has better resolution than a larger interval. Note that the main function of solution 2 is easier to read because it is shorter than the main function in the first solution.

We now look closer at the interaction between a statement that references a function and the function itself.

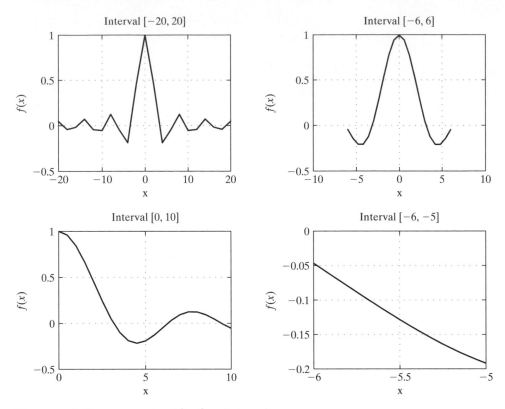

Figure 5.3 Program output for four intervals.

Function Prototype

The solution presented in program chapter5_2 contained the following statement above the main function definition:

```
double sinc(double x);
```

function prototype   This statement is a **function prototype** statement. It informs the compiler that the main function or other functions defined in the file will reference a function named *sinc*, that the *sinc* function expects a double parameter, and that the *sinc* function returns a double value. The identifier *x* is not being defined as an object; it is just used to indicate that a value is expected as an argument by the *sinc* function. In fact, it is valid to include only the argument types in the function prototype statement:

```
double sinc(double);
```

Both of these prototype statements give the same information to the compiler. We recommend using parameter identifiers in prototype statements because the identifiers help document the order and definition of the parameters.

Function prototype statements should be included for all functions referenced in a program. A function prototype is included with preprocessor directives, outside of the main function, so that the function will be known to all programmer defined function defined within the file. Header files, such as *cmath,* contain the function prototypes for the functions included in the library file; otherwise, we would need to include individual prototype statements for functions such as *log()* and *sqrt()* in our programs.

custom header file

If a program references a large number of programmer-defined functions, it becomes cumbersome to include all the function prototype statements. In these cases, a **custom header file** can be defined that contains the function prototypes and any related symbolic constants. A header file should have a file name that ends with a suffix of .h. The file is then referenced with an include statement, using double quotes around the file name. In Chapter 6, we develop a set of functions for computing common statistics from a set of values. If a header file containing the corresponding function prototypes is named *stat_lib.h*, then the prototypes are all included in a program with this statement:

```
#include "stat_lib.h"
```

Custom header files are often used to accompany routines that are shared by programmers.

5.3 Parameter Passing

formal parameters
function arguments

The function header defines the parameters that are required by the function; these are called **formal parameters.** Any statement that references the function must include values that correspond to the parameters; these are called **actual parameters** or **function arguments.** For example, consider the *sinc()* function developed earlier in this section. The function header is

```
double sinc(double x)
```

and the statement from the main program that references the function is

```
cout << new_x << " " << sinc(new_x) << endl;
```

Thus, the object *x* is the formal parameter and the object *new_x* is the function argument. When the reference to the *sinc()* function in the cout statement is executed, the value of the argument is copied to the formal parameter, and the steps in the *sinc()* function are executed using the new value in *x*. The value returned by the *sinc()* function is then printed. It is important to note that the value in the formal parameter is not moved back to the function argument when the function is completed. We illustrate these steps with a memory snapshot that shows the transfer of the value from the function argument to the formal parameter, assuming that the value of *new_x* is 5.0 at the time the *sinc()* function is called:

function argument   formal parameter

new_x $\boxed{5.0}$ →x $\boxed{5.0}$

After the value in the function argument is copied to the formal parameter, the steps in the *sinc()* function are executed. When debugging a function, it is a good idea to use *cout* statements to provide a memory snapshot of the function arguments before the function is referenced, and of the formal parameters at the beginning of the function.

Call by Value

call by value

The function reference in the *sinc()* example is a **call by value,** or a **reference by value.** When a function reference is made, the *value* of the argument is passed to the function and is used as the value of the corresponding formal parameter. In general, a C++ function cannot change the value of the function argument. Exceptions occur when the function arguments are arrays (discussed in Chapter 7) or the formal parameters are declared to be **call by reference,** which will be discussed in the next section.

Since the formal parameter x in the *sinc()* function is a call-by-value parameter, valid references to the sinc function can also include expressions and can include other function references, as shown in these references to the *sinc()* function:

```
cout << sinc(x+2.5) << endl;

double y;
cin >> y;
cout << sinc(y) << endl;

z = x*x + sinc(2.0*x);

w = sinc(fabs(y));
```

In all these references, the formal parameter is still x, but the function argument is $x +$ *2.5, y, 2.0*x,* or *fabs(y)*, depending on the reference selected.

If a function has more than one parameter, the formal parameters and the function arguments must match in number, type, and order. A mismatch between the number of formal parameters and function arguments can be detected by the compiler using the function prototype statement. If the type of an function argument is not the same as the corresponding formal parameter, then the value of the function arguments may be converted to the appropriate type; this conversion is also called **coercion of arguments** and may cause errors. The coercion occurs according to the discussion given in Chapter 2, which discussed moving values stored as one type to an object with a different type. Converting values to a higher type (such as from `float` to `double`) generally works correctly; converting values to a lower type (such as from `double` to `int`) often introduces errors. To illustrate the coercion of arguments, consider the following function that returns the maximum of two values:

```
/*-----------------------------------------------------*/
/*  This function returns the maximum of two           */
/*  integer values.                                    */

int max(int a, int b)
{
   if (a > b)
   {
      return a;
   }
   else
   {
      return b;
   }
}
/*-----------------------------------------------------*/
```

Assume that a reference to this function is *max(x_sum,y_sum)* and that *x_sum* and *y_sum* are integers containing the values 3 and 8, respectively. Then the following memory snapshot shows the transfer of values from the function arguments to the formal parameters when the reference *max(x_sum,y_sum)* is made:

function arguments   formal parameters

x_sum 3   → a 3

y sum 8   → b 8

The statements in the function will then return the value 8 as the value of the reference *max(x_sum,y_sum)*.

Now suppose that a reference to the function *max* is made using `double` objects *t_1* and *t_2*. If *t_1* and *t_2* contain the values 2.8 and 4.6, respectively, then the following transfer of parameters occurs when the reference *max(t_1,t_2)* is executed:

function arguments   formal parameters

t_1 2.8   → a 2

t_2 4.6   → b 4

The statements in the function will then return the value 4 to the statement containing the reference *max(t_1,t_2)*. Obviously, the wrong value has been returned by the function. However, the problem is not in the function; the problem is that the function was referenced with the wrong types of function arguments.

Additional errors can be introduced if the function arguments are out of order. These errors may not be detected by the compiler and can be difficult to detect upon examination of the code; therefore, be especially careful that the order of the formal parameters and the function arguments match.

Practice!

Consider the following function:

```
/*------------------.....          .............*/
/*  This function counts positive parameters.    */

int positive(double a, double b, double c)
{
   int count;

   count = 0;
   if (a >= 0)
   {
      count++;
   }
   if (b >= 0)
   {
      count++;
   }
```

```
    if (c >= 0)
    {
        count++;
    }
    return count;
}
/*------------------------------------------------*/
```

Assume that the function is referenced with the following statements:

```
x = 25;
total = positive(x, sqrt(x), x-30);
```

    1. Show the memory snapshot of the formal parameters and the function arguments.

    2. What is the new value of *total?*

Call by Reference

When a formal parameter is a call-by-value parameter, the value of the function argument cannot be changed. When the value of a function argument needs to be modified, the function must receive the **address** of the function argument, instead of the value, to allow the function call by reference to modify the argument. This type of function reference is called a **call by reference.**

      To illustrate the use of call-by-reference parameters, we develop a function that exchanges the contents of two memory locations. It takes three statements to switch the values in two location, as shown by the following statements and corresponding memory snapshots:

int hold, a(5), b(10);	a	b	hold
	5	10	?
hold = a;	a	b	hold
	5	10	5
a = b;	a	b	hold
	10	10	5
b = hold;	a	b	hold
	10	5	5

In problem solutions that require frequent switching of values, such as sorting programs, it is convenient to be able to access a function to perform the switch. Consider the following function, which **attempts** to perform the switch using standard pass-by-value parameters:

```
/*------------------------------------------------------------*/
/*   Incorrect function to switch two values.             */
```

```
void switch(int a, int b)
{
    //  Declare objects.
    int hold;

    //  Switch values in a and b.
    hold = a;
    a = b;
    b = hold;

    //  Void return.
    return;
}
```

Assume that the following statement references this function:

```
switch(x,y);
```

If *x* and *y* contain the values 5 and −2, respectively, then the transfer of the values from the function arguments to the formal parameters is the following:

function arguments   formal parameters

x 5   ⟶ a 5

y −2   ⟶ b −2

After the function is executed, the values of the function arguments and the formal parameters are as follows:

function arguments   formal parameters

x 5   ⟶ a −2

y −2   ⟶ b 5

Since this function uses call-by-value parameters, the *value* of the function arguments, not the *address,* are passed to the formal parameters. The values of the formal parameters are switched, but no change is made to the function arguments.

After considering this incorrect solution, we are now ready to develop a function that switches the contents of two simple objects using pass-by-reference parameters. The function has two formal parameters that are pass-by-reference parameters representing the two objects that we wish to switch. A prototype for this function is the following:

```
void switch2(int& a, int& b);
```

address operator

Notice that we have appended an & to the data type of each formal parameter. The & is called the **address operator.** Appending the address operator to the data type of the formal parameter results in a call by reference. When the function is referenced, the *address* of the function

argument will be passed to the formal parameters, not the value. The function definition
now follows:

```
/*-----------------------------------------------------------*/
/*  Correct function to switch values in two objects.        */
void switch2(int& a, int& b)
{
    // Declare objects.
    int hold;

    // Switch value of a and b.
    hold = a;
    a = b;
    b = hold;

    // Void return.
    return;
}
/*-----------------------------------------------------------*/
```

Assume that the following statement references this function:

```
switch2(x,y);
```

If x and y contain the values 5 and -2, respectively, then the transfer from function arguments
to the formal parameters is the following:

function arguments   formal parameters

The formal parameters receive the address of the corresponding argument. Since we do not
know what the address of x or y is, we illustrate, using an arrow, that the formal parameter a
holds the address of the argument x and that the formal parameter b holds the address of y,
and thus a *points* to x and b *points* to y. Any change to the formal parameter changes the value
of the function argument. After the function is executed, the values of the function arguments
and the formal parameters are as follows:

function arguments   formal parameters

x $\boxed{-2}$ ←————————— ⊏⊐ a

y $\boxed{5}$ ←————————— ⊏⊐ b

The function arguments that correspond to pass-by-reference parameter cannot be constants or expressions, since their values may be changed.

Practice!

In problems 1 4 consider the references to the *switch2()* function. For invalid reference, explain why the reference is invalid. For valid references, give a memory snapshot before and after the reference.

1.
```
int x=1, y=3;
...
switch2(x,y);
```

2.
```
...
switch2(10,5);
```

3.
```
int x=1, y=3;
...
switch2(x, y+5);
```

4.
```
double x=1.5, y=3.2;
...
switch2(x,y);
```

5. What is output by the following program?

```
#include<iostream>
using namespace std;

void fun_ch5(int first, int& second);

int main()
{
    int n1(0), n2(0);
    fun_ch5(n1,n2);
    cout << n1 << endl << n2 << endl;
    return 0;
}
void fun_ch5(int first, int& second)
{
        first++;
        second += 2;
        return;
}
```

Storage Class and Scope

In the sample programs presented thus far, we have declared objects within a `main` function and within programmer-defined functions, and we have placed our function prototypes before the main function. It is also possible to define an object before the `main` function. This affects the **scope** of the object, where scope refers to the portion of the program in which it is valid to reference the object. Scope is also sometimes defined in terms of the portion of the program in which the object is visible or accessible. It is important to be able to determine the scope of

scope

storage class

a function or object. Because the scope of an object is directly related to its **storage class,** we also discuss the four storage classes: automatic, external, `static`, and `register`.

local
global

First, we define the difference between **local** and **global** or **file** scope. Local objects are defined within a function and thus include the formal parameters and any other objects declared in the function. A local object can be accessed only in the function that defines it. A local object has a value when its function is being executed, but its value is not retained when the function is completed. Global objects are defined outside the main function or other programmer-defined functions. The definition of a global object is outside of all functions, so it can be accessed by any function within the program file. The **automatic storage class** is used to represent local objects; this is the default storage class, but it can also be specified with the keyword `auto` before the type designation. The **external storage class** is used to represent global objects.

automatic storage class
external storage class

Consider a program that contains the following statements:

```
#include <iostream>
using namespace std;

int count(0);
...
int main()
{
    int x, y, z;
    ...
}
int calc(int a, int b)
{
    int x;
    count += x;
    ...
}
void check(int sum)
{
    count += sum;
    ...
}
```

The object *count* is a global object that can be referenced by the functions *calc()* and *check()*. The objects *x*, *y*, and *z* are local objects that can be referenced only in the `main` program; similarly, the objects *a*, *b*, and *x* are local objects that can be referenced only in the function *calc()*, and *sum()* is a local object that can be referenced only in the function *check()*. Note that there are two local objects *x*—these are two different objects with different scopes.

The memory assigned to a global object is retained for the duration of the program. Although a global object can be referenced from a function, using global objects is generally discouraged. *In general, parameters are preferred for transferring information to a function because the parameter is evident in the function prototype, whereas the global object is not visible in the function prototype. The use of nonconstant global objects should be avoided.*

Style

Function names also have external storage class, and thus can be referenced from other functions. Function prototypes included outside of any function are also global references, and thus are available to all other functions in the program; this explains why we do not need to include *cmath()* in every function that references a mathematical function.

static storage class

The **static storage class** is used to specify that the memory for a local object should be retained during the entire program execution. Therefore, if a local object in a function is given a static storage class assignment by using the keyword static before its type specification, the object will not lose its value when the program exits the function in which it is defined. A static object could be used to count the number of times that a function was invoked, because the value of the *count* would be preserved from one function call to another. The following program illustrates the use of the static storage class:

```cpp
#include<iostream>
using namespace std;

void ch5_static();

int main()
{
    ch5_static();
    ch5_static();
    ch5_static();
}

void ch5_static()
{
    int x(0);
    static int count(0);
    x++;
    count++;
    cout << x << ',' << count;
    return;
}
```

The first time the function *ch5_static()* is called the objects *x* and *count* are defined and initialized. Since *count* is static and retains its value, the initialization is ignored on all subsequent calls to the function. The output from this program is as follows:

```
1,1
1,2
1,3
```

The keyword register is used before the type designation of an object to specify that it should be placed in a register or high speed memory location. Accessing registers is faster than accessing memory, so this class of storage is used for frequently accessed values. Because the availability of high speed memory is limited, it may not be possible to honor the request and the object will be placed in a regular memory location.

5.4 Problem Solving Applied: Calculating a Center of Gravity

When piloting an aircraft, it is necessary to know the weight and center of gravity of the aircraft before takeoff. If the aircraft is overloaded, it may be difficult or impossible to achieve lift. If the center of gravity is outside of the desinated limits, the aircraft may be difficult to control. In this section, we perform computations to determine the total weight and center of gravity of an aircraft.

1. PROBLEM STATEMENT

Determine the total weight and center of gravity of an aircraft, based on the number of crew members (a maximum of two is allowed) and the weight of the cargo (a maximum of 5,000 pounds is allowed). To compute the center of gravity, the program will take each weight and multiply it by its distance from the nose of the airplane. These products, called moments, are added together, and the sum is divided by the total weight to give us the center of gravity. The empty weight of the aircraft is known to be 9,021 pounds, and its empty center of gravity is 305 inches from the nose of the aircraft. Thus, the empty moment is 2,751,405 inch–pounds. The aircraft can hold a maximum of 540 gallons of fuel. For simplicity, we will assume that the tank is full at the time of takeoff and, with a fuel weight of 6.7 pounds per gallon, the fuel moment is known to be 1169167.3 inch–pounds.

2. INPUT/OUTPUT DESCRIPTION

The I/O diagram illustrates that the inputs to this program are the number of crew members (one to two) and the weight of the cargo. The output is a report of the total weight of the aircraft and the center of gravity. Built in data types `int` and `double` will be used for all data objects.

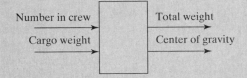

3. HAND EXAMPLE

Suppose two crew members board the aircraft with a total cargo weight of 100 pounds. Assuming an average weight of 160 pounds per person, we calculate the crew moment as follows:

Number of crew members * average weight per person *
distance from crew to nose of aircraft.

The cargo moment is calculated as follows:

cargo weight * distance from cargo bay to nose of aircraft.

The aircraft manual gives the distance in inches from nose of aircraft to the crew seats as 120 inches and the distance from the nose of the aircraft to the cargo bay as 345 inches. Thus, the crew moment is

2 * 160 * 120 = 38400 inch–pounds.

The cargo moment is

$100 * 345 = 34500$ inch–pounds.

The total weight of the aircraft is

crew weight + cargo weight + fuel weight + weight of the empty aircraft, or

$320 + 100 + 3618 + 9021 = 13059$ pounds.

The center of gravity is the sum of the moments divided by the total weight:

$$= (38400 + 34500 + 2751405 + 1169167.3) \text{ inch–pounds}/13059 \text{ pounds}$$
$$= 1438172.3 \text{ inch–pounds}/13059 \text{ pounds} = 305.802 \text{ inches.}$$

4. ALGORITHM DEVELOPMENT

We first develop the decomposition outline because it divides the solution into a series of sequential steps:

Decomposition Outline

1. Read the number of crew members and the cargo weight.

2. Calculate total weight.

3. Calculate the center of gravity.

Step 1 involves prompting the user to enter the necessary information. Since the number of crew and the amount of cargo have limits, error checking on the data is required. This step is a good candidate for a function. Step 3 requires the value of each moment. We will write value returning functions to calculate the required moments. We will use global constants for the values assumed in the problem statement. The refinement in pseudocode is as follows:

```
Refinement in Pseudocode
main:  Get_Data(crew, cargo)
       calculate total_weight
       calculate center_of_gravity
       print center_of_gravity, total_weight
```

The steps in the pseudocode are detailed enough to convert to C++:

```
/*-----------------------------------------------------------------*/
/* Program chapter5_3                                              */
/* This program calculates the total weight and                   */
/* center of gravity of an aircraft.                              */
```

```
#include<iostream>
#include<iomanip>
using namespace std;

//Program Assumptions

const double PERSON_WT(160.0);              //Average weight/person
const double FUEL_MOMENT(1169167.3);        //Fuel moment for full tank
const double EMPTY_WT(9021.0);              //Standard empty weight
const double EMPTY_MOMENT(2751405.0);       //Standard empty moment
const double FUEL_WT(3618.0);               //Full fuel weight
const double CARGO_DIST(345.0);
const double CREW_DIST(120.0);

//function prototypes

double CargoMoment(double);
double CrewMoment(int);
void GetData(int&, double&);

int main()
{

  //Declare objects.
  int crew; //number of crew on board (1 or 2)
  double cargo;   //weight of baggage, pounds
  double total_weight, center_of_gravity;

  //Set format flags.
  cout.setf(ios::fixed);
  cout.setf(ios::showpoint);
  cout.precision(1);

  GetData(crew, cargo);

  total_weight = EMPTY_WT + crew*PERSON_WT + cargo
              + FUEL_WT;

  center_of_gravity = (CargoMoment(cargo) + CrewMoment(crew)
                    + FUEL_MOMENT + EMPTY_MOMENT)/total_weight;

  cout << endl << "The total weight is " << total_weight
              << " pounds. \n"
       << "The center of gravity is " << center_of_gravity
       << " inches from the nose of the plane.\n";
  return(0);
}//end main

double CargoMoment(double weight)
{
```

```
        return(CARGO_DIST*weight);
}//end CargoMoment

double CrewMoment(int crew)
{
    return(CREW_DIST*crew*PERSON_WT);
}//end CrewMoment

void GetData(int& crew, double& cargo)
{
  cout << "enter number of crew members (Maximum of 2) ";
  cin >> crew;
  while(crew <= 0 || crew > 2)
  {
    cout << endl << crew
         << " is an invalid entry\n"
         << " re-enter number of crew, 0 < crew <= 2  ";
    cin >> crew;
  }//end while
  cout << crew << " crew members, thank you.\n\n";
  cout << "enter weight of cargo (Maximum of 5000 lbs) ";
  cin >> cargo;
  while(cargo < 0 || cargo > 5000)
  {
    cout << endl << cargo
         << " is an invalid entry"
         << " re-enter cargo weight, 0 < cargo <= 5000\n  ";
    cin >> cargo;
  }//end while
  cout << cargo << " pounds of cargo loaded.  Thank you.\n\n";
  return;
}//end getdata
```

5. TESTING

If we use the data from the hand example, we have the following interaction with the program (the total weight and center of gravity match the one that we computed by hand):

```
enter number of crew members (Maximum of 2) 2
2 crew members, thank you.

enter weight of cargo (Maximum of 5000 lbs) 100
100.0 pounds of cargo loaded.  Thank you.

The total weight is 13059.0 pounds.
The center of gravity is 332.3 inches from the nose of the plane.
```

Modify!

1. Modify the GetData() function to perform error checking and correcting for bad data, such as floating point data for the number of crew or character data. Test your function.

5.5   Random Numbers

random numbers   A sequence of **random numbers** is not defined by an equation; instead, it has certain characteristics that define it. These characteristics include the minimum and maximum values, the average, and whether the possible values are equally likely to occur or whether some values are more likely to occur than others. Sequences of random numbers can be generated from experiments, such as tossing a coin, rolling a die, or selecting numbered balls. Sequences of random numbers can also be generated using the computer.

Many engineering problems require the use of random numbers in the development of a solution. In some cases, the numbers are used to develop a simulation of a complicated problem. The simulation can be run over and over to analyze the results, and each run represents a repetition of the experiment. We also use random numbers to approximate noise sequences. For example, the static that we hear on a radio is a noise sequence. If we are testing a program that uses an input data file that represents a radio signal, we may want to generate noise and add it to a speech signal or a music signal in order to provide a more realistic signal.

Engineering applications often require random numbers distributed between specified values. For example, we may want to generate random integers between 1 and 500, or we may want to generate random floating-point values between 5 and −5. We now present discussions on generating random numbers between two specified values. The random numbers generated are equally likely to occur; that is, if the random number is supposed to be an integer between 1 and 5, each of the integers in the set 1, 2, 3, 4, 5 is equally likely to occur. Another way of saying this is that each integer has a probability of 0.20 of occurring for each run. Any values in a specified set are also called uniform random numbers or uniformly distributed random numbers.

Integer Sequences

The Standard C++ library contains a function *rand* that generates a random integer between 0 and *RAND_MAX,* where *RAND_MAX* is a system-dependent integer defined in *cstdlib*. (A common value for *RAND_MAX* is 32,767.) The rand function has no input arguments and is referenced by the expression *rand( )*. Thus, to generate and print a sequence of two random numbers, we could use this statement:

```
cout << "random numbers: " << rand() << " " << rand() << endl;
```

The same two values are printed each time that a program containing this statement is executed because the *rand* function generates integers in a specified sequence. (Because this sequence eventually begins to repeat, it is sometimes called a pseudorandom sequence instead of a random sequence.) However, if we generate additional random numbers in the same program, they will be different. Thus, this pair of statements generates four random numbers:

```
cout << "random numbers: " << rand() << " " << rand() << endl;
cout << "random numbers: " << rand() << " " << rand() << endl;
```

Each time that the *rand()* function is referenced in a program, it generates a new value; however, each time that the program is run, it generates the same sequence of values.

To cause a program to generate a new sequence of random values each time that it is executed, we need to give a new **random number seed** to the random-number generator. The function *srand()* (from cstdlib) specifies the seed for the random-number generator; for each seed value, a new sequence of random numbers is generated by *rand()*. The argument of the *srand()* function is an unsigned integer that is used in computations that initialize the sequence; the seed value is not the first value in the sequence. If an *srand()* function is not used before the *rand()* function is referenced, the computer assumes that the seed value is 1. Therefore, if you specify a seed value of 1, you will get the same sequence of values from the *rand()* function that you will get without specifying a seed value.

In the next program, the user is asked to enter a seed value, and then the program generates 10 random numbers. Each time that the user executes the program and enters the same seed, the same set of 10 random integers is generated; each time that a different seed is entered, a different set of 10 random integers is generated. The function prototype statements for *rand()* and *srand()* are included in *cstdlib*.

random number seed *(margin note)*

```
/*-------------------------------------------------------*/
/*   Program chapter5_4                                  */
/*                                                       */
/*   This program generates and prints ten              */
/*   random integers between 1 and RAND_MAX.            */

#include <iostream>
#include <cstdlib>
using namespace std;

int main()
{
   // Declare objects.
   unsigned int seed;

   // Get seed value from the user.
   cout << "Enter a positive integer seed value: \n";
   cin >> seed;
   srand(seed);

   // Generate and print ten random numbers.
   cout << "Random Numbers: \n";
   for (int k=1; k<=10; k++)
   {
      cout << rand() << ' ';
   }
   cout << endl;
```

```
   //  Exit program.
   return 0;
}
/*-------------------------------------------------------*/
```

A sample output follows, using g++ on a Linux system:

```
Enter a positive integer seed value:
123
Random Numbers:
128959393 1692901013 436085873 748533630 776550279 289139331
807385195 556889022 95168426 1888844001
```

Experiment with the program on your computer system; use the same seed to generate the same numbers, and use different seeds to generate different numbers.

Because the prototype statements for *rand()* and *srand()* are included in *cstdlib,* we do not need to include them separately in a program. However, it is instructive to analyze these prototype statements. Because the *rand()* function returns an integer and has no input, its prototype statement is

```
int rand();
```

Because the *srand()* function returns no value and has an unsigned integer as an argument, its prototype statement is

```
void srand(unsigned int);
```

Generating random integers over a specified range is simple to do with the *rand()* function. For example, suppose that we want to generate random integers between 0 and 7. The following statement first generates a random number that will be between 0 and *RAND_MAX* and then uses the modulus operator to compute the modulus of the random number and the integer 8:

```
x = rand()%8;
```

The result of the modulus operation is the remainder after *rand()* is divided by 8, so the value of *x* can assume integer values between 0 and 7.

Suppose that we want to generate a random integer between −25 and 25. The total number of possible integers is 51, and a single random number in this range can be computed with the statement

```
y = rand()%51 - 25;
```

This statement first generates a value between 0 and 50, and then subtracts 25 from the value, yielding a new value between −25 and 25.

We can now write a function that generates an integer between two specified integers, *a* and *b*. The function first computes *n*, which is the number of all integers between *a* and *b*, inclusive; this value is equal to $b - a + 1$. The function then uses the modulus operation with the *rand()* function to generate a new integer between 0 and $n - 1$. Finally, the lower limit, a, is added to the new integer to give a value between a and b. All three steps can be combined in one expression on the return statement in the function:

```
/*-------------------------------      --------------    ----*/
/*   This function generates a random integer           */
/*   between specified limits a and b (a<b).            */

int rand_int(int a, int b)
{
    return rand()%(b-a+1) + a;
}
/*-----------------      --------------------    -----------*/
```

To illustrate the use of this function, the next program generates and prints 10 random integers between user-specified limits. The user also enters the seed to initiate the sequence:

```
/*--------------------------------------------------    ----*/
/*   Program chapter5_5                                 */
/*                                                      */
/*   This program generates and prints ten random      */
/*   integers between user-specified limits.           */

#include <cstdlib>
#include <iostream>
using namespace std;

//   Function prototype.
int rand_int(int a, int b);

int main()
{
    //   Declare objects.
    unsigned int seed;
    int a, b;

    //   Get seed value and interval limits.
    cout << "Enter a positive integer seed value: \n";
    cin >> seed;
    srand(seed);
    cout << "Enter integer limits a and b (a<b): \n";
    cin >> a >> b;

    //   Generate and print ten random numbers.
    cout << "Random Numbers: \n";
    for (int k=1; k<=10; k++)
    {
        cout << rand_int(a,b) << ' ';
    }
    cout << endl;
```

```
        //  Exit program.
        return 0;
}

/*-----------------------------------------------------*/
/*  This function generates a random integer           */
/*  between specified limits a and b (a<b).            */

int rand_int(int a, int b)
{
    return rand()%(b-a+1) + a;
}
/*-----------------------------------------------------*/
```

A sample set of values generated from this program's as follows:

```
Enter a positive integer seed value:
13
Enter integer limits a and b (a<b):
-5 5
Random Numbers:
3  1 4  -4 0  4 0 0  -3 0
```

Remember that the values generated are system dependent; you should not expect to get this same set of random numbers from a different compiler.

Modify!

Use the program developed in this section to generate several sets of random integers in each of the following ranges using different seed values.

1. 0 through 500

2. −10 through 200

3. −50 through −10

4. −5 through 5

Floating-Point Sequences

In many engineering problems, we need to generate random floating-point values in a specified interval $[a, b]$. The computation to convert an integer between 0 and $RAND\_MAX$ to a floating-point value between a and b has three steps. The value from the $rand()$ function is first divided by $RAND\_MAX$ to generate a floating-point value between 0 and 1. The value between 0 and 1 is then multiplied by $(b - a)$, which is the width of the interval $[a, b]$, to give a value between 0 and $(b - a)$. The value between 0 and $b - a$ is then added to a to adjust it so that it will be between *a* and *b*. These three steps are combined in the expression on the `return` statement in the following function.

```
/*-------------------------------------     ----------*/
/*   This function generates a random                 */
/*   double value between a and b.                    */

double rand_float(double a, double b)
{
  return ((double)rand()/RAND_MAX)*(b-a) + a;
}
/*-     ---------     ------------------------------------------*/
```

Note that a cast operator was needed to convert the integer *rand()* to a `double` value so that the result of the division would be a `double` value.

The program presented earlier in this section can easily be modified to generate and print floating-point values. A sample set of values from such a modification is the following:

```
Enter a positive integer seed value:
82
Enter limits a and b (a<b):
-5 5
Random Numbers:
3.64335 -1.51118 2.9090 2.21546 -4.37439 -4.23527
0.709869 -3.41159 -4.86308 -0.958863
```

Modify!

Modify the program for generating integers to one that generates 10 random floating-point values within a user-specified range. Then, generate several sets of numbers from each of the following ranges, using different seed values:

1. 0.0 through 1.0

2. 0.1 through 1.0

3. −5.0 through −4.5

4. 5.1 through 5.1

5.6   Problem Solving Applied: Instrumentation Reliability

An analysis of the reliability of a piece of equipment is especially important if it is going to be used in situations that would be dangerous if it should fail or in environments that are not easily accessible. For example, in the application in the chapter-opening discussion that related to the Alaskan pipeline, failures in instrumentation related to the transport of oil in the pipeline could cause serious problems due to the difficulty of getting replacement equipment to the location of the failure. Also, failure of the instrumentation could cause damage to human life,

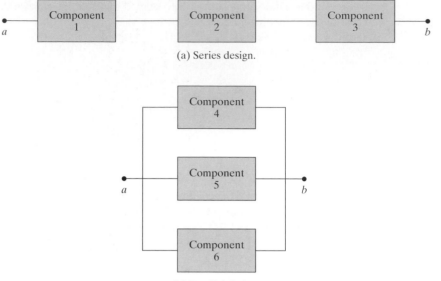

(a) Series design.

(b) Parallel design.

Figure 5.4 Series and parallel configurations.

animal life, and the environment around the pipeline. Therefore, the analysis of the reliability of equipment in applications such as this one is an important topic in engineering.

Equations for analyzing the reliability of instrumentation can be developed from the study of statistics and probability, where the reliability is the proportion of the time that the component works properly. Thus, if a component has a reliability of 0.8, then it should work properly 80% of the time. The reliability of combinations of components can also be determined if the individual component reliabilities are known. Consider the diagrams in Figure 5.4. For information to flow from point a to point b in the series design, all three components must work properly. In the parallel design, only one of the three components must work properly for information to flow from point a to point b. If we know the reliability of an individual component, then the reliability of a specific combination of components can be determined in two ways; an analytical reliability can be computed using theorems and results from probability and statistics, and a computer simulation can be developed to give an estimate of the reliability.

Consider the series configuration of Figure 5.4(a). If r is the reliability of a component and if all three components have the same reliability, then it can be shown that the reliability of the series configuration is r^3. Thus, if the reliability of each component is 0.8 (which means that a component works properly 80% of the time), then the analytical reliability of the series configuration is 0.8^3, or 0.512. That is, this series configuration should work properly 51.2% of the time.

Consider the parallel configuration of Figure 5.4(b). If r is the reliability of a component and if all three components have the same reliability, then it can be shown that the reliability of the parallel configuration is $3r - 3r^2 + r^3$. Thus, if the reliability of each component is 0.8, then the analytical reliability of the parallel configuration is $3(0.8) - 3(0.8)^2 + (0.8)^3$, or 0.992. The parallel configuration should work properly 99.2% of the time.

Your intuition probably also tells you that the parallel configuration is more reliable, because only one of the components must be working for the overall configuration to perform properly, whereas all three components must work properly for the series configuration to perform properly.

We can also estimate the reliability of these two designs using random numbers from a computer simulation. First, we need to simulate the performance of a single component. If the reliability of a component is 0.8, then it works properly 80% of the time. To simulate this performance, we could generate a random value between 0 and 1. If the value is between 0 and 0.8, we can assume that the component worked properly; otherwise, we assume that it failed. (We could also have used the values 0 to 0.2 to signify a failure and 0.2 to 1.0 to signify that a component worked properly.) To simulate the series design with three components, we would generate three floating-point random numbers between 0 and 1. If all three numbers are less than or equal to 0.8, then the design works for this one trial; if any one of the numbers is greater than 0.8, then the design does not work for this one trial. If we run hundreds or thousands of trials, we can compute the proportion of the time that the overall design works. This simulation estimate is an approximation to the analytically computed reliability.

To estimate the reliability of the parallel design with a component reliability of 0.8, we again generate three random floating-point numbers between 0 and 1. If any one of the three numbers is less than or equal to 0.8, then the design works for this one trial; if all of the numbers are greater than 0.8, then the design does not work for one trial. To estimate the reliability determined by the simulation, we divide the number of trials for which the design works by the total number of trials performed.

As indicated by the previous discussion, we can use computer simulations to provide a validation for the analytical results because the simulated reliability should approach the analytically computed reliability as the number of trials increases. There are also cases in which it is very difficult to analytically compute the reliability of a piece of instrumentation. In these cases, a computer simulation can be used to provide a good estimate of the reliability.

Develop a program to compare the analytical reliabilities of the series and parallel configurations in Figure 5.4 with simulation results. Allow the user to enter the individual component reliability and the number of trials to use in the simulation.

1. PROBLEM STATEMENT

Compare the analytical and simulation reliabilities for a series configuration with three components and for a parallel configuration with three components. Assume that all components have the same reliability.

2. INPUT/OUTPUT DESCRIPTION

The I/O diagram shows that the input values are the component reliability, the number of trials, and a random-number seed for initiating the sequence. The output consists of the analytical reliability and the simulation reliability for the series and the parallel configurations.

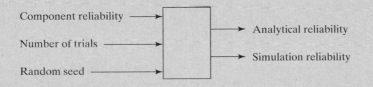

3. HAND EXAMPLE

For the hand example, we use a component reliability of 0.8 and three trials. Since each trial requires three random numbers, assume that the first nine random numbers generated are the following. (These were generated from the *rand_float* function using a seed of 6,666 for values between 0 and 1.)

The first set of three random values is

```
0.939775     0.0422243     0.929037
```

The second set of three random values is

```
0.817733     0.211689     0.9909
```

The third set of three random values is

```
0.0377037     0.103508     0.407272
```

From each group of three random numbers, we can determine whether a series configuration would work properly and whether a parallel configuration would work properly. For the first and second groups of three random numbers, two of the values are greater than 0.8, so only the parallel configuration would work properly. Both configurations work properly with the third set of random numbers. Thus, the analytical results (computed earlier in this section) and the simulation results for three trials are the following:

```
Analytical Reliability:
Series: 0.512 Parallel:  0.992
Simulation for 3 Trials
Series: 0.333333 Parallel:  1
```

As we increase the number of trials, the simulation results should approach the analytical results. If we change the random-number seed, the simulation results may also change, even with only three trials.

4. ALGORITHM DEVELOPMENT

We first develop the decomposition outline because it divides the solution into a series of sequential steps.

Decomposition Outline

1 Read component reliability, number of trials, and random-number seed.

2 Compute analytical reliabilities.

3 Compute simulation reliabilities.

4 Print comparison of reliabilities.

Step 1 involves prompting the user to enter the necessary information and then reading it. Step 2 uses the equations given earlier to compute the analytical reliabilities. Because the computations are straightforward, we compute them in the `main` function. Step 3 involves a loop to generate the random numbers and to determine whether the configurations would perform properly for each trial. The *rand_float()* function is used to compute the random numbers in the loop. In step 4, we print the results of the computations. The structure chart for this solution was shown in Figure 5.1. The refinement in pseudocode is the following:

Refinement in Pseudocode

```
main:    read component reliability, number of trials,
              and random number seed
         compute analytical reliabilities
         set series_success to zero
         set parallel_success to zero
         set k to 1
         while k <= number of trials
             generate three random numbers between 0 and 1
             if each number <= component reliability,
                 increment series_success by 1
             if any number <= component reliability,
                 increment parallel_success by 1
             increment k by 1
         print analytical reliabilities
         print simulation reliabilities
```

The steps in the pseudocode are now detailed enough to convert to C++. We also include the *rand_float()* function in the program:

```
/*-------------------------------------------------------*/
/*  Program chapter5_6                                   */
/*                                                       */
/*  This program estimates the reliability               */
/*  of a series and a parallel configuration             */
/*  using a computer simulation.                         */

#include <iostream>
#include <cstdlib>
#include <cmath>
using namespace std;

//  Function prototypes
double rand_float(double a, double b);

int main()
{
   //  Declare objects.
   unsigned int seed;
   int n;
   double component_reliability, a_series, a_parallel,
          series_success(0), parallel_success(0),
          num1, num2, num3;
```

```cpp
   //  Get information for the simulation.
   cout << "Enter individual component reliability: \n";
   cin >> component_reliability;
   cout << "Enter number of trials: \n";
   cin >> n;
   cout << "Enter unsigned integer seed: \n";
   cin >> seed;
   srand(seed);
   cout << endl;

   //  Compute analytical reliabilities.
   a_series = pow(component_reliability,3);
   a_parallel = 3*component_reliability
              - 3*pow(component_reliability,2)
              + pow(component_reliability,3);

   //  Determine simulation reliability estimates.
   for (int k=1; k<=n; k++)
   {
     num1 = rand_float(0,1);
     num2 = rand_float(0,1);
     num3 = rand_float(0,1);
     if (((num1<=component_reliability) &&
          (num2<=component_reliability)) &&
          (num3<=component_reliability))
     {
          series_success++;
     }
     if (((num1<=component_reliability) ||
          (num2<=component_reliability)) ||
          (num3<=component_reliability))
     {
          parallel_success++;
     }
   }

   //  Print results.
   cout << "Analytical Reliability \n";
   cout << "Series: " << a_series << "   "
        << "Parallel: " << a_parallel << endl;
   cout << "Simulation Reliability " << n << " trials \n";
   cout << "Series: " << (double)series_success/n << " Parallel: "
        << (double)parallel_success/n << endl;

   //  Exit program.
   return 0;
}

/*-----------------------------------------------------------*/
/*  This function generates a random                         */
```

```
/*   double value between a and b.                          */
double rand_float(double a, double b)
{
   return ((double)rand()/RAND_MAX)*(b-a) + a;
}
/*------------------------------------------------------------*/
```

5. TESTING

If we use the data from the hand example, we have the following interaction, and the output matches the data that we computed by hand:

```
Enter individual component reliability:
0.8
Enter number of trials:
3
Enter unsigned integer seed:
6666

Analytical Reliability
Series: 0.512  Parallel: 0.992
Simulation Reliability, 3 trials
Series: 0.333333  Parallel: 1
```

Here are results from two more simulations that demonstrate that the simulation results approach the analytical results as the number of trials increases:

```
Enter individual component reliability:
0.8
Enter number of trials:
100
Enter unsigned integer seed:
123

Analytical Reliability
Series: 0.512  Parallel: 0.992
Simulation Reliability, 100 trials
Series: 0.54  Parallel: 0.97
Enter individual component reliability:
0.8
Enter number of trials:
1000
Enter unsigned integer seed:
3535

Analytical Reliability
Series: 0.512  Parallel: 0.992
Simulation Reliability, 1000 trials
Series: 0.514  Parallel: 0.995
```

Modify!

These problems relate to the program developed in this section, which compares the analytical and simulated reliabilities.

1. Use this program to compute information comparing the simulation results for 10, 100, 1,000, and 10,000 trials, assuming that the component reliability is 0.85.

2. Use this program to compute information comparing the simulation results for 1,000 trials, using five different random-number seeds. Assume that the component reliability is 0.75.

3. What component reliability is necessary to give a series reliability of 0.7? (*Hint:* Use the analytical reliability equation.) Validate your answer using this program.

4. What component reliability is necessary to give a parallel reliability of 0.9? Using the analytical reliability equation is not as easy in this case. If your calculator does not find roots of polynomial equations, just experiment with the program until you are close to the desired reliability.

5.7 Numerical Technique: Roots of Polynomials*

A polynomial is a function of a single object that can be expressed in the general form

$$f(x) = a_0 x^N + a_1 x^{N-1} + a_2 x^{N-2} + \cdots + a_{N-2} x^2 + a_{N-1} x + a_N, \tag{5.1}$$

where the object is x and the coefficients are represented by $a_0, a_1, \ldots, a_N$. The degree of a polynomial is equal to the largest nonzero exponent. Therefore, the general form for a cubic (third-degree) polynomial is

$$g(x) = a_0 x^3 + a_1 x^2 + a_2 x + a_3,$$

and a specific example of a cubic polynomial is

$$h(x) = x^3 - 2x^2 + 0.5x - 6.5.$$

Note that, for each term in the equation, the sum of the coefficient subscript and the object exponent is equal to the polynomial degree using the notation in Equation (5.1).

Polynomial Roots

The solutions to many engineering problems involve finding the roots of an equation of the form

$$y = f(x),$$

where the roots are the values of x for which y is equal to zero. Examples of applications in which we need to find roots of equations include designing the control system for a robot arm, designing springs and shock absorbers for an automobile, analyzing the response of a motor, and analyzing the stability of a digital filter.

If a function $f(x)$ is a polynomial of degree N, then $f(x)$ has exactly N roots. These N roots may contain real roots or complex roots, as will be shown in the examples that follow. If we assume that the coefficients ($a_0, a_1, \dots, a_N$) of the polynomial are real values, then complex roots will always occur in complex conjugate pairs. (Recall that a complex number can be expressed as $\alpha + i\beta$, where $i = \sqrt{-1}$. The complex conjugate of $\alpha + i\beta$ is $\alpha - i\beta$.)

If a polynomial is factored into linear terms, it is easy to identify the roots of the polynomial by setting each term to zero. For example, consider the following equation:

$$f(x) = x^2 + x - 6$$
$$= (x - 2)(x + 3).$$

If $f(x)$ is equal to zero, we have

$$(x - 2)(x + 3) = 0.$$

The roots of the equation, or the values of x for which $f(x)$ is equal to zero, are then $x = 2$ and $x = -3$. These roots also correspond to the values of x where the polynomial crosses the x-axis, as shown in Figure 5.5.

If a quadratic equation (polynomial of degree two) cannot easily be factored, we can use the quadratic formula to determine the two roots of the equation. Recall that for a general quadratic equation

$$y = ax^2 + bx + c,$$

the roots can be computed as

$$x_1 = \frac{-b + \sqrt{b^2 - 4ac}}{2a}$$

and

$$x_2 = \frac{-b - \sqrt{b^2 - 4ac}}{2a}.$$

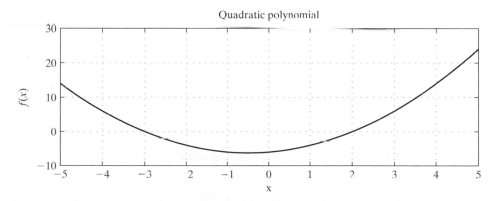

Figure 5.5 Polynomial with two real roots.

Thus, for the quadratic equation

$$f(x) = x^2 + 3x + 3,$$

the roots are

$$x_1 = \frac{-3 + \sqrt{-3}}{2} = -1.5 + 0.87\sqrt{-1}$$

and

$$x_2 = \frac{-3 - \sqrt{-3}}{2} = -1.5 - 0.87\sqrt{-1}.$$

Because a cubic polynomial is of degree three, it has exactly three roots. If we assume that the coefficients are real, then there are only these four possibilities:

- three real roots at different values (distinct roots).

- three real roots at the same value (multiple roots).

- one distinct real root and two multiple real roots.

- one real root and a complex conjugate pair of roots.

Examples of functions that illustrate each of these cases are as follows:

$$
\begin{aligned}
f_1(x) &= (x - 3)(x + 1)(x - 1) \\
&= x^3 - 3x^2 - x + 3; \\
f_2(x) &= (x - 2)^3 \\
&= x^3 - 6x^2 + 12x - 8; \\
f_3(x) &= (x + 4)(x - 2)^2 \\
&= x^3 - 12x + 16; \\
f_4(x) &= (x + 2)[x - (2 + i)][x - (2 - i)] \\
&= x^3 - 2x^2 - 3x + 10.
\end{aligned}
$$

Figure 5.6 contains plots of these functions. Note again that the real roots correspond to the points where the function crosses the x-axis.

It is relatively easy to determine the roots of polynomials of degree one or two, but it can be difficult to determine the roots of polynomials of degree three or higher. A number of numerical techniques exist for determining the roots of polynomials. Techniques such as the incremental search, the bisection method, and the false-position technique identify the real roots by searching for intervals in which the function changes sign because this indicates that the function has crossed the x-axis. Additional techniques, such as the Newton–Raphson method, can be used to find complex roots.

Incremental-Search Technique

incremental-search   The **incremental-search** technique is often used to determine the real roots of a function in an interval $[a, b]$. This technique searches for a subinterval $[a_k, b_k]$ such that the function value is negative on one end and positive on the other. We are then assured that there is at least one root in this subinterval.

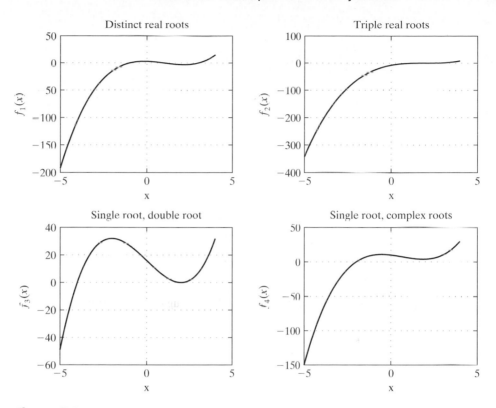

Figure 5.6 Cubic polynomials.

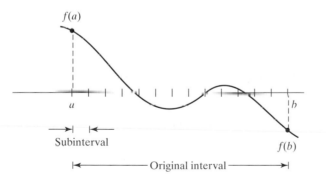

Figure 5.7 Incremental search.

There are many variations of the incremental-search technique. The one that we discuss begins with the selection of a step size that is used to subdivide the original interval into a group of smaller subintervals, as shown in Figure 5.7. For each subinterval, we evaluate the function at both endpoints. If the product of the function values is negative, then there is a root in this subinterval. (A negative product implies that one function value is positive, whereas the other function value is negative; hence, the function must cross the x-axis in the interval.) At this point, we can estimate the root to be the midpoint of this small segment, as shown in

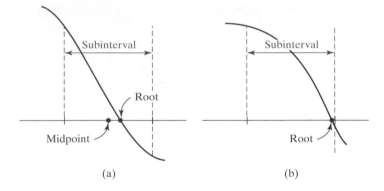

Figure 5.8 Subinterval analysis.

Figure 5.8(a). It is also possible that one of the subinterval endpoints might be a root, or be very close to a root, as shown in Figure 5.8(b). Remember that it is not likely that a floating-point value will be exactly equal to zero, so the test to determine whether an endpoint is a root should compare the function value with a very small number, but not with zero.

It is also important to recognize that there are cases in which this incremental-search technique fails. For example, suppose that there are two roots in one of the subintervals. In this case, because the function values at the endpoints will have the same sign, their product will be positive, and the algorithm will skip to the next subinterval. As another example, consider the case with three roots in one of the subintervals. In this case, because the function values at the endpoints have different signs, the estimate of the root is the midpoint of the subinterval. We then continue with the next subinterval and thus miss the other two roots in the previous subinterval. These examples are used to illustrate the fact that the incremental-search technique has some flaws, although, in general, it works reasonably well. If a technique is needed that has better performance characteristics, other root-finding methods [16] should be investigated.

 5.8   Problem Solving Applied: System Stability*

system

stable system

The term **system** is often used to represent instrumentation or equipment for which specified inputs generate specified outputs or actions. Examples of systems include the cooling equipment connected to the supports of a pipeline, a robot arm used in a manufacturing facility, and a fast "bullet" train. A simple definition of a **stable system** is the following: A system is stable if a reasonable input causes a reasonable output. For example, consider the control system of a robot arm. A reasonable input to the system would specify that the arm should move in a direction that is valid for the robot arm. If a reasonable input causes the arm to become erratic or to attempt to move in invalid directions, then the system is not stable. The analysis of the stability of the design of a system involves determining dynamic properties of the system. A discussion of the types of analyses involved, or of the functions involved, is beyond the scope of this text, but one component of the analysis requires the determination of the roots of polynomials. Usually, both the real and complex roots are needed, but the techniques for finding complex roots involve using the derivative of the polynomial, and thus they become more involved mathematically. Therefore, we reduce the scope of this problem to finding only the real roots of a polynomial given a specified interval in which to search. We also assume that the polynomial is a cubic polynomial, but the solution developed can easily be extended to handle higher degree polynomials.

Develop a program to determine the real roots of a cubic polynomial. Allow the user to enter the coefficients of the polynomial, the interval to be searched, and the step size of the subintervals used in the search.

1. PROBLEM STATEMENT

Determine the real roots of a cubic polynomial.

2. INPUT/OUTPUT DESCRIPTION

The I/O diagram shows that the input values are the polynomial coefficients, the interval endpoints, and the step size of the subintervals. The output values are the roots identified in the specified interval.

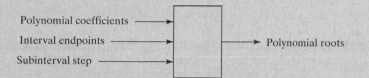

3. HAND EXAMPLE

For the hand example, we use the equation

$$y = 2x - 4.$$

This function can be described as a cubic polynomial with $a_0 = 0$, $a_1 = 0$, $a_2 = 2$, and $a_3 = -4$. If we set the polynomial to zero, we easily observe that the root is 2. To examine the incremental-search technique, we first use a step size such that the root falls on one of the endpoints of a subinterval, and then we use a step size such that the root does not fall on one of the endpoints of a subinterval. If the root falls on an endpoint, we can easily identify it because the polynomial value will be very close to zero. If the root falls within a subinterval, the product of the function values at the endpoints will be negative, and we then estimate the root to be the midpoint of the interval.

First, consider the interval [1, 3] with a step size of 0.5. The subintervals and the corresponding information derived from them are as follows:

Subinterval 1:   [1.0, 1.5]
$f(1.0) * f(1.5) = (-2) * (-1) = 2$
No root in this interval.

Subinterval 2:   [1.5, 2.0]
When we evaluate the endpoints, we detect the root at $x = 2.0$.

Subinterval 3:   [2.0, 2.5]

When we evaluate the endpoints, we again detect the root at $x = 2.0$. Note that we will need to be careful that we do not identify this root twice in the program.

Subinterval 4:   [2.5, 3.0]

$f(2.5) * f(3.0) = (1) * (2) = 2$

No root in this interval.

We now consider the interval [1,3] with a step size of 0.3. The subintervals and the corresponding information derived from them are as follows:

Subinterval 1:   [1.0, 1.3]

$f(1.0) * f(1.3) = (-2) * (-1.4) = 2.8$

No root in this interval.

Subinterval 2:   [1.3, 1.6]

$f(1.3) * f(1.6) = (-1.4) * (-0.8) = 1.12$

No root in this interval.

Subinterval 3:   [1.6, 1.9]

$f(1.6) * f(1.9) = (-0.8) * (-0.2) = 1.6$

No root in this interval.

Subinterval 4:   [1.9, 2.2]

$f(1.9) * f(2.2) = (-0.2) * (0.4) = -0.08$

The root in this interval is estimated to occur at the midpoint.

Subinterval 5:   [2.2, 2.5]

$f(2.2) * f(2.5) = (0.4) * (1.0) = 0.4$

No root in this interval.

Subinterval 6:   [2.5, 2.8]

$f(2.5) * f(2.8) = (1.0) * (1.6) = 1.6$

No root in this interval.

Subinterval 7:   [2.8, 3.1]

Note that the right endpoint exceeds the overall endpoint. In the program, we will modify such an interval so that it ends on the original right endpoint.

$f(2.8) * f(3.0) = (1.6) * (2.0) = 3.2$

No root in this interval.

4. ALGORITHM DEVELOPMENT

We first develop the decomposition outline because it breaks the solution into a series of sequential steps.

Decomposition Outline

1. Read polynomial coefficients, interval of interest, and step size.

2. Locate roots using subintervals.

Step 1 involves prompting the user to enter the necessary information and then reading it. Step 2 requires a loop to compute the subinterval endpoints and then to determine whether a root occurs on an endpoint or in the subinterval. When a root is located, a corresponding message is printed. There are a number of operations involved in step 2, so we should consider using functions to keep the main function from getting long. Because we need to evaluate the cubic polynomial several places in the program, it is a good candidate for a function. Within each subinterval, we need to search for a root; this search is also a good candidate for a function. The structure chart for this solution was shown in Figure 5.1. The refinement in pseudocode is the following:

```
Refinement in Pseudocode
main:   read coefficients, interval endpoints a and b,
             and step size
        compute the number of subintervals, n
        set k to 0
        while k<= n-1
            compute left subinterval endpoint
            compute right subinterval endpoint
            check_roots (left, right, coefficients)
            increment k by 1
        check_roots (b,b,coefficients)

check_roots (left, right, coefficients):
        set f_left to poly(left,coefficients)
        set f_right to poly(right,coefficients)
        if f_left is near zero
            print root at left endpoint
        else
            if f_left * f_right < 0
                    print root at midpoint of subinterval
        return
poly(x,a0,a1,a2,a3):
return a0x^3 + a1x^2 + a2x + a3
```

Note in the pseudocode for the *check_root()* function that we check to see whether the left subinterval endpoint is a root, but we do not check the right subinterval endpoint. This is necessary to avoid identifying the same root twice: when it is a right endpoint for one interval and also when it is a left endpoint for the next subinterval. Because we only check the left endpoints, we need to check the final point in the interval because it never becomes a left endpoint.

The steps in the pseudocode are detailed enough to convert to C++:

```
/*-------------------------------------------------------*/
/*  Program chapter5_7                                   */
/*                                                       */
/*  This program estimates the real roots of a           */
/*  polynomial function using incremental search.        */
```

```cpp
#include <iostream>
#include <cmath>
using namespace std;

// Function Prototypes
void check_roots(double left, double right, double a0,
                 double a1, double a2, double a3);
double poly(double x, double a0, double a1,
            double a2, double a3);

int main()
{
   // Declare objects and function prototypes.
   int n;
   double a0, a1, a2, a3, a, b, step, left, right;

   // Get user input.
   cout << "Enter coefficients a0, a1, a2, a3: \n";
   cin >> a0 >> a1 >> a2 >> a3;
   cout << "Enter interval limits a, b (a<b): \n";
   cin >> a >> b;
   cout << "Enter step size: \n";
   cin >> step;

   // Check subintervals for roots.
   n = ceil((b - a)/step);
   for (int k=0; k<=n-1; k++)
   {
      left = a + k*step;
      if (k == n-1)
      {
         right = b;
      }
      else
      {
         right = left + step;
      }
      check_roots(left,right,a0,a1,a2,a3);
   }
   check_roots(b,b,a0,a1,a2,a3);

   // Exit program.
   return 0;
}
/*-------------------------------------------------------------*/
/*  This function checks a subinterval for a root.    */

void check_roots(double left, double right, double a0,
                 double a1, double a2, double a3)
```

```
{
    // Declare objects and function prototypes.
    double f_left, f_right;

    // Evaluate subinterval endpoints and
    // test for roots.
    f_left = poly(left,a0,a1,a2,a3);
    f_right = poly(right,a0,a1,a2,a3);
    if (fabs(f_left) < 0.1e-04)
    {
        cout << "Root detected at " << left << endl;
    }
    else
    {
        if (fabs(f_right) < 0.1e-04)
            ;
        else
        {
            if (f_left*f_right < 0)
            {
                cout << "Root detected at " << (left+right)/2 << endl;
            }
        }
    }
    // Exit function.
    return;
}
/*-------------------------------------------------------*/
/*  This function evaluates a cubic polynomial.          */

double poly(double x, double a0, double a1, double a2,
            double a3)
{
    return a0*x*x*x + a1*x*x + a2*x + a3;
}
/*-------------------------------------------------------*/
```

5. TESTING

If we use the data from the hand example, we have the following interaction with the program (the roots match the ones that we computed by hand):

```
Enter coefficients a0, a1, a2, a3:
0 0 2 -4
Enter interval limits a, b (a<b):
1 3
Enter step size:
0.5
Root detected at 2.000
```

```
Enter coefficients a0, a1, a2, a3:
0  0  2  -4
Enter interval limits a, b (a<b):
1  3
Enter step size:
0.3
Root detected at 2.050
```

Use the polynomials given on page 196 to test this program. Use intervals and step sizes so that the roots do not always fall on subinterval endpoints.

Modify!

1. The size of the interval affects the estimate of the root if the root is not on an endpoint of a subinterval. Using the polynomial from the hand example, experiment with several step sizes, including 1.1, 0.75, 0.5, 0.3, and 0.14, for the interval [0.5, 3].

2. Using the first cubic polynomial given on page 196, test the program using intervals in which the roots fall on the endpoints of the interval [a, b] entered as input.

3. Using the first cubic polynomial given on page 196, find a step size that cause the program to miss some of the roots for an initial interval of [−10, 10]. Explain why the roots were missed by the program. Is this an error in the program?

4. Modify the program so that it checks to see whether the right endpoint of a subinterval is a root, instead of checking the left endpoint of a subinterval. Be sure to include a check for the first point of the interval [a, b].

5. Modify the program so that it can accept and locate the real roots of a fourth-degree polynomial.

6. Use this program to help answer Problem 4 of the previous Modify! problems on page 194.

Newton–Raphson method

Newton–Raphson Method*

The **Newton–Raphson method** is a popular root-finding technique that relies on information about the equation. It is also known as the tangent method because of the root-estimation technique it uses. The Newton–Raphson method uses both the function $f(x)$ and its derivative $f'(x)$ to compute the slope of a tangent line, which is then used as a straight-line approximation of the curve at each iteration point. The intersection of the tangent line and the x-axis becomes the next estimate for the root and the next point at which the tangent line is computed. The process is repeated until the root is found. Since the Newton–Raphson method makes a better estimate for the root at each step, it typically requires significantly fewer iterations to converge than the incremental-search technique.

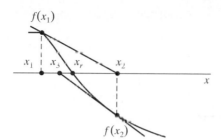

Figure 5.9 Newton–Raphson method.

Using the graph shown in Figure 5.9, we find that the Newton–Raphson method can be described with the following series of steps. An initial guess, x_1, is made for the root of the function $f(x)$. The slope of the curve at x_1 is then computed using $f'(x_1)$, and a tangent line with that slope is drawn through $f(x_1)$. The point x_2 where the tangent line intersects the x-axis becomes the new estimate for the root. The process then repeats using $f'(x_2)$ as the slope of the tangent line drawn through $f(x_2)$, which intersects the x-axis at x_3 and so on until it converges on the root at x_r.

The algorithm for finding the next estimate for the root, x_{k+1}, given the current estimate for the root, x_k, is obtained by noting that the slope of the tangent line at $f(x_k)$ can be computed by dividing the change in y by the change in x:

$$f'(x_k) = \frac{f(x_k) - 0}{x_k - x_{k+1}}.$$

Solving this equation for x_{k+1} provides the algorithm we need for the next estimate of the root:

$$x_{k+1} = x_k - \frac{f(x_k)}{f'(x_k)}.$$

As stated earlier, an advantage of the Newton–Raphson method is that it generally requires fewer iterations and, therefore, is computationally more efficient than the incremental-search method. In addition, it can be used to find complex roots when complex objects are used and when the initial guess is a complex value. The method can also be generalized to multiple dimensions for use in solving systems of nonlinear equations.

The method also has some limitations. The most important limitation relates to the initial guess; if the initial guess for the root is not good enough, the algorithm may miss the root entirely, finding instead one of the other roots or not finding a root at all. Other problems can arise, depending on the equation itself. Places where $f'(x)$ is zero or close to zero at peaks or inflection points in the curve can cause both the function and its derivative to be zero and result in the method failing at the origin. But these problems can usually be avoided if the initial guess for a root is close enough. It may also not be easy or even possible to compute the derivative of the function. Methods that do not require the derivative, such as the secant method, can be used in these situations.

To illustrate the Newton–Raphson method, we will write a program to determine the real roots of a polynomial $p(x)$ where $p(x)$ has the following form:

$$y = p(x)$$

$$= a_0 x^3 + a_1 x^2 + a_2 x + a_3.$$

We will assume that a root has been located if the absolute value of $p(x)$ is less than 0.001. For a test case, assume that the polynomial equation is

$$y = p(x)$$
$$= x^2 + 4x + 3.$$

We can use factoring to determine that the roots of this equation are $x = -1$ and $x = -3$. The Newton–Raphson method also requires the derivative of the polynomial, which in this case is

$$p'(x) = 2x + 4.$$

We begin with an initial guess and compute the value of the function and its derivative. The tolerance measure is the absolute value of the function. When the tolerance is less than 0.001, the process is terminated; otherwise, the next estimate for the root is determined using the equation for x_{k+1} given previously.

We now present a program to implement the Newton–Raphson method. Since the program is short and straightforward, no modules are needed:

```
/*-------------------------------------------------------------*/
/*  Program chapter5_8                                         */
/*                                                             */
/*  This program finds the real roots of a cubic polynomial    */
/*  using the Newton-Raphson method.                           */

#include <iostream>
#include <cmath>
using namespace std;

int main()
{
// Declare objects.
     int iterations(0);
     double a0, a1, a2, a3, x, p, dp, tol;

// Get user input.
     cout << "Enter coefficients a0, a1, a2, a3\n";
     cin >> a0 >> a1 >> a2 >> a3;
     cout << "Enter initial guess for root\n";
     cin >> x;

// Evaluate p at initial guess.
     p = a0*pow(x,3) + a1*x*x + a2*x + a3;

// Determine tolerance.
     tol = fabs(p);
     while(tol > 0.001 && iterations < 100)
     {
          // Calculate the derivative.
          dp = 3*a0*x*x + 2*a1*x + a2;

          // Calculate next estimated root.
          x = x - p/dp;
```

```
                    //  Evaluate p at estimated root.
                    p = a0*x*x*x + a1*x*x + a2*x + a3;
                    tol = abs(p);
                    iterations++;
        }
        if(tol < 0.001)
        {
                    cout << "Root is " << x << endl
                         << iterations << " iterations\n";
        }
        else
                    cout << "Did not converge after 100 iterations\n";
        return 0;
}
```

The following are some sample runs of the program:

```
Enter coefficients a0, a1, a2, a3
0 1 4 3
Enter initial guess for root
0
Root is -0.999695
 3 iterations
- - - - - - - - - - - - - - - - - - - - - - - - - - - - - - - - - - - - - - - - -
Enter coefficients a0, a1, a2, a3
0 1 4 3
Enter initial guess for root
5
Root is -0.999799
5 iterations
- - - - - - - - - - - - - - - - - - - - - - - - - - - - - - - - - - - - - - - - -
Enter coefficients a0, a1, a2, a3
0 1 4 3
Enter initial guess for root
-4
Root is -3.000305
 3 iterations
```

Modify!

1. Run the Newton–Raphson program using an initial guess of -1.

2. Run the Newton–Raphson program using an initial guess of -2. Explain what happens.

3. Modify the Newton–Raphson program to allow the user to input the tolerance used to stop the iterations.

4. Modify the Newton–Raphson program to find the roots of a fifth-degree polynomial.

5.9 Numerical Technique: Integration*

trapezoidal rule

The operation of integration gives engineers and scientists important information about functions or data sets. For example, distance, velocity and acceleration all relate to each other through integration. Velocity is the integral of acceleration and distance is the integral of velocity. The topic of integration is covered in detail in calculus courses, but the underlying principles can be explained simply in terms of area. The integral of a function over an interval represents the area under the graph of the function. Integration can be numerically approximated using any one of several different techniques. In this chapter, we will present a technique for performing numerical integration using the **trapezoidal rule.**

Integration Using the Trapezoidal Rule

To use the analytical techniques of calculus to obtain the integral of a function over an interval, we must have an equation for the function. In many engineering and scientific applications, we have data points or measurements from the function, but we do not have an explicit equation. Therefore, we need a method that requires only points of the function to numerically compute the integral. In other applications, we may have an equation that defines the function, but it is difficult or impossible to determine the integral analytically. In this case, we would also like to have a method that allows us to compute points or values of the function and then numerically evaluate the integral. The technique that we present in this section is a simple way to numerically estimate the area under a curve, given points on the curve. The technique uses the areas of trapezoids and thus is called integration using the trapezoidal rule.

The integral of the function $f(x)$, evaluated from a to b, is expressed as

$$\int_a^b f(x)\,dx$$

and represents the area under the function $f(x)$ from $x = a$ to $x = b$, as shown in Figure 5.10. If we are given the function that represents the curve, we can evaluate the function at points spaced along the interval of interest, as shown in Figure 5.11. Note that since $y = f(x)$, we can represent $f(x_1)$ as y_1, $f(x_2)$ as y_2, and so on.

If we join the points on the curve with straight-line segments, we form a group of trapezoids whose combined areas approximate the area under the curve. The closer the points are together on the curve, the more trapezoids there are in the interval, and thus the more accurate will be our approximation to the integral. In Figure 5.12, we use five points on the curve to generate four trapezoids, and the sum of the areas of the four trapezoids is then an approximation to the integral of the function between a and b.

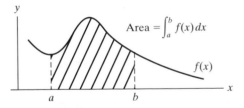

Figure 5.10 Area under a curve.

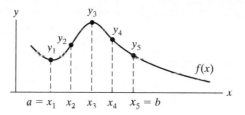

Figure 5.11 Spaced intervals.

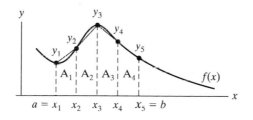

Figure 5.12 Four trapezoids.

The area of a trapezoid is one-half times the base times the sum of the two heights (or sides):

$$Area = 1.2 * base * (height_1 + height_2).$$

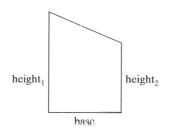

Thus, the area of the first trapezoid, A_1, is computed using the pair of points (x_1, y_1) and (x_2, y_2):

$$A_1 = 1/2 * (x_2 - x_1) * (y_1 + y_2).$$

Since the points on the curve are equally spaced along the x-axis in this example, the base of each of the trapezoids is the same value. We can then compute the individual areas of the trapezoids as

$$A1 = 1/2 * base * (y_1 + y_2),$$

$$A2 = 1/2 * base * (y_2 + y_3),$$

$$A3 = 1/2 * base * (y_3 + y_4),$$

$$A4 = 1/2 * base * (y_4 + y_5).$$

Thus, the total area between a and b can be approximated by the sum of the areas of the four trapezoids:

$$\int_a^b f(x)\,dx \approx \frac{\text{base}}{2}((y_1 + y_2) + (y_2 + y_3) + (y_3 + y_4) + (y_4 + y_5))$$

$$\approx \frac{\text{base}}{2}(y_1 + 2y_2 + 2y_3 + 2y_4 + y_5).$$

In general, if the area under a curve is divided into N trapezoids with equal bases, the area can be approximated by the following equation:

$$\int_a^b f(x)\,dx \approx \frac{\text{base}}{2}\left(y_1 + 2\sum_{k=2}^{N} y_k + y_{N+1}\right).$$

This equation is referred to as the trapezoidal rule.

When computing an integral with this numerical technique, we need to remember that the data points on the curve could come from different sources. If we have the equation for the curve, a C++ program can compute the data points that we use as the height of the trapezoids; in this case, we can choose the data points to be as close together or as far apart as we wish. Another possibility is that the points are experimentally collected data; in this case, we have a set of x-coordinates that represent the trapezoid base values and the y-coordinates that represent the heights of the trapezoids. We can still use the trapezoid areas to estimate the integral, but we cannot choose data points that are closer together or farther apart, because we do not have a function to evaluate; we only have the available data to use. If the bases of the trapezoids determined by the data points are not of equal value, we have to add the areas of the trapezoids individually instead of using the equation that assumes that the bases are equal.

We will now present a C++ program that determines an estimate of the integral (between two specified points) of the following equation:

$$y = f(x)$$

$$= 4e^{-x}.$$

```
/*-----------------------------------------------------------------*/
/*   Program chapter5_9                                            */
/*                                                                 */
/*   This program estimates the area under a given curve          */
/*   using trapezoids with equal bases.                           */

#include <iostream>
#include <cmath>
using namespace std;

//  Function prototypes.
double integrate(double a, double b, int n);
double f(double x);

int main()
{
   //  Declare objects
   int num_trapezoids;
   double a, b, area;
```

```cpp
   //  Get input from user.
   cout << "Enter the interval endpoints, a and b\n";
   cin >> a >> b;
   cout << "Enter the number of trapezoids\n";
   cin >> num_trapezoids;

   //  Estimate area under the curve of 4e^-x
   area = integrate(a, b, num_trapezoids);

   //  Print result.
   cout << "Using " << num_trapezoids
        << " trapezoids, the estimated area is "
        << area << endl;

   return 0;
}
/*--------------------------------------------------------------------*/

/*--------------------------------------------------------------------*/
double integrate(double a, double b, int n)
{
   //  Declare objects.
      double sum(0), x, base, area;

      base = (b-a)/n;
      for(int k=2; k<=n; k++)
      {
              x = a + base*(k-1);
              sum = sum + f(x);
      }
      area = 0.5*base*(f(a) + 2*sum + f(b));
      return area;
}
double f(double x)
{
      return(4*exp(-x));
}
/*--------------------------------------------------------------------*/
```

The following are some sample runs of the preceding program:

```
Enter the interval endpoints, a and b
0 1
Enter the number of trapezoids
5
Using 5 trapezoids, the estimated area is 2.536905
-------------------------------------------------------------
Enter the interval endpoints, a and b
0 1
Enter the number of trapezoids
50
Using 50 trapezoids, the estimated area is 2.528567
-------------------------------------------------------------
```

```
Enter the interval endpoints, a and b
0 1
Enter the number of trapezoids
100
Using 100 trapezoids, the estimated area is 2.528503
```

If we use calculus to integrate the specified function over the interval [0, 1], the theoretical answer to seven digits of accuracy is 2.528482.

5.10 Recursion*

A function that invokes itself (or calls itself) is a recursive function. Recursion can be a powerful tool for solving certain classes of problems in which the solution can be defined in terms of a similar, but smaller, problem, and then the smaller problem can be defined in terms of a similar, but still smaller, problem. This redefinition of the problem into smaller problems continues until the smaller problem has a unique solution that is then used to determine the overall solution. There are system-dependent limitations to the number of times that a recursive function can call itself as it is continually redefining a problem into smaller and smaller problems, but these limitations do not usually cause difficulties.

In the next two examples, we illustrate problems that can be solved with a recursive algorithm. In the examples, note the two parts to a recursive solution: First, the solution has to be redefined in terms of a similar, but smaller, problem; second, the smaller problems must reach a point at which there is a unique solution.

Factorial Computation

A simple example of recursion can be shown using the factorial computation. Recall that $k!$ (read as k factorial) is defined as

$$k! = (k)(k-1)(k-2)\cdots(3)(2)(1),$$

where k is a nonnegative integer and $0! = 1$. Thus,

```
5! = 5 * 4 * 3 * 2 * 1 = 120.
```

We could also compute 5! using the following steps:

```
5! = 5 * 4!
4! = 4 * 3!
3! = 3 * 2!
2! = 2 * 1!
1! = 1 * 0!
0! = 1.
```

Thus, we have defined a factorial in terms of a product that involves smaller factorials. The smaller factorial is continually redefined until we reach 0!. We substitute the value of 0! in the last equation and then begin going back up the list of equations, substituting values for the factorials:

```
1! = 1 * 1
2! = 2 * 1! = 2
3! = 3 * 2! = 6
4! = 4 * 3! = 24
5! = 5 * 4! = 120.
```

We have now developed a recursive algorithm for computing a factorial.

We present a program with two functions to compute a factorial: The first function is a nonrecursive (iterative) function, and the second is a recursive function. A factorial value becomes large quickly, so we use long integers for the factorial value. Note that both functions are referenced similarly in the main function:

```cpp
/*-------------------------      ------------------------------*/
/*   Program chapter5_10                                      */
/*                                                            */
/*   This program compares a recursive function and          */
/*   a nonrecursive function for computing factorials.  */

#include <iostream>
using namespace std;

// Function prototypes.
long factorial(int k);
long factorial_r(int k);

int main()
{
   //  Declare objects
   int n;

   //  Get user input.
   cout << "Enter positive integer: \n";
   cin >> n;

   //  Compute and print factorials.
   cout << "Nonrecursive: " << n << "! = " << factorial(n) << endl;
   cout << "Recursive: " << n << "! = " << factorial_r(n) << endl;

   //  Exit program.
   return 0;
}
/*-----------------------------------------------------------*/
/*   This function computes a factorial with a loop.    */

long factorial(int k)
{
   //  Declare objects.
   long term;
```

```
//  Compute factorial with multiplications.   */
term = 1;
for (int j=2; j<=k; j++)
{
   term *= j;
}

//  Return factorial value.
return term;
}
/*----------------------------------------------------------*/
/*  This function computes a factorial recursively.   */

long factorial_r(int k)
{
   /*  Recursive reference until k is equal to 0.   */
   if (k == 0)
   {
      return 1;
   }
   else
   {
      return k*factorial_r(k - 1);
   }
}
/*----------------------------------------------------------*/
```

The condition $k == 0$ keeps the recursive routine from becoming an infinite loop; this routine calls itself recursively with an argument that is continually being decremented by 1, until the argument reaches zero.

For large values of k, the value of $k!$ can exceed even long integers. In these cases, the computations should be done using double or long double values. An interesting approximation to $k!$ is also discussed in the end-of-chapter problems.

Fibonacci Sequence

A Fibonacci sequence is a sequence of numbers f_0, f_1, f_2, f_3, . . . in which the first two values (f_0 and f_1) are equal to 1, and each succeeding number is the sum of the previous two numbers. Thus, the first few values of the Fibonacci sequence are

```
1  1  2  3  5  8  13  21  34
```

This sequence was first described in the year 1202, and it has applications that range from biology to electrical engineering. For example, Fibonacci sequences are often used in studies of rabbit population growth.

A function to compute the kth value in the Fibonacci sequence is a good candidate for a recursive function because each new value in the sequence is computed from the two previous values. The following functions implement both nonrecursive and recursive algorithms for computing a Fibonacci number:

```
/*------------------------------------------- --------*/
/*  This function computes the kth Fibonacci        */
/*  number using a nonrecursive algorithm.          */

int fibonacci(int k)
{
   //  Declare objects.
   int term, prev1, prev2, n;

   //  Compute kth Fibonacci number with a loop.
   term = 1;
   if (k > 1)
   {
      prev1 = prev2 = 1;
      for (n=2; n<=k; n++)
      {
         term = prev1 + prev2;
         prev2 = prev1;
         prev1 = term;
      }
   }

   //  Return kth Fibonacci number.
   return term;
}
/*--------------------------------- --------------*/
/*                                                */
/*  This function computes the kth Fibonacci      */
/*  number using a recursive algorithm.           */

int fibonacci_r(int k)
{
   //  Declare objects.
   int term;

   //  Compute kth Fibonacci number recursively
   //  until k is equal to 1.
   term = 1;
   if (k > 1)
   {
      term = fibonacci_r(k-1) + fibonacci_r(k-2);
   }
   // Return kth Fibonacci number.   */
   return term;
}
/*----------- ------------------------------------*/
```

In the recursive function, the condition $k > 1$ keeps the function from getting into an infinite loop.

Modify!

1. Use program chapter5_10 to compute values of 1!, 2!, and so on, until you reach the limits for long integers. What kind of error message occurred when the value of $k!$ exceeded the limits on your system?

2. Modify chapter5_10 so that it uses `double` values instead of integers to compute factorials. Explain why the number of digits of precision determines the maximum value of $k!$ that can be correctly computed using `double` values. What is the maximum value of $k!$ that can be computed using `double` values on your system?

3. Write a `main` function to test the Fibonacci functions. What is the maximum Fibonacci value that can be correctly computed with integers on your system?

SUMMARY

Most programs in C++ benefit from using both library and programmer-defined functions. Functions allow us to reuse software and to employ abstraction in our solution, and, hence, reduce development time and increase the quality of the software. Numerous examples were developed to illustrate using value returning programmer-defined functions to solve problems, including examples of recursive functions. Specific applications were presented to illustrate generating random numbers (integers or floating-point values) and to implement the incremental search technique and Newton–Raphson method for identifying real roots of polynomials as well as numerical integration using the trapezoidal rule.

Key Terms

abstraction	incremental search
address operator	library function
automatic storage class	local scope
call by reference	modularity
call by value	module
center of gravity	module chart
coercion of arguments	moment
computer simulation	Newton–Raphson method
custom header file	numerical integration
external storage class	parameter declarations
factorial	programmer-defined function
function argument	random number
Fibonacci sequence	random number seed
formal parameter	recursion
function	register class
function argument	reliability
function body	re-usability
function header	root
function prototype	scope
global scope	stable system

static storage class

storage class

structure chart

system

trapezoidal rule

C++ Statement Summary

Function definition:

```
return_type function_name(parameter types)
{
    declarations;
    statements;
}
```

Return statement:

void function:

```
return;
```

Value returning function:

```
return (a + b)/2;
```

Function prototype:

```
double sinc(double x);
double sinc(double);
void check_roots(double left, double right, double a0,
                 double a1, double a2, double a3);
```

Style Notes

1. A program with several modules is easier to read and understand than one long main function.
2. Select the name of the function to indicate the purpose of the function.
3. Use a special line, such as a line of dashes, to separate programmer-defined functions from the main function and other programmer-defined functions.
4. Use a consistent order for functions, such as the main function first, followed by additional functions in the order in which they are referenced.
5. Use parameter identifiers in prototype statements to help document the order and definition of the parameters.
6. List the function prototypes on separate lines so that they are easy to identify.
7. Use the parameter list instead of global objects to transmit information to a function.

Debugging Notes

1. If you are having difficulty understanding the error messages from a compiler, try running the program on another compiler to obtain different error messages.
2. When debugging a long program, add comment indicators (/* and */) around some sections of the code so that you can focus on other parts of the program.

3. Test a complicated function by itself using a driver program.
4. Make sure that the value returned from a function matches the function return type. If necessary, use the cast operator to convert a value to the proper type.
5. Functions can be defined before or after the `main` function, but not within it.
6. Always use function prototype statements to avoid errors in parameter passing.
7. Use *cout* statements to generate memory snapshots of the function argument before a function is referenced, and of the formal arguments at the beginning of the function.
8. Carefully match the type, order, and number of function argument with the formal parameters of a function.
9. System-dependent limitations can occasionally cause problems with recursive solutions to a problem.

Problems

Exam Practice!

True/False Problems
Indicate whether the following statements are true (T) of false (F).

1. The body of a function is contained in braces. T F
2. The parameter list (or argument list) contains all objects used by the function. T F
3. In a call by value, a function cannot change the value of an function argument. T F
4. A static object is declared inside a function, but it retains its value from one reference call to another. T F

Multiple Choice Problems
Circle the letter for the best answer to complete each statement or for the correct answer to each question.

5. Which of the following is a valid function definition statement?
   (a) function cube (double x)
   (b) double cube (double x)
   (c) double cube (x)
   (d) cube (double x)
6. In a function call, the function arguments are separated by
   (a) commas.
   (b) semicolons.
   (c) colons.
   (d) spaces.
7. The definition of the statements in which an identifier is known (or can be used) is its
   (a) global.
   (b) local.
   (c) static.
   (d) scope.

Program Analysis

Use the following function for Problems 8–11:

```
/*---------------------------------------------- */
/* This function returns 0 or 1.                 */
/*                                               */
int fives (int n)
{
//   Declare objects.
    int result;
//    Compute result to return.
    if ((n%5) == 0)
    {
        return 1;
    }
    else
    {
        return 0;
    }
}
/*---------------------------------------------- */
```

8. What is the value of fives(15) ;
9. What is the value of fives(26) ;
10. What is the value fives(ceil(sqrt(62.5))) ;
    (*Hint:* You don't need a calculator to determine this value.)
11. Does the function work properly for all integers? If not, what are its limitations?

Programming Problems

  Simple Simulations.   In the problems that follow, develop simple simulations using the functions *randint* and *randfloat* developed in this chapter.

12. Write a program to simulate tossing a "fair" coin. Allow the user to enter the number of tosses. Print the number of tosses that yielded heads and the number of tosses that yielded tails. What should be the percentage distribution of heads and tails?
13. Write a program to simulate tossing a coin that has been weighted such that it lands with heads up 60 percent of the time. Have the user enter the number of tosses. Print the number of tosses that yielded heads and the number of tosses that yielded tails.
14. Write a program to simulate rolling a six-sided "fair" die with one dot on one side, two dots on another side, three dots on another side, and so on. Allow the user to enter the number of rolls. Print the number of rolls that gave one dot, the number of rolls that gave two dots, and so on. What should be the percentage distribution of the number of dots from the rolls?
15. Write a program to simulate an experiment rolling two six-sided "fair" dice. Allow the user to enter the number of rolls of the dice to simulate. What percentage of the time does the sum of the dots on the dice equal eight in the simulation?

16. Write a program to simulate a lottery drawing that uses balls numbered from 1 to 10. Assume that three balls are drawn at random. Allow the user to enter the number of lottery drawings to simulate. What percentage of the time does the result contain three even numbers in the simulation? What percentage of the time does the number 7 occur in the three numbers in the simulation? What percentage of the time do the numbers 1, 2, and 3 occur in the simulation?

Component Reliability.   The following problems specify computer simulations to evaluate the reliability of several component configurations. Use the function *randfloat* developed in this chapter.

17. Write a program that simulates the design shown in Figure 5.13 using a component reliability of 0.8 for component 1, 0.85 for component 2, and 0.95 for component 3. Print the estimate of the reliability using 5,000 simulations. (The analytical reliability of this system is 0.794.)

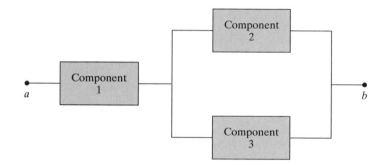

Figure 5.13 Configuration 1.

18. Write a program that simulates the design shown in Figure 5.14, using a component reliability of 0.8 for components 1 and 2, and 0.95 for components 3 and 4. Print the estimate of the reliability, using 5,000 simulations. (The analytical reliability of this system is 0.9649.)

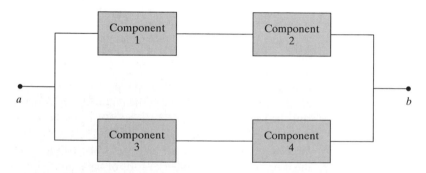

Figure 5.14 Configuration 2.

19. Write a program that simulates the design shown in Figure 5.15, using a component reliability of 0.95 for all components. Print the estimate of the reliability using 5000 simulations. (The analytical reliability of this system is 0.99976.)

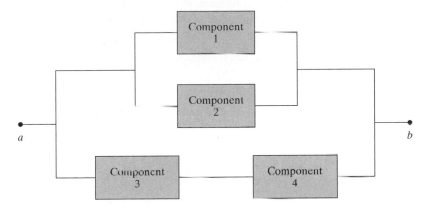

Figure 5.15 Configuration 3.

Flight Simulator Wind Speed.   This set of problems relates to a computer simulation of wind speed for a flight simulator. Assume that the wind speed for a particular region can be modeled by using an average value and a range of gust values that is added to the average. For example, the wind speed might be 10 miles an hour, with added noise (which represents gusts) that ranges from 22 miles per hour to 2 miles per hour, as shown in Figure 5.16. Use the function *randfloat* developed in this chapter.

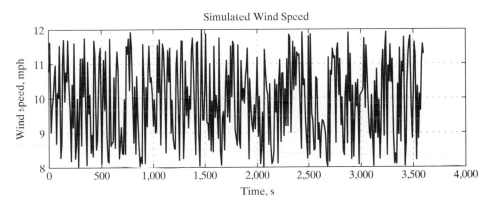

Figure 5.16 Simulated wind speed.

20. Write a program to generate a data file named **wind.dat** that contains 1 hour of simulated wind speeds. Each line of the data file should contain the time in seconds and the corresponding wind speed. The time should start with 0 seconds. The increment in time should be 10 seconds and the final line of the data file should correspond to 3,600 seconds. The user should be prompted to enter the average wind speed and the range of values of the gusts.

21. In Problem 20, assume that we want the flight simulator wind data to include a 0.5% possibility of encountering a small storm at each time step. Therefore, modify the solution to Problem 20 so that the average wind speed is increased by 10 mph for a period of 5 minutes when a storm is encountered. A plot of an example data file with three storms is shown in Figure 5.17.

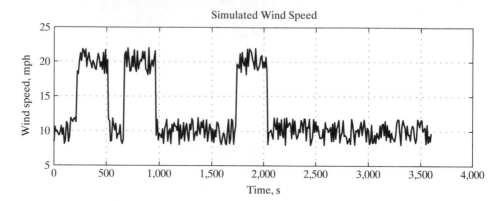

Figure 5.17 Simulated wind speeds with three storms.

22. In Problem 21, assume that there is a 1% possibility of encountering a microburst at each time step in a small storm. Therefore, modify the solution to Problem 22 so that the wind speed is increased by 50 mph over the storm values for a period of 1 minute if a microburst is encountered. A plot of a sample data file with a microburst within a storm is shown in Figure 5.18.

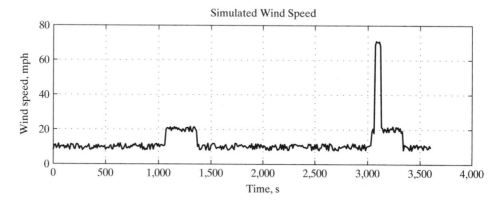

Figure 5.18 Simulated wind speeds with a microburst.

23. Modify the program in Problem 21 so that the user enters the possibility of encountering a storm.
24. Modify the program in Problem 21 so that the user enters the length in minutes for the duration of a storm.
25. Modify the program in Problem 21 so that the length of a storm is a random number that varies between 3 and 5 minutes.

Roots of Functions.   The following problems relate to finding real roots for functions:

26. Write a program to determine the real roots of a quadratic equation, assuming that the user enters the coefficients of the quadratic equation. If the roots are complex, print an appropriate message.
27. Modify the program in Problem 26 so that the program also computes the real and imaginary parts of the roots if they are complex.
28. Write a C++ function to evaluate this mathematical function:

$$f(x) = 0.1x^2 - x \ln x.$$

Assume that the corresponding function prototype is

```
double f(double x);
```

Then modify the program developed in Section 5.6 so that it searches for roots of this new function instead of searching for roots of polynomials. Test the program by searching for a root in [1, 2] for this new function.

29. Modify the program developed in Section 5.6 to find the roots of this function in a user-specified interval:

$$f(x) = \text{sinc}(x).$$

Use the sinc function developed in this chapter.

30. In the program developed in Section 5.6, we searched for subintervals for which the function values at the endpoints had different signs; we then estimated the root location to be the midpoint of the subinterval. A more accurate estimate of the root location is usually the intersection of a straight line through the function values with the x-axis, as shown in Figure 5.19.

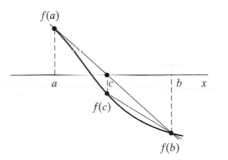

Figure 5.19 Straight line intersection in (a, b).

Using similar triangles, it can be shown that the intersection point c can be computed using the following equation:

$$c = \frac{a * f(b) - b * f(a)}{f(b) - f(a)}.$$

Modify program chapter5_6 to estimate the root of a subinterval using this approximation.

31. Write functions that could be used by the Newton–Raphson method program to evaluate the polynomial and its derivative. These functions would be useful if the evaluations of the polynomial and its derivative were complicated. Show the changes that would be necessary in the program.

Numerical Integration.   The following set of problems relates to performing numerical integration using the trapezoidal rule.

32. Modify program chapter5_9 to estimate the integral of the function

$$f(x) = 3x - 2x^2.$$

33. Modify program chapter5_9 so that it stores the x- and y-coordinates of the endpoints of the trapezoids in a data file so that they can be plotted later.

34. Write a program that estimates the integral of a function where the function is represented by a collection of experimental data points stored in a file rather than by an equation. The file contains a set of x-coordinates that represent the trapezoid base values and the y-coordinates that represent the heights of the trapezoids. Note that the number of data points determines the number of trapezoids. You must recalculate the base of the trapezoid for each new pair of data points because you cannot assume that all of the x-coordinates are equally spaced across the interval.

Factorials.   The following set of problems relates to computing factorials. If you did not cover the section on recursion, read the material on page 212 for the definition of a factorial and then review the nonrecursive function for computing the factorial.

35. A convenient approximation for computing the factorial $n!$ for large values of n is given by the Stirling formula [18]

$$n! = \sqrt{2\pi n}\left(\frac{n}{e}\right)^n,$$

where e is the base for natural logarithms, or approximately 2.718282. Write an integer function for computing this approximation to a factorial. Assume that the corresponding prototype is

```
int n_fact(int n);
```

36. Suppose that we have n distinct objects. There are many different orders that we can select to line up the objects in a row. In fact, there are $n!$ orderings, or permutations, that can be obtained with n objects. If we have n objects and select k of the objects, then there are $n!/(n - k)!$ possible orderings of k objects. That is, the number of different permutations of n different objects taken k at a time is $n!/(n - k)!$. Write a function named **permute** that receives values for n and k, and then returns the number of permutations of the n objects taken k at a time. (If we consider the set of

digits 1, 2, 3, the different permutations of two digits are 1, 2, 2, 1, 1, 3, 3, 1, 2, 3 and 3, 2.) Assume that the corresponding prototype is

```
int permute(int n; int k);
```

37. Whereas permutations (Problem 36) are concerned with order; combinations are not. Thus, given n distinct objects, there is only one combination of n objects taken k at a time, but there are $n!$ permutations of n distinct objects taken n at a time. The number of combinations of n objects, taken k at a time, is equal to $n!/((k!)(n-k)!)$. Write a function named combine that receives values for n and k and then returns the number of combinations of the n objects taken k at a time. (If we consider the set of digits 1, 2, 3, the different combinations of two digits are 1, 2, 1, 3 and 2, 3.) Assume that the corresponding prototype is

```
int combine(int n, int k);
```

38. The cosine of an angle can be computed from the following infinite series:

$$\cos x = 1 - \frac{x^2}{2!} + \frac{x^4}{4!} + \frac{x^6}{6!} + \cdots .$$

Write a program that reads an angle x (in radians) from the keyboard. Then, in a function, compute the cosine of the angle using the first five terms of this series. Print the value computed along with the value of the cosine computed using the C++ library function.

39. Modify the program in Problem 38 so that the approximation uses terms from the series as long as the absolute value of a term is greater than 0.0001. Also, print the number of terms used in the series approximation.

CHAPTER 6

GRAND CHALLENGE:
Speech Recognition

The modern jet cockpit has literally hundreds of switches and gauges. Several research programs are investigating the feasibility of using a speech-recognition system in the cockpit to serve as a pilot's assistant. The system would respond to verbal requests from the pilot for information such as fuel status or altitude. The pilot would use words from a small vocabulary that the computer had been trained to understand. In addition to understanding a specific vocabulary, the system would also have to be trained using the speech of the pilot who would be using the system. This training information could be stored on a disk and inserted into the onboard computer at the beginning of a flight so that the system could recognize the current pilot. The computer system would also use speech synthesis to respond to the pilot's request for information.

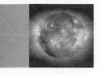

One-Dimensional Arrays

Chapter Outline

Objectives

Summary, Key Terms, C++ Statement Summary, Function Templates, Style Notes, Debugging Notes, Problems

OBJECTIVES

This chapter introduces **arrays,** a data structure used frequently in solving engineering problems. One-dimensional arrays are discussed in detail, with examples that illustrate defining and initializing arrays, that perform computations with arrays, that use arrays in input and output statements, and that use arrays as function arguments. A set of functions for performing statistical measurements on one-dimensional arrays is developed and used to analyze a speech signal. **Function overloading** and **function templates** are introduced. Character strings are introduced, with examples that illustrate defining and manipulating strings, and using string functions. A program is developed that determines if a character string represents a palindrome. The string class is revisited, and the **vector class** is introduced as an object-based alternative to arrays.

6.1 Arrays

When solving engineering problems, it is important to be able to visualize the data related to the problem. Sometimes the data consist of just a single number, such as the radius of a circle. Other times the data may be a coordinate in a plane that can be represented as a pair of numbers, with one number representing the *x*-coordinate and the other number representing the *y*-coordinate. There are also times when we want to work with a set of similar data values, but we do not want to give each value a separate name. For example, suppose that we have a set of 100 temperature measurements that we want to use to perform several computations. Obviously, we do not want to use 100 different names for the temperature measurements, so we need a method for working with a group of values using a single identifier. One solution to this problem uses a data structure called an **array.**

one-dimensional
array

A **one-dimensional array** can be visualized as a list of values arranged in either a row or a column, as follows:

0.5	0.0	–0.1	0.2	0.15	0.2
s[0]	s[1]	s[2]	s[3]	s[4]	s[5]

'a'	v[0]
'e'	v[1]
'i'	v[2]
'o'	v[3]
'u'	v[4]

elements
offsets

We assign an identifier to an array and then distinguish between **elements,** or values, in the array using **offsets,** also referred to as **subscripts.** Thus, by using the example arrays, the first value in the *s* array is referenced by *s[0],* the second value in the *s* array is reference by *s[1],* and the last value in the array *v* is referenced by *v[4].* In C++, the array identifier holds the *address of the first element,* so the offsets always start at 0 and are incremented by 1.

Definition and Initialization

An array is defined using declaration statements. An integer expression in brackets follows the identifier and specifies the number of elements in the array. Note that all elements in an array must be of the same data type. The declaration statements for the two example arrays are as follows:

```
double s[6];
char v[5];
```

An array can be initialized with declaration statements or assigned values with program statements. To initialize the array with the declaration statement, the values are specified in a sequence that is separated by commas and enclosed in braces. The following statements define and initialize the sample arrays *s* and *v*:

```
int s[6]={0.5, 0.0, -0.1, 0.2, 0.15, 0.2};
char v[5] = {'a', 'e', 'i', 'o', 'u'};
```

If the initializing sequence is shorter than the array, then the rest of the values are initialized to zero. Hence, the following statement defines an integer array of 100 values; each value is also initialized to zero:

```
int t[100]={0};
```

If an array is specified without a size, but with an initialization sequence, the size is defined to be equal to the number of values in the sequence:

```
double s[]={0.5, 0.0, -0.1, 0.2, 0.15, 0.2};
int t[]={0, 1, 2, 3};
```

The size of an array must be specified in the declaration statement, using either a constant within brackets or by an initialization sequence within braces.

Arrays can also be assigned initial values with program statements. For example, suppose that we want to fill a double array g with the values 0.0, 0.5, 1.0, 1.5, ..., 10.0. Because there are 21 values, listing the values in the declaration statement would be tedious. Thus, we use the following statements to define and initialize this array:

```
//  Declare objects.
double g[21];
...
//  Initialize the array g.
for (int k=0; k<=20; k++)
{
    g[k] = k*0.5;
}
```

It is important to recognize that the condition in this for statement must specify a final offset value of 20, and not 21 (since the array elements are g[0] through g[20]). It is a common mistake to specify an offset that is one value more than the largest valid offset. This error can be very difficult to find because it **accesses values outside the array.** Accessing values outside of an array can produce execution errors such as "segmentation fault" or "bus error". More often this error is not detected during the program execution, but will cause unpredictable program results, since your program has modified a memory location outside of your array. It is important to be careful about exceeding the bounds of an array. In our programs, we *Style* select conditions in for loops that specifically use the final value as a reminder to ourselves to carefully write the condition to avoid errors. *Thus, in this example, we use the condition $k <= 20$ instead of $k < 21$, although both work properly. Also, we will generally use k as the subscript for a one-dimensional array.*

Arrays are often used to store information that is read from data files. For example, suppose that we have a data file named *sensor3.dat* that contains 10 time and motion measurements collected from a seismometer. To read these values into arrays named time and motion, we could use these statements:

```
//  Declare objects.
double time[10], motion[10];
ifstream sensor3("sensor3.dat");
...
//  Check for succesfull open and read data into arrays.
if(!sensor3.fail())
{
    for (int k=0; k<=9; k++)
    {
        sensor3 >> time[k] >> motion[k];
    }
}
...
```

If the data file *sensor3.dat* held the set of data

```
0.0        1
0.1        1
0.2        2.5
0.3        1.7
0.4        2
0.5        2.5
0.6        3.5
0.7        1.5
0.8        1.5
0.9        1
```

then the arrays time and motion would contain the following values:

time	motion
0.0	1
0.1	1
0.2	2.5
0.3	1.7
0.4	2
0.5	2.5
0.6	3.5
0.7	1.5
0.8	1.5
0.9	1

Practice!

Show the contents of the arrays defined in each of the following sets of statements.

1. `int x[10]={-5, 4, 3};`

2. `char letters[] = {'a', 'b', 'c'};`

3. ```
double z[4];
  . . .
  z[1] = -5.5;
  z[2] = z[3] = fabs(z[1]);
```

4. ```
double time[9];
  . . .
  for (int k=0; k<=8; k++)
  {
      time[k] = (k-4)*0.1;
  }
```

Computation and Output

Computations with array elements are specified just like computations with simple objects, but an offset must be used to specify an individual array element. To illustrate, the next program reads an array y of 100 floating-point values from a data file. The program determines the average value of the array, and stores it in y_ave. Then, the number of values in the array y that are greater than the average are counted and printed.

```cpp
/*----------------------------------------------------------*/
/*   Program chapter6_1                                     */
/*                                                          */
/*   This program reads 100 values from a data file         */
/*   and determines the number of values greater            */
/*   than the average.                                      */

#include <fstream>
#include <string>
using namespace std;

const int N=100;

int main()
{
   //  Declare and initialize objects.
   string filename;
   int count(0);
   double y[N], y_ave, sum(0);
   ifstream lab;

   //  Prompt user for name of input file
   cout << "Enter name of the input file ";
   cin >> filename;

   //  Open data file and read data into an array.
   //  Compute a sum of the values.
   lab.open(filename.c_str());
   if(lab.fail())
   {
      cout << "Error opening input file\n";
   }
   else
   {
      for (int k=0; k<=N-1; k++)
      {
         lab >> y[k];
         sum += y[k];
      }

      //  Compute average and count values that
      //  are greater than the average.
      y_ave = sum/N;
      for (int k=0; k<=N-1; k++)
```

```
         {
            if (y[k] > y_ave)
               count++;
         }

         //  Print count.
         cout << count << " values greater than the average \n";

         //  Close file and exit program.
         lab.close();
      }
   return 0;
   }
   /*- - - - - - - - - - - - - - - - - - - - - - - - - - - - - - - - - - - - - - - - - - - - - - -*/
```

If the purpose of this program had been to determine the average of the values in the data file, an array would not have been necessary. The loop to read values could read each value into the same object, adding its value to a sum before the next value is read. However, because we needed to compare each value to the average in order to count the number of values greater than the average, an array was needed so that we could access each value again.

Array values are printed using an offset to specify the individual value desired. For example, the following statement prints the first and last values of the array *y* used in the previous example:

```
cout << "first and last array values: \n";
cout << y[0] << "   " << y[N-1] << endl;
```

The following loop prints all 100 values of *y*, one per line:

```
cout << "y values: \n";
for (int k=0; k<=N-1; k++)
{
   cout << y[k] << endl;
}
```

When printing a large array such as this one, we probably would like to print several numbers on the same line. The following statements use the modulus operator to skip to a new line before each group of five values is printed:

```
cout << "y values: \n";
for (int k=0; k<=N-1; k++)
{
   if (k%5 == 0)
      cout << y[k] << endl;
   else
      cout << y[k] << "   ";
}
cout << endl;
```

Statements similar to the ones illustrated here can also be used to write array values to a data file. For example, the following statement will print the value of *y[k]* on a line in a data

TABLE 6.1   Operator Precedence

Precedence	Operation	Associativity
1	( ) []	innermost first
2	++ — + — ! (*type*)	right to left (unary)
3	* / %	left to right
4	+ —	left to right
5	< <= > >=	left to right
6	== !=	left to right
7	&&	left to right
8	||	left to right
9	? :	right to left
10	= += —= *= /= %=	right to left
11	,	left to right

file using the file stream object *sensor:*

```
sensor << y[k] << endl;
```

Since the *endl* manipulator is included, the next value written to the file will be on a new line.

The number of elements in an array is used in the array declaration and in loops used to access the elements in the array. If the number of elements is changed, then there are several places in the program that need to be modified. *Changing the size of an array is simplified if a symbolic constant is used to specify the size of the array.* Then, to change the size, only the const definition needs to be changed. This style suggestion is especially important in programs that contain many modules or in programming environments in which several programmers are working on the same software project. Many of the following programs illustrate the use of a symbolic constant to define the size of an array.

Style

Table 6.1 gives an updated precedence order that includes offset brackets. Brackets and parentheses are associated before the other operators. If parentheses and brackets are in the same statement, they are associated from left to right; if they are nested, the innermost set is evaluated first.

Practice!

Assume that the array *s* has been defined with the following statement:

```
int s[]={3, 8, 15, 21, 30, 41};
```

Determine, by hand, the output for each of the following sets of statements.

```
1. for (int k=0; k<=5; k+=2)
   {
       cout << s[k] << ' ' <<  s[k+1] << endl;
   }
```

```
2. for (int k=0; k<=5; k++)
   {
       if (s[k]%2 == 0)
          cout << s[k] << ' ';
   }
   cout << endl;
```

Function Arguments

When the information in an array is passed to a function, two parameters are usually used; one parameter specifies the specific array, and the other parameter specifies the number of elements used in the array. By specifying the number of elements of the array that are to be used, the function becomes more flexible. For example, if the function specifies an integer array, then the function can be used with any integer array; the parameter that specifies the number of elements assures that we use the correct size. Also, the number of elements used in an array may vary from one time to another. For example, the array may use elements read from a data file; the number of elements then depends on the specific data file used when the program is run. In all these examples, though, the array must be declared to be a maximum size, and then the actual number of elements used can be less than or equal to that maximum size.

Consider the program presented next, which reads an array from a data file and then references a function to determine the maximum value in the array. The object *npts* is used to count the actual number of values that are read from the data file and stored in the array; the value of *npts* can be less than or equal to the defined size of the array, which is 100. We must be careful not to assign more than 100 values to the array, and we must also keep an accurate count of the **actual number of values** that are assigned to the array. The function has two formal parameters: the name of the array and the actual number of points in the array, as indicated in the function prototype statement.

actual number of values

```
/*----------------------------------------------------------*/
/*   Program chapter6_2                                      */
/*                                                           */
/*   This program reads values from a data file and         */
/*   calls a function to determine the maximum value.       */
/*                                                           */

#include <fstream>
#include <string>
using namespace std;

// Define constants and declare function prototypes.
const int N=100;
double maxval(double x[], int n);

int main()
{
```

```cpp
   //   Declare objects.
   int npts(0);
   double y[N], temp;
   string filename;
   ifstream lab;

   //   Prompt user for file name and open data file.
   cout << "Enter the name of the data file ";
   cin >> filename;
   lab.open(filename.c_str());
   if(lab.fail())
   {
      cout << "Error opening input file\n";
   }
   else
   {
      //   Read a data value from the file.
      lab >> temp;

      //   While there is room in the array and
      //   and end of file was not encountered,
      //   assign the value to the array and
      //   input the next value.
      while (npts <= (N-1) && !lab.eof() )
      {
         y[npts] = temp;    //  Assign data value to array.
         npts++;            //  Increment npts.
         lab >> temp;       //  Input next value
      }

      //   Find and print the maximum value.
      cout << "Maximum value: " << maxval(y,npts) << endl;

      //   Close file and exit program.
      lab.close();
   }
   return 0;
}
/*-------------------------------------------------------*/
/*   This function returns the maximum                  */
/*   value in the array x with n elements.              */

double maxval(double x[], int n)
{
   //   Declare local objects.
   double max_x;

   //   Determine maximum value in the array.
   max_x = x[0];
   for (int k=1; k<=n-1; k++)
   {
```

```
      if (x[k] > max_x)
         max_x = x[k];
   }

   //  Return maximum value. /
   return max_x;
}
/*- - - - - - - - - - - - - - - - - - - - - - - - - - - - - - - - - - - - - - - - - -*/
```

In the next example, we modify the `while` loop that checks both the state of the input stream the value of *npts* before executing the loop:

```
int main()
{
   //  Declare objects.
   int npts(0);
   double y[N];
   string filename;
   ifstream lab;

   //  Prompt user for file name and open data file.
   cout << "Enter the name of the data file ";
   cin >> filename;
   lab.open(filename.c_str());
   if(lab.fail())
   {
      cout << "Error opening input file\n";
   }
   else
   {
      //  Read a data value from the file.
      while (npts <= (N-1) && lab >> y[npts] )
      {
         npts++;            //  Increment npts.
      }

      //  Find and print the maximum value.
      cout << "Maximum value: " << maxval(y,npts) << endl;

      //  Close file and exit program.
      lab.close();
   }
   return 0;
}
/*- - - - - - - - - - - - - - - - - - - - - - - - - - - - - - - - - - - - - - - - -*/
```

This `while` loops checks the value returned by the *ifstream* object *labs* directly to determine whether a new value has been assigned to the array *y*. It is important to check the value of *npts* in the expression before the input statement. Since we are taking the and of two expressions, if the value of *npts* is not less than or equal to $N - 1$, the entire condition will be false, and the input statement will not be executed. If the input statement appears first in the expression, an assignment to the array may occur before determining that *npts* is greater than the max size of the array, and the program may not continue to execute correctly.

Both main functions will correctly read and count the data in a data file, and assign the data to an array. In both examples, the array offset is not allowed to exceed the size of the array. We will use the first method when reading data from a file and storing it in an array.

There is a very significant difference in using arrays as parameters, and using simple objects as parameters. When a simple object is used as a parameter, the default is always a call by value. When an array is used as a parameter, it is always a call by reference. Recall that a call by reference means that the memory address of the argument, rather than the value, is passed to the formal parameter. When an array is used as a parameter, the address of the first element is passed to the function. The function uses this address to reference values in the original array. Any changes made to the array in the function are made to the original array argument. Because a function accesses the original array, we must be very careful that we do not inadvertently change values in an array within a function. Of course, there may be occasions when we wish to change the values in the array, as we will see in later examples in this chapter.

If we want to insure that a function will not change the values in an array, we can use the const modifier in the function prototype and the function header. This will prevent the function from assigning new values to the array. Our function to determine the maximum value in an array should not modify the values in the array, so we will now rewrite the function definition using the const modifier:

```
/*-----------------------------------------------------------*/
/*  This function returns the maximum                        */
/*  value in the array x with n elements.                    */

double maxval(const double x[], int n)
{
   //  Declare local objects.
   double max_x;

   //  Determine maximum value in the array.
   max_x = x[0];
   for (int k=1; k<=n-1; k++)
   {
      if (x[k] > max_x)
         max_x = x[k];
   }

   //  Return maximum value. /
   return max_x;
}
/*-----------------------------------------------------------*/
```

The prototype for this function is

```
double maxval(const double x[], int n);
```

Assume that the following objects are defined:

```
int k=6;
double data[]={1.5, 3.2, -6.1, 9.8, 8.7, 5.2};
```

Give the values of the expressions that follow, which reference the *maxval* function presented in this section. Both versions of the *maxval* function will produce the same results.

1. maxval(data,6);

2. maxval(data,5);

3. maxval(data,k-3);

4. maxval(data,k%5);

6.2 Statistical Measurements

Analyzing data collected from engineering experiments is an important part of evaluating the experiments. This analysis ranges from simple computations on the data, such as calculating the average value, to more complicated analysis. Many of the computations or measurements using data are **statistical measurements** because they have statistical properties that change from one set of data to another. For example, the sine of 60 degrees is an exact value that is the same value every time we compute it, but the number of miles to the gallon that we get with our car is a statistical measurement because it varies somewhat, depending on parameters such as the temperature, the speed that we travel, the type of road, and whether we are in the mountains or the desert.

statistical measurements

Simple Analysis

*mean
median*

When evaluating a set of experimental data, we often compute the maximum value, minimum value, **mean** or average value, and the **median**. In this section, we develop functions that can be used to compute these values using an array as input. These functions (stored in a file *stat_lib.cpp*) will be useful in many of the programs that we develop later in the text and in solutions to problems at the end of the chapters. It is important to note that the functions assume that there is at least one value in the array. The functions also assume that the array contains `double` values.

Maximum, Minimum.   A function for determining the maximum value in an array was presented in the previous section; a similar function for determining the minimum value is presented here:

```
/*----------------------------------------------------*/
/*  This function returns the minimum                 */
/*  value in an array x with n elements.              */
```

```
double minval(const double x[], int n)
{
// Declare objects.
   double min_x;
// Determine minimum value in the array.
   min_x = x[0];
   for (int k=1; k<=n-1; k++)
   {
      if (x[k] < min_x)
         min_x = x[k];
   }

// Return minimum value.
   return min_x;
}
/*-------------------------------------------------------------*/
```

Average. The Greek symbol μ is used to represent the average, or mean, value, as shown in the following equation, which uses summation notation:

$$\mu = \frac{\sum_{k=0}^{n-1} x_k}{n},$$

where

$$\sum_{k=0}^{n-1} x_k = x_0 + x_1 + x_2 + \cdots + x_{n-1}.$$

The average of a set of values is always a floating-point value, even if all the data values are integers. This function computes the mean value of a double array of n values:

```
/*-------------------------------------------------------------*/
/*   This function returns the average or                      */
/*   mean value of an array with n elements.                   */

double mean(const double x[], int n)
{
   // Declare and initialize objects.
   double sum(0);

   // Determine mean value.
   for (int k=0; k<=n-1; k++)
   {
      sum += x[k];
   }

   // Return mean value.
   return sum/n;
}
/*-------------------------------------------------------------*/
```

Note that the object *sum* was initialized to zero in the declaration statement. It could also have been initialized to zero with an assignment statement. In either case, the value of *sum* is initialized to zero when the function is referenced.

Median.   The **median** is the value in the middle of a group of values, assuming that the values are sorted. If there is an odd number of values, the median is the value in the middle; if there is an even number of values, the median is the average of the values in the two middle positions. For example, the median of the values 1, 6, 18, 39, 86 is the middle value, or 18; the median of the values 1, 6, 18, 39, 86, 91 is the average of the two middle values, or $(18+39)/2$, or 28.5. Assume that a group of sorted values is stored in an array, and that n contains the number of values in the array. If n is odd, then the offset of the middle value can be represented by *floor(n/2)*, as in *floor(5/2)*, which is 2. If n is even, then the offsets of the two middle values can be represented by *floor(n/2)−1* and *floor(n/2)*, as in *floor(6/2)−1* and *floor(6/2)*, which are 2 and 3. The next function determines the median of a set of values stored in an array. We assume that the values are sorted (into either ascending or descending order). If the array is not sorted, a function developed later in this chapter can be referenced from the median function to sort the values.

```
/*-------------------------------------------------------*/
/*  This function returns the median                     */
/*  value in an array x with n elements                  */
/*  The values in x are assumed to be ordered.           */

double median(const double x[], int n)
{
   //  Declare objects.
   double median_x;
   int k;

   //  Determine median value.
   k = floor(n/2);
   if (n%2 != 0)
      median_x = x[k];
   else
      median_x = (x[k-1] + x[k])/2;

   //  Return median value.
   return median_x;
}
/*-------------------------------------------------------*/
```

Go through this function by hand, using the two sets of data values given in this discussion.

Variance and Standard Deviation

One of the most important statistical measurements for a set of data is the variance. Before we give the mathematical definition for variance, it is useful to develop an intuitive understanding. Consider the values of arrays *data1* and *data2* that are plotted in Figure 6.1. If we attempted to draw a horizontal line through the middle of the values in each plot, this line would be at approximately 3.0.

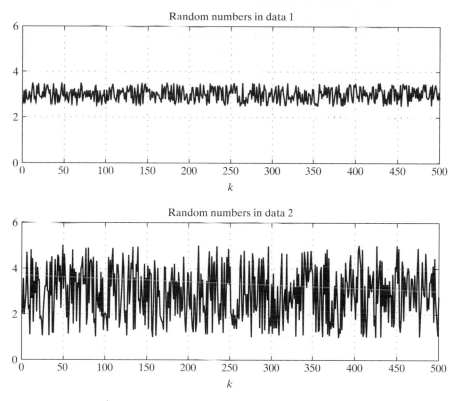

Figure 6.1 Random Sequence.

Thus, both arrays have approximately the same average, or mean, value of 3.0. However, the data in the two arrays clearly have some distinguishing characteristics. The values in *data2* vary more from the mean, or deviate more from the mean value. The **variance** of a set of values is defined to be the average squared deviation from the mean; the **standard deviation** is defined to be the square root of the variance. Thus, the variance and the standard deviation of the values in *data2* are greater than the variance and standard deviation for the values in *data1*. Intuitively, the larger the variance (or the standard deviation), the further the values fluctuate around the mean value.

Mathematically, the variance is represented by σ^2, where σ is the Greek symbol sigma. The variance for a set of data values (which we assume are stored in an array x) can be computed using the following equation:

$$\sigma^2 = \frac{\sum_{k=0}^{n-1}(x_k - \mu)^2}{n - 1}.$$

(6.2)

This equation is a bit intimidating at first, but if you look at it closely, it becomes much simpler. The term $x_k - \mu$ is the difference between x_k and the mean, or the deviation of x_k from the mean. This value is squared so that we always have a positive value. We then add the squared deviations for all data points. This sum is then divided by $n - 1$, which approximates an average. The definition of variance has two forms: The denominator of a **sample variance**

variance

standard deviation

sample variance

population variance   is $n - 1$, and the denominator of a **population variance** is n. Most engineering applications use the sample variance, as shown in Equation (6.2.) Thus, Equation (6.2) computes the average squared deviation of the data from the mean. The standard deviation is defined to be the square root of the variance:

$$\sigma = \sqrt{\sigma^2}. \tag{6.3}$$

Both the variance and the standard deviation are commonly used in analyzing engineering data, so we give functions for computing both values. Note that the function for computing the standard deviation references the variance function and that the variance function references the mean function; thus, these functions must include the proper function prototype statements. Also, note that there must be at least two values in the array, or the variance function will attempt to perform a division by zero.

```
/*-------------------------------------------------------*/
/*  This function returns the variance                   */
/*  of an array with n elements.                         */

//  Declare function prototypes.
double mean(const double x[], int n);

double variance(const double x[], int n)
{
   //  Declare objects.
   double sum(0), mu;

   //  Determine variance.
   mu = mean(x,n);
   for (int k=0; k<=n-1; k++)
   {
      sum += (x[k] - mu)*(x[k] - mu);
   }

   //  Return variance.
   return sum/(n-1);
}
/*-------------------------------------------------------*/
/*  This function returns the standard deviation         */
/*  of an array with n elements.                         */

//  Declare function prototypes.
double variance(const double x[], int n);

double std_dev(const double x[], int n)
{

   //  Return standard deviation.
   return sqrt(variance(x,n));
}
/*-------------------------------------------------------*/
```

Practice!

Assume that the array x is defined and initialized with the following statement:

```
double x[]={2.5, 5.5, 6.0, 6.25, 9.0};
```

Compute by hand the values returned by the following function references:

1. maxval(x,5)

2. median(x,5)

3. variance(x,5)

4. std_dev(x,5)

5. minval(x,4)

6. median(x,4)

OOP **6.3** **Functions Revisited**

In the previous section, we developed a set of functions that are useful when performing simple analysis on a set of experimental data. These functions expect the data arrays to be of type `double` and cannot be used for other types of data without modification. To work with different data types, we would need to write multiple version of the same function; one version for different data type.

Function Overloading

function overloading

C++ supports **function overloading,** which means that a function name can have more than one definition. For example, we could write multiple versions of the function *maxval,* where the only difference would be the type of value returned by the function and the data type of the array. The prototypes for three possible versions of the *maxval* function are as follows:

```
double maxval(const double x[], int n);
int maxval(const int x[], int n);
char maxval(const char x[], int n);
```

function signature

Function overloading requires that each function definition has a unique **function signature.** A function signature includes the name of the function and the parameter list. Looking at the three function prototypes for the function *maxval,* we see that each function signature is unique because the data type of the arrays are different. A second definition for the function maxval is as follows:

```
/*------------------------------------------------------*/
/*  This function returns the maximum                   */
/*  value in an array x with n elements.                */

char maxval(const char x[], int n)
{
// Declare objects.
   char max_x;
// Determine maximum value in the array.
   max_x = x[0];
   for (int k=1; k<=n-1; k++)
   {
      if (x[k] > max_x)
         max_x = x[k];
   }

// Return maximum value.
   return max_x;
}
/*------------------------------------------------------*/
```

Compare this function definition with the definition in the previous section. The data type of the formal parameter *x* has been changed to char , the data type of the local object *max_x* has been changed to char and the return value of the function has also been changed to char . The algorithm for finding a maximum value is unchanged.

When an overloaded function is referenced, the function signature determines which function definition will be executed. This is illustrated in the following example:

```
/*------------------------------------------------------*/
/* Function Overloading                                 */
#include<iostream>
using namespace std;

// Function prototypes.
char maxval(const char x[], int n);
int maxval(const int x[], int n);

int main()
{
   int a[] = {55, 42, 99, 7};
   char ch[] = {'H', 'E', 'L', 'L', 'O'};

   // Function call matches first prototype.
   cout << maxval(a,4) << ' ';

   // Function call matches second prototype.
   cout << maxval(ch, 5) << endl;
   return 0;
}
```

Each function call looks for a function prototype with a matching function signature. Since the array *a* in main is of type int, the first function call matches the second prototype and the corresponding function is executed. The second function call matches the first prototype, since the array *ch* is an array of type char. The output from this program is

```
99 o
```

Function Templates

Writing multiple version of functions can become very tedious. Fortunately, C++ supports **function templates.** Function templates allow a programmer to provides a generic algorithm for a function that is not tied to a specific data type. The function template is then used to automatically generate a function definition for a specific data type when the function template is referenced. A specific definition of a function is also referred to as an **instance of a function.**

function templates

instance of a function

As an example, we will write a function template for our function *minval:*

```
/*-------------       -------------------------       ------*/
/* Function returns the minimum value in an          */
/* array x having n elements.                        */

template <class D_type>
D_type minval(const D_type x[], int n)
{

// Declare objects.
   D_type min_x;
// Determine minimum value in the array.
   min_x = x[0];
   for (int k=1; k<=n-1; k++)
   {
      it (x[k] < min_x)
         min_x = x[k];
   }

// Return minimum value.
   return min_x;
}
/*---------------------------------------------------*/
```

The prototype for this function template is

```
template <class D_type>
D_type minval(const D_type x[], int n);
```

 The keyword template, followed by a list of template type parameters enclosed within < > symbols, always begins a function template definition and the prototype. Within the template type parameter list, the keyword class precedes each identifier in the list, indicating that the identifier represents a potential built-in or programmer-defined data type. The identifiers are then used in the function `template` definition and prototype to replace specific data types. If multiple parameters are used, they are separated with commas. The template type parameter list must include at least one parameter.

In our example, we use the identifier *D_type* to represent a potential data type. Since the value returned by the function *minval* depends on the data type of the array, we use *D_type,* in both the function header and the function prototype, to specify the type of value returned by the function and the data type of the array *x*. The parameter *n* represents the size of the array, and thus remains an `int`. We also use *D_type* in the body of our function definition to declare and initialize the local object *minx*. The remainder of the function body is unchanged.

The following program illustrates the use of this function `template` with arrays of type `int` and `double`:

```
/*-----------------------------------------------------------*/
/*   Program chapter6_3                                      */
/*                                                            */
/*   This program reads values from a data file and         */
/*   determines the minimum value in each column of          *
/*   the file with a template function.                      */

#include <fstream>
#include <string>
using namespace std;

// Define global constants.
const int N(100);

// Function prototype.
template<class D_type>
D_type maxval(D_type x[], int n);

int main()
{
   //  Declare objects.
   int npts(0);
   int x[N], xtemp;
   double y[n], ytemp;
   string filename;
   ifstream lab;

   //  Prompt user for file name and open data file.
   cout << "Enter the name of the data file ";
   cin >> filename;
   lab.open(filename.c_str());
   if(lab.fail())
   {
      cout << "Error opening input file\n";
   }
   else
   {
```

```
    //  Read two data values from the file.
    lab >> xtemp >> ytemp;

    //  While there is room in the arrays and
    //  and end of file was not encountered,
    //  assign values to the arrays and
    //  input the next values.
    while (npts <= (N-1) && !lab.eof() )
    {
        x[npts] = xtemp;        //  Assign data value to array.
        y[npts] = ytemp;        //  Assign data value to array.
        npts++;                 //  Increment npts.
        lab >> xtemp >> ytemp;  //  Input next value
    }

    //  Find and print the maximum values.
    cout << "Maximum x value: " << maxval(x,npts) << endl;
    cout << "Maximum y value: " << maxval(y,npts) << endl;

    //  Close file and exit program.
    lab.close();
    }
return 0;
}
```

The foregoing program defines one array, *x*, of type `int` and a second array, *y*, of type `double`. The function *minval* is referenced twice; once with the array *x* as an argument and again with the array *y* as an argument. Each reference executes a different instance of the function. When the program is compiled, the function `template` is used to create two instances of the function *minval*. In one instance, the identifier Dtype is replaced with the keyword **int.** In the other instance, the identifier *D_type* is replace with the keyword `double`. When the function *minval* is referenced, the program executes the version of the function that has a matching function signature.

As you can see in this example, using function `templates` can greatly reduce the amount of code that a programmer must write.

Custom Header Files

The functions developed in the previous sections are frequently used in solving engineering problems. To facilitate their use, we generate a custom header file that contains the prototypes for these function. Then, instead of writing all the function prototypes in a main function, a preprocessor directive can be used that includes the custom header file.

The custom header file named *stat_lib.h* contains the following function prototypes:

```
double maxval(const double x[], int n);
double minval(const double x[], int n);
double mean(const double x[], int n);
double median(const double x[], int n);
double variance(const double x[], int n);
double std_dev(const double x[], int n);
```

The statement that includes these in a `main` function is

```
#include "stat_lib.h"
```

The use of this custom header is illustrated in the program in the next section.

In addition to accessing the custom header file with the include statement, a program must also have access to the file *stat_lib.cpp* containing the statistical functions. The specific details of providing this access are platform dependent and may involve adding a file name to the operating system command that performs the compilation and linking/loading operations.

Modify!

Modify the *stat_lib.h* and the *stat_lib.cpp* files to incorporate function `templates`.

6.4 Problem Solving Applied: Speech Signal Analysis

A speech signal is an acoustical signal that can be converted into an electrical signal with a microphone. The electrical signal can then be converted into a series of numbers that represents the amplitudes of the electrical signal values. These numbers can be stored in data files so that the speech signal can be analyzed using computer programs. Suppose that we are interested in analyzing speech signals for the words "zero," "one," "two," ..., "nine." The goal of this analysis would be to develop ways of identifying the correct digit from a data file containing the utterance of an unknown digit.

Figure 6.2 contains a plot of an utterance of the digit "zero." The analysis of a complicated signal like this one often starts with computing some of the statistical measurements discussed in the last section. Other measurements used with speech signals include the average magnitude, or average absolute value, which is computed as shown, where n is the number of data values:

$$\text{Average magnitude} = \frac{\sum_{k=0}^{n-1} |x_k|}{n}. \tag{6.4}$$

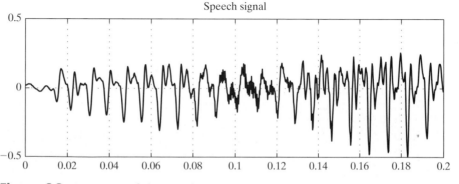

Figure 6.2 Utterance of the word "zero".

Another metric used in speech analysis is the average power of the signal, which is the average squared value:

$$\text{Average power} = \frac{\sum_{k=0}^{n-1} x_k^2}{n}. \tag{6.5}$$

The number of zero crossings in a speech signal is also a useful statistical measurement. This value is the number of times that the speech signal transitions from a negative to a positive value or from a positive value to a negative value: Transition from a nonzero value to a zero value is not a zero crossing.

Write a program to read a speech signal from a data file named *zero.dat*. This file contains values that represent an utterance of the word "zero." Each line of the file contains a single value representing a measurement from the microphone taken in time increments of 0.0002 second, so 5,000 measurements represent 1 second of data. The data file contains only valid data, with no header or trailer line; a maximum of 2,500 values is contained in the file. Compute and print the following statistical measurements from the file: mean, standard deviation, variance, average power, average magnitude, and number of zero crossings.

1. PROBLEM DESCRIPTION

Compute the following statistical measurements for a speech utterance: mean, standard deviation, variance, average power, average magnitude, and number of zero crossings.

2. INPUT/OUTPUT DESCRIPTION

The I/O diagram shows the data file as the input and the statistical measurements as output.

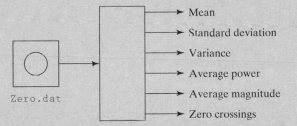

3. HAND EXAMPLE

For a hand example, assume that the file contains the following values:

```
2.5   8.2   -1.1   -0.2   1.5
```

Using a calculator, we can compute the following values:

$$\text{Mean} = \mu = \frac{(2.5 + 8.2 - 1.1 - 0.2 + 1.5)}{5}$$

$$= 2.18;$$

$$\text{Variance} = [(2.5 - \mu)^2 + (8.2 - \mu)^2 + (-1.1 - \mu)^2$$
$$+ (-0.2 - \mu)^2 + (1.5 - \mu)2]/4$$

$$= 13.307;$$

$$\text{Standard deviation} = \sqrt{13.307}$$

$$= 3.648;$$

$$\text{Average power} = \frac{[(2.5)^2 + (8.2)^2 + (-1.1)^2 + (-0.2)^2 + (1.5)^2]}{5}$$

$$= 15.398;$$

$$\text{Average magnitude} = \frac{(|2.5| + |8.2| + |-1.1| + |-0.2| + |1.5|)}{5}$$

$$= 2.7;$$

$$\text{Number of zero crossings} = 2.$$

4. ALGORITHM DEVELOPMENT

We first develop the decomposition outline, because it divides the solution into a series of sequential steps.

Decomposition Outline

1. Read the speech signal into an array.

2. Compute and print statistical measurements.

Step 1 involves reading the data file and determining the number of data points. Step 2 involves computing and printing the statistical k measurements, using the functions already developed when possible. The refinement in pseudocode for the `main` function and for the additional statistical functions needed is shown next; the structure chart was shown in Figure 5.1 to illustrate an example of a main function that references several programmer-defined functions.

Refinement in Pseudocode

```
main:   read speech signal from data file and
        determine the number of points, n
        compute and print mean
        compute and print standard deviation
```

```
            compute and print variance
            compute and print average power
            compute and print average magnitude
            compute and print zero crossings
Additional Functions
ave_power(x, n):
            set sum to zero
            set k to zero
            while k <=n - 1
              add x[k]^2 to sum
              increment k by 1
            return sum/n
ave_magn(x, n):
            set sum to zero
            set k to zero
            while k <= n - 1
              add | x[k] | to sum
              increment k by 1
            return sum/n
crossings(x, n):
            set count to zero
            set k to zero
            while k <= n-2
              if x[k]*x[k + 1] < 0
                 increment count by 1
              increment k by 1
            return count
```

Note that the number of potential zero crossings for a set of n data points is $n - 1$ crossings, because each crossing is determined by a pair of values. Thus, the last pair of values tested will be at offsets $n - 2$ and $n - 1$. The steps in the pseudocode are detailed enough to convert to C++:

```
/*-----------------------------------------------------*/
/*  Program chapter6_3                                 */
/*                                                     */
/*  This program computes a set of statistical         */
/*  measurements from a speech signal.                 */

#include <fstream>
#include <string>
#include <cmath>
#include "stat_lib.h"
using namespace std;

// Declare function prototypes and define constants.
double ave_power(double x[], int n);
double ave_magn(double x[], int n);
```

```
int crossings(double x[], int n);
const int MAXIMUM = 2500;

int main()
{
   // Declare objects.
   int npts(0);
   double speech[MAXIMUM];
   string filename;
   ifstream file_1;

   // Prompt user for file name and
   // open file.
   cout << "Enter filename ";
   cin >> filename;
   file_1.open(filename.c_str());
   if( file_1.fail() )
   {
        cout << "error opening file " << filename
             << endl;
        return 0;
   {
   // Read information from a data file.  *
      while (npts <= MAXIMUM-1 && file_1 >> speech[npts])
      {
        npts++;
      } //end while

   // Compute and print statistics.
      cout << "Digit Statistics \n";
      cout << "\tmean: " << mean(speech,npts) << endl;
      cout << "\tstandard deviation: "
           << std_dev(speech,npts) << endl;
      cout << "\tvariance: " << variance(speech,npts)
           << endl;
      cout << "\taverage power: " << ave_power(speech,npts)
           << endl;
      cout << "\taverage magnitude: "
           << ave_magn(speech,npts) << endl;
      cout << "\tzero crossings: " << crossings(speech,npts)
           << endl;

   // Close file and exit program.
   file_1.close();
   return 0;
}
/*------------------------------------------------------*/
/*  This function returns the average power           */
```

```
/*   of an array x with n elements.                              */

double ave_power(double x[], int n)
{
   // Declare and initialize objects.
   double sum(0);

   // Determine average power.
   for (int k=0; k<=n-1; k++)
   {
      sum += x[k]*x[k];
   }

   // Return average power.
   return sum/n;
}
/*------------------------------------------------------------*/
/*   This function returns the average magnitude              */
/*   of an array x with n values.                             */

double ave_magn(double x[], int n)
{
   // Declare and initialize objects.
   double sum(0);

   // Determine average magnitude.
   for (int k=0; k<=n-1; k++)
   {
      sum += abs(x[k]);
   }

   // Return average magnitude.
   return sum/n;
}
/*------------------------------------------------------------*/
/*   This function returns a count of the number              */
/*   of zero crossings in an array x with n values.           */

int crossings(double x[], int n)
{
   // Declare and initialize objects.
   int count(0);

   // Determine number of zero crossings.
   for (int k=0; k<=n-2; k++)
   {
      if (x[k]*x[k+1] < 0)
         count++;
   }
```

```
//  Return number of zero crossings.
    return count;
}
/*------------------------------------------------------------*/
```

5. TESTING

This program requires access to the *stat_lib.h* header file and to the *stat_lib.cpp* file developed in the previous section. The following values were computed for the utterance "zero" using the file zero.dat:

```
Digit Statistics
        mean: 0.002931
        standard deviation: 0.121763
        variance: 0.014826
        average power: 0.014820
        average magnitude: 0.089753
        zero crossings: 106
```

Modify!

1. Run this program using the files *two_a.dat, two_b.dat,* and *two_c.dat,* available on your instructor's resource CD. These utterances are all of the word "two," but they are spoken by different people.

2. Compare the program output from Problem 1 for the three files. The output illustrates some of the difficulty in designing speech-recognition systems that are speaker independent.

6.5 Sorting Algorithms

Sorting

Sorting a group of data values is another operation that is routinely used when analyzing data. Entire texts are available that present many different sorting algorithms. One of the reasons that there are so many sorting algorithms is that there is not one "best" sorting algorithm. Some algorithms are faster if the data are already close to the correct order, but these algorithms may be very inefficient if the order is random or is close to the opposite order. Therefore, to choose the best sorting algorithm for a particular application, you usually need to know something about the order of the original data. Rather than try to present a complete discussion of sorting algorithms, we present two algorithms in this text. We encourage you to reference additional texts for a more completes discussion of sorting algorithms. In this section, we present a selection sort that is simple to understand and simple to code in a function. We also present a quicksort function that uses a recursive algorithm to sort a set of values.

Selection Sort

selection sort

The **selection sort** algorithm begins by finding the position of the minimum value and exchanging the minimum with the value in the first position in the array. Then, the algorithm finds the minimum value beginning with the second element, and exchanges this minimum with the second element. This process continues until reaching the next-to-last element, which is compared to the last element; the values are exchanged if they are out of order. At this point, the entire array of values is now in ascending order. This process is illustrated in the following sequences that reorder an array:

Original order:

| 5 | 3 | 12 | 8 | 1 | 9 |

Exchange the minimum with the value in the first position:

| 1 | 3 | 12 | 8 | 5 | 9 |

Exchange the next minimum with the value in the second position:

| 1 | 3 | 12 | 8 | 5 | 9 |

Exchange the next minimum with the value in the third position:

| 1 | 3 | 5 | 8 | 12 | 9 |

Exchange the next minimum with the value in the fourth position:

| 1 | 3 | 5 | 8 | 12 | 9 |

Exchange the next minimum with the value in the fifth position:

| 1 | 3 | 5 | 8 | 9 | 12 |

Array values are now in ascending order:

| 1 | 3 | 5 | 8 | 9 | 12 |

The steps in the following function are short, but it is still a good idea to go through this function using the data in this example. Follow the changes in the subscripts k, m, and j within the loops. Also, note that it takes three steps (not two) to exchange values in two objects. Because the function does not return a value, its return type is void.

```
/*-------------------------------------------------------------*/
/*   This function sorts an array with n elements      */
/*   into ascending order.                             */

void sort(double x[], int n)
{
   //  Declare objects.
   int m;
   double hold;
```

```
   //  Implement selection sort algorithm.
   for (int k=0; k<=n-2; k++)
   {
      // Find position of largest value in array
      // beginning at k
      m = k;
      for (int j=k+1; j<=n-1; j++)
      {
         if (x[j] < x[m])
            m = j;
      }
      // Exchange largest value with value at k
      hold = x[m];
      x[m] = x[k];
      x[k] = hold;
   }

   //  Void return.
   return;
}
/*-----------------------------------------------------------*/
```

To change this function into one that sorts an array into descending values, the inner loop should search for a maximum instead of a minimum.

The function prototype statement that should be used to refer to this sort function is

```
void sort(double x[], int n);
```

It is also important to note that this function modifies the original array. To keep the original order, an array should be copied into another array before this function is executed; then the data are available in the original order and in the sorted order.

Modify!

1. Rewrite the sort function as a function `template`.

2. Write a `main` function that initializes an array, references this *sort* function, and then prints the array values in the new order.

3. Modify the **sort** function so that it sorts values in descending order instead of ascending order. Test the function with the program written in Problem 2.

Quicksort

quicksort

In this section, a **quicksort** algorithm is implemented with a recursive function. The first step in the quicksort algorithm is to select a value, called a pivot value, and then separate the rest of the values into two groups—one group containing values less than the pivot value and one group containing values greater than the pivot value. We select the pivot value to be the first element in the list, but the midpoint of the list is also often used as the pivot value. When this separation is done, the correct position in the list for the pivot value is determined; it goes between the two groups of values. Since the values in the two groups are not necessarily in the correct order, we take the group of smaller values and select a new pivot value. This group is separated into two new groups of values: ones smaller than the new pivot value and ones larger than the new pivot value. This process continues until we eventually have a group of smaller values that contains no values, one value, or two values. If this group contains two values, their order is switched if necessary, and then the original group of values smaller than the original pivot value are in order. We repeat the process with the original group of values that are larger than the original pivot value. When these are in order, the entire list is in order. This algorithm can be described recursively because each step is defined in terms of a similar process with a smaller group of values, and because it has a stopping point that is encountered when the group of values has two or fewer values. A hand example is as follows:

```
Original list:
4      10     3      6     -1     0      2      5
```

Separate into groups of values smaller and larger than the pivot value:

```
[3     -1     0      2]     4      [10     6      5]
```

Separate each remaining group into groups of values smaller and larger than the pivot value of each group:

```
[-1     0      2]     3      4      [6      5]     10
```

Separate each remaining group into groups of values smaller and larger than the pivot of each group:

```
-1      [0     2]     3      4      5      6      10
```

Separate each remaining group into groups of values smaller and larger than the pivot of each group:

```
-1      0      2      3      4      5      6      10
```

The implementation of the quicksort algorithm that we present references an additional function named *separate()*. This function switches values in the array that it receives such that the pivot value is correctly positioned in the position referenced by *break_pt*. All values less than the pivot value are to the left in the array (if we visualize the array as a row), and all values greater than the pivot value are to the right. Then, the *quicksort* function is recursively called, using a statement which specifies that a total of *break_pt* values, starting with x[0], should be sorted:

```
quicksort(x, break_pt);
```

The *quicksort()* function is also recursively called, using a statement that specifies that a total of *n-break_pt-1* values, starting with *x[break_pt+1]*, should be sorted:

```
quicksort(x[break_pt+1], n-break_pt-1];
```

The *quicksort()* function and the *separate()* function use the *switch()* function developed on page 174. Since the quicksort algorithm is a complicated algorithm, a good way to begin is to use the hand example and work through the statements using that data. (The order of the values in the intermediate groups varies from the order in the hand example.)

```
/*-----------------------------------------------------*/
/*  This function implements a quicksort algorithm.  */

void quicksort(int x[], int n)
{
   // Declare objects.
   int break_pt;

   // If only two elements, order them correctly.
   if (n == 2)
   {
      if (x[0] > x[1])
         switch2(x[0],x[1]);
   }
   else
   // If more than two elements, separate into those
   // greater than and those less than a breakpoint.
   {
      if (n > 2)
      {
         break_pt = separate(x,n);
         quicksort(x,break_pt);
         quicksort(x[break_pt+1],n-break_pt-1);
      }
   }
   return;
}
/*-----------------------------------------------------*/
/*  This function reorders the array such that       */
/*  y[0] is correctly positioned and the values      */
/*  less than it are to the left and the values      */
/*  greater than it are to the right.                */

int separate(int y[], int m)
{
   // Declare objects.
   int k1(1), k2(1), count(0), pivot;

   // Separate values into two groups.
   pivot = y[0];
```

```
        while ((k1<m) && (k2<m))
        {
            while ((k1<m) && (y[k1]>pivot))
                k1++;
            while ((k2<m) && (y[k2]<pivot))
                k2++;
            if ((k1<m) && (k2<m))
            {
                switch2(y[k1],y[k2]);
                count++;
            }
        }

        //  Put pivot value in correct position.
        if (count > 0)
            switch2(y[0],y[count]);
        else
        {
            k1 = 0;
            while ((k1<m-1) && (y[k1]>y[k1+1]))
            {
                switch2(y[k1],y[k1+1]);
                k1++;
            }
            count = k1;
        }

        return count;
}
/* - - - - - - - - - - - - - - - - - - - - - - - - - - - - - - - - - - - - - */
```

Modify!

1. Write a program that reads a set of values from the keyboard, calls the *quicksort()* function to sort them, and prints the sorted values.

2. Modify this program so that the values are sorted into descending order.

6.6 Search Algorithms

Another very common operation performed with arrays is searching the array for a specific value. We may want to know whether a particular value is in the array, how many times it occurs in the array, or where it first occurs in the array. All these forms of searches determine a single value, and thus are good candidates for functions. In this section, we will develop several functions for searching an array; then, when you need to perform a search in a program, you can probably use one of these functions with little or no modification to the function.

Searching algorithms fall into two groups: those for searching an unordered list and those for searching an ordered list.

Unordered Lists

sequential search

We first consider searching an unordered list; thus, we assume that the elements are not necessarily sorted into an ascending numerical order, or any other order that may aid us in searching the array. The algorithm to search an unordered array is just a simple **sequential search:** check the first element, check the second element, and so on. There are several ways that we could implement this function. We could develop the function as an integer function that returns the position of the desired value in the array or the value -1 if the desired value is not in the array. We could develop the function as an integer function that returns the number of times the element occurs in the array. We could also develop the function as a logical function that returns a value of true (1) if the element is in the array or false (0) if the element is not in the array. All of these ideas represent valid functions, and we could think of programs that would use each of these forms. Here we present a function that returns the position of the desired value in an unordered array or -1 if the value is not found.

```
int search(const int A[], int n, int value)
/* This function returns the position of value in array A.   */
/*   Returns -1 if value is not found in A.                  */
/*   Function assumes array A is unordered.                  */
{
int index(0);
while (index < n && A[index]!=value)
        {
                index++;
        }
        if(index < n && A[index] == value)
                return(index);
        else
                return(-1);
}
```

Ordered Lists

We now consider searching an ordered or sorted list of values. Consider the following list of ordered values, and assume that we are searching for the value 25:

-7
2
14
38
52
77
105

As soon as we reach the value 38, we know that 25 is not in the list, because we know that the list is ordered in ascending numerical order. Therefore, we do not have to search the entire list, as we would have to do for an unordered list; we only need to search past the point where the value we are looking for should have been. If the list is in ascending order, we search until the current value in the list is larger than the value we are searching for; if the list is in descending order we search until the current value is smaller than the value we are looking for. We now present a function that performs a **sequential search on an ordered list.** The function returns the position of the desired value in an ordered array or −1 if the value is not found:

sequential search
on an ordered list

```
/*------------------------------------------------------------*/
/*  This function returns the position of value in array A.  */
/*  Returns -1 if value is not found in A.                   */
/*  Function assumes:                                        */
/*     the array A has n elements in ascending order.        */

int search(const int A[], int n, int value)
{
int index(0);
while (index < n && A[index] < value)
        {
                index++;
        }
        if(index < n && A[index] == value)
                return(index);
        else
                return( 1);
}
/*------------------------------------------------------------*/
```

binary search

Another popular and more efficient algorithm for searching an ordered list is the **binary search.** The binary search algorithm is sometimes referred to as the divide-and-conquer algorithm because it begins at the middle of the list and determines if the value being searched for is in the top half or the bottom half of the list. If the value belongs in the top half of the list, the algorithm checks the middle of the top half and repeats, dividing the search space in half at each iteration until the value is found or it is determined that the value is not in the list. The following is a function that implements a binary search:

```
/*------------------------------------------------------------*/
/*  This function returns the position of value in array list. */
/*  Returns a value of -1 if value is not found in list.      */
/*  Function assumes:                                         */
/*     the array list has n elements in ascending order.      */

int bSearch(const int list[], int n, int value)
{
int top(0), bottom(n-1), mid;
```

```
while(top<=bottom)
{
    //  Determine mid point of list.
    mid = (top + bottom)/2;

    //  Value is found.
    if(list[mid] == value)
        return mid;

    //  Look for value in top half of list.
    else if(list[mid] > value)
        bottom=mid-1;

    //  Look for value in bottom half of list.
    else
        top=mid+1;
}
//  Value was not found in the list.
return -1;
}
```

Modify!

1. Modify either of the sequential search functions to form a function `template`. Write a `main` program to test your function.

2. Modify the sequential search on an ordered list to return a count of the number of times a specified value occurred in an ordered list.

3. Modify the binary-search function so that it correctly searches a list that is ordered in descending order instead of ascending order. Write a `main` program to test your function.

6.7 Character Strings

character string

C-style string

A character array is an array in which the individual elements are stored as characters. A **character string** can be represented using a character array in which the last array element is a null character, '\0', which has an ASCII integer equivalent of zero. This representation of strings is referred to as a **C-style string,** because it originated with the C programming language and is still supported by C++.

Character strings can also be represented using the *string* class type introduced in Chapter 2. In this section, we discuss both methods of representing character strings.

C Style String Definition and I/O

Character string constants are enclosed in double quotes, as in "sensor1.dat", "r", and "15762". A character string object can be defined and initialized using string constants or using character constants, as shown in the following statements:

```
// Define string objects using string constants.
char filename1[15] = "sensor1.dat";
char filename2[] = "zero.dat";

// Define string object using character constants
char filename3[] = {'s','p','e','a','c','h',
                    '.','d','a','t','\0'};
```

Each of the preceding statements defines a C-style string object as illustrated with the following memory snapshot:

filename1 | s | e | n | s | o | r | 1 | . | d | a | t | \0 | 0 | 0 | 0 |

filename2 | z | e | r | o | . | d | a | t | \0 |

filename3 | s | p | e | a | c | h | . | d | a | t | \0 |

Note that the null character occupies one element of the array.

The following statements use the input operator to read two strings from the keyboard and the output operator to print the strings to the screen:

```
//   Declare objects.
char unit_length[10], unit_time[10];
...
//   Read data into string.
cin >> unit_length >> unit_time;
cout << unit_length << ' ' << unit_time << endl;
...
```

Suppose the following data were entered at the keyboard:

```
inch second
```

The input operator will input a character string and assign the null character to the end of the string, as illustrated with the following memory snapshot:

unit_length | i | n | c | h | \0 | ? | ? | ? | ? | ? |

unit_time | s | e | c | o | n | d | \0 | ? | ? | ? |

However, the input operator does not do any checking on the maximum size of the array. If the input data has more characters than the maximum size of the character array, the input operator will assign values beyond the bounds of the array, and an error will occur.

Recall that the input operator ignores all whitespace. If whitespace is desired as part of a string, the function *getline()* can be used to read strings, as illustrated in the next example

peek()

that reads comment lines from the header of an ASCII image file and prints the comment lines on the screen. Our example uses the **peek()** function to look at the next character on the input stream. The function *peek()* is a member function of the *istream* class and can be called by any *istream* object. The function *peek()* returns the value of the next character on the input stream but does not remove the character from the input stream:

```
. . .
// Declare objects
ifstream image("Io.ppm");
char comment_line[100];
. . .
// Read and print a comment line from a data file.
// Comment lines begin with a #.
while(image.peek() == '#')
{
        image.getline(comment_line, 100);
        cout << comment_line << endl;
}
. . .
```

getline()

The function **getline()** is a member function of the *istream* class and can be called by any input stream object. The first argument is the name of a character array. The second argument is the maximum length of the array. The *getline()* function will read and store characters until the newline character is encountered or until $maximum\_length - 1$ characters have been read. The function will assign the null character as the last character in the string. If the newline character is encountered, the *getline()* function will read and discard the character. A third argument can be used with the *getline()* to specify a character other than the newline to signal the end of the input.

Practice!

Assume that the following text is entered from the keyboard:

```
The mice, Sniff and Scurry,
had only simple brains.
```

Show the output generated by the following program segments (assume that each segment uses the entire input stream):

1. ```
   char cstring1[10], cstring2[] = "Cheese";
   cin >> cstring1;
   cout << cstring1 << ' ' << cstring2 << endl;
   ```

2. ```
   char cstring1[10], cstring2[] = "Cheese";
   cin.getline(cstring1,10);
   cout << cstring1 << cstring2 << endl;
   ```

```
3. char cstring1[50], cstring2[50];
   cin.getline(cstring1,50);
   cin.getline(cstring2,50);
   cout << cstring1 << cstring2 << endl;
```

String Functions

The Standard C++ library contains numerous functions for working with C-style strings, such as the ones listed next. The header file *cstring* must be included for these functions to be used in a program:

```
strlen(s)    // Returns the length of the string s.
strcpy(s,t)  // Copies string t to string s.
strcat(s,t)  // Concatenates string t to the end of string s.
strcmp(s,t)  // Compares ASCII values of string s to string t
             // in an character-by-character comparison.
             // Returns a negative value if s<t.
             // Returns zero if s is equal to t.
             // Returns a positive value if s>t.
```

A complete list of the functions included in the **cstring** library file can be found in Appendix A. To illustrate the use of these functions, we now present a simple example:

```
/*-----------------------------------------------------------*/
/*   Program chapter6_5                                       */
/*   This program illustrates the use of several             */
/*   C style string functions.                               */

#include <iostream>
#include <cstring>

int main()
{
// Declare and initialize objects.
char strg1[]="Engineering Problem Solving: ";
char strg2[]="Object Based Approach", strg3[75] = "";

// Print the length of each string.
cout << "String lengths: " << strlen(strg1) << ' '
     << strlen(strg2) << ' ' << strlen(strg3) << endl;

// Swap strings if strg1 is larger than strg2
if(strcmp(strg1,strg2) > 0)
```

```
{
  strcpy(strg3,strg2);
  strcpy(strg2,strg1);
  strcpy(strg1,strg3);
}

//  Combine two strings into one.
strcpy(strg3,strg1);
strcat(strg3,strg2);
cout << "strg3: " << strg3 << endl;
cout << "strg3 length: " << strlen(strg3) << endl;
return 0;
}
/*-----------------------------------------------------*/
```

The output from this program is the following:

```
String lengths: 29 21 0
strg3: Engineering Problem Solving: Object Based Approach
strg3 length: 50
```

6.8 Problem Solving Applied: Palindromes

palindrome

A **palindrome** is a word (noon), sentence (Draw a level award), or number (18781) that reads the same backward or forward. Write a program that reads a line from a data file and determines whether the line contains a palindrome. (Note that whitespace is ignored when determining whether a word, sentence, or number is a palindrome.) The program should read each line in the data file (read lines until an end of file is encountered), print each line, and also print a message that indicates whether the line is a palindrome.

1. PROBLEM DESCRIPTION

Write a program that identifies palindromes read from a file.

2. INPUT/OUTPUT DESCRIPTION

The input to the program are lines from a data file and the output is the same line along with a message indicating whether or not the line is a palindrome.

one line ⟶ ☐ ⟶ one line and appropriate message

3. HAND EXAMPLE

If the data file contained the lines

```
noon
draw a level award
this sight
18781
187761
```

the output would be as follows:

```
noon (this is a palindrome)
draw a level award (this is a palindrome)
this sight (this is NOT a palindrome)
18781 (this is a palindrome)
187761 (this is NOT a palindrome)
```

4. ALGORITHM DEVELOPMENT

We first develop the decomposition outline because it breaks the solution into a series of sequential steps:

Decomposition Outline

1. Read one line from the data file
2. Remove all white space and punctuation
3. Determine if data is a palindrome
4. Print original data and appropriate message

Step 1 in the decomposition outline involves a loop in which we read a single line from the file and store it in a C-style character string. The *getline()* function looks for the '\n' character to determine the end of the line. The condition to exit the loop will be a test for the end of the file. Step two requires a loop to copy only the alphanumeric characters from the input string to a new string. The condition to terminate this loop will be the length of the input string. Step 3 requires a loop to compare corresponding characters within the new string to determine whether the new string is a palindrome. We will use a function to perform this task. Step 4 prints the original character string, and the appropriate message. The refinement in pseudocode is the following:

```
Refinement in Pseudocode
main:    while not at end of file
             read a line from the file and store in string
             set count to zero
```

```
                    while count < length of string
                       if(string[count] is alpha numeric character)
                         copy character to new string
                         increment count
                    add null character to end of new string
                    print original string
                    if(is_palindrome(new_string)
                         print("this is a palindrome)
                    else
                         print("this is NOT a palindrome)
        is_palindrome(string):
                    set begin to zero
                    set end to length of string - 1
                    set is_pal to true
                    while(is_pal && begin <= end)
                       if(string[begin] != string[end]
                         set is_pal to false
                       increment begin
                       decrement endl
                    return is_pal
```

The steps in the pseudocode are now detailed enough to convert into C++:

```
/*----------------------------------------------------------------------*/
/* Program chapter6_6                                                 */
/* This program looks at a character string and determines            */
/* if the string is a palindrome.                                     */

#include<fstream>
#include<cstring>
#include<cctype>

//Function Prototypes
bool is_palindrome(char string[]);

//Global constant for string maximum string length
const int BUFFERSIZE = 180;

int main()
{
  // Declare objects.
  char buffer[BUFFERSIZE], new_string[BUFFERSIZE], filename[50];
  int count;
  ifstream palindromes;

  // Prompt user for file name and open input file.
  cout << "Enter the name of the input file ";
```

```
      cin >> filename;
      palindromes.open(filename);
      if(palindromes.fail())
      {
        cout << "error opening file " << filename << endl;
      }
      else
      {
        // Input first line from the data file.
        palindromes.getline(buffer, BUFFERSIZE);

        // While not end of file, process string.
        while(!palindromes.eof())
        {
          count = 0;
          for(int k=0; k<strlen(buffer); k++)
          {
            if(isalnum(buffer[k]))
            {
              new_string[count] = buffer[k];
              count++;
            }
          }

          // Assign null character to end of new_string.
          new_string[count] = '\0';

          // Output original string and check new_string.
          cout << buffer;
          if(is_palindrome(new_string))
          {
            cout << " (this is a palindrome)\n";
          }
          else
          {
            cout << " (this is NOT a palindrome)\n";
          }

          // Input next string.
          palindromes.getline(buffer, BUFFERSIZE);
        }
        return 0;
      }
}
/*-------------------------------------------------------------  */
/*-------------------------------------------------------------  */
/* This function returns a value of true if string is  a palindrome.  */
/* The function returns false otherwise.                              */
```

```
bool is_palindrome(char string[])
{
  bool is_pal = true;
  int begin(0), end;

  // Find the offset of the last character.
  end = strlen(string) - 1;
  while(is_pal && begin <= end)
  {
    if(string[begin] != string[end])
    {
      is_pal = false;
    }
    begin++;
    end--;
  }
  return(is_pal);
}
/*------------------------------------------------------------------*/
```

5. TESTING

If we use the data from the hand example, we get the following output:

```
noon (this is a palindrome)
draw a level award (this is a palindrome)
this sight (this is NOT a palindrome)
18781 (this is a palindrome)
187761 (this is NOT a palindrome)
```

6.9 The string Class

The *string* class provides and object-based alternative to the C-style string. The following are a few of the commonly used member functions included in the *string* class:

```
size()            // Returns the length of the calling string.
empty()           // Returns true if the calling string
                  // Contains no characters.
                  // Return false otherwise.
substr(int start, // Returns the substring of length len,
       int len)   // Beginning at start of the calling string.
c_str()           // Returns the equivalent C-style string.
```

Numerous operators have been overloaded in the *string* class to support the use of *string* objects. The assignment operator, as well as the relational operators <, >, <=, >=, ==, and the operators + and +—, can be used with string objects. The binary operator + concatenates two strings, and the binary operator += appends one string to the end of the other. To illustrate the use of some of these operators and functions, we will rewrite program6_5, adding a few additional statements and using the *string* class instead of C-style strings (recall that we must include the header file *string* in order to use the *string* class):

```
/*------------------------------------------------------------*/
/*   Program chapter6_7                                        */
/*   This program illustrates the use of several              */
/*   operators and functions supported by the string class.   */

#include <iostream>
#include <string>

int main()
{
// Declare and initialize string objects.
string strg1 = "Engineering Problem Solving: ";
string strg2 = "Object Based Approach", strg3;

// Print the length of each string.
cout << "String lengths: " << strg1.size() << ' '
     << strg2.size() << ' ' << strg3.size() << endl;

// Swap strings if strg1 is larger than strg2
if(strg1 > strg2)
{
  strg3 = strg2;
  strg2 = strg1;
  strg1 = strg3;
}

// Append a string.
strg2 += " Using C++";

// Concatenate two strings.
strg3 = strg1 + strg2;

cout << "strg3: " << strg3 << endl;
cout << "strg3 length: " << strg3.size() << endl;
return 0;
}
/*------------------------------------------------------------*/
```

The output from this program is the following:

```
String lengths: 29 21 0
strg3: Engineering Problem Solving: Object Based Approach Using C++
strg3 length: 60
```

Modify!

1. Modify the function *is_palindrome()* so that it uses the *string* class instead of C-style strings. Write a program to test the function.

2. Modify the *sort()* function so that it sorts an array of strings in alphabetical order. Use the *string* class. Write a program to test the function.

3. Modify the *bSearch()* function so that it searches an ordered list of strings. Use the **string** class. Write a program to test the function.

6.10 The vector Class

vector class

Working with arrays has several pitfalls that were discussed in this chapter. When working with arrays, we must be careful not to exceed the bounds of the array when referencing an element. We must always declare the array to be as large as, or larger than, the maximum number of values we expect to store, which can result in inefficient use of memory. Passing and array as an argument to a function is always a pass by reference, so we must either use the keyword `const`, or take care not to inadvertently change the array values within the function. These problems can be avoided with the use of the **vector class.**

The *vector* class is included in the Standard C++ library and provides an object-based alternative to the built-in array. To use the *vector* class, we must include the header file *vector* in our programs as follows:

```
#include<vector>
```

The following are a few of the commonly used member functions included in the *vector* class:

```
begin()              // Returns address of first element.
empty()              // Returns true if the calling vector
                     // Contains no value.
                     // Returns false otherwise.
end()                // Returns address 1 past last element
                     // of calling vector.
erase()              // Delete specified element from calling vector.
insert()             // Add element to calling vector at
                     // specified location.
pop_back()           // Delete last element from calling vector.
push_back()          // Add element to end of calling vector.
resize()             // Changes the size of the calling vector.
size()               // Returns the size of the calling vector.
```

iterator

You will notice that many of these member functions return addresses. These functions are designed to be used with a special kind of pointer, called an **iterator.** Using iterators to access elements in a *vector* object is one convenient way of using the *vector* class. Pointers and iterators will be discussed in detail in Chapter 9. A second way to use the *vector* class models the built-in array. This is the method presented in this chapter.

We can define a *vector* object in a type declaration statement, as illustrated:

Define an integer *vector v2*, with space for 10 integers:

```
vector<int> v2(10);
```

v2 | ? | ? | ? | ? | ? | ? | ? | ? | ? | ? |
   [0][1][2][3][4][5][6][7][8][9]

Defines a *vector v3* of strings with space for *n* strings:

```
vector<string> v3(n);
```

v3 | ? | ? | ? | ? | ? | ? | ··· | ? |
   [0][1][2][3] . . . [n-1]

Define an integer *vector v4* with space for *n* integers (each element in the vector is initialized to −1):

```
vector<int> v4(n,-1);
```

v4 | -1 | -1 | -1 | -1 | -1 | ··· | -1 |
    [0] [1] [2] [3] . . . [n-1]

The last two examples illustrate that the size of a *vector* can be specified using a nonconstant value. This provides greater flexibility and efficiency than the built-in array. The current size of a *vector* can be determined by referencing the function *size()*.

Once a *vector* object has been defined, standard array notation can be used to access elements in the *vector*. The following program uses a for loop to sum the elements in the *vector v:*

```
/*-----------------------------------------------------------*/
#include<iostream>
#include<vector>
using namespace std;

int main()
{
//Declare objects.
   double sum(0);
   vector<double> v(5, -1.2);

// Sum elements in v.  Use size of v as a limit.
   for(int i=0; i<v.size(); i++)
   {
       sum+= v[i];
   }
   cout << sum << endl;
   return 0;
}
/*-----------------------------------------------------------*/
```

The output from this program is

-6

Unlike the situation with a built-in array, when a *vector* is required as a formal parameter in a function definition, a pass by value is the default. A pass by reference can be specified by appending "&" to the data type of the vector.

Another feature of the *vector* class is the definition of the assignment operator. A *vector* object can be assigned to another object of the same type in a single statement. These features are illustrated in the next example:

```
/*-------------------------------------------------------*/
/* Program chapter6_5                                    */
/* This program reads a set of experimental data and    */
/* scales the data to values between 0 and 1            */

#include<fstream>
#include<string>
#include<vector>
using namespace std;

// Function prototypes.
double maximum(vector<double> v);
void scale(vector<double>& v, double m);
int main()
{
 //Declare objects.
   double maxv(0);
   int npts;
   string filename;
   ifstream file_1;

   // Prompt user for file name and
   // open file.
   cout << "Enter filename ";
   cin >> filename;
   file_1.open(filename.c_str());
   if( file_1.fail() )
   {
        cout << "error opening file " << filename
             << endl;
        return 0;
   }
   // Read number of data points.
   file_1 >> npts;

   // Define vectors.
   vector<double> v(npts), vscaled(npts);

   // Read data and store in speech vector.
   for (int i=0; i<npts; i++)
   {
        file_1 >> v[i];
   }
```

```
   // Format output.
      cout.setf(ios::fixed);
      cout.precision(2);

   // Print original vector.
      cout << "Original vector:\n";
      for(int i=0; i<v.size(); i++)
      {
         cout << v[i] << ' ';
      }
   // Find max value in v.
      maxv =  maximum(v);
   // Assign vector v to vscaled
      vscaled = v;

   // Scale vector.
      scale(vscaled, maxv);

   // Print scaled vector.
      cout << endl << "Scaled vector:\n";
      for(int i=0; i<vscaled.size(); i++)
      {
         cout << vscaled[i] << ' ';
      }
   return 0;
}
/*----------------------------------------------------*/
/*            ------------------------------------*/
/* This function returns the largest value in v.      */

double maximum(vector<double> v)
{
   double temp = v[0];
   for(int i=1; i<v.size(); i++)
   {
     if(v[i] > temp)
       temp = v[i];
   }
   return temp;
}
/*----------------------------------------------------*/
/* This functions scales the vector v to values       */
/* between 0 and 1.                                   */

void scale(vector<double>& v, double m)
{
  for(int i=0; i<v.size(); i++)
  {
    v[i] = v[i]/m;
  }
}
/*----------------------------------------------------*/
```

A sample run of this program generated the following output:

```
input filename testdata
Original vector:
55.00 49.50 45.00 26.00 17.89
Scaled vector:
1.00 0.90 0.82 0.47 0.33
```

As you can see in the preceding example, the *vector* class provides an easy-to-use alternative to the built-in array.

SUMMARY

Key Terms

alphanumeric character	one-dimensional array
array	palindrome
binary search	power
C-style string	quicksort algorithm
character string	selection sort algorithm
element	sequential search
function overloading	sorting
function template	standard deviation
function signature	statistical measurements
instance of a function	string class
iterator	subscripts
magnitude	utterance
mean	variance
median	vector class
null character	whitespace
offset	zero crossing

C++ Statement Summary

Include C-style string header file

```
#include<cstring>
```

Include string class header file

```
#include<string>
```

Array declaration:

```
int a[5], b[]={2, 3, -1};
char vowels[]={'a', 'e', 'i', 'o', 'u'};
string words[100];
```

Function Templates

```
template <class D_type>
D_type minval(const D_type x[], int n);
```

Style **Notes**

1. The object k is commonly used as a subscript for a one-dimensional array.
2. Use symbolic constants to declare the size of an array so that it is easy to modify.

Debugging Notes

1. Use arrays only when it is necessary to keep all the data available in memory.
2. If unexpected characters are printed at the end of a C-style string, the null character may be missing from the string.
3. Be careful not to exceed the maximum offset value when referencing an element in an array.
4. Select conditions in **for** loops to specifically use an equality with the maximum offset value; this helps avoid errors with offset ranges.
5. An array must be declared to be as large as, or larger than, the maximum number of values to be stored in it.
6. Because an array reference in a function is always a call by address, be careful that you do not inadvertently change values in an array in the function.

Problems

Exam Practice!

True/False Problems
Indicate whether the following statements are true (T) or false (F).

1. If the initializing sequence is shorter than an array, then the rest of the values are initialized to zero.
2. If an array is defined without a size, but with an initialization sequence, then the array size is arbitrary.
3. When the value of a subscript or offset is greater than the largest valid offset of an array, it will always cause an execution error.
4. All values of an array are printed if we specify the identifier of the array without an offset.
5. In ASCII, the string "Smith" is less than the string "Johnson".

Multiple Choice

6. An array is
   (a) a group of values having a common object name and all of the same data type.
   (b) a collection of elements of different data types which are stored in adjacent memory locations.
   (c) an object that contains multiple values of the same data type.
   (d) a location in memory that holds multiple values of the same data type.

7. An individual element in an array is addressed by specifying
    (a) the name of the array and the offset of the element.
    (b) the name of the array.
    (c) the offset of the element within the array followed by the name of the array.
    (d) the offset of the element in the array.
8. The offset identifies the _____ of a particular element in the array.
    (a) location
    (b) value
    (c) range
    (d) name

Memory Snapshot Problems

Give the corresponding snapshots of memory after each of the following sets of statements is executed. Use ? to indicate an array element that is not initialized.

9.
```
int t[5];
...
t[0] = 5;
for(int k=0; k<4; k++)
    t[k+1] = t[k] + 3;
```

10.
```
char s[] = "Hello", t[] = {'a', 'e', 'i', 'o', 'u'}, name[10];
strcpy(name,"Sue");
```

Program Output

Problems 11–13 refer to the following statements:

```
string strng1 = "K", strng2 = "265", strng3 = "xyz";
```

11. What is the output of the following statement?

```
cout << strng1.size() << endl;
```

12. What is the output of the following statement?

```
strng1 =  strng2;
cout << strng1 << endl;
```

13. What is the output of the following statements?

```
strng1 += string2;
cout << strng1 << endl;
```

Programming Exercises

Linear Interpolation.   The following problems refer to the wind-tunnel test data stored in the file *tunnel.dat*. The file contains the set of data discussed in Chapter 2, which consists of a flight-path angle (in degrees) and its corresponding coefficient of lift on each line in the file. The flight-path angles will be in ascending order.

14. Write a program that reads the wind-tunnel test data and then allows the user to enter a flight-path angle. If the angle is within the bounds of the data set, the program should then use linear interpolation to compute the corresponding coefficient of lift. (You may need to refer to the section on linear interpolation in Section 2.0.)

15. Modify the program in Problem 14 so that it prints a message to the user giving the range of angles that are covered in the data file after reading the values.

16. Write a function that could be used to verify that the flight-path angles are in ascending order. The function should return a zero if the angles are not in order and a 1 if they are in order. Assume that the corresponding function prototype is

```
int ordered(double x[], int num_pts);
```

17. Write a function that receives two one-dimensional vectors that correspond to the flight-path angles and the corresponding coefficients of lift. The function should sort the flight-path angles into ascending order while maintaining the correspondence between the flight-path angles and the corresponding coefficients of lift. Assume that the corresponding function prototype is

```
void reorder(vector <double> & x, vector <double> & y);
```

18. Modify the program developed in Problem 14 such that it uses the function developed in Problem 16 to determine whether the data are in the desired order. If they are not in the desired order, use the function developed in Problem 17 to reorder them.

Noise Signals. In engineering simulations, we often want to generate a floating-point sequence of values with a specified mean and variance. The function developed in this chapter allows us to generate numbers between limits a and b, but it does not allow us to specify the mean and variance. By using results from probability, the following relationships can be derived between the limits of a uniform random sequence and its theoretical mean μ and variance σ^2:

$$\sigma^2 = \frac{(b-a)^2}{12}, \qquad \mu = \frac{(a+b)}{2}.$$

19. Write a program that uses the **rand_float** function developed in Chapter 4 to generate sequences of random floating-point values between 4 and 10. Then compare the computed mean and variance to the theoretical values computed. As you use more and more random numbers, the computed values and the theoretical values should become closer.

20. Write a program that uses the **rand_float** function developed in Chapter 4 to generate two sequences of 500 points. Each sequence should have a theoretical mean of 4, but one sequence should have a variance of 0.5, and the other should have a variance of 2. Check the computed means and compare to the theoretical means. (*Hint:* Use the two previous equations to write two equations with two unknowns. Then solve for the unknowns by hand.)

21. Write a program that uses the **rand_float** function developed in Chapter 4 to generate two sequences of 500 points. Each sequence should have the same variance of 3.0,

but one sequence should have a mean of 0.0, and the other should have a mean of −4.0. Compare the theoretical and computed values for mean and variance. (*Hint:* Use the two previous equations to write two equations with two unknowns. Then solve for the unknowns by hand.)

22. Write a function named **rand_mv** that generates a random floating-point value with a specified mean and variance that are input parameters to the function. Assume that the corresponding function prototype is

```
double rand_mv(double mean, double var);
```

Use the rand_float function developed in Chapter 4.

Cryptography.   The science of developing secret codes has interested many people for centuries. Some of the simplest codes involve replacing a character, or a group of characters with another character, or group of characters. To easily decode these messages, the decoder needs the "key" that shows the replacement characters. In recent times, computers have been used very successfully to decode many codes that initially were assumed to be unbreakable. The next set of problems considers simple codes and schemes for decoding them. Generate files to test the programs.

23. One step in decoding a simple code without knowing the coding scheme, involves counting the number of occurrences of each character. Then, knowing that the most common letter in English is 'e,' the letter that occurs most commonly in the coded message is replaced by 'e.' Similar replacements are then made based on the number of occurrences of characters in the coded message and the known occurrences of characters in the English language. This decoding often provides enough of the correct replacements that the incorrect replacements can then be determined. For this problem, write a program that reads a data file and determines the number of occurrences of each of the characters in the file. Then, print the characters and the number of times that they occurred. If a character does not occur, do not print it. (*Hint:* Use an array to store the occurrences of the characters based on their ASCII codes.)

24. Another simple code encodes a message in text such that the true message is represented by the first letter of each word. There are no spaces between the words, but the decoded string of characters can easily be separated into words by a person. Write a program to read a data file and determine the secret message stored by the sequence of first letters of the words. (*Hint:* Use the **string** class, and store the first letter of each word in a character string.)

25. Assume that the true secret message in Problem 00 is stored in the second letter of each word. Write a program to read a data file and determine the secret message stored in the file. (*Hint:* Use the **string** class, and store the first letter of each word in a character string.)

26. Assume that the true secret message in Problem 00 is represented by the characters that are three characters to the right in the collating sequence from the first letters of the words. Write a program to read a data file and determine the secret message stored in the file using this decoding scheme. (*Hint:* Use the **string** class, and store the first letter of each word in a character string.)

27. Write a program that encodes the text in a data file using a character array named **key** that contains 26 characters. This key is read from the keyboard; the first letter contains the character that is to replace the letter a in the data file, the second letter contains the letter that is to replace the letter b in the data file, and so on. Assume that all punctuation is to be replaced by spaces. Check to be sure that the key does not map two different characters to the same one during the encoding.

28. Write a program which decodes the file that is the output of Problem 27. Assume that the same integer key is read from the keyboard by this program and is used in the decoding steps. Note that you will not be able to restore the punctuation characters.

CHAPTER 7

GRAND CHALLENGE:
Image Processing

Launched in 1989, the Galileo spacecraft arrived at Jupiter on December 7, 1995, when it fired its main engine for a successful orbit capture around Jupiter. The Galileo Solid State Imaging Team has been studying Jupiter and its moons (encountering one moon during each orbit) and returning a steady stream of images and scientific data. Image products, which are of special interest to the public, have been available on an ongoing basis during the spacecraft's journey through the Jovian system in order to share with the public the excitement of exploration and new discoveries being made via the Galileo spacecraft.

Two-Dimensional Arrays and Matrices

Chapter Outline

Objectives

Summary, Key Terms, C++ Statement Summary, Style Notes, Debugging Notes, Problems

OBJECTIVES   This chapter introduces **two-dimensional arrays** with examples that illustrate defining and initializing arrays, that perform computations with two-dimensional arrays, that use two-dimensional arrays in input and output statements, and that use two-dimensional arrays as function arguments. Two-dimensional arrays are used to solve a **terrain navigation problem.** The *vector* class is revisited as an alternative to two-dimensional arrays. In addition, matrices are defined, along with some of the common operations performed with them. Finally, the **Gauss elimination technique** for solving a system of simultaneous equations is presented, and a program is developed to solve a system of equations using arrays.

7.1 Two-Dimensional Arrays

A set of data values that is visualized as a row or column is easily represented by a one-dimensional array. However, there are many examples in which the best way to visualize a set of data is with a grid or a table of data, which has both rows and columns, as shown in this array, which has four rows and three columns:

```
row 0 ⟶  | 2  | 3  | −1 |
row 1 ⟶  | 0  | −3 | 5  |
row 2 ⟶  | 2  | 6  | 3  |
row 3 ⟶  | −2 | 10 | 4  |
            ↑    ↑    ↑
          col0 col1 col2
```

two-dimensional
array
row offsets
column offsets

In C++, a grid or table of data is represented with a **two-dimensional array.** Each element in a two-dimensional array is referenced using an identifier followed by two offsets: a **row offsets** and a **column offsets.** The offset values for both rows and columns begin with 0, and each offset has its own set of brackets. Thus, assuming that the previous array has an identifier *x*, we see that the value in position *x*[2][1] is 6.

Common errors in array references include using parentheses instead of brackets, as in x(2)(3), or using only one set of brackets or parentheses, as in x[2,3] or x(2,3).

All values in a two dimensional array must have the same data type. An array cannot have a column of integers followed by a column of floating-point numbers, and so on.

Definition and Initialization

To define a two-dimensional array, we specify the number of rows and the number of columns in the declaration statement, with the row number first. Both the row number and the column number are in brackets, as shown in this statement:

```
int x[4][3];
```

A two-dimensional array can be initialized with a declaration statement. The values are specified in a sequence separated by commas, and each row is contained in braces. An additional set of braces is included around the complete set of values, as in

```
int x[4][3] = {{2,3,-1},{0,-3,5},{2,6,3},{-2,10,4}};
```

If the initializing sequence is shorter than the array, then the rest of the values are initialized to zero. If the array is specified with the first subscript empty, but with an initialization sequence, the size is determined by the sequence. Thus, the following statement also defines the array x:

```
int x[][3] = {{2,3,-1},{0,-3,5},{2,6,3},{-2,10,4}};
```

Style

Arrays can also be assigned values with program statements. *For two-dimensional arrays, two nested **for** loops are usually required to initialize an array; i and j are commonly used as offsets.* The following statements define and initialize an array such that each row contains the row number:

```
//  Declare objects.
int t[5][4];
...
```

```
//  Assign values to array.
for (int i=0; i<=4; i++)
}
   for (int j=0; j<=3; j++)
   {
       t[i][j] = i;
   }
}
```

The following are the values in the array *t* after these statements are executed:

0	0	0	0
1	1	1	1
2	2	2	2
3	3	3	3
4	4	4	4

Style

Two-dimensional arrays can also be assigned values read from a data file. In this set of statements, we assume that a data file named *engine.dat* contains 50 temperature values that we read and store in the array. Symbolic constants *NROWS* and *NCOLS* are used to represent the number of rows and columns. *Changing the size of an array is easier to do when the numbers of rows and columns are specified as symbolic constants; otherwise, the change requires modifications to several statements.*

```
#include<fstream>
. . .
const int NROWS = 10;
const int NCOLS = 5;
. . .
int main()
{
// Declare objects.
double temps[NROWS][NCOLS];
ifstream data_1;
. . .
// Open file and read data into array.
data_1.open("engine.dat");
if(!data_1.fail())
{
  for (int i=0; i<=NROWS-1; i++)
  {
    for (int j=0; j<=NCOLS-1; j++)
    {
      data_1 >> temps[i][j];
    }
  }
}
data_1.close();
. . .
```

Practice!

Show the contents of the arrays defined in each of the following sets of statements. Use a question mark to indicate an element that has not been initialized.

1. `int d[3][1]={{1},{4},{6}};`

2. `int g[6][2]={{5,2},{-2,3}};`

3. `double h[4][4]={{0,0}};`

4. `int p[3][3]={{0,0,0}};`

```
...
for (int k=0; k<=2; k++)
{
   p[k][k] = 1;
}
```

5. `int g[5][5];`

```
...
for (int i=0; i<=4; i++)
{
   for (int j=0; j<=4; j++)
   {
      g[i][j] = i + j;
   }
}
```

6. `int g[5][5];`

```
...
for (int i=0; i<=4; i++)
{
   for (int j=0; j<=4; j++)
   {
      g[i][j] = pow(-1,j);
   }
}
```

Computations and Output

Computations and output with two-dimensional arrays must always specify two offsets when referencing an array element. To illustrate, consider the next program, which reads a data file containing power output for an electrical plant for a 10-week period. Each line of the data file contains seven values representing the daily power output for a week. The data are stored in a two-dimensional array, and then a report is printed giving the average power for the first day of the week during the period, the average power for the second day of the week during the period, and so on:

```
/*--------------------------------------------------------*/
/*   Program chapter7_1                                   */
/*                                                        */
/*   This program computes power averages                 */
/*   over a 10-week period.                               */

#include <fstream>
#include <string>
using namespace std;

const int NROWS = 10;
const int NCOLS = 7;

int main()
{

   //   Declare objects.
   double power[NROWS][NCOLS], col_sum;
   string filename;
   ifstream data1;

   //   Open file and read data into array.
   cout << "Enter name of input file.\n";
   cin >> filename;
   data1.open(filename.c_str());
   if(data1.fail())
   {
     cout << "Error opening data file\n";
   }
   else
   {
     // Set format flags.
     cout.setf(ios::fixed);
     cout.setf(ios::showpoint);
     cout.presicion(1);
     for (int i=0; i<=NROWS-1; i++)
     {
        for (int j=0; j<=NCOLS-1; j++)
       {
           data1 >> power[i][j];
        }
     }

   //   Compute and print daily averages.
     for (int j=0; j<=NCOLS-1; j++)
     {
        col_sum = 0;
        for (int i=0; i<=NROWS-1; i++)
```

```
      {
          col_sum += power[i][j];
      }
      cout << "Day" << j+1 <<": Average =" << col_sum/NROWS << endl;
    }

  //  Close file and exit program.
  data1.close();
  }
  return 0;
}
/*-------------------------------------------------------------*/
```

Note that the daily averages are computed by adding each column and then dividing the column sum by the number of rows (which is also the number of weeks). The column number is then used to compute the day number. A sample output from this program is as follows:

```
Day 1: Average = 238.4
Day 2: Average = 199.5
Day 3: Average = 274.8
Day 4: Average = 239.1
Day 5: Average = 277.0
Day 6: Average = 305.8
Day 7: Average = 276.1
```

Writing information from a two-dimensional array to a data file is similar to writing the information from a one-dimensional array. In both cases, a newline indicator must be used to specify when the values are to begin a new line. The following statements will write a set of distance measurements to a data file named *dist.dat,* with five values per line:

```
//  Declare objects.
double dist[20][5];
ofstream data_1;
...
//  Write information from the array to a file.
data_1.open("dist.dat");
for (int i=0; i<=19; i++)
{
   for (int j=0, j<=4; j++)
   {
      data_1 << dist[i][j] << ' ';
   }
   data_1 << endl;
}
```

The space printed after the value of **dist[i][j]** in the output statement is necessary in order that the values be separated by a space.

Practice!

Assume the following declaration for the array g:

```
int g[3][3]={{0,0,0},{1,1,1},{2,2,2}};
```

Give the value of sum after each of the following sets of statements are executed.

1.
```
sum = 0;
for (int i=0; i<=2; i++)
{
   for (int j=0; j<=2; j++)
   {
      sum += g[i][j];
   }
}
```

2.
```
sum = 1;
for (int i=1; i<=2; i++)
{
   for (int j=0; j<=1; j++)
   {
      sum *= g[i][j];
   }
}
```

3.
```
sum = 0;
for (int j=0; j<=2; j++)
{
   sum -= g[2][j];
}
```

4.
```
sum = 0;
for (int i=0; i<=2; i++)
{
      sum += g[i][1];
}
```

Function Arguments

When arrays are used as function parameters, the references are call by reference, instead of call by value. As discussed in Chapter 6, this means that array references in a function refer to the original array and not to a copy of the array. Thus, we must be careful that we do not change values in the original array when we do not intend to make changes.

When using a one-dimensional array as a function argument, the function needs only the address of the first element in the array, which is specified by the array name. When using a two-dimensional array as a function argument, the function also needs information about

declared
column size

the **declared column size** of the array. In general, the function header and function prototype need to give the declared column size of a two-dimensional array. To illustrate, suppose that we need to write a program that computes the sum of the elements in an array containing four rows and four columns. Computing this sum requires two nested loops, so the program will be more readable if we put the steps to compute the sum in a function. The program can then reference the function with a single statement, as in the following:

```
*-------------------------------------------------------------------*
#include <iostream>
using namespace std;
const int NROWS=4, NCOLS=4;

//  Function prototypes.
int sum(int x[][NCOLS]);
...
int main()
{
//  Declare objects.
int a[NROWS][NCOLS];
...
//  Use function to compute array sum.
cout << "Array sum = " << sum(a) << endl;
```

If we need to recompute the array sum in several places in the program, the function becomes even more effective. If there are several different arrays, we can use the same function to compute their sums:

```
#include <iostream>
using namespace std;
const int NROWS=4, NCOLS=4;

//  Function prototypes.
int sum(int x[][NCOLS]);
...
int main()
{
//  Declare objects.
int a[NROWS][NCOLS], b[NROWS][NCOLS];
...
//  Use function to compute array sums.
cout << "Sum of a = " << sum(a) << endl;
cout << "Sum of b = " << sum(b) << endl;
```

We now present the function referenced in these statements:

```
/*-----------------------------------------------------------*/
/*  This function returns the sum of the values in    */
/*  an array with four rows and four columns.         */
```

```
int sum(int x[][NCOLS])
{
   // Declare and initialize objects.
   int total(0);

   // Compute a sum of the array values.
   for (int i=0; i<=NCOLS-1; i++)
   {
      for (int j=0; j<=NCOLS-1; j++)
      {
         total += x[i][j];
      }
   }

   // Return sum of array values.
   return total;
}
/*--------------------------------------------------------*/
```

In a final example, we develop a function that computes a partial sum of the elements in an array. The elements to be summed are assumed to be in a **subarray** in the upper left corner of the array. The arguments of the function include the original array, and the numbers of rows and columns in the subarray. The function prototype is

subarray

```
// Function prototype
int partial_sum(int x[][NCOLS], int m, int n);
```

Thus, if we want to sum the elements shown in the *shaded area* in the array *a*, we would use the reference

```
partial_sum(a,2,3);
```

2	3	-1	9
0	-3	5	7
2	6	3	2
-2	10	4	6

This reference should then compute the sum of the elements in the subarray beginning in the upper left corner and consisting of two rows and three columns; the function should return a value of 6. This function is as follows:

```
/*--------------------------------------------------------*/
/*  This function returns the sum of the values           */
/*  in a subarray of an array with four rows              */
/*  and four columns.                                     */
```

```
int partial_sum(int x[][NCOLS],int m, int n)
{
    //  Declare and initialize objects.
    int total(0);
    //  Compute a sum of subarray values.
    for (int i=0; i<=m-1; i++)
    {
        for (int j=0; j<=n-1; j++)
        {
            total += x[i][j];
        }
    }

    //  Return sum of subarray values.
    return total;
}
/*-------------------------------------------------------*/
```

 This function can be used with two-dimensional arrays of various sizes provided the symbolic constant **NCOLS** is within the scope of the function.

Practice!

Assume that the following statement is from a `main` function:

```
int a[4][4] = {{2, 3, -1, 9}, {0, -3, 5, 7},
               {2, 6, 3, 2}, {-2, 10, 4, 6}};
```

Determine by hand the values of the following references to the *partial_sum* function developed in this section.

     1. `partialsum(a,1,4);`

     2. `partialsum(a,1,1);`

     3. `partialsum(a,4,2);`

     4. `partialsum(a,2,4);`

7.2 Problem Solving Applied: Terrain Navigation

Terrain navigation is a key component in the design of remotely piloted vehicles (RPVs); these vehicles can travel on land, such as a robot or a car, or they can fly above the land, as in a drone or a plane. An RPV system contains an onboard computer that has stored the terrain information for the area in which it is to be operated. By knowing at any time where it is (perhaps with the aid of a global positioning system [GPS] receiver), the vehicle can then select the best path to get to a designated spot. If the destination changes, the vehicle can refer to its internal maps to recompute the new path.

The computer software that guides these vehicles must be tested over a variety of land formations and topologies. Elevation information for large grids of land is available in computer databases. One way of measuring the "difficulty" of a land grid with respect to terrain navigation is to determine the number of peaks in the grid, where a peak is a point that has lower elevations all around it. For this problem, we will assume that the values in the four positions shown in the following diagram are the ones adjacent to grid position [m][n] for purposes of determining if the value in grid position [m][n] is a peak:

	grid [m−1][n]	
grid [m][n−1]	grid [m][n]	grid [m][n+1]
	grid [m+1][n]	

Write a program that reads elevation data from a data file named *grid1.dat* and then prints the number of peaks and their locations. Assume that the first line of the data file contains the number of rows and the number of columns for the grid of information. These values are then followed by the elevation values, in row order. The maximum size grid is 25 rows by 25 columns.

1. PROBLEM STATEMENT

Determine and print the number of peaks and their locations in an elevation grid.

2. INPUT/OUTPUT DESCRIPTION

The I/O diagram shows that the input is a file containing the elevation data, and that the output is a listing of the locations of the peaks.

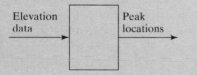

Elevation data → Peak locations

3. HAND EXAMPLE

Assume that the following data represent elevation for a grid that has six points along the side and seven points along the top. The peaks have been underlined in the data:

```
5039 5127 5238 5259 5248 5310 5299
5150 5392 5410 5401 5320 5820 5321
5290 5560 5490 5421 5530 5831 5210
5110 5429 5430 5411 5459 5630 5319
4920 5129 4921 5821 4722 4921 5129
5023 5129 4822 4872 4794 4862 4245
```

To specify the location of the peaks, we need to assign an addressing scheme to the data. Because we are going to be implementing this solution in C++, we choose its two-dimensional array-offset notation. Thus, we assume that the top-left corner is position [0][0], that the row numbers increase by 1 as we move down the page, and that the column numbers increase by 1 as we move to the right. These peaks then occur at positions [2][1], [2][5], and [4][3].

To determine the peaks, we compare a potential peak with its four neighboring points. If all four neighboring points are less than the potential peak, then the potential peak is a real peak. Note that the points on the edges of the array or grid cannot be potential peaks because we do not have elevation information on all four sides of the points.

4. ALGORITHM DEVELOPMENT

We first develop the decomposition outline because it divides the solution into a series of sequential steps:

Decomposition Outline

1. Read the terrain data into an array.

2. Determine and print the location of the peaks.

Step 1 involves reading the data file and storing the information in a two-dimensional array. Step 2 is a loop that evaluates all potential peaks and prints their locations if they are determined to be real peaks. We will write a boolean function to determine whether a location is a peak.

Refinement in Pseudocode

```
main:   read nrows and ncols from the data file
        read the terrain data into an array
        set i to 1
        while i <= nrows - 2
          set j to 1
          while j <= ncols- 2
            if (ispeak(grid,i,j))
               print peak location
            increment j by 1
          increment i by 1
peak:
        if ((grid[i-1][j]<grid[i][j]) &&
            (grid[i+1][j]<grid[i][j]) &&
            (grid[i][j-1]<grid[i][j]) &&
            (grid[i][j+1]<grid[i][j]))
            return true;
        else
            return false;
```

The steps in the pseudocode are now detailed enough to convert to C++:

```cpp
/*-------------------------------------------------------------*/
/*  Program chapter7_2                                         */
/*                                                             */
/*  This program determines the locations of                  */
/*  peaks in an elevation grid of data.                       */

#include <fstream>
#include <string>
using namespace std;

int const N = 25;

// Function prototypes.
bool ispeak(double grid[][N], int r, int c);

int main()
{
   //  Declare objects.
   int nrows, ncols;
   double elevation[N][N];
   string filename;
   ifstream file1;

   //  Prompt user for file name and open file for input.
   cout << "Enter the name of the input file.\n";
   cin >> filename;
   file1.open(filename.c_str());
   if(file1.fail())
   {
     cerr << "Error opening input file\n";
     return 0;
   }
   file1 >> nrows >> ncols;
   if(nrows > N || ncols > N)
   {
     cerr << "Grid is too large, adjust program.";
     return 0;
   }
   //  Read information from data file into array.
   for (int i=0; i<=nrows-1; i++)
   {
     for (int j=0; j<=ncols-1; j++)
     {
        file1 >> elevation[i][j];
     }
   }
```

```
        // Determine and print peak locations.
        cout << "Top left point defined as row 0, column 0 \n";
        for (int i=1; i<=nrows-2; i++)
        {
           for (int j=1; j<=ncols-2; j++)
           {
              if(ispeak(elevation, i, j))
              {
                   cout << "Peak at row: " << i
                        << " column: " << j << endl;
              }
           }
        }
        // Exit program.
        return 0;
}
bool ispeak(double grid[][N], int i, int j)
{
   if ((grid[i-1][j]<grid[i][j]) &&
       (grid[i+1][j]<grid[i][j]) &&
       (grid[i][j-1]<grid[i][j]) &&
       (grid[i][j+1]<grid[i][j]))
        return true;
   else
        return false;
}
/*----------------------------------------------------------*/
```

5. TESTING

The following output was printed using a data file that corresponds to the hand example (recall that this file must contain a special first line that specifies the number of rows and columns in the elevation data):

```
Top Left point defined as row 0, column 0
Peak at row: 2 column: 1
Peak at row: 2 column: 5
Peak at row: 4 column: 3
```

Modify!

Modify the peak-finding program as follows:

1. Print a count of the number of peaks in the grid.

Modify!

2. Print the location of valleys instead of peaks. Assume that a valley is a point with an elevation lower than the four surrounding elevations. Write a boolean function named isvalley to be called by your program.

3. Find and print the location and elevation of the highest point and the lowest point in the elevation data. Write a function named extremes to be called by your program.

4. Assuming that the distance between points in a vertical and horizontal direction is 100 feet, give the location of the peaks in feet from the lower left corner of the grid.

5. Modify the function ispeak() to use all eight neighboring points in determining a peak instead of only four neighboring points.

 7.3 *vector* **Class Revisited**

vector of *vectors*

The **vector** class can be used to model a two-dimensional array by defining a *vector* **of** *vectors* of a defined data type, as in:

```
vector< vector<double> > v1(row_size, col_size);
```

 The space between the last two > > characters is required. The desired row size and column size are specified insides parentheses, separated with a comma. Consider the following example:

```
#include<iostream>
#include<vector>
using namespace std;

int main()
{
  vector< vector<double> > v1(10, 5);
  cout << "The row size of v1 is " << v1.size() << endl;
  cout << "The column size of v1 is " << v1[0].size() << endl;
  return 0;
}
```

The output generated by this program is

```
The row size of v1 is 10
The column size of v1 is 5
```

Member functions of the *vector* class can be applied to the row vectors of a two-dimensional vector.

To illustrate using the *vector* class to implement a two dimensional array and passing a two dimensional *vector* as an argument to a function, we rewrite program chapter7_2 using the *vector* class:

```
/*-------------------------------------------------------*/
/*   Program chapter7_3                                  */
/*                                                       */
/*   This program determines the locations of            */
/*   peaks in an elevation grid of data.                 */
/*   The vector class is used to store grid data.        */

#include <fstream>
#include <string>
#include <vector>
using namespace std;

// Function prototypes.
bool ispeak(vector< vector<double> >, int r, int c);

int main()
{
   //   Declare objects.
   int nrows, ncols;
   string filename;
   ifstream file1;

   // Prompt user for file name and open file for input.
   cout << "Enter the name of the input file.\n";
   cin >> filename;
   file1.open(filename.c_str());
   if(file1.fail())
   {
     cerr << "Error opening input file\n";
     return 0;
   }
   // Read grid size from file.
   file1 >> nrows >> ncols;

   // Define a vector to hold grid data.
   vector< vector<double> > elevation(nrows, ncols);

   //   Read information from data file into vector.
   for (int i=0; i<=nrows-1; i++)
   {
     for (int j=0; j<=ncols-1; j++)
     {
        file1 >> elevation[i][j];
     }
   }

   //   Determine and print peak locations.
    cout << "Top left point defined as row 0, column 0 \n";
    for (int i=1; i<=nrows-2; i++)
```

```
    {
      for (int j=1; j<=ncols-2; j++)
      {
         if(ispeak(elevation, i, j))
         {
                cout << "Peak at row: " << i
                     << " column: " << j << endl;
         }
      }
    }
    // Exit program.
    return 0;
}
bool ispeak(vector< vector<double> > grid, int i, int j)
{
  if ((grid[i-1][j]<grid[i][j]) &&
      (grid[i+1][j]<grid[i][j]) &&
      (grid[i][j-1]<grid[i][j]) &&
      (grid[i][j+1]<grid[i][j]))
      return true;
  else
      return false;
}
/*-----------------------------------------------------------*/
```

Using the *vector* class, we can define the elevation *vector* after we have input the actual size of the grid. Standard array notation can be used to access elements within the vector. The

```
#include<vector>
```

compiler directive must be added to our program in order to use the vector class. A run of our program produces the same output as program chapter7_2.

7.4 Matrices*

matrix

A **matrix** is a set of numbers arranged in a rectangular grid with rows and columns, as shown in the following matrix with four rows and three columns, whose size is also specified as 4×3:

$$A = \begin{bmatrix} -1 & 0 & 0 \\ 1 & 1 & 0 \\ 1 & -2 & 3 \\ 0 & 2 & 1 \end{bmatrix}.$$

Note that the values within a matrix are written within large brackets.

In mathematical notation, matrices are usually given names with uppercase boldface letters. To refer to individual elements in the matrix, the row and column number are used, with both the row and column numbers starting with the value 1. In formal mathematical notation, the uppercase name refers to the entire matrix, and the lowercase name with subscrips refer to

square matrix

a specific element. Thus, by using the matrix **A**, the value of $a_{3,2}$ is -2. If a matrix has the same number of rows and columns, it is a **square matrix.**

A two-dimensional array can be used to store a matrix, but we must be careful translating equations in matrix notation into C++ statements because of the difference in subscripting. Matrix notation assumes that the row and column numbers begin with the value 1, whereas C++ statements assume that the row and column offsets of a two-dimensional array begin with the value 0.

Matrix operations are frequently used in engineering problem solutions, so we now present common operations with matrices. C++ statements for performing some of the operations are included; the problems at the end of the chapter relate to developing C++ statements for the remaining operations.

Determinant

determinant

The **determinant** of a matrix is a value computed from the entries in the matrix. Determinants have various applications in engineering, including computing inverses and solving systems of simultaneous equations. For a 2×2 matrix A, the determinant is defined as

$$|A| = a_{1,1}a_{2,2} - a_{2,1}a_{1,2}.$$

Therefore, the determinant of A is equal to 8 for the following matrix:

$$A = \begin{bmatrix} 1 & 3 \\ -1 & 5 \end{bmatrix}.$$

For a 3×3 matrix A, the determinant is defined to be the following:

$$|A| = a_{1,1}a_{2,2}a_{3,3} + a_{1,2}a_{2,3}a_{3,1} + a_{1,3}a_{2,1}a_{3,2} - a_{3,1}a_{2,2}a_{1,3}$$
$$- a_{3,2}a_{2,3}a_{1,1} - a_{3,3}a_{2,1}a_{1,2}.$$

If A is the matrix

$$A = \begin{bmatrix} 1 & 3 & 0 \\ -1 & 5 & 2 \\ 1 & 2 & 1 \end{bmatrix},$$

then $|A|$ is equal to $5 + 6 + 0 - 0 - 4 - (-3)$, or 10.

A more involved process is necessary for computing determinants of matrices with more than three rows and columns. This process is discussed in the problems at the end of this chapter.

Transpose

transpose

The **transpose** of a matrix is a new matrix in which the rows of the original matrix are the columns of the new matrix. We use a superscript T after a matrix name to refer to the transpose. For example, consider the following matrix and its transpose:

$$B = \begin{bmatrix} 2 & 5 & 1 \\ 7 & 3 & 8 \\ 4 & 5 & 21 \\ 16 & 13 & 0 \end{bmatrix}, \quad B^T = \begin{bmatrix} 2 & 7 & 4 & 16 \\ 5 & 3 & 5 & 13 \\ 1 & 8 & 21 & 0 \end{bmatrix}.$$

If we consider a couple of the elements, we see that the value in position (3, 1), has now moved to position (1, 3) and that the value in position (4, 2) has now moved to position (2, 4). In fact, we have interchanged the row and column offset so that we are moving the value in position (i, j) to position (j, i). Also, note that the size of the transpose is different from the size of the original matrix unless the original is a square matrix (i.e., a matrix with the same number of rows as columns).

We now develop a function that generates the transpose of a matrix. The formal arguments of the function must include two-dimensional arrays that represent the original matrix and the matrix that is to contain the transpose of the original matrix. To allow some flexibility with this function, we assume that symbolic constants have been defined that specify the number of rows and the number of columns in the original matrix; these symbolic constants are *NROWS* and *NCOLS*. Note that the function does not return a value; hence, the return type is void. Note also that the symbolic constants *NROWS* and *NCOLS* must be defined in a program that uses this function:

```
/*----------------------------------------------------*/
/*   This function generates a matrix transpose.    */
/*   NROWS and NCOLS are symbolic constants         */
/*   that must be defined in the calling program.   */

void transpose(int b[][NCOLS], int bt[][NROWS])
{
   //   Declare objects.

   //   Transfer values to the transpose matrix.
   for (int i=0; i<=NROWS-1; i++)
   {
      for (int j=0; j<=NCOLS-1; j++)
      {
         bt[j][i] = b[i][j];
      }
   }

   //   Void return.
   return;
}
/*----------------------------------------------------*/
```

Matrix Addition and Subtraction

The addition (or subtraction) of two matrices is performed by adding (or subtracting) the elements in corresponding positions in the matrices. Therefore, matrices that are added (or subtracted) must be of the same size; the result of the operation is another matrix of the same size. Consider the following matrices:

$$A = \begin{bmatrix} 2 & 5 & 1 \\ 0 & 3 & -1 \end{bmatrix}, \quad B = \begin{bmatrix} 1 & 0 & 2 \\ -1 & 4 & -2 \end{bmatrix}.$$

Several matrix sums and differences follow:

$$A + B = \begin{bmatrix} 3 & 5 & 3 \\ -1 & 7 & -3 \end{bmatrix}, \quad A - B = \begin{bmatrix} 1 & 5 & -1 \\ 1 & -1 & 1 \end{bmatrix},$$

$$B - A = \begin{bmatrix} -1 & -5 & 1 \\ -1 & 1 & -1 \end{bmatrix}.$$

Matrix Multiplication

Matrix
multiplication

Matrix multiplication is not computed by multiplying corresponding elements of the two matrices. The value in position $c_{i,j}$ of the product C of two matrices A and B is the product of row i of the first matrix and column j of the second matrix:

$$c_{i,j} = \sum_{k=1}^{n} a_{i,k} b_{k,j}.$$

The product of row i and column j requires that the row i and the column j have the same number of elements. Therefore, the first matrix (A) must have the same number of elements in each row as there are in the columns of the second matrix (B). Thus, if A and B both have five rows and five columns, their product has five rows and five columns. Furthermore, for these matrices, we can compute both AB and BA, but, in general, they will not be equal.

If A has two rows and three columns and B has three rows and three columns, the product AB will have two rows and three columns. To illustrate, consider the following matrices:

$$A = \begin{bmatrix} 2 & 5 & 1 \\ 0 & 3 & -1 \end{bmatrix}, \quad B = \begin{bmatrix} 1 & 0 & 2 \\ -1 & 4 & -2 \\ 5 & 2 & 1 \end{bmatrix}.$$

The first element in the product $C = AB$ is

$$\begin{aligned} c_{1,1} &= \sum_{k=1}^{3} a_{1,k} b_{k,1} \\ &= a_{1,1} b_{1,1} + a_{1,2} b_{2,1} + a_{1,3} b_{3,1} \\ &= 2(1) + 5(-1) + 1(5) \\ &= 2. \end{aligned}$$

Similarly, we can compute the rest of the elements in the product of A and B:

$$AB = C = \begin{bmatrix} 2 & 22 & -5 \\ -8 & 10 & -7 \end{bmatrix}.$$

In this example, we cannot compute BA, because B does not have the same number of elements in each row as A has in each column.

An easy way to decide whether a matrix product exists is to write the sizes of the two matrices side by side. If the two inside numbers are the same, the product exists; the size of the product is determined by the two outside numbers. To illustrate, in the previous example, the size of A is 2×3 and the size of B is 3×3. Therefore, if we want to compute AB, we write the sizes side by side:

$$2 \times 3 \quad 3 \times 3$$

The two inner numbers are both the value 3, so AB exists, and its size is determined by the two outer numbers, 2×3. If we want to compute BA we again write the sizes side by side:

$$3 \times 3 \quad 2 \times 3$$

The two inner numbers are not the same, so BA does not exist.

We now present a function to compute the product $C = AB$. In this function, the arrays are each of size $N \times N$, where N is a symbolic constant.

```
/*--------------------------------------------------------------*/
/*   This function performs a matrix multiplication    */
/*   of two NxN matrices using sums of products.       */
/*   N is a symbolic constant that must be defined     */
/*   within the scope of the function.                 */

void matrix_mult(int a[][N], int b[][N], int c[][N])
{

    //  Compute sums of products.
    for (int i=0; i<=N-1; i++)
    {
        for (int j=0; j<=N-1; j++)
        {
            c[i][j] = 0;
            for (int k=0; k<=N-1; k++)
            {
                c[i][j] += a[i][k]*b[k][j];
            }
        }
    }
    //  Void return.
    return;
}
/*--------------------------------------------------------------*/
```

Practice!

Use the matrices A, B, and C presented next to evaluate by hand the expressions in these problems. Then write programs to test your answers using the functions developed in this section. The functions are available in a file *matrix.cpp* on the instructor's resource CD.

$$A = \begin{bmatrix} 2 & 1 \\ 0 & -1 \\ 3 & 0 \end{bmatrix}, \quad B = \begin{bmatrix} -2 & 2 \\ -1 & 5 \end{bmatrix},$$

$$C = \begin{bmatrix} 3 & 2 \\ -1 & -2 \\ 0 & 2 \end{bmatrix}$$

Practice!

1. $|B|$

2. $C^T + A^T$

3. AB

4. $B(C^T)$

5. $(CB)C^T$

The problems at the end of the chapter use the matrix operations discussed in this section and also define additional matrix operations.

7.5 Numerical Technique: Solution to Simultaneous Equations*

The need to solve a system of simultaneous equations occurs frequently in engineering problems. A number of methods exist for solving a system of equations, and each method has

Gauss elimination
simultaneous linear
equations

its advantages and disadvantages. In this section, we present the **Gauss elimination** method of solving a set of **simultaneous linear equations;** the equations are called linear equations because the equations contain only linear (degree-1) terms such as x, y, and z. However, before we present the details of this technique, we first present a graphical interpretation of the solution to a set of equations.

Graphical Interpretation

A linear equation with two variables, such as $2x - y = 3$, defines a straight line and is often written in the form $y = mx + b$, where m represents the slope of the line and b represents the y-intercept. Thus, $2x - y = 3$ can also be written as $y = 2x - 3$. If we have two linear equations, they can represent two different lines that intersect in a single point, they can represent two parallel lines that never intersect, or they can represent the same line; these possibilities are shown in Figure 7.1.

Equations that represent two intersecting lines can be easily identified because they will have different slopes, as in $y = 2x - 3$ and $y = -x + 3$. Equations that represent two parallel lines will have the same slope, but different y-intercepts, as in $y = 2x - 3$ and $y = 2x + 1$. Equations that represent the same line have the same slope and y-intercept, as in $y = 2x - 3$ and $3y = 6x - 9$.

If a linear equation contains three variables, x, y, and z, then it represents a plane in three-dimensional space. If we have two equations with three variables, they can represent two planes that intersect in a straight line, they can represent two parallel planes, or they can represent the same plane; these possibilities are shown in Figure 7.2. If we have three equations with three variables, the three planes can intersect in a single point, they can intersect in a plane, they can have no common intersection point, or they can represent the same plane. Examples of the possibilities that exist if the three equations define three different planes are shown in

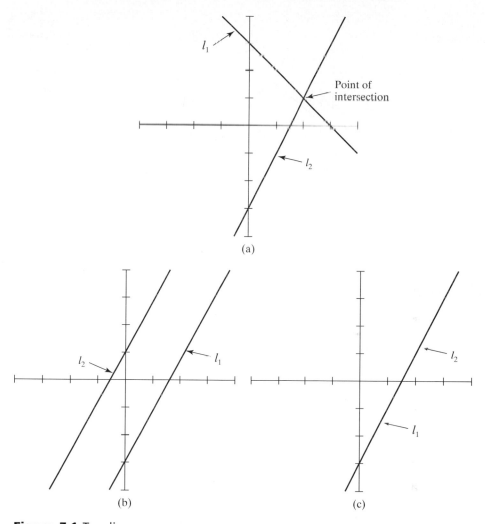

Figure 7.1 Two lines.

Figure 7.3. These ideas can be extended to more than three variables, although it is harder to visualize the corresponding situations.

hyperplane   We call the set of points defined by an equation with more than three variables a **hyperplane.** In general, we consider a set of m linear equations that contain n unknowns, where each equation defines a hyperplane that is not identical to another hyperplane in the set of equations. If $m < n$ then the system is underspecified, and a unique solution does not exist. If $m = n$, then a unique solution will exist if none of the equations represents parallel hyperplanes. If $m > n$, then the system is overspecified, and a unique solution does not exist. A set of

system of equations   equations is also called a **system of equations.** A system with a unique solution is called a
nonsingular   **nonsingular** system of equations, and a system with no unique solution is called a singular set of equations.

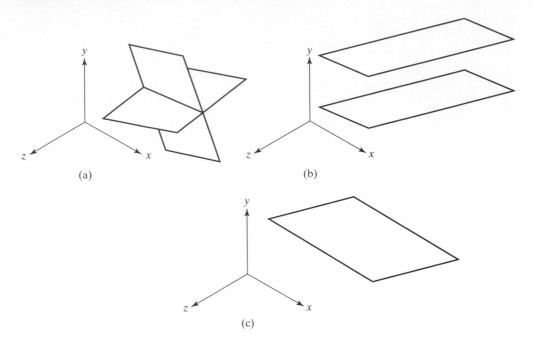

(a)   (b)

(c)

Figure 7.2 Two planes.

As a specific example, consider the following system of equations:

$$3x + 2y - z = 10,$$
$$-x + 3y + 2z = 5,$$
$$x - y - z = -1.$$

The solution to this set of equations is the point $(-2, 5, -6)$. Substitute these values in each of the questions to confirm that this point is a solution to the set of equations.

The material in the previous section on matrices is not required for the development of the solution presented in this section. However, if you did cover that material, it is interesting to observe that a system of linear equations can be expressed in terms of a matrix multiplication. To illustrate, let the information in the previous equations be expressed using the following matrices:

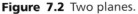

$$A = \begin{bmatrix} 3 & 2 & -1 \\ -1 & 3 & 2 \\ 1 & -1 & -1 \end{bmatrix}, \quad X = \begin{bmatrix} x \\ y \\ z \end{bmatrix}, \quad B = \begin{bmatrix} 10 \\ 5 \\ -1 \end{bmatrix}.$$

Then, using matrix multiplication, we find that the system of equations can be written in the form

$$AX = B.$$

Go through the multiplication to convince yourself that this matrix equation yields the original set of equations.

In many engineering problems, we are interested in determining whether a common solution exists to a system of equations. If the common solution exists, then we want to

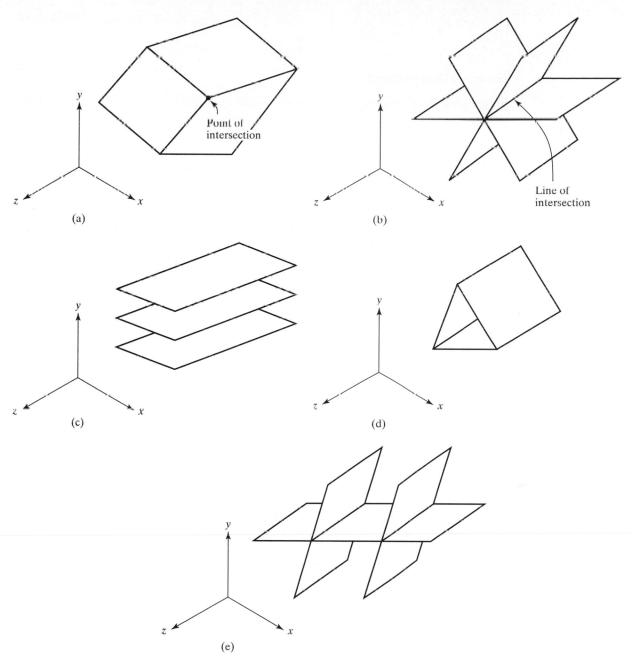

Figure 7.3 Three distinct planes.

determine it. In the next part of this section, we present the Gauss elimination technique for solving a set of simultaneous linear equations.

Gauss Ellimination

Before presenting a general description of the Gauss elimination technique, we illustrate the technique with a specific example, using the set of equations presented earlier:

$$3x + 2y - z = 10, \quad \text{(first equation)}$$

$$-x + 3y + 2z = 5, \quad \text{(second equation)}$$

$$x - y - z = -1. \quad \text{(third equation)}$$

elimination   The first step is an **elimination** step in which the first variable is eliminated from each equation that follows the first equation. This elimination is achieved by adding a scaled form of the first equation to each of the other equations. The term involving the first variable, x, in the second equation is $-x$. Therefore, if we multiply the first equation by $1/3$ and add it to equation 2, we obtain a new equation in which the x variable has been eliminated:

$$-x + 3y + 2z = 5 \quad \text{(second equation)}$$

$$x + \frac{2}{3}y - \frac{1}{3}z = \frac{10}{3} \quad \left(\text{first equation times } \frac{1}{3}\right),$$

$$\overline{0x + \frac{11}{3}y + \frac{5}{3}z = \frac{25}{3}} \quad \text{(sum).}$$

The modified set of equations is then

$$3x + 2y - z = 10,$$

$$0x + \frac{11}{3}y + \frac{5}{3}z = \frac{25}{3},$$

$$x - y - z = -1.$$

We now eliminate the first variable from the third equation, using a similar process:

$$x - y - z = -1 \quad \text{(third equation)},$$

$$-x - \frac{2}{3}y + \frac{1}{3}z = -\frac{10}{3} \quad \left(\text{first equation times } -\frac{1}{3}\right),$$

$$\overline{0x - \frac{5}{3}y - \frac{2}{3}z = -\frac{13}{3}} \quad \text{(sum).}$$

The modified set of equations is then

$$3x + 2y - z = 10,$$

$$0x + \frac{11}{3}y + \frac{5}{3}z = \frac{25}{3},$$

$$0x - \frac{5}{3}y - \frac{2}{3}z = -\frac{13}{3}.$$

We have now eliminated the first variable in all equations except for the first.

The next step is to eliminate the second variable in all equations except for the first and second, by adding the equations to a scaled form of the second equation:

$$0x - \frac{5}{3}y - \frac{2}{3}z = -\frac{13}{3} \quad \text{(third equation)},$$

$$0x + \frac{5}{3}y + \frac{25}{33}z = \frac{125}{33} \quad \left(\text{second equation times } \frac{5}{11}\right),$$

$$\overline{0x + 0y + \frac{3}{33}z = -\frac{18}{33}} \quad \text{(sum)}.$$

The modified set of equations is then

$$3x + 2y - z = 10,$$

$$0x + \frac{11}{3}y + \frac{5}{3}z = \frac{25}{3},$$

$$0x + 0y + \frac{3}{33}z = -\frac{18}{33}.$$

Because there are no equations following the third equation, this part of the algorithm is completed.

back substitution   We now perform a **back substitution** to determine the solution of the equations. The last equation has only one variable, so we can multiply the equation by a scale factor chosen to make the variable's coefficient equal to 1. Thus, we multiply the last equation by $\frac{33}{3}$, or 11, giving

$$0x + 0y + z = -6.$$

This value of z is substituted in the next-to-last equation, giving

$$0x + \frac{11}{3}y + \frac{5}{3}(-6) = \frac{25}{3}.$$

Reducing the equation so that all constant terms are on the right side, we have

$$0x + \frac{11}{3}y = \frac{55}{3}.$$

This equation has only one variable, so we now multiply it by a scale factor chosen to make the new coefficient equal to 1:

$$0x + y = 5.$$

We back up to the next equation, which is the last equation in this example:

$$3x + 2y - z = 10.$$

Substituting the values already determined, we have

$$3x + 2(5) - (-6) = 10,$$

or

$$3x = -6$$

Thus, the value of x is -2.

The Gauss elimination technique thus has two parts: elimination and back substitution. First, the equations are modified such that the kth variable is eliminated in all equations following the kth equation. Then, starting with the last equation, we compute the value of the last variable. Next, using this value and the next-to-last equation, we compute the value of the next-to-last variable. This back substitution continues until we have determined the values of

ill conditioned   all the variables. The system is **ill conditioned** or does not have a unique solution if all the coefficients for a variable are zero or are very close to zero.

pivoting   A process called **pivoting** can be applied to improve the accuracy of Gauss elimination. Row pivoting involves reordering the rows before perfoming Gauss elimination, and column pivoting involves reordering the columns before performing the process. Complete pivoting involves reordering both rows and columns. These processes are discussed in the problems at the end of the chapter.

Practice!

Use the Gauss elimination numerical technique to find the solution of the following sets of simultaneous linear equations:

1. $-2x + y = -3$
   $x + y = 3$

2. $3x + 5y + 2z = 8$
   $2x + 3y - z = 1$
   $x - 2y - 3z = -1$

7.6 Problem Solving Applied: Electrical Circuit Analysis*

The analysis of an electrical circuit frequently involves finding the solution of a set of simultaneous equations. These equations are often derived using either current equations that describe the currents entering and leaving a node or voltage equations that describe the voltages around mesh loops in the circuit. For example, consider the circuit shown in Figure 7.4. The equations

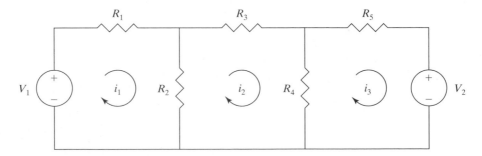

Figure 7.4 Circuit with two voltage sources.

that describe the voltages around the three loops are the following:

$$-V_1 + R_1 i_1 + R_2(i_1 - i_2) = 0,$$
$$R_2(i_2 - i_1) + R_3 i_2 + R_4(i_2 - i_3) = 0,$$
$$R_4(i_3 - i_2) + R_5 i_3 + V_2 = 0.$$

If we assume that the values of the resistors (R_1, R_2, R_3, R_4, and R_5) and the voltage sources (V_1 and V_2) are known, then the unknowns in the system of equations are the mesh currents (i_1, i_2, and i_3). We can then rearrange the system of equations to the following form:

$$(R_1 + R_2)i_1 - R_2 i_2 + 0 i_3 = V_1,$$
$$-R_2 i_1 + (R_2 + R_3 + R_4)i_2 - R_4 i_3 = 0,$$
$$0 i_1 - R_4 i_2 + (R_4 + R_5)i_3 = -V_2.$$

Write a program that allows the user to enter the values of the five resistors and the values of the two voltage sources. The program should then compute the three mesh currents.

1. PROBLEM DESCRIPTION

Compute the three mesh currents in the circuit shown in Figure 7.4.

2. INPUT/OUTPUT DESCRIPTION

The I/O diagram shows that the resistor values and the voltage values are the input values. The three mesh currents are the output values.

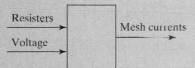

3. HAND EXAMPLE

By using the resistor values and the voltage values, a system of three equations can be defined, using this rearranged set of equations from the definition of the problem:

$$(R_1 + R_2)i_1 - R_2 i_2 + 0 i_3 = V_1,$$
$$-R_2 i_1 + (R_2 + R_3 + R_4)i_2 - R_4 i_3 = 0,$$
$$0 i_1 - R_4 i_2 + (R_4 + R_5)i_3 = -V_2.$$

For example, suppose that each of the resistor values is 1 ohm and that both of the voltage sources are 5 volts. Then the corresponding set of equations is the following:

$$2i_1 - i_2 + 0i_3 = 5,$$
$$-i_1 + 3i_2 - i_3 = 0,$$
$$0i_1 - i_2 + 2i_3 = -5.$$

Once the system of equations is determined, the solution follows the steps illustrated in the hand example in the previous section. For this set of equations, the solution is $i_1 = 2.5$, $i_2 = 0$, and $i_3 = -2.5$.

4. ALGORITHM DEVELOPMENT

We first develop the decomposition outline, because it breaks the solution into a series of sequential steps:

Decomposition Outline

1. Read the resistor values and the voltage values.

2. Specify the coefficients for the system of equations.

3. Perform Gauss elimination to determine currents.

4. Print currents.

In step 1 we read the information necessary to specify the circuit values, and in step 2 we use this information to specify the coefficients for the system of equations. Then, in step 3, we develop the details of the elimination and back-substitution steps. To keep the main function short and readable, functions are used for both the elimination and the back substitution. The structure chart for this solution was used in Figure 4.1.

The coefficients of the simultaneous equations are stored in a two-dimensional array; the solution is stored in a one-dimensional array. The variable index indicates which variable is being eliminated in the elimination function; this variable ranges from 0 to $n - 1$ to match the subscripting in C++.

The algorithm for Gauss elimination is a difficult algorithm to describe in pseudocode because of the detailed subscripting that must be specified. Go through this pseudocode with the hand example to be sure that you are comfortable with the subscript handling.

```
Refinement in Pseudocode
main:    read resistor values and voltage values
         specify array coefficients, a[i][j]
         set index to zero
         while index <= n - 2
                eliminate(a,n,index)
                increment index by 1
```

```
                    back_substitute(a,n,soln)
                    print current values
eliminate(a,n,index):
            set row to index +1
            while row <= n-1
                                  -a[row][index]
                    set scale_factor to ─────────────
                                   a[index][index]
                    set a[row][index] to zero
                    set col to index +1
                    while col <= n
                            add a[index][col] · scale_factor
                                  to a[row][col]
                            increment col by 1
                    increment row by 1
back_substitute(a,n,soln):
                                  a[n-1][n]
            set soln[n-1] to ─────────────
                                 a[n-1][n-1]
            set row to n-2
            while row >= 0
                    set col to n-1
                    while col >= row +1
                            subtract soln[col] · a[row][col]
                                  from a[row][n]
                            subtract 1 from col
                                           a[row][n]
                    set soln[row] to ───────────
                                          a[row][row]
                    subtract 1 from row
```

Once we are comfortable with the pseudocode, it is relatively straightforward to convert it to C++:

```
/*-------------------------------------------------------*/
/*   Program chapter7_3                                   */
/*                                                        */
/*   This program uses Gauss elimination to              */
/*   determine the mesh currents for a circuit.          */

#include <iostream>
using namespace std;

// Define global constant for number of unknowns.
const int N = 3;

//  Declare function prototypes.
void eliminate(double a[][N+1], int n, int index);
void back_substitute(double a[][N+1],
                     int n, double soln[N]);
int main()
{
```

```
   //  Declare objects.
   double r1, r2, r3, r4, r5, v1, v2,
          a[N][N+1], soln[N];

   //  Get user input.
   cout << "Enter resistor values in ohms: \n"
        << "(R1, R2, R3, R4, R5) \n";
   cin >> r1 >> r2 >> r3 >> r4 >> r5;
   cout << "Enter voltage values in volts: \n"
        << "(V1, V2) \n";
   cin >> v1 >> v2;

   //  Specify equation coefficients.
   a[0][0] = r1 + r2;
   a[0][1] = a[1][0] = -r2;
   a[0][2] = a[2][0] = a[1][3] = 0;
   a[1][1] = r2 + r3 + r4;
   a[1][2] = a[2][1] = -r4;
   a[2][2] = r4 + r5;
   a[0][3] = v1;
   a[2][3] = -v2;

   //  Perform elimination step.
   for (int index=0; index<=N-2; index++)
   {
     eliminate(a,N,index);
   }

   //  Perform back substitution step.
   back_substitute(a,N,soln);

   //  Print solution.
   cout << "\nSolution: \n";
   for (int i=0; i<=N-1; i++)
   {
     cout << "Mesh Current " << i+1 << ": "<< soln[i] << endl;
   }

   //  Exit program.
   return 0;
}
/*--------------------------------------------------*/
/*  This function performs the elimination step.  */

void eliminate(double a[][N+1], int n, int index)
{
   //  Declare objects.
   double scale_factor;

   //  Eliminate object from equations.
   for (int row=index+1; row<=n-1; row++)
```

```
      {
          scale_factor = -a[row][index]/a[index][index];
          a[row][index] = 0;
          for (int col=index+1; col<=n; col++)
          {
              a[row][col] += a[index][col]*scale_factor;
          }
      }

      // Void return.
      return;
}
/*-------------------------------------     -------------*/
/*  This function performs the back substitution.  */

void back_substitute(double a[][N+1], int n,
                     double soln[])
{
      // Perform back substitution in each equation.
      soln[n-1] = a[n-1][n]/a[n-1][n-1];
      for (int row=n-2; row>=0; row--)
      {
          for (int col=n-1; col>=row+1; col--)
          {
              a[row][n] -= soln[col]*a[row][col];
          }
          soln[row] = a[row][n]/a[row][row];
      }

      // Void return.
      return;
}
/*----------------------------------------------------*/
```

To handle larger systems of equations, the symbolic constant N must be changed; the steps in the Gauss elimination do not need any modifications. The program interaction using the data from the hand example is as follows:

```
Enter resistor values in ohms:
(R1, R2, R3, R4, R5)
1 1 1 1 1
Enter voltage values in volts:
(V1, V2)
5 5

Solution:
Mesh Current 1: 2.5
Mesh Current 2: 0
Mesh Current 3: -2.5
```

The program assumes that the system of equations has a solution, which means that none of the equations represents the same equation or parallel equations. Modifications to the program to check for these conditions could be added with additional statements or functions.

Modify!

Use the program developed in this section to answer the following questions.

1. Determine the mesh currents if all five resistors are 5 ohms and both voltage sources are 10 volts.

2. Verify your answer in Problem 1 by using matrix multiplication as discussed in this section. (This problem assumes that you covered the previous section on matrices and vectors.)

3. Determine the mesh currents if the resistors have the values of 2, 8, 6, 6, and 4 ohms and the voltage sources have the values of 40 and 20 volts.

4. Verify your answer from Problem 3 by substituting back in the original set of three equations.

7.7   Higher Dimensional Arrays*

C++ allows arrays to be defined with more than two dimension. For example, the following statement defines a **three-dimensional array:**

```
int b[3][4][2];
```

The three offsets, which are necessary to specify a specific element, correspond to the x-, y-, and z-coordinates if you position the array at the origin of a three-dimensional space, as shown in Figure 7.5. Thus, the position that is shaded corresponds to $b[2][0][1]$.

Most engineering problems that need arrays can be solved using one-dimensional or two-dimensional arrays. However, there are occasionally problems that are good candidates for using higher dimensional arrays. These problems typically involve data that are specified by several parameters; in addition, the parameters either are integers that are sequential or parameters that can easily be converted into sequential parameters. For example, suppose that a set of data representing temperature measurements is taken from the floor of a large chemical reaction chamber. Furthermore, this set of temperatures is taken at specified intervals of time during a chemical reaction. In this case, we might choose to use a three-dimensional array, using the first offset to indicate a specific time, and the other two offset to indicate the location within the floor. The offsets would need to begin with zero to match the requirements of C++ offsets. The offsets [3][2][5] would then specify the value taken at the fourth time value and at position [2][5] in the grid of temperatures.

Arrays with more than three offsets are seldom used because it is difficult to visualize them. However, a simple way to visualize arrays with more than three offsets can be developed.

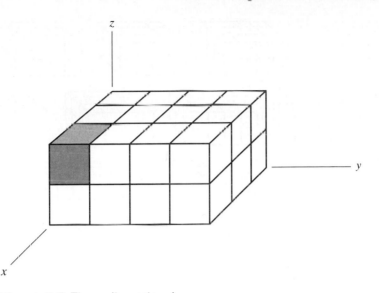

Figure 7.5 Three-dimensional array.

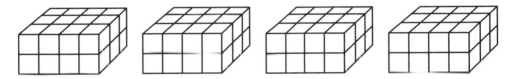

Figure 7.6 Four-dimensional array.

First, consider a three-dimensional array to be a building. The building has floors and a rectangular grid of rooms on each floor. Assume that each room can contain a single value. The three-dimensional array representing the building uses three offsets to specify a room; the first offset is the floor number, and the other two offsets specify the row and column number of the room on the specified floor.

A **four-dimensional array** is a row of buildings, as shown in Figure 7.6. The first offset specifies the building, and the remaining three offsets specify the room in the building.

A **five-dimensional array** is a block of buildings, as shown in Figure 7.7. The first two offsets specify the building in the block, and the remaining three offsets specify the room in the building.

This analogy could continue with a row of blocks, a city of blocks, a group of cities, a state of cities, and so on. Although we have shown you how to visualize higher dimensional arrays, we also want to caution you about using higher order arrays. Higher order arrays have a lot of overhead related to the offsetting; not only are there extra offsets required, but extra loops are necessary each time you want to work with groups of values in the array. In general, higher order arrays also complicate the debugging and maintenance of the program. Therefore, higher order arrays should be used only when they simplify the overall visualization of the problem and the steps to solve it.

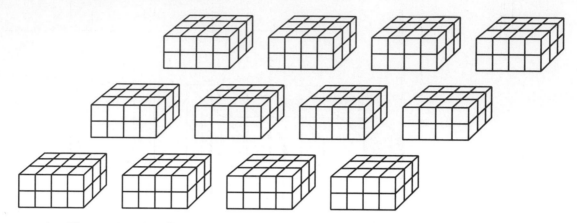

Figure 7.7 Five-dimensional array.

SUMMARY

An array is a data structure often used to store engineering data that are analyzed in a program. If the data are best represented by a table or grid of information, a two-dimensional array is used. Many examples were developed in this chapter to illustrate definitions, initializations, computations and input and output with two-dimensional arrays, and two-dimensional arrays as function parameters. The Gauss elimination technique for solving a system of simultaneous linear equations was also presented, and a C++ program developed to implement this technique. The *vector* class was used in an example to model a two-dimensional array.

Key Terms

column offset	pivoting
declared column size	row offset
determinant	simultaneous linear equations
Gauss elimination	square matrix
hyperplane	subarray
ill conditioned	system of equations
inner product	transpose
matrix	two-dimensional array
matrix multiplication	vector of vectors
nonsingular	

C++ Statement Summary

Two-dimensional Array declaration:

```
double x[10][5];
```

Two-dimensional vector declaration:

```
vector< vector<double> > x(10,5);
```

Style **Notes**
_____

1. Use symbolic constants to declare the size of an array so that it is easy to modify.
2. In documentation, describe a two-dimensional array as a grid with rows and columns.
3. The objects i and j are commonly used as offsets for a two-dimensional array.

Debugging Notes
_____

1. The declared column size of an array must be specified in the formal parameter list and in the function prototype.
2. Be careful not to exceed the maximum offset value when referencing an element in a multidimensional array.
3. Be sure to enclose each offset in its own set of brackets when referencing elements of a multidimensional array.
4. When translating matrix notation to C++, remember that the first row and column in a matrix is referenced with the number 1, not 0.
5. Multidimensional matrices complicate the logic of a program and should be used only when they are necessary.

Problems
_____

Exam Practice!

Give the corresponding snapshots of memory after each of the following sets of statements is executed. Use ? to indicate an array element that is not initialized.

```
1.  int x[4][5];
    . . .
    for(int r=0; r<=3; r++)
      for(int c=0; c<=4; c++)
        x[r][c] = r + c;
2.  int x[4][5];
    for(int c=0; c<=4; c++)
      for(int r=0; r<=3; r++)
        x[r][c] = r;
```

Program Output

Problems 3 and 4 refer to the following statements:

```
int sum, k, i, j;
int x[4][4] = {{1,2,3,4}, {5,6,7,8}, {9,8,7,3}, {2,1,7,1}};
```

3. Give the value in sum after the following statements are executed.

```
sum = x[0][0];
for(int k=1; k<=3; k++)
  sum += x[k][k];
```

4. Give the value in sum after the following statements are executed.

```
sum = 0;
for(int i=1; i<=3; i++)
   for(int j=0; j<=3; j++)
      if(x[i][j] > x[i-1][j])
         sum++;
```

Programming Exercises

Power Plant Data.   The data file *power1.dat* contains a power plant output in megawatts over a period of 10 weeks. Each row of data contains 7 floating-point numbers that represent 1 week's data. In developing the following programs, use symbolic constants NROWS and NCOLS to represent the number of rows and columns in the array used to store the data.

5. Write a program to compute and print the average power output over this period. Also print the number of days with greater-than-average power output.

6. Write a program to print the day of the week and the number of the week on which the minimum power output occurred. If there are several days with the minimum power output, print the information for each of these days.

7. Write a function to compute the average of a specified column of a two dimensional array that has NROWS rows and NCOLS columns. The parameters should be the floating-point array and the desired column. Assume that the corresponding function prototype is

```
double col_ave(double x[]NCOLS],int col);
```

8. Write a program to print a report that lists the average power output for the first day of the week, then for the second day of the week, and so on. Print the information in the following format:

```
Day x: Average Power Output in Megawatts:   xxxx.xx
```

9. Write a function to compute the average of a specified row of a two-dimensional array that has NROWS rows and NCOLS columns. The parameters should be the floating-point array and the desired row. Assume that the corresponding function prototype is

```
double row_ave(double x[]NCOLS],int row);
```

10. Write a function to compute the average of a specified row of a two-dimensional vector. The parameters should be include the vector and the desired row. Assume that the corresponding function prototype is

```
double row_ave(vector< vector<double> > x, int row);
```

11. Write a program to print a report that lists the average power output for the first week, the second week, and so on. Print the information in the following format:

```
Week x: Average Power Output in Megawatts:   xxxx.xx
```

12. Write a program to compute and print the mean and variance of the power plant output data.

Temperature Distribution. The temperature distribution in a thin metal plate with constant (or isothermal) temperatures on each side can be modeled using a two-dimensional grid, as shown in Figure 7.8. Typically, the number of points in the grid are specified, as are the constant temperatures on the four sides. The temperatures of the interior points are usually initialized to zero, but they change according to the temperatures around them. Assume that the temperature of an interior point can be computed as the average of the four adjacent temperatures; the points shaded in Figure 7.8 represent the adjacent temperatures for the point labeled x in the grid. Each time that the temperature of an interior point changes, the temperatures of the points adjacent to it change. These changes continue until a thermal equilibrium is achieved and all temperatures become constant.

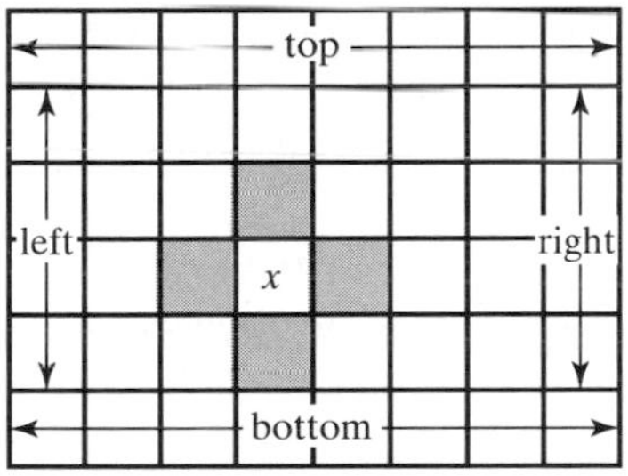

Figure 7.8 Temperature grid in a metal plate.

13. Write a program to model this temperature distribution for a grid with six rows and eight columns. Allow the user to enter the temperatures for the four sides. Use one grid to store the temperatures. Thus, when a point is updated, its new value is used to update the next point. Continue updating the points, moving across the rows until the temperature differences for all updates are less than a user-entered tolerance value. Use the *vector* class to implement the grid.
14. Modify the program generated in Problem 13 so that the updates are performed down the columns. Compare the equilibrium values for the two programs using different tolerance values. The equilibrium values should be very close for small tolerance values.
15. Modify the program in Problem 13 so that two grids are used and so that the program can perform the updates as if they all happen at the same time. Thus, all temperatures are updated using one set of grid values. The two grids are needed so that all the old temperatures are available to compute each new temperature.

Gauss Elimination. The accuracy of the Gauss elimination technique can be improved using a process called pivoting. To perform row pivoting, we first reorder the equations so that the equation with the largest absolute value for the first coefficient is the first equation. We then eliminate the first object from the equations that follow the first equation. Then, starting with the second equation, we reorder the equations such that the second equation has the largest coefficient (in absolute value) for the second object. We then eliminate the second object from all equations after the second equation. The process continues similarly for the rest of the objects. Assume that a symbolic constant N contains the number of equations.

16. Use the program developed in Section 7.4 as a guide to develop a function that receives a double array a of size N by $N+1$. A second parameter is a double array soln of size $N+1$. The function should solve the system of equations represented by array a, and return the solution in array *soln*. Assume that the corresponding function prototype is

    ```
    void gauss(double a[][N+1], double soln[N+1]);
    ```

17. Write a function that receives a two-dimensional array and a pivot value that specifies the coefficient of interest j. The function should then reorder all equations starting with the jth equation such that the jth equation will have the largest coefficient (in absolute value) in the jth position. Assume that the function can reference the size of the array as N by $N+1$, and that the corresponding function prototype is

    ```
    void pivot_r(double a[][N+1], int j);
    ```

18. Modify the function developed for Problem 16 so that the row pivoting is performed before each variable is eliminated. Use the function developed in Problem 17.

19. Column pivoting is performed in a similar fashion to row pivoting by exchanging columns such that the largest coefficient (in absolute value) will be in the position of interest. When columns are exchanged, it is important to keep track of the changes in the order of the objects. Write a function to perform column pivoting. Include parameters to specify changes in the order of the objects. Assume that the corresponding function prototype is

    ```
    void pivot_c(double a[][N+1], int j, int reorder k[N]);
    ```

20. Modify the function developed for Problem 16 so that column pivoting is performed before each object is eliminated. Use the function developed in Problem 19.

21. Modify the function developed for Problem 16 so that both row pivoting and column pivoting are performed before each object is eliminated. Use the functions developed in Problems 17 and 19.

Determinants.   The following problems define cofactors and minors of a square matrix and then use them to evaluate a determinant.

22. The **minor** of an element $a(i, j)$ of a matrix A is the determinant of the matrix obtained by removing the row and column to which the given element $a(i, j)$ belongs. Thus, if the original matrix has four rows and four columns, the minor is the determinant of a matrix with three rows and columns. Write a function to compute the minor of a square matrix with four rows and four columns. The input arguments should be the matrix A and the values of i and j. Assume that the corresponding function prototype is

    ```
    double minor(double a[][4], int i, int j);
    ```

23. A **cofactor** $A(i, j)$ of a matrix A is the product of the minor of $a(i, j)$ and the factor $(-1)i + j$. Write a function to compute a cofactor of a square matrix with four rows and four columns. The arguments should be the matrix A and the values of i and j. You may want to reference the function in problem 22. Assume that the corresponding function prototype is

```
double cofactor(double a[][4], int i, int j);
```

The determinant of a square matrix A can be computed in the following way:
(a) Select any column.
(b) Multiply each element in the column by its cofactor.
(c) Add the products obtained in step (b).

24. Write a function **det_c** to compute the determinant of a square matrix with four rows and four columns using this technique. You may want to reference the function developed in Problem 23. Assume that the corresponding function prototype is

```
double det_c(double a[][4]);
```

25. The determinant of a square matrix A can be computed in the following way:
(a) Select any row.
(b) Multiply each element in the row by its cofactor.
(c) Add the products obtained in step (b).

26. Write a function det_r to compute the determinant of a square matrix with four rows and four columns using this technique. You may want to reference the function developed in Problem 23. Assume that the corresponding function prototype is:

```
double det_r(double a[][4]);
```

CHAPTER 8

GRAND CHALLENGE:
Simulation Design of Advanced Composite Materials

Simulation has become recognized as the third paradigm of science, the first two being experimentation and theory. In some cases, it is the only approach available for further advancing knowledge. Experimentation may not be possible, due to size, speed, distance, dangers to health and safety, or the economics of conducting the experiments. In simulations, mathematical models of physical phenomena are translated into computer software that specifies how calculations are performed using input data that may include both experimental data and estimated values of unknown parameters in the mathematical models. By repeatedly running the software using different data and different parameter values, we attain an understanding of the phenomenon of interest.

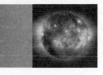

An Introduction to Classes

Chapter Outline

OBJECTIVES   This chapter introduces the `class` **mechanism,** a mechanism that allows programmers to define their own data types. We discuss how classes are defined. The building of a **rectangle class** illustrates the development of the **class declaration** and the **class implementation.** Class **data members** and **member functions,** including **constructor functions** and **accessor functions** are discussed along with keywords `public` and `private`. A program is developed to test the rectangle class and introduce **separate compilation.** A **UnitVector** `class` is developed to illustrate the use of `private` member functions, **class types as arguments to functions** and **class types as data members.** A program using classes is developed to aid in the design of **advanced composite materials.**

8.1 | Object-Based Programming with Classes

In the previous chapters we have used the built in data types supported by C++, including `int`, `double` and `char` to solve a variety of small problems. We have also used various `class` definitions from the Standard C++ library, including *ifstream* and *ofstream* to provide data types to support file input and output, and the *string* class to provide an easy to use data type for working with character data. Each of these classes includes a set of member functions that can be called by objects of that class. Object oriented programming languages such as C++ allow programmers to define their own `class` data types for use in application programs.

Many programming applications today require working with complex objects. Consider what is required to program even a simple video game. When writing a video game, a programmer needs to manipulate objects that represent the game characters and the backdrop of the game. Each of these graphical objects requires numerous fields of data for definition, and each object requires a set of rules, or functions, that define how the object can move, change and interact with other objects. An object oriented programming language allows a programmer to define new data types to represent game objects and define their rules of interaction.

In scientific programming, simulation is a powerful tool for the advancement of knowledge. In this chapter, for example, we develop a program to perform a simulation to aid in the design of a composite material. For this problem we are interested in calculating the rate of migration of particles. For our application a particle is defined as having a radius, a density, a magnitude and a position/direction. Our program will need to manipulate particle objects and calculate the migration rate of particles within a cylinder. An object based approach to this problem suggests that we define a new data type to represent a particle, and define rules, or functions, that define the behavior of particles within the simulation.

The ability to define a new data type to represent an object is beneficial in many ways. It insures that all programmers working on a particular application program are using the same physical definition of the object and that the objects are being manipulated in ways that are consistent with the rules that define the behavior of the object. Another benefit of defining new data types is that the implementation of the data type is hidden from the application program. Since the application program manipulates data objects via the member functions, changes to the implementation of the data type does not require changes to the application program. The design, development and testing of a new data type requires time, but once the implementation is complete, the new data type is reliable and as easy to use as a built in data type. This reduces the time required to develop and maintain application programs.

class definition
class declaration
class implementation

In C++ we use the keyword `class` to define a new data type. A **class definition** consists of two parts; the **class declaration** which provides the interface between the application program and the `class`, and the **class implementation.**

Class Declaration

In a `class` declaration, the name of the class is specified using the keyword `class`. The body of the `class` declaration is enclosed within braces and includes the type declaration statements for the **data members** of the `class`, and function prototypes for the **member functions.** The keywords `public` and `private` are used to restrict access to the `class` members. To illustrate how classes are defined, we will begin with the definition of a simple *rectangle* `class`. The internal representation of a rectangle requires four data members: an *x*-coordinate, a *y*-coordinate, a *width,* and a *height,* as illustrated in Figure 8.1.

data members
member functions

To begin with, our *rectangle* `class` will have only three member functions: one to set the value of a rectangle, one to move (translate) a rectangle in a plane, and one to return the area of the rectangle. We will add to the functionality of our `class` as we continue our discussion of member functions. We will now write a `class` declaration for our *rectangle* `class`. The declaration will be written in a file named *rectangle.h:*

```
/*-------------------------------------------------------------------*/
/*   Class declaration for the rectangle class.                    */
/*   Filename:  rectangle.h                                        */
```

```
class rectangle
{
public:
// Member function prototypes
void set_value(double x, double y, double w, double h);
void translate(double dx, double dy);
double area() const;

private:
// Declaration of data members;
double x_coord, y_coord, width, height;
};
/*-------------------------------------------------------------------*/
```

Notice that a semicolon is required to follow the body of the class declaration.

Our *rectangle* class has four private data members and three public member functions. The public member functions can be called by *rectangle* objects within a program to manipulate the objects. However, the keyword private restricts access to the data members. The private data members *x_coord*, *y_coord*, *width*, and *height* can be accessed only by the member functions *set_value()*, *translate()*, and *area()* of the *rectangle* class.

information hiding   They cannot be accessed within any other function. This is known as **information hiding.** Since the data members are private, the internal representation of the *rectangle* class is hidden from any program that uses it. This allows for changes to be made to the internal

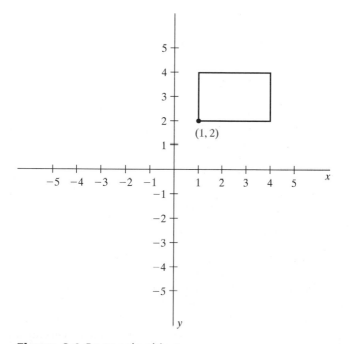

Figure 8.1 Rectangle object.

Style

representation of a `class` without affecting the application programs that use the `class`. Information hiding is fundamental to object-based programming. *It is recommended that all data members of a class be declared under the keyword* `private`.

Class Implementation

class implementation

scope resolution operator

To complete the definition of our *rectangle* `class`, we need to write a function definition for each of the member functions. This is called the **class implementation.** When writing the definition of a member function the **scope resolution operator** (::) is used in the function header. The :: operator is placed between the `class` name and the function name to identify the function as a member of the `class`. The implementation of our *rectangle* `class` follows:

```
/*-------------------------------------------------------------------*/
/*  Class implementation for the rectangle class.                    */
/*                                                                   */
void rectangle::set_value(double x, double y, double w, double h)
{
  // Set the value of the calling object.
  x_coord = x;
  y_coord = y;
  width = w;
  height = h;

  // Void return
  return;
}
void rectangle::translate(double dx, double dy)
{
  // Translate calling object
  x_coord += dx;
  y_coord += dy;

  // Void return
  return;
}
double rectangle::area() const
{
  // Return the area of the calling object.
  return(width*height);
}
/*-------------------------------------------------------------------*/
```

Notice that the member functions reference the `private` data members declared in the class declaration, even though these identifiers do not appear in the function header and are not defined as local objects inside the body of the function. A member function has access to all of the data members of its `class`. The values of the data members are provided by the object that calls the member function, referred to as the **calling object.**

calling object

The member function *set_value()* modifies all of the data members of the calling object by assigning values that are provided through the function header. The member function *translate()* modifies only the values of the data members *x_coord* and *y_coord*. The member function *area()* references the data members *width* and *height* to return the area of the calling object. However, this value-returning function does not, and should not, modify the values of any of the data members. The keyword const is appended to the end of the function prototype and the function header of the *area()* function to prevent the function from modifying the data members of the calling object. When the const modifier is used, any attempt to modifiy the value of one of the data members will result in a error reported by the compiler.

Style

Since all member functions have the ability to modify the data members of the calling object, it is good programming practice to use the keyword const in the definition of all member function that are not intended to modify the data members of the calling object.

With the introduction of the *rectangle* class, a program can declare objects of type *rectangle*, and these objects can call the member functions of the *rectangle* class as illustrated in the following program:

```
/*----------------------------------------------------   -------------*/
/*Program chapter 8.1                                                 */
/*This program illustrates use of the rectangle class.        */
#include<iostream>
#include "rectangle.h"
using namespace std;

int main()
{
  // Declare two rectangle objects.
  rectangle r1, r2;

  // Set the value of r1.
  r1.set_value(0,0,1.5,1.5);

  // Assign the value of r1 to r2.
  r2=r1;

  // Translate r2
  r2.translate(2,1);

  // Output the area of r2.
  cout << "Area of r2 is " << r2.area() << endl;
  return 0;
}
/*--------------------------------------------------------------*/
```

The output from this program is:

```
Area of r2 is 2.25
```

The assignment operator is used in the above example to assign the value of *r1* to the object *r2*. The assignment operator can only be used with class objects *of the same class type*. The

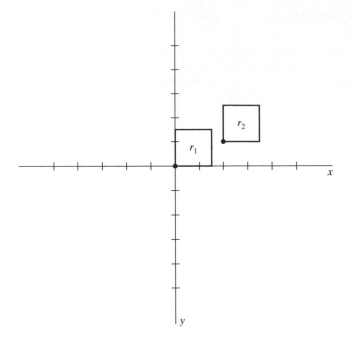

Figure 8.2 Rectangles r1 and r2.

memory snapshot after executing the statements in this program is the following:

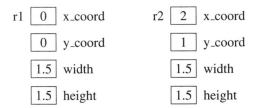

A diagram of the rectangles *r1* and *r2* is shown in Figure 8.2.

Practice!

Assume that the *rectangle* class declaration included the following function prototype:

```
void resize(double dw, double dh);
```

1. Write the function **header** for this function.

2. Where would the complete function definition be written, in the class declaration or the class implementation?

8.2   Member Functions

The member functions of a `class` define the operations that can be performed on an object, including the operation of initializing an object at the time the object is defined. Recall that we can initialize and object in a type declaration statement as follows:

```
double sum(0);
```

To allow the initialization of programmer-defined `class` objects, we need to include a special set of member functions, referred to as **constructor functions** in our class definition.

Constructor Functions

constructor
functions

A **constructor function** is a special member function used to initialize the data members of a `class` object. Constructor functions have three important properties:

1. A constructor is called automatically when a `class` object is defined.

2. The name of a constructor function is the name of the `class`.

3. No return value can be associated with a constructor function, not even `void`.

Since a constructor function has the same name as the `class`, all constructor functions in a `class` will have the same name. Overloading of constructor functions provides flexibility when initializing objects. There is no limit to the number of constructor functions that can be included in a `class` definition, as long as each function has a unique function signature.

default constructor

We will add two constructor functions to our *rectangle* `class`: a **default constructor** and a constructor with four formal parameters. The **default constructor** is called automatically whenever a rectangle object is defined in a declaration statement as follows:

```
rectangle r1; // Default constructor is called.
```

The data members of the object *r1* are initialized with values provided by the default constructor function. The constructor function with four formal parameters is called automatically whenever a *rectangle* object is defined in a declaration statement as follows:

```
rectangle r2(0,0,1,1); // Constructor with 4 parameters is called
```

The data members of the object *r2* are initialized with the values provided by the parameter list.

If a `class` definition does not include a constructor function, the system will provide a default constructor. However, if any constructors are included in a `class` definition, then a default constructor must also be included. When constructor functions are included in `class` definition, the function prototypes are added to the `class` declaration and the function definitions are added to the `class` implementation. The new definition of the *rectangle* `class` is as follows:

```
/*------------------------------------------------------------*/
/*   Rectangle class declaration.                          */
```

```cpp
class rectangle
{
public:
// Member function prototypes.

// Default constructor.
rectangle();

// Constructor with four formal parameters.
rectangle(double x, double y, double w, double h);

void set_value(double x, double y, double w, double h);
void translate(double dx, double dy);
double area() const;

private:
// Declaration of data members.
double x_coord, y_coord, width, height;
};
/*------------------------------------------------------------------*/

/*------------------------------------------------------------------*/
/*   Rectangle class implementation.                                */
/*                                                                  */
// Definition of default constructor.
rectangle::rectangle() : x_coord(0), y_coord(0), width(1), height(1)
{
}

// Definition of constructor with four parameters.
rectangle::rectangle(double x, double y, double w, double h) :
                     x_coord(x), y_coord(y), width(w), height(h)
{
}

void rectangle::set_value(double x, double y, double w, double h)
{
  // Set the value of the calling object.
  x_coord = x;
  y_coord = y;
  width = w;
  height = h;

  // Void return.
  return;
}
void rectangle::translate(double dx, double dy)
{
  // Translate calling object
  x_coord += dx;
  y_coord += dy;
```

```
  // Void return.
  return;
}
double rectangle::area() const
{
    return(width*height);
}
/*- - - - - - - - - -       - - - - - - - - - - - -     - - - - - - - - - - - - - -*/
```

Notice the syntax used in the definitions of the constructor functions. Each constructor function definition has an empty function body. The data members of the calling object are initialized using the **member initialization list.** The member initialization list lists the names of the data members followed by the desired initial value enclosed within parentheses. The member initialization list follows the function header and is outside the body of the function. A colon separates the function header from the member initialization list.

member initialization list

A constructor function can have statements inside the body of the function definition, if needed. We could have written the definition of the default constructor as follows:

```
rectangle::rectangle()
{
  x_coord = 0;
  y_coord = 0;
  width = 1;
  height = 1;
}
```

However, in the preceding function definition, the data members are not initialized. Rather, they are assigned values in the body of the function definition. This subtle difference can be significant in certain cases. *For correct initialization of programmer-defined class objects, it is recommended that constructor function definitions use the member initialization list.*

Style

Accessor Functions

When the data members of a class are specified as private, their values cannot be accessed directly within a program. A set of member functions, referred to as **accessor functions,** are often included in a class definition. An accessor function is a public member function that returns the value of a private data member. Our *rectangle* class has four private data members. When using the *rectangle* class in a program, we may want to access the value of one or more of the data members. For example, we may want to compare the *width* of one *rectangle* to the *width* of another *rectangle*. To allow access to the private data members of our rectangle class, we will add a complete set of four accessor functions to our class definition. Each accessor function will return the value of one of the private data members. The prototypes for the four accessor functions are as follows:

accessor functions

```
double get_x_coord() const;
double get_y_coord() const;
double get_width() const;
double get_height() const;
```

It is a common convention to name accessor functions get_ followed by the name of the data member. The keyword `const` prevents the function from changing the values of the private data members. We will now write the function definitions for the four accessor functions:

```
// Filename: rectangle.cpp
double rectangle::get_x_coord() const
{
   return x_coord;
}
double rectangle::get_y_coord() const
{
   return y_coord;
}
double rectangle::get_width() const
{
   return width;
}
double rectangle::get_height() const
{
   return height;
}
```

As illustrated in program chapter8_1, the assignment operator can be used with class objects of the same type. In the code

```
. . .
   rectangle r1, r2(1,1,2,3);
   r1 = r2;
```

each data member of *r1* is assigned the value of the corresponding data member of *r2*. Other C++ operators, including the arithmetic operators, the relational operators, and the input and output operators cannot be used with `class` objects unless the operator has been defined in the `class` definition. For example, the following comparison between the objects *r1* and *r2* is **not valid:**

```
rectangle r1,r2;
. . .
if( r1 == r2) (invalid comparison)
   . . .
```

However, we can use the accessor functions to compare r1 and r2 as follows:

```
rectangle r1,r2;
. . .
if( r1.get_x_coord() == r2.get_x_coord() &&
    r1.get_y_coord() == r2.get_y_coord() &&
    r1.get_width() == r2.get_width() &&
    r1.get_height() == r2.height() )
{
    cout << "Rectangles r1 and r2 are equivalent" << endl;
}
```

In the foregoing example, the equality operator is used to compare values of type `double` that are returned by each of the accessor functions.

The condition in the `if` statement is long and rather cumbersome. Thus, it is desirable to write member functions to define operators for `class` objects. This is referred to as **operator overloading** and is discussed in detail in Chapter 10.

Before we write a program to test the *rectangle* `class`, we will introduce two additional member functions: one to allow us to print the value of a *rectangle* and one to read the value of a *rectangle* from an input stream.

Member Functions for Input and Output

The input operator and the output operator cannot be used with `class` objects unless the operators have been defined in the `class` definition. For example, the following statements that attempt to input and output the value of *r1* are not valid for our *rectangle* `class`:

```
rectangle r1;
cin >> r1;        // Invalid statement.
cout << r1;       // Invalid statement.
```

To allow input and output of *rectangle* objects without overloading operators, we will write a member function named *input* to read the value of a *rectangle* from an input stream and a member function named *print* to display the value of a *rectangle*. The function prototypes are

```
void input(istream& in);
void print(ostream& out) const;
```

We use a formal parameter of type *istream* with the function *input()*. This provides flexibility when calling the function. The function *input()* can be called using *cin* as an argument if we want to input data from the keyboard. The function can also be called with an argument of type *ifstream* if we want to input data from a file. The same flexibility is provided by using a formal parameter of type *ostream* with the function *output()*. The function *output()* can be called with *cout* as an argument if we want to display the output on the screen. The function can also be called with an argument of type *ofstream* if we want to print the output to a file. We will now write the definitions for these functions:

```
void rectangle::input(istream& in)
{
    in >> x_coord >> y_coord >> width >> height;
}
void rectangle::print(ostream& out) const
{
    out << "Fixed point at: ("
        << x_coord << ',' << y_coord << ')' << endl
        << "Width: " << width << endl
        << "Height: " << height << endl;
}
```

Assume that a *rectangle* class is defined having the following class declaration:

```
/*-------------------------------------------------------------*/
/*  Class declaration for the rectangle class.                 */
class rectangle
{
public:
// Default constructor.
rectangle();

// Constructor with four parameters.
rectangle(double x, double y, double w, double h);

// Accessor functions.
double get_x_coord() const;
double get_y_coord() const;
double get_width() const;
double get_height() const;

// Functions for input and output.
void input(istream& in);
void print(ostream& out) const;

// Additional member function prototypes.
void set_value(double x, double y, double w, double h);
void translate(double dx, double dy);
double area() const;

private:
// Declaration of data members;
double x_coord, y_coord, width, height;
};
/*-------------------------------------------------------------*/
```

Determine whether the following statements are valid or invalid with respect to the class declaration.

1. rectangle r1;

2. rectangle r2(0,0,2,4);

3. rectangle r3();

4. rectangle r4(0,0);

5. cin ≫ r1;

6. cout ≪ r2;

Practice!

7. cout ≪ r2.get_width();

8. r2.print(cout);

9. cout ≪ r2.print();

10. cout ≪ r2.print(cout);

11. r1 = r2;

12. r1 = r1 + r2;

8.3   Separate Compilation

In this section, we will develop a program to test the functionality of our *rectangle* class. We will write the test program in a file named *chapter8_2.cpp*. To use the *rectangle* class, our program must have access to the class declaration and the class implementation. The class declaration for the *rectangle* class is written in a file named *rectangle.h,* and the class implementation is written in a file named *rectangle.cpp.* The implementation file for the *rectangle* class can be compiled separately. This separation allows us to build our own libraries of programmer-defined classes that can be used by many application programs in the same way the standard libraries are used. The application program must include the following declaration file and must be linked to the implementation file:

```
#ifndef RECTANGLE_H
#define RECTANGLE_H
/*-------------------------------------------------------------------*/
/*   Class declaration for the rectangle class.                      */
/*   Filename: rectangle.h                                           */

#include <iostream>
using namespace std;

class rectangle
{
public:
// Default constructor.
rectangle();

// Constructor with four parameters.
rectangle(double x, double y, double w, double h);

// Accessor functions.
double get_x_coord() const;
double get_y_coord() const;
#endif
```

```
double get_width() const;
double get_height() const;

// Functions for input and output.
void input(istream& in);
void print(ostream& out) const;

// Additional member function prototypes.
void set_value(double x, double y, double w, double h);
void translate(double dx, double dy);
double area() const;

private:
// Declaration of data members.
double x_coord, y_coord, width, height;
};
*-------------------------------------------------------------------------*/
```

 The new compiler directives prevent multiple includes.
    The program to test the *rectangle* class is given below.

```
/*-------------------------------------------------------------------------*/
/* Program chapter8_2                                                    */
/*                                                                       */
/* This program tests each of the functions in the rectangle class.*/

#include<iostream>
#include "rectangle.h"
using namespace std;

int main()
{
// Test default constructor.
  rectangle r1;

// Test constructor with 4 arguments.
  rectangle r2(0,0,1,2);

// Test print function and verify constructors.
  cout << "Value of r1:\n ";
  r1.print(cout);
  cout << endl;
  cout << "Value of r2:\n ";
  r2.print(cout);
  cout << endl;

// Test accessor functions.
  cout << "Accessor function test:\n";
  cout << r2.get_x_coord() << ' ' << r2.get_y_coord() << ' '
       << r2.get_width() << ' ' << r2.get_height() << endl;
```

```
// Test input function.
  cout << "\nEnter values to define a rectangle:\n"
       << "x-coordinate, y-coordinate, width and height\n";
  r1.input(cin);
  r1.print(cout);
  return 0;
}
```

The implementation file must also include the class declaration file, *rectangle.h;* as illustrated below, and must be linked to, or included in the same project as, the application.

```
/*   Class implementation for the rectangle class.               */
/*                                                               */
#include "rectangle.h"
#include <iostream>

// Definition of default constructor
rectangle::rectangle(): x_coord(0), y_coord(0), width(1), height(1)
{
}

// Definition of constructor with four formal parameters
rectangle::rectangle(double x, double y, double w, double h):
     x_coord(x), y_coord(y), width(w), height(h)
{
}

void rectangle::set_value(double x, double y, double w, double h)
{
  // Set the value of the calling object.
  x_coord = x;
  y_coord = y;
  width = w;
  height = h;

  // Void return
  return;
}
void rectangle::translate(double dx, double dy)
{
  // Translate calling object
  x_coord += dx;
  y_coord += dy;
  // Void return
  return;
}
double rectangle::area() const
{
    return(width*height);
}
```

```
double rectangle::get_x_coord() const
{
   return x_coord;
}
double rectangle::get_y_coord() const
{
   return y_coord;
}
double rectangle::get_width() const
{
   return width;
}
double rectangle::get_height() const
{
   return height;
}
void rectangle::input(istream& in)
{
   in >> x_coord >> y_coord >> width >> height;
}
void rectangle::print(ostream& out) const
{
   out << "Rectangle has fixed point at: ("
       << x_coord << ',' << y_coord << ')' << endl
       << "The width of the rectangle is " << width << endl
       << "The height of the rectangle is " << height << endl;
}
/*-------------------------------------------------------------------*/
```

The output from a sample run of our test program is as follows:

```
Value of r1:
Fixed point at: (0,0)
Width: 1
Height: 1

Value of r2:
Fixed point at: (0,0)
Width: 1
Height: 2

Accessor function test:
0 0 1 2

Enter values to define a rectangle:
x-coordinate, y-coordinate, width and height
1 2 3.5 7.4
Fixed point at: (1,2)
Width: 3.5
Height: 7.4
```

Modify!

1.   Add a member function to the *rectangle* class that will change the size of a rectangle by adding *dw* to the width and *dh* to the height. The prototype is:

```
void resize(double dw, double dh);
```

2. Add a member function to the *rectangle* class that will change the change the size of a rectangle by multiplying the *width* and *height* by a positive scale factor. The prototype is

```
void scale(double scale_factor);
```

8.4 The UnitVector Class

private member functions

class types as formal parameters

In this section, we will develop a new `class` data type to illustrate the use of ***private member functions*** and member functions that have `class` **types as formal parameters.** Suppose we want to define a new `class` data type to represent a unit vector as illustrated in Figure 8.3.

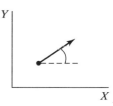

Figure 8.3 Unit Vector.

The internal representation of a unit vector requires three data members: an *x*-coordinate and a *y*-coordinate to represent the anchor point and an angle to represent the orientation of the vector. The class declaration is given next:

```
#ifndef UNITVECTOR_H
#define UNITVECTOR_H
/*-----------------------------------------------------------*/
/*        UnitVector class declaration.                    */
/*        Filename is UnitVector.h                         */

#include <fstream>
using namespace std;
{
public:
/* Constructor functions. */
```

```cpp
// Default constructor.
   UnitVector();

// Constructor with 3 parameters.
   UnitVector(double x_val,         // x coordinate.
              double y_val,         // y coordinate.
              double or);           // orientation in degrees.

/* Accessor functions.  */

   double get_x() const;
   double get_y() const;
   double get_orientation() const;

/* Functions for input and output. */

// Input anchor point and orientation measured in degrees.
   void input(istream& fin);

// Print the value of a unit vector.
   void print(ostream& fout) const;

/* Function to test for equality of two vectors. */
   bool equal(UnitVector v2) const;

private:
// Internal representation of data
   double x, y;                     // Vector anchor point.
   double orientation;              // Vector orientation.

// Helper functions
   void to_radians();               // Convert degrees to radians.
   double to_degrees() const;       // Convert radians to degrees.
};
/*--------------------------------------------------------------*/
#endif
```

Private Member Functions

helper functions

The member functions *to_radians()* and *to_degrees()* are declared under the keyword `private`. A `private` member function can be called by member functions of the `class`. These functions are sometimes referred to as **helper functions,** because they are designed to help the other member functions and can assist in information hiding.

  Our *UnitVector* class has three `private` data members and two `private` member functions. The `private` data member *orientation* will be stored as an angle measured in radians for compatibility with functions in the standard *cmath* library. However, the `public` member functions that interface with the user of the *UnitVector* `class` will input and print the value of *orientation* in degrees, since degrees are easier for most users to interpret. The `private` member functions *to_radians()* and *to_degrees()* are called by other member functions of the *UnitVector* class to perform the necessary conversions.

The *UnitVector* class implementation is as follows:

```
/*-------------------------------------------------------------------*/
/* Implementation of the UnitVector class                          */

#include "UnitVector.h"
#include <cmath>
const double PI = acos(-1.0);

/* Constructor function definitions.   */

UnitVector::UnitVector(): x(1), y(1), orientation(0)
{
  // Default constructor.
  // Initialize all data members.
}

UnitVector::UnitVector(double x_val, double y_val, double or):
    x(x_val), y(y_val), orientation(or)
  // Constructor function with three arguments.
  // Initialize data members to parameter values.
{
  to_radians(); // Convert orientation to radians.
}

/* Accessor functions.   */

double UnitVector::get_x() const
{
  return x;
}
double UnitVector::get_y() const
{
  return y;
}
double UnitVector::get_orientation() const
{
  return(to_degrees());
}

/* Member function for input and output.   */

void UnitVector::input(istream& fin)
{
  // Orientation is input as a value measured in degrees.
  fin >> x >> y >> orientation;

  // Convert orientation to radians.
  to_radians();
}
```

```
void UnitVector::print(ostream& fout) const
{
  // Print the value of a UnitVector.
  // Print the anchor point.
  fout << "( " << x << ',' << y << " ) : ";

  // Print the orientation in degrees.
  fout << "orientation is "<< to_degrees() << " degrees";
}

/* Function to test for equality of two vectors. */
bool UnitVector::equal(UnitVector v2) const
{
  if(x == v2.x && y == v2.y && orientation == v2.orientation)
    return true;
  return false;
}

/* Helper function definitions. */

void UnitVector::to_radians()
{
  // Convert orientation to radians.
  orientation = PI/180*orientation;
}

double UnitVector::to_degrees() const
{
  // Convert orientation to degrees.
  return(180/PI*orientation);
}
/*----------------------------------------------------------------*/
```

In the foregoing implementation, notice how the `private` member functions *to_radians()* and *to_degrees()* are called within the `public` member functions. No calling object is required; the implicit calling object is the calling object of the `public` member function.

Class Objects as Arguments to Member Functions

Our *UnitVector* class includes a boolean function named *equal()* that returns a true value if the object that is passed as an argument to the function is equivalent to the calling object. In the expression

```
if(x == v2.x && y == v2.y && orientation == v2.orientation)
```

the dot (.) operator is used to access the `private` data members of the formal parameter *v2*. These values are compared to the `private` data members of the calling object.

With the introduction of the *UnitVector* class, a program can compare objects of type *UnitVector* as follows:

```
. . .
// Declare two UnitVector objects.
UnitVector v1;                        // Default constructor.
UnitVector v2(1.0,1.0,180.0);   // Constructor with 3 arguments.

// Compare v1 and v2.
if( v1.equal(v2) )
  cout << "Vectors are equivalent\n";
else
  cout << "Vectors are not equivalent\n";
. . .
```

The memory snapshot after executing these statements is the following:

```
v1 | 1 | x           v2 |    1    | x
   | 1 | y              |    1    | y
   | 0 | orientation     | 3.14159 | orientation
```

Since the orientation of *v1* is different from the orientation of *v2,* the message

```
Vectors are not equivalent
```

will be printed to the screen.

When passing a `class` object as an argument to a function, the argument can be a pass by value or a pass by reference. The function *equal()* uses a pass by value, and thus the value of the argument cannot be modified. The following program tests the functionality of the UnitVector class:

```
/*-------------------------------------------------------------------*/
/* Program Chapter8_3                                                */
/*  This program tests the UnitVector class                         */

#include<iostream>
#include "UnitVector.h"
using namespace std;
int main()
{
// Test constructor functions.
UnitVector v1, v2(2,3,45);

// Test print function.
cout << "value of unit vector v1:   ";
```

```
v1.print(cout);
cout << endl << "value of unit vector v2:   ";
v2.print(cout);

// Test input function.
cout << "\nenter anchor point, followed by the orientation\n";
v1.input(cin);

// Test the accessor functions.
cout << "\nVector v1 - Anchor point: " << v1.get_x() << ','
                                        << v1.get_y()
     << " Orientation: " << v1.get_orientation() << endl;

return 0;
}
```

A sample run of our test program gives the following results:

```
value of unit vector v1:   ( 1,1 ) : orientation is 0 degrees
value of unit vector v2:   ( 2,3 ) : orientation is 45 degrees
enter anchor point, followed by the orientation
0 0 90
Vector v1 - Anchor point: 0,0 Orientation: 90
```

Modify!

These problems relate to the *UnitVector* class developed in this section.

1. Add a `public` member function named *translate()* to the *UnitVector* class. The prototype for this function is

   ```
   void translate(double dx, double dy); // add dx to x, dy to y
   ```

2. Add a `public` member function named *rotate()* to the *UnitVector* class. The prototype for this function is

   ```
   void rotate(double degrees); // add degrees to orientation
   ```

3. Add a `private` member function named *fix_orientation()* to the *UnitVector* class. The prototype for this function is

   ```
   void fix_orientation();
   ```

   This function will keep the value of *orientation* within the range of 0 to 2π.

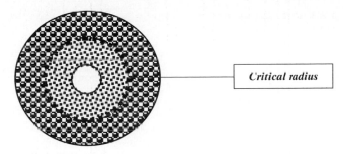

Figure 8.4 Particles suspended between two cylinders.

8.5 Problem Solving Applied: Simulation

The design of advanced composite materials is an important problem in many areas of science and engineering. As an example, encapsulating materials are now being engineered to insulate critical components in electronic assemblies from thermal and mechanical shock. It may be important for an encapsulating material to be tough against penetration on the outside while providing damping from vibration on the inside near the electronic assembly.

In this example, we are modeling a molten plastic material containing suspended alumina particles in a space between two cylinders. We are interested in calculating the rate of migration of the alumina particles. Initially, the alumina particles are uniformly distributed. When the inner cylinder is rotated, the alumina particles migrate away from the inner cylinder towards the outer cylinder. More toughness exists with a higher concentration of alumina particles and better vibrational dampening occurs with fewer particles.

We can measure the rate of migration at a critical radius by summing the mass flux of all particles within a particle's radius of the critical radius as illustrated in Figure 8.4.

The mass flux is determined by taking the dot product of the particle velocity with the unit normal to the circle at the critical radius and multiplying by the particle volume and density.

For this program, we will define a *particle* class as follows:

```
/*------------------------------------------------------------------*/
/* Particle class declaration                                       */
/* File named Particle.h                                            */

#include <cmath>
#include "UnitVector.h"
const double PI=acos(-1.0);

class Particle
{
public:
// Constructor functions.
   Particle();
   Particle(UnitVector v, double m, double d, double r);
```

```
// Functions for input and output.
   void input(istream&);
   void print(ostream&);

// Accessor functions.
   UnitVector get_position_dir();
   double get_magnitude();
   double get_density();
   double get_radius();

// Return mass flux of a particle
   double mass_flux();
private:
   UnitVector position_dir;    //particle position and direction
   double magnitude;           //particle magnitude
   double density;             //particle density
   double radius;              //particle radius
};
/*-----------------------------------------------------------------*/
```

The UnitVector class is used to define one of the private data members of the *Particle* class, thus the file *UnitVector.h* must be included in the declaration of the *Particle* class.

The implementation of the *Particle* class is as follows:

```
/*-----------------------------------------------------------------*/
/* Particle class implementation                                   */
/* Filename Particle.cpp                                           */

#include "Particle.h"

Particle::Particle(): magnitude(0), density(0), radius(0)
{
\\ position_dir initialized by implicit call to default constructor
}
Particle::Particle(UnitVector v, double m, double d, double r):
   position_dir(v), magnitude(m), density(d), radius(r)
{
}
double Particle::mass_flux()
{
   double dp, mf;
   dp = cos( position_dir.get_orientation() -
   atan2(position_dir.get_y(),position_dir.get_x()) );
   mf = dp * magnitude*density*(4.0/3.0)*PI*pow(radius,3);
   return mf;
}
void Particle::input(istream& in)
{
   position_dir.input(in);
   in >>magnitude >>density >> radius;
}
```

```
void Particle::print(ostream& out)
{
  position_dir.print(out);
  out << endl << magnitude << endl << density <<  endl << radius;
}

UnitVector Particle::get_position_dir()
{
  return(position_dir);
}

double Particle::get_magnitude()
{
  return(magnitude);
}

double Particle::get_density()
{
  return(density);
}

double Particle::get_radius()
{
  return(radius);
}
```

Our *Particle* class has four private data members and nine member functions. Our *UnitVector* class is used to define the *position_dir* data member of the *Particle* class. The *mass_flux()* function requires access to the values of the *private* data members of the *position_dir* data member, but since the *mass_flux()* function is not a member of the *UnitVector* class, it must use the accessor functions provided by the *UnitVector* class to access these values.

1. PROBLEM STATEMENT

A data file named *particles.dat* has particle data for 1,000 alumina particles. Using the *UnitVector* and the *Particle* classes, write a program to calculate the rate of migration at a critical radius of 2.57 centimeters.

2. INPUT/OUTPUT DESCRIPTION

The inputs to this program are a data file named *particles.dat*. and the critical radius. The critical radius is entered by the user from the keyboard. The output is the rate of migration at the critical radius.

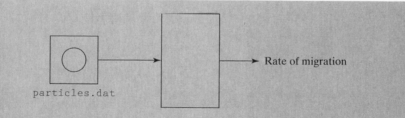

3. HAND EXAMPLE

We will work a hand example using only four particles as illustrated in the following diagram:

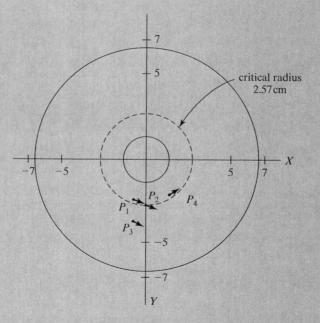

Our data file for this hand example is

```
-1 -2.27 -15.5 2.5 0.98 0.1
0 -2.57 -5 2.5 0.98 0.1
-0.5 -3.2 -7.5 2.5 0.98 0.1
1.5 -2.1 25.0 2.5 0.98 0.1
```

and we are using a critical radius of 2.57 cm. Looking at the first particle, we determine whether the particle is within a particle radius of the critical radius. The particle radius is given in the data file as 0.1. Calculating the distance from the critical radius, we get

0.089496, which is within range, so we calculate the mass flux contribution for this particle and get the value 0.00147702. We add this value to our total and continue with the remaining three points as follows:

```
P2:    distance:  0. mass flux: 0.000894435
P3:    distance:  0.668827 (not within a particle radius)
P4:    distance:  0.0106976, mass flux 0.00187685
```

Thus, our rate of migration at the critical radius is: 0.129427E-02

4. ALGORITHM DEVELOPMENT

We first develop the decomposition outline because it divides the solution into a series of sequential steps.

Decomposition Outline

1. Read the critical radius from the keyboard and the particle data from the data file
2. Compute the rate of migration at the critical radius
3. Print the rate of migration

Step 1 involves reading the particle data. Since the number of particles can be quite large in a real simulation, the particles will be read one at a time from the file and not stored in an array. We will read the critical radius from the keyboard to allow for multiple simulations to be run on the same data set. Because we need to determine the distance from the critical radius for each particle, we implement the distance measurement as a function. The mass flux calculation is implemented as a member function of the Particle class. The refinement for main can now be developed:

```
Refinement in Pseudocode
main: read critical radius from keyboard
read nparticles from input file input
set sum_migration_rate to 0
set p to 1
while p <= nparticles
  read a particle
  set dist to distance( particle.position_dir, critical_radius)
  if(dist <= particle.radius )
    add mf to sum_migration_rate
  increment p
  print sum migration_rate
```

```
distance(v, r):
 set d to sqrt(v.x*v.x + v.y*v.y) - r
return abs(r)
```

We now convert the pseudocode to C++:

```cpp
/*-------------------------------------------------------------------*/
/*                                                                   */
/* This program calculates the rate of migration of particles.   */

#include <fstream>
#include <string>
#include "Particle.h"
using namespace std;

// Function prototypes.
double dist(UnitVector, double);

int main()
{
// Declare objects.
   double critical_radius, d, sum_mf=0;
   int num_particles, p=1;
   string filename;
   ifstream fin;
   Particle particle;

// Prompt user for file name and open file for input.
   cout << "enter name of input file\n";
   cin >> filename;
   fin.open(filename.c_str());
   if( fin.fail() )
   {
     cout << "error opening input file\n";
   }
   else
   {

     cout << "enter critical radius: ";
     cin >> critical_radius;
     fin >> num_particles;
     while(p<=num_particles)
     {
     // Input a particle.
       particle.input(fin);

     // Calculate distance.
        d =  dist(particle.get_position_dir(), critical_radius);
```

```
                    if( d <= particle.get_radius() )
                    {
                        sum_mf += particle.mass_flux();
                    }
                    p++;
                }//end while
                cout << "migration rate is: " << sum_mf;
            }//end else
            return 0;
        }
        double dist(UnitVector v, double r)
        {
            double d;
            d = sqrt( pow( v.get_x(),2 ) + pow( v.get_y(),2 ) ) - r;
            return (fabs(d));
        }
```

5. TESTING

The output from the program using the data file from the hand example is as follows:

```
migration rate is: 0.00129427
```

Since the output matches our hand example, we can test our program on a larger data set.

SUMMARY

In this chapter, we introduced the class mechanism. The definition of a class, including the class declaration and the class implementation, were discussed and separate compilation of files was introduced. A *rectangle* class was developed to illustrate the use of public and private class members. Accessor functions and constructor functions were defined, and programs were developed to test newly defined classes. An application problem in simulation of composite materials was developed to illustrated the use of object based programming.

Key Terms

accessor functions   class declaration
calling object   class implementation
class   constructor functions
class definition   default constructor

data members   member initialization list
dot operator   private
helper functions   public
information hiding   scope resolution operator
member functions   separate compilation

C++ Statement Summary

Class declaration:

General Form:

```
class identifier
{
public:
  function prototypes;
private:
  type declaration statements;
  function prototypes;
};
```

Member function definition:

General Form:

```
return_type class_name::function_name(parameter list)
{
statements;
}
```

Member initialization list:

General Form:

```
class_name::class_name (parameter list):
 member_name (initial_value), member_name (initial_value)
{
statements;
}
```

Style **Notes**

1. All data members of a class should be specified as `private`.
2. A well-designed `class` should provide a complete set of accessor functions.
3. A well-designed `class` should provide a set of constructor functions.
4. A `class` declaration should be placed in a separate file named *classname.h*
5. A `class` implementation should be placed in a separate file named *classname.cpp*

Debugging Notes

1. Test each member function definition as you write it.

2. The assignment operator is the only operator automatically defined for class objects.

3. A semicolon is required following the body of a `class` declaration.

Problems

Exam Practice!

Indicate whether each of the following statements is true (T) or false (F).

1. An object is an instance of a class.
2. All data members of a class must be of the same data type.
3. Member functions designed to initialize the data members of a class are called accessor functions.
4. Member functions designed to initialize the data members of a class are called constructor functions.
5. Member functions are called using the dot operator.
6. The dot operator is required as part of a member function definition.
7. Member functions have access to all private data members.
8. Constructor functions are member functions.
9. A constructor function may not be overloaded.

Memory Snapshot Problem

Give the corresponding snapshots of memory after each of the following sets of statements is executed. Use the following abbreviated class definition to answer questions 10–12:

```
//Class Declaration
class UnitVector
{
public:
//constructor functions
  UnitVector(); //default constructor
  UnitVector(double x_val,  // constructor with 3 parameters
             double y_val,
             double or);
private:
//data members
double x, y; //vector anchor point
double orientation; //vector orientation
};
//Class implementation
UnitVector::UnitVector():  x(1), y(1), orientation(3.1415)
{
}
```

```
UnitVector::UnitVector(double x_val, double y_val, double o):
  x(x_val), y(y_val), orientation(o)
{
}
```

10. UnitVector v1, v2;

11. UnitVector v1(0,0,0), v2;

12. UnitVector v1(1,1,3), v2(1,4,3.2);

Programming Problems

13. Define a class to represent circle. Your class should have three private data members: *radius, xp,* and *yp.* Include a complete set of accessor functions, constructor functions and member functions to

  - input a circle

  - print location and radius of a circle

  - move (translate) a circle

  - resize a circle

14. Define a class to represent a date. Your class should have three data members: month, day, and year. Include a complete set of accessor functions, constructor functions, and member functions to

  - input a date

  - print a date as month/day/year (10/1/2002)

  - print a date as month day, year (October 1, 2002)

  - initialize a date object

15. Define a class to represent time in military format. Your class should have three private data member: hours, minutes, and seconds. Military time is represented with times ranging from 00:00:00 (12 A.M.) to 23:59:59 (11:59:59 P.M.). Include a complete set of accessor functions, constructor functions, and other member functions to

  - input a time;

  - print a time in 12-hour format;

  - calculate the difference between two times;

  - initialize a time object.

16. Define a card class. Your class should have two private data members: suit and rank. Include a complete set of accessor functions, constructor functions and a

function to

- display a card (ie Jack of Spades).

17. Define a deck class. Your class should keep a complete deck of 52 cards. (Use the card class defined in the previous problem.) Include accessor functions, constructor functions, and other member functions to

- test for an empty deck;
- draw a card from the top of the deck;
- shuffle the deck.

CHAPTER 9

GRAND CHALLENGE:
Oil and Gas Exploration

The identification of underground oil and gas reserves can be performed using a group of sensors that measure earth motion. These sensors, also called seismometers, are arranged in a predetermined pattern and are collectively called a sensor array. A ground-shock signal can be generated near the sensor array using an explosive charge in a hole that has been drilled near the array. Ground-shock signals can also be generated by an explosive charge on the surface, or by a special truck that uses a hydraulic hammer to pound the earth several times per second. The ground-shock signals that are transferred into the earth are reflected by the different geologic layer boundaries and are collected by the sensors on the surface. By using sophisticated signal processing, one can map the boundary layers and make predictions about the materials (such as sandstone, shale, water, and oil) for the various layers.

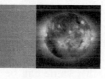

An Introduction to Pointers

Chapter Outline

Objectives

9.1 Addresses and Pointers
9.2 Pointers to Array Elements
9.3 Dynamic Memory Allocation
9.4 Problem Solving Applied: Seismic Event Detection
9.5 Common Errors Using new and delete
9.6 Data Structures*
9.7 Problem Solving Applied: Concordance of a Text File*

Summary, Key Terms, C++ Statement Summary, Style Notes, Debugging Notes, Problems

OBJECTIVES

The relationships between the value stored in an object, the identifier assigned to an object, and the address of the memory location used to store the value of an object are examined. The **pointer data type** is described to store the address of a value associated with an object. Examples are presented to demonstrate the use of pointers to reference array elements and character strings. The process of **dynamic memory allocation** is defined. The functions **new** and **delete** are examined. Data structures, including **linked list, stacks,** and **queues,** are discussed, with examples that utilize the **list, stack,** and **queue** classes.

9.1 Addresses and Pointers

When a C++ program is executed, memory locations are assigned to the objects used in the program. Each of these memory locations has a positive integer address that uniquely defines the location. When an object is assigned a value, this value is stored in the corresponding memory location. The value of an object can be used by statements in the program, and it can be changed by statements in the program. The specific addresses used for the objects are determined each time that the program is executed, and may vary from one execution to another.

It is sometimes helpful to compare memory allocation with the allocation of a group of post office boxes. If the post office has 100 boxes numbered from 1 to 100, then the box number corresponds to the memory address. Each box is assigned to an individual, using the individual's name; this name corresponds to the identifier assigned to a memory location. The contents of the box corresponds to the value in the memory location; this value can be examined, and it can be changed:

post office box number	individual name	contents
78	John Ruiz	utility bill

memory address	identifier	contents
oxbffff8d8	x	105

This analogy is not completely valid, because two individuals might have the same name, but two identifiers cannot be exactly the same. Also, a mail box might be empty, or it might contain a number of items, whereas a memory location always contains a single value.

Address Operator

address operator

In C++, the address of an object can be referenced using the **address operator &.** This operator was introduced in Chapter 5 in conjunction with pass by reference. Recall that when the address operator is appended to the data type of a formal parameter in a function prototype and function header, the formal parameter receives the address of the corresponding argument when the function is called. To illustrate the use of the address operator to obtain the memory address of a object, consider the following program:

```
/*------------------------------------------------------------------*/
/*  Program chapter9_1                                            */
/*                                                                */
/*  This program demonstrates the relationship                   */
/*  between objects and addresses.                               */

#include <iostream>
using namespace std;
int main()
{
//  Declare and initialize objects.
    int a(1), b(2);

//  Print the contents and addresses of a and b.
    cout << "a= " << a << ";  address of a = " << &a << endl;
    cout << "b= " << b << ";  address of b = " << &b << endl;
    return 0;
}
/*------------------------------------------------------------------*/
```

A sample output from this program is the following:

```
a = 1:   address of a = 0xbffff8d8
b = 2;   address of b = 0xbffff8d4
```

The following memory snapshot shows the values in the two memory locations at the time that the *cout* statements are executed:

a 1   b 2

We do not usually indicate the memory addresses in these diagrams because the addresses used are system dependent and change with every run of the program.

In the next example, which is a modification to the previous program, there are no initial values given to objects *a* and *b*:

```
/*-------------------------------------------------------------------------*/
/*  Program chapter9_2                                                     */
/*                                                                         */
/*  This program demonstrates the relationship                            */
/*  between objects and addresses.                                        */

#include <iostream>
using namespace std;
int main()
{
//  Declare and initialize objects.
    int a, b;

//  Print the contents and addresses of a and b.
    cout << "a= " << a << ";   address of a = " << &a << endl;
    cout << "b= " << b << ";   address of b = " << &b << endl;
    return 0;
}
/*-------------------------------------------------------------------------*/
```

A sample output from this program is the following:

```
a = -1073743608;   address of a = 0xbffff8e8
b = 1073784016;   address of b = 0xbffff8e4
```

A memory snapshot at the time that the *cout* statements are executed should show a question mark in the objects contents because the values are undefined:

a ?   b ?

While we see that there are values in the objects, even though we have not assigned any in the program, we should not assume anything about these values. This example illustrates the importance of being sure that a program initializes an object before using its value in other statements in a program.

Modify!

1. Run program chapter9_1 two times on the computer that you are using for class assignments. Did your computer use the same addresses or different addresses? Compare the results with your classmates.

2. Run program chapter9_2 presented in this section. What values were in the locations assigned to a and b? Do the values change from one execution of the program to another?

Pointer Assignment

pointer

base type

dereference
indirection

The C++ language allows us to store the address of a memory location in a special type of object called a **pointer.** When a pointer is defined, the type of object to which it will point must also be defined. The type of object to which a pointer will point is referred to as the pointer's **base type.** The base type of a pointer determines how the object being pointed to will be interpreted. Thus, a pointer defined to point to an integer object cannot also be used to point to a floating-point object. The following statement defines two integer objects and a pointer to an integer value. Note that an asterisk is used to indicate that the object is a pointer; this asterisk is also called a **dereference** or **indirection** operator:

```
int a, b, *ptr;
```

This statement specifies that memory addresses should be assigned to three objects—two integer objects and a pointer to an integer object. The statement does not specify the initial values for *a*, *b*, and *ptr*. Thus, the memory snapshot after this declaration indicates that the initial contents of all objects are not specified; the diagram uses an arrow to indicate that ptr is a pointer object:

a ? b ? ptr ? →

To specify that *ptr* should point to the object *a*, we could use an assignment statement that stores the address of *a* in *ptr*:

```
int a, b, *ptr;
ptr = &a;
```

This assignment could also have been made on the declaration statement:

```
int a, b, *ptr=&a;
```

In either case, the memory snapshot after the declaration is the following:

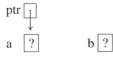

Note that it is not necessary to show the contents of ptr, as long as the object to which it points is specified.

Consider this set of statements:

```
//  Declare and initialize objects.
int a(5), b(9), *ptr(&a);
. . .
//  Assign the value pointed to by ptr to b.
b = *ptr;
```

This last statement is read as "b is assigned the value at the address contained in ptr," or "b is assigned the value pointed to by ptr." The memory snapshot before the assignment statement is executed is the following:

The memory snapshot after the assignment statement is executed is the following:

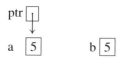

Thus, *b* is assigned the value pointed to by *ptr*. Now consider this set of statements:

```
//  Declare and initialize objects.
int a=5, b=9, *ptr=&a;
. . .
//  Assign the value of b to the object
//  pointed to by ptr.
*ptr = b;
```

The memory snapshot before the assignment statement is executed is the following:

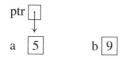

The memory snapshot after the assignment statement is executed is the following:

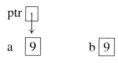

Thus, the value pointed to by *ptr* is assigned the value in *b*.

We now extend program chapter9_1 to demonstrate the relationship between objects, addresses, and pointers. Consider the following program:

```
/*------------------------------------------------------------------*/
/*  Program chapter9_3                                            */
/*                                                                */
/*  This program demonstrates the relationship                   */
/*  between objects, addresses, and pointers.                    */

#include <iostream>
using namespace std;
int main()
{
// Declare and initialize objects.
int a(1), b(2), *ptr(&a);

// Print address and contents of all objects.
   cout << "a = " << a << "; address of a = " << &a << endl;
   cout << "b = " << b << "; address of b = " << &b << endl;
   cout << "ptr = " << ptr << "; address of ptr = " << &ptr << endl;
   cout << "ptr points to the value " << *ptr << endl;
   return 0;
}
/*------------------------------------------------------------------*/
```

A sample output from this program is the following:

```
a = 1; address of a = 0xbffff8d8
b = 2; address of b = 0xbffff8d4
ptr = 0xbffff8d8; address of ptr = 0xbffff8d0
ptr points to the value 1
```

Note that the values of the pointer to *a* and the address of *a* are the same.

Practice!

Give memory snapshots after each of these sets of statements are executed.

1. `int a(1), b(2), *ptr;`
   `ptr = &b;`

2. `int a(1), b(2), *ptr=&b;`
   `a = *ptr;`

3. `int a(1), b(2), c(5), *ptr=&c;`
   `b = *ptr;`
   `*ptr = a;`

4. `int a(1), b(2), c(5), *ptr;`
   `ptr = &c;`
   `c = b;`
   `a = *ptr;`

Pointer Arithmetic

The operations that can be performed with pointers (or addresses) are limited to the following:
A pointer can be assigned to another pointer of the same type; an integer value can be added
to or subtracted from a pointer; and a pointer can be assigned or compared to the integer zero,
or, equivalently, to the symbolic constant *NULL*, which is defined in *<iostream>*. In addition,
pointers to elements of the same array can be subtracted or compared as a means to accessing
elements in the array.

A pointer can point to only one location, but several pointers can point to the same
location, as illustrated in this next example. Both *ptr_1* and *ptr_2* point to the same object after
the following statements are executed:

```
// Declare and initialize objects.
int x(-5), y(8), *ptr_1, *ptr_2;
...
// Assign both pointers to x.
ptr_1 = &x;
ptr_2 = ptr_1;
```

The memory snapshot after these statements are executed is

We now present several invalid statements using these objects to illustrate some common
errors that can be made when working with pointers:

```
&y = ptr_1;        // invalid statement: attempts
                   // to change the address of y

ptr_1 - y;         // invalid statement: attempts
                   // to change ptr_1 to a
                   // nonaddress value

*ptr_1 = ptr_2;    // invalid statement: attempts
                   // to assign an address to an
                   // integer object

ptr_1 = *ptr_2;    // invalid statement: attempts
                   // to change ptr_1 to a
                   // nonaddress value
```

It is recommended, as an instructive exercise, to attempt to draw memory snapshots of
these invalid statements; in each statement we are attempting to store an object value in a
Style   pointer, or we are attempting to store a pointer in an object. *To help avoid these errors, use identifier
names for pointers that clearly indicate that the identifiers are associated with pointers.*

When simple objects are defined, we should not make any assumptions about the relation-ships of the memory locations assigned to the objects. For example, if a declaration statement defines two integers, *a* and *b*, we should not assume that the values are adjacent in memory; we also should not make assumptions about which value occurs first in memory. The memory assignments of simple objects are system dependent. However, the memory assignment for an array is guaranteed to be a sequential group of memory locations. Thus, if array *x* contains five integers, then the memory location for *x[1]* will immediately follow the memory location for *x[0]*, the memory location for *x[2]* will follow the memory location for *x[1]*, and so on. Therefore, if *ptr_x* is a pointer to an integer, we can initialize it to point to the integer *x[0]* with the statement

```
ptr_x = &x[0];
```

The statement

```
ptr_x = x;
```

is equivalent, since the identifier *x* holds a pointer to the first element in *x*. To move the pointer to *x[1]*, we can increment *ptr_x* by 1, which causes it to point to the value that follows *x[0]*, or we can assign *ptr_x* the address of *x[1]*. Thus, any of the following statements would cause *ptr_x*, which currently points to *x[0]*, to be changed to point to *x[1]*:

```
++ptr_x;              // increment ptr_x to point to the
                      // next value in memory

ptr_x++;              // increment ptr_x to point to the
                      // next value in memory

ptr_x = ptr_x + 1;    // increment ptr_x to point to
                      // the next value in memory

ptr_x += 1;           // increment ptr_x to point to
                      // the next value in memory

ptr_x = &x[1];        // ptr_x is assigned the
                      // address of x[1]
```

Similarly, the statement

```
ptr_x += k;
```

refers to the address of the value that is *k* values past the one pointed to by *ptr_x* before this statement was executed. These are all examples of adding integers to pointers. Similarly, integers can also be subtracted from pointers. Section 9.2 expands this discussion for one-dimensional arrays.

When an integer value is added to or subtracted from a pointer, it is assumed that the integer refers to the number of values from the one referenced by the pointer before the addition or subtraction is performed. For example, the statement

```
ptr++;
```

indicates that *ptr* should be modified such that it points to the next value in memory, which is the value that follows the one pointed to by *ptr* before *ptr* is incremented. Because different types of values require different amounts of memory, the actual integer value added to *ptr* depends on the base type of the pointer. A value of type `double` requires more memory than an integer, and thus the address increment for a pointer to `double` will be more than an address increment for a pointer to `int`. For example, if the size of an `int` on your system is four bytes, and the size of a `double` is eight bytes, the memory addresses for consecutive integers might be 0xbffff8d4 and 0xbffff8d8, and memory addresses for consecutive values of type `double` might be 0xbffff8c0 and 0xbffff8c8. In this case, an address increment for a pointer to `int` will add 4 to the address and an address increment for a pointer to `double` will add 8. Fortunately, the compiler will determine the correct address increment for us when we add an integer to a pointer or when we subtract an integer from a pointer.

A pointer operation can be included in a statement with other operations, so it is important to be sure that the precedence of the operations is specified correctly. An address operator is a unary operation, and thus it is performed before binary operations; unary operations are also performed from right to left if there are more than one in a statement. These precedence rules are summarized in Table 9.1. Remember that parentheses can always be used to change the precedence of operations.

Style

Errors with pointers can cause problems that are difficult to debug. Even worse, pointer errors can often cause a program to give incorrect results while appearing to work properly. Many pointer errors are caused by pointers that were not initialized before being used. *Therefore, it is a good habit to initialize all pointers at the beginning of the program. If a pointer is not initially assigned to a memory location, assign it a NULL value.* A pointer that is assigned a *NULL* value does not point to any memory location. You can determine whether the pointer named *ptr_1* has been assigned to a memory location at some point in the program in an `if` statement that contains a condition such as (*NULL == ptr_1*).

TABLE 9.1   Operator Precedence

Precedence	Operation	Associativity
1	( ) [ ]	innermost first
2	++ −− + − ! (type) & ∗	right to left (unary)
3	∗ / %	left to right
4	+ −	left to right
5	< <= > >=	left to right
6	== !−	left to right
7	&&	left to right
8	‖	left to right
9	?:	right to left
10	= += −= ∗= /= %=	right to left
11	,	left to right

Practice!

For each of the problems that follow, give a memory snapshot that includes all objects after the problem statements are executed. Include as much information as possible. Use question marks to indicate memory locations that have not been initialized.

1. `double x(15.6), y(10.2), *ptr_1(&y), *ptr_2(&x);`
   `*ptr_1 = *ptr_2 + x;`

2. `int w(10), x(2), *ptr_2(&x);`
   `*ptr_2 -= w;`

3. `int x[5]={2,4,6,8,3};`
   `int *ptr_1=NULL, *ptr_2=NULL, *ptr_3=NULL;`
   `ptr_3 = &x[0];`
   `ptr_1 = ptr_2 = ptr_3 + 2;`

4. `int w[4], *first_ptr(NULL), *last_ptr(NULL);`
   `first_ptr = w;`
   `last_ptr =first_ptr + 3;`

9.2 Pointers to Array Elements

Arrays and array handling were covered in detail in Chapters 6 and 7 using offsets to specify individual array elements. Pointers can also be used to specify individual array elements. Array references using pointers and addresses are almost always faster than references using offsets; thus, pointer references for arrays are generally preferred if speed is a concern. As discussed in Section 9.2, pointer references to array values are based on the knowledge that memory assignment of array values is always sequential.

One-Dimensional Arrays

Consider the following declaration that defines and initializes a one-dimensional array with floating-point values:

`double x[6]={1.5, 2.2, 4.3, 7.5, 9.1, 10.5};`

The memory snapshot after this statement is executed is the following:

x[0]	1.5
x[1]	2.2
x[2]	4.3
x[3]	7.5
x[4]	9.1
x[5]	10.5

In referencing the array *x* using standard array notation, reference *x[0]* refers to the first element in the array, reference *x[1]* refers to the second element in the array, and reference *x[k]* refers to the *k*th element in the array. Similar references to an array can be generated with pointers. Assume that a pointer *ptr* has been defined to be a pointer to `double` and is then initialized with the statement

```
ptr = &x[0];
```

The address of the first element in the array is then stored in the pointer *ptr*. Thus, reference **ptr* refers to *x[0]*, reference **(ptr+1)* refers to *x[1]*, and reference **(ptr+k)* refers to *x[k]*. The value of *k* in reference **(ptr+k)* is the offset from the first element in the array.

The following statements compute the sum of the values in the array *x* using array notation and a `for` loop:

```
// Declare and initialize objects.
double x[6], sum(0);
...
// Sum the values in the array x.
for (int k=0; k<=5; k++)
{
    sum += x[k];
}
```

An equivalent set of statements that uses pointers instead of array notation is the following:

```
// Declare and initialize objects.
double x[6], sum(0), *ptr=&x[0];
...
// Sum the values in the array x.
for (int k=0; k<=5; k++)
{
    sum += *(ptr+k);
}
```

Note that reference **(ptr+k)* requires parentheses to perform the operations in the correct order; *k* is added to the address in *ptr*, and then the indirection operator is used to refer to the value pointed to by *ptr+k*. Reference **ptr+k* would be computed as *(*ptr)+k* because a unary operator has precedence over a binary operator.

In the discussion on arrays in Chapters 6, we saw that the name of an array is the address of the first element. Thus, an array name can also be used as a pointer to reference elements in the array. For example, the following two statements are equivalent:

```
ptr = &x[0];
ptr = x;
```

Similarly, reference **(ptr+k)* is also equivalent to **(x+k)*. Thus, the statements to sum array *x* can be simplified to the following:

```
// Declare and initialize objects.
double x[6], sum(0);
...
```

```
//  Sum the values in the array x.
for (int k=0; k<=5; k++)
{
   sum += *(x+k);
}
```

 This example illustrates the use of an array name as an address. The array name can be used in most statements in place of a pointer, but it cannot be used on the left side of an assignment statement, because its value cannot be changed.

Practice!

Assume that an array *g* is defined with the following statement:

```
int g[] = {2, 4, 5, 8, 10, 32, 78};
int *ptr1(g), *ptr2(&g[3]);
```

Give a diagram of the memory allocation, including the array values. Also indicate the offset values from the initial value in the array. Using this information, give the value of the following references.

1. `*g`
2. `*(g+1)`
3. `*g+1`
4. `*(g+5)`
5. `*ptr1`
6. `*ptr2`
7. `*(ptr1 + 1)`
8. `*(ptr2 + 2)`

Character Strings

Recall from Chapter 6 that a character array is an array in which the individual elements are stored as characters. A C-style character string is a character array in which the last array element is a null character. Character strings are used in many engineering applications, including cryptography and pattern recognition. It is often convenient to manipulate character strings via pointers to the strings. Many of the character functions in the header file *cstring*, introduced in Chapter 6, require pointers to strings as arguments, and many return pointers to strings. In this section, we will look at the syntax required to reference C-style character strings using pointers.

One of the functions included in the header file *cstring* is the function named *strstr()*. The function *strstr(ps,pt)* takes a pointer to string *s* and a pointer to string *t* as arguments and returns a pointer to the start of the string *t* within the string *s*. If *t* does not occur in *s*, a *NULL* pointer is returned. We will use this function in our next example.

Assume that we want to count the occurrences of one string in another string. For example, suppose we want to count the number of times that the string *"bb"* occurs in the string *"abbcfgwdbibbw"*. The *strstr()* function will return a pointer to the start of the first occurrence of *"bb"* in *"abbcfgwdbibbw"*, or a *NULL* pointer if *"bb"* is not found. In this example, the *strstr()* function will return a pointer to the beginning of the first occurrence of *"bb"*, as follows:

```
"abbcfgwdbibbw"
   ^
```

To find the next occurrence of the string *"bb"*, we need to search the portion of the string that follows the first position of the occurrence of *"bb"*. The *strstr()* function will then return a pointer to the beginning of the first occurrence of *"bb"* in the new portion of the string as follows:

```
"bcfgwdbibbw"
         ^
```

We repeat the process until the *strstr()* function returns a *NULL* value. The complete program to implement this process follows:

```
/*------------------------------------------------------------------*/
/* Program chapter9_4                                               */
/*                                                                  */
/*   This program counts and prints the number of                  */
/*   times one string appears within another string.               */
/*
#include <iostream>
#include <cstring>
using namespace std;

int main()
{
// Declare and initialize objects.
int count(0);
char strg1[] ="abbcfgwdbibbw" , strg2[] = "bb";
char *ptr1(strg1), *ptr2(strg2);

// Count  number of occurrences of strg2 in strg1.
// While function strstr does not return NULL
// increment count and move ptr1 to next section
// of strg1.
while ((ptr1=strstr(ptr1,ptr2)) != NULL)
```

```
{
  count++;
  ptr1++;
}

//  Print the number of occurrences.
cout << "Count: " << count << endl;

return 0;
}
/*----------------------------------------------------------------*/
```

The output from this program is:

```
count: 2
```

Pointers as Function Arguments

When a pointer is passed as an argument to a function, the pointer can be passed by value or passed by reference. If a pointer is passed by value, the pointer can be used to modify the object it points to, but the value of the pointer argument cannot be modified by the function. If a pointer is passed by reference, the pointer can be used to modify the object it points to, and the value of the pointer argument in can also be modified.

Consider the following program that calls a function to convert a string to uppercase:

```
/*----------------------------------------------------------------*/
/* Program chapter9_5                                             */
/*                                                                */
/* This program converts a string to all upper case.             */
/*                                                                */
#include <iostream>
#include <cstring>
#include <cctype>
using namespace std;

//Function prototypes
void stringupper(char*);

int main()
{
// Declare and initialize objects.
char strg1[] ="abbcfgwdbibbw";
char *ptr_strg1(strg1);

// Ouput string before and after call to function.
cout << ptr_strg1 << endl;
stringupper(ptr_strg1);
cout << ptr_strg1 << endl;

return 0;
}
/*----------------------------------------------------------------*/
```

```
/*--------------------------------------------------------------------*/
/*                                                                  */
/*   This function converts each character in                       */
/*   the string pointed to by ptr_strg to upper case.               */
/*                                                                  */
void stringupper(char* ptr_strg)
{
  // While not end of string (while character is not null).
  while(*ptr_strg)
  {
     // Convert character to upper case
     *ptr_strg = toupper(*ptr_strg);

     // Mover pointer to next character
     ptr_strg++;
  }
}
/*--------------------------         --------------------------------*/
```

In this example, the pointer *ptr_str1* is passed to the function *stringupper()*, and the string pointed to by *ptr_str* is converted to uppercase. The formal parameter *ptr_strg* is incremented in the function to traverse the string, but no change is made to the argument in `main` because a pass by value is used. The output from this program is

```
abbcfgwdbibbw
ABBCFGWDBIBBW
```

The next program modifies the function in program 9_5 to use pass by reference instead of pass by value:

```
/*--------------------------------------------------------------------*/
/* Program chapter9_6                                               */
/*                                                                  */
/*   This program converts a string to all upper case.              */
/*                                                                  */
#include <iostream>
#include <cstring>
#include <cctype>
using namespace std;

//Function prototypes
void stringupper(char*&);

int main()
{
// Declare and initialize objects.
char strg1[] ="abbcfgwdbibbw";
char *ptr_strg1 = strg1;

// Ouput string before and after call to function.
cout << ptr_strg1 << endl;
```

```
stringupper(ptr_strg1);
cout << ptr_strg1 << endl;
return 0;
}
/*-----------------------------------------------------------------*/
/*-----------------------------------------------------------------*/
/*                                                                 */
/*  This function converts each character in the string            */
/*  pointed to by ptr_strg to upper case.                          */
/*                                                                 */
void stringupper(char* &ptr_strg)
{
  // While not end of string.
  while(*ptr_strg)
  {
     // Convert character to upper case
     *ptr_strg = toupper(*ptr_strg);

     // Mover pointer to next character
     ptr_strg++;
  }
}
/*-----------------------------------------------------------------*/
```

Notice the order of operators in the function prototype and the function header. When passing a pointer by reference the address operator must follow the dereference operator.

In this version of the program, the string is converted to uppercase just as it was in program *chapter9_6*. However, in this version, incrementing the formal parameter in the function changes the argument in main because a pass by reference is used. After the call to the function *stringupper()*, the pointer *ptr_strg1* points to the null character at the end of the string. Thus, the uppercase string will not be printed. A sample output from this program is

```
abbcfgwdbibbw
```

In both examples, the function *stringupper()* was able to modify the string being pointed to by the formal parameter.

Sometimes it is desirable to pass a pointer as an argument to a function and also ensure that the function will not inadvertently modify the object being pointed to. We can use the const modifier in the function prototype, and the function header, to protect the object being pointer to, as illustrated in the next example. The definition for the function *stringupper()* is not included in this example:

```
/*-----------------------------------------------------------------*/
/* Program chapter9_7                                              */
/*                                                                 */
/*  This program counts the number of times a specified            */
/*  letter appears in an upper case string.                        */
/*                                                                 */
```

```cpp
#include <iostream>
#include <cstring>
#include <cctype>
using namespace std;

//Function prototypes.
void stringupper(char*);
int countchar(const char*, char);

int main()
{
// Declare and initialize objects.
char strg1[] ="abbcfgwdbibbw";
char *ptr_strg1 =strg1, ch='B';

// Convert string to upper case.
stringupper(ptr_strg1);

cout << "The letter " << ch << " appears "
    << countchar(ptr_strg1, ch) << " times in the string "
    << ptr_strg1 << endl;

return 0;
}
/*-----------------------------------------------------------------*/
/*-----------------------------------------------------------------*/
/*                                                                 */
/*   This function counts the number of times the character ch     */
/*   appears in the string pointed to by ptr_strg.                 */
/*                                                                 */
int countchar(const char* ptr_strg, char ch)
{
   // Declare and initialize local objects.
   int cnt(0);

   // While not end of string.
   while(*ptr_strg)
   {
   // Look for ch and increment cnt.
     if( *ptr_strg == ch)
       cnt++;

   // Mover pointer to next character
     ptr_strg++;
   }
   return cnt;
}
/*-----------------------------------------------------------------*/
```

This program generates the following output:

```
The letter B appears 5 times in the string ABBCFGWDBIBBW
```

The function *countchar( )* cannot modify the object pointed to by *ptr_strg*. For example, if we were to make the nagging error of using the assignment operator instead of the equality operator in the `if` statement, as in

```
if ( *ptr_strg = ch);
```

the compiler would flag it as an error.

The **const** modifier can also be used in a type declaration statement when defining pointers, as in the following statement:

```
const char *cptr = "abbcfgwdbibbw";
```

pointer to a
constant

In the preceding statement, *cptr* is defined to be a **pointer to a constant.** It is important to note that the pointer *cptr* is not constant, but what's pointed to by *cptr* is considered to be constant. Thus, the value of *cptr* can be reassigned, but we cannot use *cptr* to modify an object. The following code segment illustrates this use of the `const` modifier:

```
// Declare and initialize objects.
int x(5), y(10), *ptr1(&x);
const int *cptr(&y);

// Print values.
cout << *ptr1 <<',' << *cptr << endl;
cout << x << ',' << y << endl;

// Increment x.
(*ptr1)++;

// Print values.
cout << *ptr1 <<',' << *cptr << endl;
cout << x << ',' << y << endl;

// Reassign both pointers.
ptr1 = &y;
cptr = &x;

// Increment y.
(*ptr1)++;

// Print values.
cout << *ptr1 <<',' << *cptr << endl;
cout << x << ',' << y << endl;
```

The output generated by this code segment is shown below:

```
5,10
5,10
6,10
6,10
11,6
6,11
```

constant pointer

A **constant pointer** can be declared in a type declaration statement, as in the statement

```
char *const cptr = "A standard message.";
```

Using this syntax, the value of *cptr* cannot be reassigned, but the object pointed to by *cptr* can be modified.

Practice!

Assume that objects have been defined with the following statements:

```
int i(5), j(10);
int *iptr(&i);
const int *cptr(&j);
int *const jptr(&j);
```

Determine whether the following statements are valid or invalid.

    1. cptr = jptr;

    2. jptr = cptr;

    3. *cptr = *jptr;

    4. *cptr = *iptr;

    5. *jptr = *cptr;

    6. iptr = cptr;

9.3   Dynamic Memory Allocation

Dynamic memory allocation allows a program to allocate memory for objects during execution of the program rather than determining memory requirements at the time the program is compiled. This is important when a program uses an array thats size is not determined until the program is executed; without dynamic memory allocation, the program would have to specify the maximum size anticipated for the array. For systems with limited memory, it is possible that there would not be enough memory to run a program if all arrays had to be specified to the maximum size anticipated. Dynamic memory is allocated from a region of available memory

free store

referred to as the program's **free store**. Dynamic memory is allocated on the free store using the new operator and returned to the free store using the delete operator.

The new Operator

Dynamic memory allocation is specified using the keyword new, followed by a type specifier to indicate the data type of the object to be allocated. The new expression returns the address of the new object in memory. To allocate memory for a single object of type int we could use either of the following sets of statements:

```
//  Example 1
//  Dynamically allocate memory for one integer object.
//  No initial value is given to the object.
int *ptr;
ptr = new int;


//  Example 2
//  Dynamically allocate memory for one integer object.
//  Give an initial value of -1 to the object.
int *ptr;
ptr = new int(-1);
```

In both of the preceding examples, the `new` expression returns a value that is assigned to a pointer. If memory is available on the free store, the pointer will contain the address of the memory. In the first example, no initial value is assigned to the newly allocated memory, as illustrated in Figure 9.1. In the second example, a value of -1 is specified as an initial value and is assigned to the newly allocated memory, as illustrated in Figure 9.2.

Since the free store is finite there is always a possibility that a request for new memory cannot be honored. If there is insufficient memory on the free store for a memory request, in general, the `new` operator will `throw` **an exception** called *bad_alloc*. This exception will terminate execution of the program. There is a mechanism supported by C++ that allows a program to detect an exception and recover from the potential error. This mechanism is referred to as **exception handling.** A good reference on exception handling is "C++ How to Program," Second Edition, by Deitel and Deitel, Prentice Hall, © 1998, Upper Saddle River, NJ.

`throw` an exception

exception handling

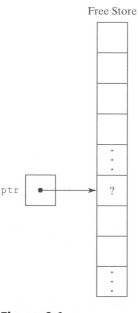

Figure 9.1

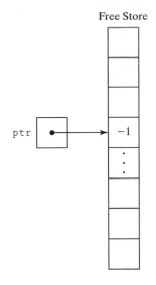

Free Store

ptr

Figure 9.2

Dynamically Allocated Arrays

Dynamic memory
allocation

Dynamic memory allocation is very useful in solving engineering problems that require large arrays. Assume that we want to dynamically allocate a block of memory to store a `double` array containing *npts* elements. (In this example, we assign a small value to *npts* for illustration, but more commonly it would be a large value, computed by other statements in the program or read from the keyboard or a data file.) The following set of statements specify the desired allocation:

```
//  Declare objects.
int npts = 10;
double *dptr;
...
//  Dynamically allocate memory.
dptr = new double[npts];
```

As illustrated in Figure 9.3, a contiguous block of memory is allocated on the free store to hold 10 objects of type `double`. The pointer *dptr* is assigned the memory address of the first element in the array. References to the array can be made using pointer notation, such as **(dptr+2)*. References to the array can also be made using standard array notation, such as *dptr[2]*.

When using `new` to dynamically allocate objects, the data type specified for the object can be any built in data type or any programmer-defined class type.

The delete Operator

de-allocated

When a program is finished using memory that has been dynamically allocated using `new`, the memory can be returned to the free-store, or **de-allocated,** using the operator `delete`. The

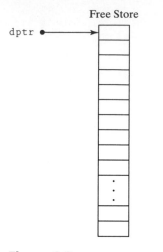

Figure 9.3

following program illustrates the use of the operators new and delete:

```
/*----------------------------------------------------------------*/
/*  Program chapter9_8                                            */
/*  This program illustrates the use of operators new and delete.  */

#include<iostream>
using namespace std;

int main()
{
// Declare objects.
int *ptr, npts(10);
double *darr_ptr;

// Dynamically allocate one integer object.
ptr = new int(-1);

// Dynamically allocate array of type double.
darr_ptr = new double[npts];

// Assign what is pointed to by ptr to all elements of dynamic array.
for(int i=0; i<=npts-1; i++)
{
    darr_ptr[i] = *ptr;
}

// Print all values in dynamic array.
for(int i=0; i<=npts-1; i++)
```

```
{
    cout << darr_ptr[i] << ' ';
}
cout << endl;

//  Return memory to free-store.
delete ptr;
delete [] darr_ptr;
return 0;
}
/*- - - - - - - - - - - - - - - - - - - - - - - - - - - - - - - - - - - - - - - - - - - - - - - - - - - - - - - - - - - - - -*/
```

The output from this program is as follows:

```
-1 -1 -1 -1 -1 -1 -1 -1 -1 -1
```

 When deallocating an array, the empty square brackets are required with the `delete` operator. If we omit the brackets, our program may not continue to execute correctly.

9.4   Problem Solving Applied: Seismic Event Detection

Special sensors called seismometers are used to collect earth motion information. These seismometers can be used in a passive environment, in which they record the earth's motion, which includes earthquakes and tidal motion. By analyzing ground motion from an earthquake using data from several seismometers, it is possible to determine the epicenter of the earthquake and the intensity of the earthquake. The earthquake intensity is usually measured using the Richter scale, which is a scale from 1 to 10 named after U.S. seismologist C. F. Richter.

Write a program that reads a set of seismometer data from a data file named *seismic.dat*. The first line of the file contains two values: the number of seismometer data readings that follow in the file and the time interval in seconds that occurred between consecutive measurements. Array memory is dynamically allocated based on the number of seismometer data readings in the seismic data file. The time interval is a floating-point value, and we assume that all the measurements were taken with the same time interval between them. After reading and storing the data measurements, the program should identify possible earthquakes, which are also called seismic events, using a power ratio. At a specific point in time, this ratio is the quotient of a short-time power measurement divided by a longtime power measurement. If the ratio is greater than a given threshold, an event may have occurred at that point in time. Given a specific point in the data measurements, the short-time power is the average power, or average squared value, of the measurements using the specified point plus a small number of points that occurred just previous to the specified point. The longtime power is the average power of the measurements using the specified point plus a larger number of points that occurred just previous to the specified point. (The set of points used in a calculation is sometimes referred to as a data window.) The threshold is generally greater than 1 to avoid detecting events in constant data because the short-time power is equal to the longtime power if the data values are all the same value. Assume that the numbers of measurements for the short-time power and for the longtime power are read from the keyboard. Set the threshold value to 1.5.

1. PROBLEM STATEMENT

Determine the locations of possible seismic events using a set of seismometer measurements from a data file.

2. INPUT/OUTPUT DESCRIPTION

The inputs to this program are a data file named *seismic.dat* and the number of measurements to use for short-time power and longtime power. The output is a report giving the times of potential seismic events.

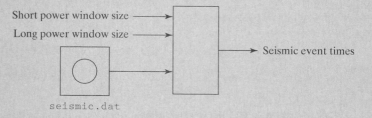

Short power window size ⟶

Long power window size ⟶

⟶ Seismic event times

seismic.dat

3. HAND EXAMPLE

Suppose that a data file contains the following data, which includes number of points to follow (11) and time interval between points (0.01), followed by the 11 values that correspond to a sequence of values $x_0, x_1, \ldots x_1 0$:

```
11 0.01
1    2    1    1    1    5    4    2    1    1    1
```

If the short-time power measurement is made using two samples and the longtime power measurement is made using five measurements, then we can compute power ratios, beginning with the rightmost point, in a window:

```
1 2 1 1 1 5 4 2 1 1 1
      └─┘

short window
└──────────┘

long window

Point x4:     Short-time power = (1 + 1)/2 = 1

Long-time power= (1 + 1 + 1 + 4 + 1 )/5 = 1.6
Ratio = 1/1.6 = 0.63

1 2 1 1 1 5 4 2 1 1 1
      └─┘

short window
└──────────┘

long window
```

Point x5:   Short-time power = (25 + 1)/2 = 13

Long-time power = (25 + 1 + 1 + 1 + 4)/5 = 6.4

Ratio = 13/6.4 = 2.03

1 2 1 1 1 5 4 2 1 1 1

short window

long window

Point x6:   Short-time power = (16 + 25)/2 = 20.5

Long-time power = (16 + 25 + 1 + 1 + 1)/5 = 8.8

Ratio = 20.5/8.8 = 2.33

1 2 1 1 1 5 4 2 1 1 1

short window

long window

Point x7:   Short-time power = (4 + 16)/2 = 10

Long-time power = (4 + 16 + 25 + 1 + 1)/5 = 9.4

Ratio = 10/9.4 = 1.06

1 2 1 1 1 5 4 2 1 1 1
short window

long window

Point x8:   Short-time power = (1 + 4)/2 = 2.5

Long-time power = (1 + 4 + 16 + 25 + 1)/5 = 9.4

Ratio = 2.5/9.4 = 0.27

1 2 1 1 1 5 4 2 1 1 1

short window

long window

```
Point x9:     Short-time power = (1 + 1)/2 = 1

Long-time power = (1 + 1 + 4 + 16 + 25 )/5 = 9.4

Ratio = 1/9.4 = 0.11

1 2 1 1 1 5 4 2 1 1 1
                  └─┘
short window

long window  └─────┘

Point x10:    Short-time power = (1 + 1)/2 = 1

Long-time power = (1 + 1 + 1 + 4 + 16 )/5 = 4.6

Ratio = 1/4.6 = 0.22
```

By using the previous ratios computed, possible seismic events occurred at points x5 and x6. Because the time interval between points is 0.01 second, the times that correspond to the seismic events are 0.05 and 0.06 second. (We assume that the first point in the file occurred at 0.0 second.)

4. ALGORITHM DEVELOPMENT

We first develop the decomposition outline because it divides the solution into a series of sequential steps.

Decomposition Outline

    (a) Read data header and allocate memory.

    (b) Read seismic data from the data file and read numbers of measurement for power from the keyboard.

    (c) Compute power ratios and print possible seismic event times.

Step 3 involves computing power ratios and comparing them to the threshold to determine whether a possible event occurred. Because we need to compute two power measurements for each possible event location, we implement the power measurement as a function. The refinement in pseudocode for the main function and the power function can now be developed:

Refinement in Pseudocode

```
main:  set threshold to 1.5
       read npts and time-interval
       allocate memory for sensor array
```

```
            read the values into sensor array
            read short-window, long-window from keyboard
            set k to long-window - 1
            while k<= npts-1
                set short-power to power(sensor,short-window,k)
                set long-power to power(sensor,long-window,k)
                set ratio to short-power/long-power
                if ratio > threshold
                    print k*time-interval
                increment k by 1
power(x,length,n):
    set xsquare to zero
    set k to 0
    while k<=n 1
        add x[length-k]*x[length-k] to xsquare
    return xsquare/length
```

We are now ready to convert the pseudocode to C++:

```cpp
/*-------------------------------------------------------------*/
/*  Program chapter9_9                                     */
/*                                                         */
/*  This program reads a seismic data file and then        */
/*  determines the times of possible seismic events.       */
/*  Dynamic memory allocation is used.                     */

#include <fstream>
#include <string>
#include <cmath>
using namespace std;

// Set threshold.
const double THRESHOLD = 1.5;

// Function prototypes.
double power_w(double arr[], int length, int n);
int main()
{
   // Declare objects.
   int k, npts, short_window, long_window;
   double time_incr, *sensor, short_power, long_power,
          ratio;
   string filename;
   ifstream fin;

   // Prompt user for file name and open file for input.
   cout << "Enter name of input file\n";
   cin >> filename;
   fin.open(filename.c_str());
```

```
      if(fin.fail())
      {
         cerr << "error opening input file" << endl;
      }
      else
      {
      //  Read data header and allocate memory.
         fin >> npts >> time_incr;
         sensor = new double[npts];

      //  Program continues if no exception is thrown.
         cout << "Memory allocated." << endl;

      //  Read data into an array.
         for (k=0; k<=npts-1; k++)
             fin >> sensor[k];
      //  Read window sizes from the keyboard.
         cout << "Enter number of points for short-window: \n";
         cin >> short_window;
         cout << "Enter number of points for long-window: \n";
         cin >> long_window;

      //  Compute power ratios and search for events.
         for (k=long_window-1; k<=npts-1; k++)
         {
             short_power = power_w(sensor, k, short_window);
             long_power = power_w(sensor, k, long_window);
             ratio = short_power/long_power;
             if (ratio > THRESHOLD)
                 cout << "Possible event at " << time_incr*k
                                              << " seconds \n";

         }
      //  Return memory to free-store, close file, and exit program.
         delete [] sensor;
         fin.close();
      }
   return 0;
}
/*-----------------------------------------------------*/
/*-----------------------------------------------------*/
/*  This function computes the average power in a      */
/*  specified window of a double array.                */
double power_w(double arr[], int length,  int n)
{
   //  Declare and initialize objects.
   double xsquare(0);

   //  Compute sum of values squared in the array x.
   for (int k=0; k<=n-1; k++)
```

```
      {
          xsquare += pow(arr[length-k],2);
      }

      /*  Return the average squared value.  */
      return xsquare/n;
   }
   /*                                                    */
```

5. TESTING

The output from the program using the data file from the hand example is as follows:

```
Memory allocated.
Enter number of points for short-window:
2
Enter number of points for long-window:
5
Possible event at 0.05 seconds
Possible event at 0.06 seconds
```

Modify!

Modify the event-detection program to include the following new capabilities.

1. Allow the user to enter the threshold value. Check the value to be sure that it is a positive value greater than 1.

2. Print the number of events detected by the program. (Assume that events with contiguous times are all part of the same event. Thus, for the hand example, one event was detected.)

3. Use the *vector* class instead of an array, eliminating the need for new and delete.

9.5   Common Errors Using new and delete

Dynamically allocated memory should always be returned to the free store once it is no longer needed so that the memory becomes available for use with another dynamic allocation. This requires being careful to keep track of all pointers to the memory space. After the delete operator is used with a pointer to return memory to the *free store,* the pointer will point to an invalid memory space or, depending on the compiler, it may retain the memory address of the deleted memory. In either case, the pointer should not be referenced again until it has been assigned a new, valid address.

It is easy to make errors when working with pointers and dynamic memory allocation and difficult to find these errors. The following are some of the more common errors:

- Referencing a pointer to dynamically allocated memory after the delete operator has been used to return the memory to the free store.

memory leak

- Failing to return memory to the free store when it is no longer being used. This is often referred to as a **memory leak.**

- Using the delete operator with a pointer that does not reference memory that has been dynamically allocated using the new operator.

- Omitting the square brackets when using delete to free a dynamically allocated array.

To avoid many of the errors associated with dynamic memory allocation of arrays, we recommend using the *vector* class.

Practice!

Assume that the pointers *iptr, jptr,* and *arr_ptr* have been defined with the following statements:

```
int *iptr, *jptr, *arr_ptr;
iptr = new int(10);
arr_ptr = new int[5];
```

Draw a memory allocation diagram, and show the output line (or lines) generated by each of the following set of statements. We recommend that you program each example and run it to determine the output generated on your system.

1. ```
   jptr = iptr;
   cout << *iptr << ' ' << *jptr << endl;
   cout <<  iptr << ' ' <<  jptr << endl;
   delete iptr;
   cout << iptr  << ' ' <<  jptr << endl;
   ```

2. ```
   cout << arr_ptr << endl;
   for(int i=0; i<=4; i++)
      arr_ptr[i] = i;
   for(int i=0; i<=4; i++)
      cout << *(arr_ptr)++ << ' ';
   cout << endl << arr_ptr << endl;
   for(int i=0; i<=4; i++)
      cout << arr_ptr[i] << ' ';
   ```

Practice!

```
3. for(int i=0; i<=4; i++)
     arr_ptr[i] = i;
   jptr = &arr_ptr[2];
   cout << arr_ptr << ' ' << jptr << endl;
   cout << *arr_ptr << ' ' << *jptr << endl;
   delete [] arr_ptr;
   cout << arr_ptr << ' ' << jptr << ' ' << *jptr << endl;
```

9.6   Data Structures*

When we work with data structures such as arrays and vectors, we are working with a contiguous block of memory. It is easy to access individual elements of an array or a *vector* because each access is a fixed offset from the starting address. However, it is not easy to insert or remove an element unless the element is the last element. To insert or remove an element at any location other than the last requires copying all elements below the inserted or removed element into a new memory location. This is very inefficient, especially when working with very large amounts of data.

Linked data structures

Linked data structures, such as linked lists, stacks and queues, are designed for efficient inserts and removals. Memory is allocated and deleted as needed during execution of the program, and pointers are used to link the elements, since the elements do not form a contiguous block of memory. Using pointers to link the elements allows for efficient inserting and removing of elements; links need to be reassigned, but no coping of elements is required. However, accessing elements in a linked structure is less efficient than array access because

traverse

we must **traverse** the structure for each access. To traverse a linked data structure, we must begin at the first element in the structure and follow the links to successive elements until we reach the element to be accessed.

The link Class

linked list

A **linked list** is a data structure organized as a group of elements that are linked by pointers. An individual element consists of data and a pointer to the next element. We generally assume that there is some order to the data stored in the elements, such as an ascending order, and that we may want to insert new elements or remove elements from this ordered list.

Figure 9.4 illustrates a linked list with four elements, containing the ordered information 10, 14, 21, 35. A separate pointer, which we have labeled *head,* points to the first element in the linked list.

To access data in a linked list, we use the *head* pointer to reference the information in the first element (the element containing the value 10 in this example). Then, since the first element contains a pointer to the next element (the element containing the value 14), we can use this information to move to the second element. Similarly, we use the pointer in the second element to move to the third element. The last element in a linked list will contain a pointer value of *NULL* to indicate that we have reached the last element in the list. We use the symbol Ω to indicate a value of *NULL* in our diagrams.

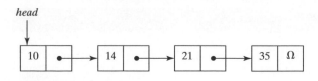

Figure 9.4 Linked list.

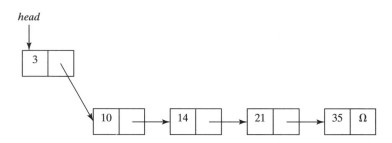

Figure 9.5 Insert before the first element (requires updating the head pointer).

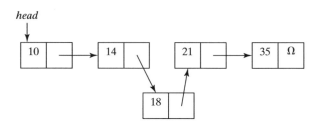

Figure 9.6 Insert between two elements.

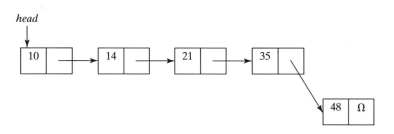

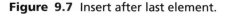

Figure 9.7 Insert after last element.

To insert a value into a linked list, we must traverse the list to find the location for the insert. We begin at the *head* of the list and move from one element to another using the pointer in the current element, until we find the desired location for the insert. The insertion location can be one of four places: before the first element, between two elements, after the last element, or in an empty list. Figures 9.5 through 9.8 outline each of these cases assuming that we started with the linked list given in Figure 9.4 for each of the first three cases.

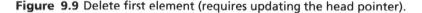

Figure 9.8 Insert in an empty list (requires updating the head pointer).

Figure 9.9 Delete first element (requires updating the head pointer).

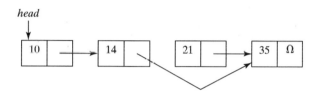

Figure 9.10 Delete an element between two elements.

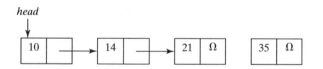

Figure 9.11 Delete the last element.

To delete a value from a linked list, we must traverse the list to find the element to be deleted. We begin at the head of the list and move from one element to another using the pointer in the current element. If the element to be deleted is found, it can be the first element, an element between two other elements, or the last element. Figures 9.9 through 9.11 outline each of these three cases. For each case we start with the linked list given in Figure 9.4.

Writing programmer-defined functions to insert and remove elements from a linked list requires careful memory management and reassignment of pointers. The Standard C++ library includes the **list class,** which provides an object based implementation of a linked list. The header file *list* must be included to use the *list* class.

list class

When a *list* is defined, the data type of the elements in the *list* must be specified. The following statement defines an empty list of integers, named *alist:*

```
list<int> alist;
```

To systematically insert and remove elements from a *list,* we must be able to traverse the list. The *list* class provides a special type of pointer, called an *iterator,* to support accessing

TABLE 9.2   Member Functions of the list class

begin( )	returns an iterator that points to first element in the list.
end( )	returns an iterator that points to *one past the last element in the list*.
empty( )	returns true if the list is empty, false otherwise
insert(iterator, value)	insert value at location specified by the iterator.
remove(value)	remove all instances of value from the list.
sort( )	arranges elements in ascending order.

successive elements in a list. An *iterator* is basically a pointer to an element in a list. We can define an *iterator* named *iter* to access elements in our *list* of integers with the following statement:

```
list<int>::iterator iter;
```

The *list* class includes numerous member functions to support a *list* structure, including functions to insert and remove elements from a list. Table 9.2 lists several of the commonly used member functions of the *list* class.

The following program illustrates the use of several of these functions:

```
/*------------------------------------------------------------------*/
/* Program chapter9_10                                              */
/*                                                                  */
/* This programs creates a list of data entered from
   standard input.                                                  */
/* The list is sorted and printed to standard output.              */

#include<iostream>
#include<list>
using namespace std;

int main()
{

  // Declare objects.
  list<int> alist;
  list<int>::iterator iter;
  int ivalue;

  // Set iter to beginning of alist.
  iter = alist.begin();

  cout << "enter integer values, 's' to stop\n";

  // While valid data, read value and insert into list.
  while(cin >> ivalue)
```

```
  {
    alist.insert(iter, ivalue);
    iter++;
  }

  // Sort the list in ascending order.
  alist.sort();

  // Print the list to standard output.
  cout << "Sorted list: \n";
  for(iter=alist.begin(); iter!=alist.end(); iter++)
  {
    cout << *iter << endl;
  }
  return 0;
}
```

If the data

```
35 18 21 14 10 2 s
```

were entered from the keyboard, the program would generate the following output:

```
Enter integer values, 's' to stop
Sorted List:
2
10
14
18
21
35
```

The statement

```
iter++;
```

does not do standard pointer arithmetic, but rather reassigns *iter* to point to the next element in the *list*.

The stack Class

stack

A **stack** is known as a last-in-first-out (LIFO) data structure. You can insert (*push*) and remove (*pop*) elements only from the top of the stack. Thus, the element removed from a stack is always the last element that was added to the stack.

Stacks are essential in the design of compilers and in unraveling the flow of function calls within a program. For example, each time a function is called, a return address is added to the stack. Each `return` statement references the last address added to the stack. Figure 9.12 illustrates the behavior of a stack.

stack class

The Standard C++ library includes the **stack** `class`, which provides an object-based implementation of a stack. The header file *stack* must be included to use the *stack* `class`.

TABLE 9.3	Member Functions of the stack class
empty( )	returns true if the stack is empty, false otherwise.
pop( )	remove top element from the stack. Does not return a value.
push(value)	add *value* to top of stack.
size( )	returns the number of elements in the stack.
top( )	returns the value of the first element in the stack. The element is not removed from the stack.

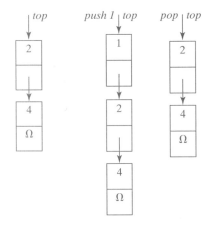

Figure 9.12 Behavior of a stack.

When a *stack* is defined, the data type of the elements in the *stack* must be specified. The following statement defines an empty *stack* of integers named *astack:*

```
stack<int> astack;
```

Table 9.3 lists member functions of the stack class. The following program illustrates the use of several of these functions:

```
/*--------------------------------------------------------------------*/
/* Program chapter9_11                                                */
/*                                                                    */
/* This programs creates a stack of data entered from
   standard input.                                                   */
/* The stack is printed to standard output.                         */

#include<iostream>
#include<stack>
using namespace std;
```

```
int main()
{

    // Declare objects.
    stack<int> astack;
    int ivalue;

    cout << "enter integer values, 's' to stop\n";

    // While valid data, read value and add to stack.
    while(cin >> ivalue)
    {
        astack.push(ivalue);
    }

    // Print values to standard output.
    cout << "Elements from the stack: \n";
    while(!astack.empty())
    {
    // Access the top element
        cout << astack.top() << endl;

    // Remove top element from the stack.
        astack.pop();
    }
    return 0;
}
```

If the data

```
35 18 21 14 s
```

were entered from the keyboard, the program would generate the following output:

```
Enter integer values, 's' to stop
Elements from the stack:
14
21
18
35
```

Notice that the order of the elements has been reversed.

The queue Class

queue

A **queue** is known as a first-in-first-out (FIFO) data structure. You can add (*push*) elements only to the back of a queue and remove (*pop*) elements only from the front of the queue. Thus, the element removed from a queue is always the first element that was added to the queue.

TABLE 9.4   Member Functions of the queue class

empty( )	returns true if the queue is empty and false otherwise.
pop( )	removes front element from the queue. Does not return a value.
push(value)	adds value to front of queue.
size( )	returns the number of elements in the queue.
top( )	returns value of the element at the front of the queue. The element is not removed from the queue.

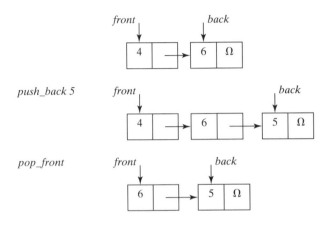

Figure 9.13 Behavior of a queue.

Queues are useful data structures in computer engineering and computer science application. For example, operating systems use queues to process job requests. Job requests, such as a request for a printer, wait in a queue to be processed. The job request at the front of the queue is the first to be processed. Figure 9.13 illustrates the behavior of a queue.

The Standard C++ library includes the *queue* class, which provides an object-based implementation of a queue. The header file *queue* must be included to use the *queue* class. When a *queue* is defined, the data type of the elements in the *queue* must be specified. The following statement defines an empty *queue* of integers, named *aqueue:*

```
queue<int> aqueue;
```

Table 9.4 lists some of the member functions of the *queue* class. The following program illustrates the use of several of these functions:

```
/*-------------------------------------------------------------*/
/* Program chapter9_12                                         */
/*                                                             */
/* This programs creates a queue of data entered from
   standard input.                                             */
/* The queue is printed to standard output.                    */
#include<iostream>
#include<queue>
using namespace std;
```

```
int main()
{

   // Declare objects.
   queue<int> aqueue;
   int ivalue;

   cout << "enter integer values, 's' to stop\n";

   // While valid data, read value and add to back of queue.
   while(cin >> ivalue)
   {
      aqueue.push(ivalue);
   }

   // Print values to standard output.
   cout << "Elements in the queue: \n";
   while(!aqueue.empty())
   {
   // Access element at the front of the queue.
      cout << aqueue.top() << endl;

   // Remove element from the front of the queue.
      aqueue.pop();
   }
   return 0;
}
```

If the data

```
35 18 21 14 s
```

were entered from the keyboard, the program would generate the following output:

```
Enter integer values, 's' to stop
Elements in the queue:
35
18
21
14
```

 ## 9.7 Problem Solving Applied: Concordance of a Text File*

A concordance of a text file is an alphabetical list of the unique words in the text file. Here is a concordance of the preceding sentence:

```
a
an
alphabetical
concordance
```

```
file
in
is
list
of
text
the
unique
words
```

Write a programs that prompts the user for the name of a input text file, and output file. Build a concordance of the file and print the concordance to an output file.

1. PROBLEM STATEMENT

Build a concordance of a text file. Write the concordance, along with a count of the unique words in the text file, to an output file.

2. INPUT/OUTPUT DESCRIPTION

The following diagram shows that the input to the program is a text file, and that the output is a concordance of the text file along with the count of unique words. We will use the *list* class to define a list, where each element in the list is of type *string*.

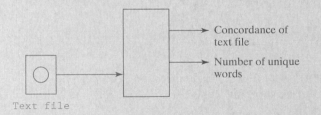

Concordance of text file

Number of unique words

Text file

3. HAND EXAMPLE

Suppose our text file contained only the following text:

```
A concordance of a text file is an alphabetical list of
the unique words in the text file.
```

Our program would generate the following output file:

```
There are 13 distinct words in the text file:
a
an
alphabetical
```

```
concordance
file
in
is
list
of
text
the
unique
words
```

4. ALGORITHM DEVELOPMENT

We first develop the decomposition outline to break the solution into a series of sequential steps:

Decomposition Outline

1. Open input and output files.

2. Read a word from the input file.

3. Insert word if the word is not already in the list.

4. Alphabetize list of unique words.

5. Write the size and contents of the list to output file.

Step 2 in the decomposition outline involves a loop that reads the text file one character at a time until a nonalpha character is reached. A nonalpha character will signal the end of a word. Other than their use as delimiters between words, all nonalpha characters will be ignored. All alpha characters will be converted to lowercase. We will use a function to perform this task. Step 3 requires that we insert a word if it is not already in the list. We will use a function that utilizes member functions of the *list* class. Step 4 involves sorting the list in ascending order. We will use the generic *sort()* function. Since the list may be long, step 5 will print the list three words per line. We will use a function to perform this task. The refinement in pseudocode is the following:

Refinement in Pseudocode

```
main:  open input file
          get_word(istream,string)
          while(string size in not 0)
            insert_word(list,string)
            get_word(string)
          sort(list)
          print size of list
          display_list(ostream,list)
```

```
get_word(istream,string):
      clear string
      read a character
      while(not end of file and character is not alpha)
          read next character
      while(not end of file and character is an alpha)
          append lower case character to string
          input next character
insert_word(list, string)
      if(string is not in list)
          insert string
display_list(ostream,list)
      set counter to 0
      while(not end of list)
        print list element
        increment counter
        if(counter mod 3 is zero)
            print newline
```

The steps in the pseudocode are now detailed enough to convert into C++ code:

```cpp
/*-------------------------------------------------------------------*/
/* Program chapter9_13                                               */
/* This program builds a concordance of a text file.                */
/*                                                                   */
#include <fstream>
#include <string>
#include <cctype>
#include <iomanip>
#include <list>
#include <algorithm>
using namespace std;

// Function prototypes.
void get_word(istream& in_stream, string& w);
void insert_word(string word, list<string> &wordlist);
void display_list(ostream& out_stream, list <string> wordlist);

int main()
{
// Declare objects.
ifstream in_stream;
ofstream out_stream;

string infile, outfile;//filenames
string word;          // string to hold current word

// Prompt for filenames and open files
cout << "Enter the input file name ";
```

```
      cin >> infile;
      cout << "Enter the output file name ";
      cin >> outfile;

      in_stream.open(infile.c_str());
      if(in_stream.fail())
        cout << "fail to open file " << infile << endl;
      else
      {
        out_stream.open(outfile.c_str());
        list <string> wordlist;
        list <string>::iterator iter;
        get_word(in_stream,word);   // get a word

        // While non-empty word was returned
        while(word.size())
        {
          insert_word(word, wordlist);
          get_word(in_stream,word);   // get a word
        }
        wordlist.sort();
        out_stream << "There were " << wordlist.size()
                   << " distinct words. \n";
        out_stream << "\nHere is the ordered list of words\n";
        display_list(out_stream,wordlist);

      }//end else
      return 0;
      }
      /*------------------------------------------------------------*/


      /*------------------------------------------------------------*/
      /* This function will insert word into wordlist               */
      /* if word is not found in wordlist.                          */
      /*                                                            */
      void insert_word(string word, list<string> &wordlist)
      {
        list<string>::iterator iter;

        iter = find(wordlist.begin(), wordlist.end(), word);

        if( iter == wordlist.end() )
        {
        // Word is not in list.  Insert word.
          wordlist.insert(iter, word);
        }
      }
      /*------------------------------------------------------------*/
```

```
/*------------------------------------------------------------------*/
/* This function returns the next word from the input stream.    */
/* All non-alpha characters are treated as delimiters.           */
/* The function will ignore all leading non-alpha characters,    */
/* then read and store the following alpha characters            */
/* until it reaches the next non alpha character.                */
void get_word(istream& in_stream, string& w)
{
  char ch;
  w = ""; //clear word

  in_stream.get(ch);
  while( !isalpha(ch)&& !in_stream.eof() )// skip non-alpha
  {
    in_stream.get(ch);
  }

  while( isalpha(ch) && !in_stream.eof() ) // read and store alpha
  {
    ch = tolower(ch);
    w += ch;
    in_stream.get(ch);
  }
}
/*------------------------------------------------------------------*/


/*------------------------------------------------------------------*/
/* This function outputs the list of words to an output stream.  */
/* Three words per column are printer.                           */
void display_list(ostream& out_stream, list<string> wordlist)
{
  int columns(3), counter(0);
  list<string>::iterator iter;
  out_stream << setiosflags(ios::left);

  // Position iter at beginning of list.
  iter = wordlist.begin();
  while(iter != wordlist.end())
  {
    out_stream << setw(20) << (*iter).c_str();
    iter++;
    counter++;
    if(counter%columns == 0)
    {
      out_stream << endl;
    }
  }
}
```

5. TESTING

If we use the text from the hand example, we get the following information written to a data file:

```
There are 13 distinct words in the text file:
a                an             alphabetical
concordance      file           in
is               list           of
text             the            unique
words
```

SUMMARY

In this chapter, we looked at the relationships between the value stored in an object, the identifier assigned to a object, and the address of the memory location used to store the value of a object. A new pointer data type was defined that can be use to hold the address of another object. Examples were presented to demonstrate the use of pointers to reference array elements and character strings. The process of dynamic memory allocation was defined. The operators `new` and `delete` were examined, and the *vector* class was revisited as an alternative to dynamic memory allocation. Data structures, including linked list, stacks and queues, were discussed, with examples that utilize the *list, stack,* and *queue* classes.

Key Terms

address	linked data structures
address operator	list
deallocation	new
delete	offset
dereference	pointer
dynamic data structures	queue
dynamic memory allocation	stack
indirection	

C++ Statement Summary

Pointer declaration:

General Form:

```
data type *identifier [,*identifier];
```

Example:

```
int *ptr_1;
double a, *ptr_2=&a;
```

Dynamic memory allocation:

General Form:

```
pointer_object = new datatype;
```

Example:

```
ptr = new double;
```

Deallocation of dynamic memory:

General Form:

```
delete pointer_object;
```

Dynamic array memory allocation:

```
arr_ptr = new double[100];
```

Deallocation of dynamic array:

General Form:

```
delete pointer_object[];
```

Style **Notes**

1. Choose identifiers for pointers that clearly indicate that the identifiers are associated with pointer objects.
2. If a pointer is not initially assigned to a memory location, give it a value of NULL to indicate that it has not yet been assigned.

Debugging Notes

1. Be sure that a program initializes an object before using its value in other statements.
2. Be sure that a pointer object is initialized before it is used to reference a value.
3. The actual parameter that corresponds to a pointer argument in a function must be an address or a pointer.

Problems

Exam Practice!

True/False Problems
Indicate whether the following statements are true (T) or false (F).

1. Both the address operator and the indirection operator are unary operators.
2. A pointer provides an indirect means of accessing the value of a particular data item.
3. An object must always be declared and initialized before a pointer can point to it.
4. The memory locations given to dynamic memory space are determined when the program is compiled.

Multiple Choice Problems

Circle the letter for the best answer to complete each statement or for the correct answer to each question.

5. A location in memory
   (a) is reserved whenever an object is declared.
   (b) is reserved when an object is used in a program.
   (c) can hold several different values at the same time.
   (d) cannot be reused once it is assigned a value.

6. A pointer object
   (a) contains the data stored at a location in memory.
   (b) contains the address of a memory location.
   (c) can be used in input statements, but not output statements.
   (d) can be changed to different values in both input and output statements.

7. How would you assign to the object *name* the value of an object referenced by the pointer *a*?
   (a) *a = &name;*
   (b) *name = &a;*
   (c) *a = *name;*
   (d) *name = *a;*

8. Assume that *a* and *b* are pointers to integers and that *a* points to the object *name*. What is the effect of the statement

   ```
   b = a;
   ```

   (a) The value of *name* is copied into *b*.
   (b) The memory address stored in *a* is copied into *b*.
   (c) The memory address stored in *b* is copied into *a*.
   (d) The pointer *a* is now pointing to a different object.

Memory Snapshot Problem

Give the corresponding snapshot of memory after the set of statements is executed:

```
double name, x(20.5);
double *a - &x;
name = *a;
```

Assume the address of *name* is 10 and the address of x is *14*. (That is, *name* is stored in memory location *10*, and *x* is stored in memory location 14.) Problems 9–12 refer to the following statements:

```
int i1, i2;
int *p1, *p2;
i1 = 5;
p1 =   &i1;
i2 = *p1/2 + 10;
p2 = p1;
```

9. What is the value of *i1*?
10. What is the value of *i2*?
11. What is the value of **p1*?
12. What is the value of **p2*?

Vector Functions.   These problems develop functions for manipulating values within a vector. Use pointer notation instead of offsets in the functions.

13. Write a function that creates a vector of size n, with each element assigned the value v. Assume that the function prototype statement is

    ```
    void assign_n(vector <double> &x, int n, double v);
    ```

14. Write a function that creates a vector of n random numbers between a and b. Assume that the function prototype statement is

    ```
    void assign_random(vector <int> &x, int n, int a, int b);
    ```

15. Write a function that computes the sum of a vector. Assume that the function prototype statement is

    ```
    int v_sum(vector<int> x);
    ```

16. Write a function that replaces values in a vector with their absolute values. Assume that the function prototype statement is

    ```
    void v_abs(vector<int>&x);
    ```

Character Functions: Pattern Recognition.   Many areas of engineering use problem solutions in which we search for a specific pattern of information in a signal. Problems 17–24 develop a set of functions for this purpose.

17. Write a function that receives a pointer to a character string and a character. The function should return the number of times that the character occurred in the string. Assume that the function has the prototype statement

    ```
    int charcnt(char *ptr, char c);
    ```

18. Write a function that receives a pointer to a character string and returns the number of repeated characters that occur in the string. For example, the string "Mississippi" has three repeated characters. Do not count repeated blanks in the string. If a character occurs more than two times, it should still only count as one repeated character; thus, "hisssss" would have only one repeated character. Assume that the function has the prototype statement

    ```
    int repeat(char *ptr);
    ```

19. Rewrite the function from Problem 24 so that each pair of characters is counted as a repeat. Thus, the string "hisssss" would have four repeated characters. Assume

that the function has the prototype statement

```
int repeat2(char *ptr);
```

20. Write a function that receives pointers to two character strings and returns a count of the number of times that the second character string occurs in the first character string. Do not allow overlap of the occurrences. Thus, the string "110101" contains only one occurrence of "101." Assume that the function has the prototype statement

```
int pattern(char *ptr1, char *ptr2);
```

21. Rewrite the function from Problem 26 so that overlap of the occurrences of the second string in the first string is allowed. Thus, the string "110101" contains two occurrences of "101." Assume that the function has the prototype statement

```
int overlap(char *ptr1, char *ptr2);
```

22. Rewrite the function in Problem 24 using the **string** class instead of C-style strings. Assume that the function has the prototype statement

```
int repeat(string);
```

23. Rewrite the function in Problem 25 using the **string** class instead of C-style strings. Assume that the function has the prototype statement

```
int repeat2(string);
```

24. Rewrite the function in Problem 26 using the **string** class instead of C-style strings. Assume that the function has the prototype statement

```
int pattern(string, string);
```

25. Modify Program chapter 9_13 to insert all word into the list, then call the member function *unique()* to remove duplicate words.
26. Modify Program chapter 9_13 to keep a count of how many times each unique word appears in the text file.

GRAND CHALLENGE:
Artificial Intelligence

Artificial Intelligence (AI) is an intriguing area of science that focuses on creating intelligent machines that have the ability to "think." Research in the areas of cognitive science, language, computing, and sensory perception have advanced the creation of intelligent machines. Today, software exists that conducts a dialog with a human client, can beat world-class chess player, and aids in the diagnosis of disease. Virtual pets are available that "learn" about their environment and respond to their owners. The intelligent software that exists today is only a hint of what is to come.

Additional Topics in Programming with Classes

Chapter Outline

Objectives

10.1 Overloading Operators
10.2 Problem Solving Applied: Color Image Processing
10.3 Inheritance
10.4 `virtual` Functions
10.5 Problem Solving Applied: Iterated Prisoner's Dilemma

Summary, Key Terms, C++ Statement Summary, Style Notes, Debugging Notes, Problems

OBJECTIVES   In this chapter we introduce several advanced topics in programming with classes. **Overloading of operators,** including arithmetic operators and the stream insertion (≪) and stream extraction (≫) operators, is introduced along with `friend` **functions.** The power of overloaded operators is illustrated in an application program that uses a **pixel class,** developed in this chapter, to perform simple **color image processing.** The use of **inheritance** and **virtual functions** is illustrated with the development of two new classes **derived from the rectangle class** developed in Chapter 8, and an implementation of the **iterated prisoner's dilemma** game.

10.1 Overloading Operators

In Chapter 8, we introduced programmer-defined classes and defined a *rectangle* `class` with the following `class` declaration:

```
/*-----------------------------------------------------------------*/
/*  Class declaration for the rectangle class.                    */
class rectangle
```

```
{
public:
// Default constructor.
rectangle();

// Constructor with four parameters.
rectangle(double x, double y, double w, double h);

// Accessor functions.
double get_x_coord() const;
double get_y_coord() const;
double get_width() const;
double get_height() const;

// Functions for input and output.
void input(istream& in);
void print(ostream& out) const;

// Additional member function prototypes.
void set_value(double x, double y, double w, double h);
void translate(double dx, double dy);
double area() const;

private:
// Declaration of data members;
double x_coord, y_coord, width, height;
};
/*------------------------------------------------------------------*/
```

Recall that the only operator predefined for programmer-defined data types is the assignment (=) operator

Our *rectangle* class has 11 public member functions, including a set of 4 accessor functions, the function *input()*, and the function *output()*. When we define a rectangle object, the object must call the *input()* function to receive input from a specified input stream, since the input operator $\gg$ is not defined for the *rectangle* class. If we define two *rectangle* objects and we wish to determine whether the two objects are equivalent, we must compare values returned by the accessor functions to compare the private data members of the objects, since the equality (==) operator is not defined for the *rectangle* class. **Recall that the only operator predefined for programmer-defined data types is the assignment (=) operator.**

Not being able to use the standard operators supported by C++ makes our *rectangle* class less convenient to use than a built-in data type. Anyone using our *rectangle* class must know and remember the names of our functions for input and output rather than relying on the standard operators. Using accessor functions to test for equality can become very cumbersome when an object has multiple data members.

overloading of operators
friend functions

Fortunately, C++ supports **overloading of operators.** Recall that overloading allows functions to share a common name, as long as each function definition has a unique parameter list. Overloading of operators allows a programmer to write member functions and **friend functions** that define the standard C++ operators for use with programmer-defined class objects. Only predefined operators may be overloaded. You may not, for example, define a new operator ∗∗ to perform exponentiation, since this operator is not one of the predefined operators in C++. All of the predefined operators, with the exception of four, may be overloaded. The four operators that cannot be overloaded are as follows:

```
::     Scope Resolution Operator
.      Dot Operator
.*     Pointer to Member Operator
?:     Conditional Operator
```

color image processing

To illustrate overloading of operators, we will develop a *pixel* class to be used for **color image processing** on a digital image. We will return to our *rectangle* class in section 3.

The pixel Class

picture elements
pixel
red, green and blue triple

A digital image can be represented as a collection of **picture elements.** A picture element is a small rectangular region, also referred to as a **pixel.** In the case of a color image each pixel represents a **red, green and blue triple.** Typically, each value in the triple ranges from 0 to 255, where 0 indicates that none of that primary color is present in the pixel and 255 indicates a maximum amount of that primary color. Thus, a pixel displaying the color white will have a value of (255,255,255), and a black pixel will have a value of (0,0,0).

Digital images can be modified by manipulating the pixels that represent an image. For example, we can uniformly **brighten** an image by multiplying each pixel by a small positive value greater than 1, bringing each pixel closer to white. We can uniformly **darken** an image by multiplying each pixel by a positive value less than 1, bringing each pixel closer to black.

When we multiply a pixel by a value, we want to multiply each of the three color values of the pixel—the red value, the green value and the blue value—by the same amount, and we would like to do this in a single multiplication using the multiplication * operator. Thus, we will overload the multiplication operator when we define our pixel class.

neighborhood

Another modification we can perform on a digital image is called **smoothing.** To smooth an image, we replace each pixel with an average of the surrounding pixels. The number of surrounding pixels we choose to include is referred to as the **neighborhood.** The size of the neighborhood determines the degree of smoothing: the larger the neighborhood, the more dramatic the smoothing's. For example, we can uniformly smooth an image by replacing each pixel, except the pixels on the boundaries of the image, with an average of four surrounding pixels; the pixel above, the pixel below, the pixel to the right and the pixel to the left. To calculate an average, we need to sum the pixel values and divide by the number of pixels. When we sum two pixels, we want to add the red values, the green values, and the blue values of the two pixels. When we divide a pixel by a value, we want to divide the red value, the green value, and the blue value by the same value. Thus, we will overload the addition operator and the division operator.

We have identified the attributes of a pixel, a red, green and blue triple, and we have defined three arithmetic operations (addition, multiplication, and division) required to brighten, darken, or smooth an image. However, there are numerous creative ways to modify an image using these overloaded operators. We will now develop a functional *Pixel* class. We begin by providing the class declaration:

```
/*-------------------------------------------------  -------------------*/
/* Pixel class declaration.                                           */
/* File name:  pixel.h                                                */
```

```
#ifndef PIXEL_H
#define PIXEL_H
#include <fstream>
#include <iostream>
using namespace std;
class pixel
{
public:
// Constructor Functions
pixel(); // initialize data members to zero.
pixel(int);
pixel(int, int, int);

// Accessor Functions
int get_red() const;
int get_green() const;
int get_blue() const;

// Functions to set the value of pixel
void set_pixel_value(int r, int g, int b);
void set_red(int);
void set_blue(int);
void set_green(int);

// Overloaded operators.

// Addition.
// Add two pixel.
pixel operator+(pixel p) const;

// Multiplication.
// Multiply a pixel by a floating point value.
pixel operator*(double v) const;

// Division.
// Divide a pixel by an integer value.
pixel operator/(int v) const;

// Input operator.
friend istream& operator >>(istream& in, Pixel& p);

// Output operator.
friend ostream& operator <<(ostream& out, Pixel p);
private:
unsigned int red, green, blue;
};
#endif
/*-------------------------------------------------------------------------*/
```

The class declaration includes function prototypes for a set of constructor functions, a set of accessor functions, and a set of functions to set the value of a *pixel*. Function prototypes for the arithmetic operators $+$, $-$, and $*$ and the operators $\ll$ and $\gg$ are also included. Notice that the function prototypes for the operators use the keyword `operator` followed by the operator that is being overloaded as the function name. The keyword `friend` is used in the prototypes for the input and output operators. Overloading of operators and `friend` functions are discussed in detail in the sections that follow.

Arithmetic Operators

Our *pixel* `class` declaration includes the following function prototypes:

```
pixel operator+(pixel p) const;
pixel operator*(double v) const;
pixel operator/(int v) const;
```

Each prototype specifies a return type of *pixel*, indicating that each function will return a value of type *pixel*, and each function has one formal parameter. In each function, the formal parameter is a pass-by-value parameter, which prevents modification of the function argument. The keyword `const` prevents modification of the data members of the calling object.

The + Operator   The function *pixel operator+(pixel p)* `const` has one formal parameter of type *pixel*. Since we are defining this function as a member function of the *pixel* `class`, this function will be called by a *pixel* object. The calling object will provide the first operand for the $+$ operator, and the function argument will provide the second operand. The following is the function definition:

```
/*-----                -------------    -----------------------------------------*/
/* Addition (+) operator.                                                       */
/* File name: pixel.cpp                                                         */

pixel pixel:: operator+(pixel p) const
{
    pixel temp;
    temp.red = red + p.red;
    temp.green = green + p.green;
    temp.blue = blue + p.blue;
    return temp;
}
/*---------------------------------------------------------------------------*/
```

We can call the $+$ operator as illustrated here:

```
pixel p1, p2(100,200,100), p3(10,20,30);
p1 = p2 + p3;   //function call
cout << p1;
...
```

In the statement

```
p1 = p2 + p3;
```

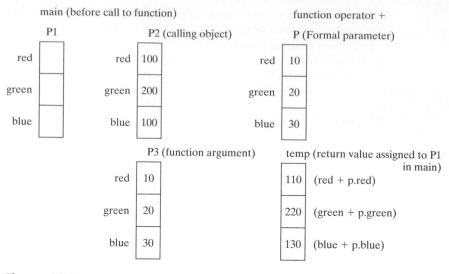

Figure 10.1

p2 is the calling object and *p3* is the function argument for the operator +. When the + function is called, the formal parameter *p* receives the value of the argument, *p3*. The function references the `private` data members, *red, green,* and *blue,* of the calling object and the `private` data members, *p.red, p.green,* and *p.blue,* of the formal parameter. The function also references the `private` data members of the local object *temp; temp.red, temp.green* and *temp.blue.* The three assignment statements in the function definition

```
temp.red = red + p.red;
temp.green = green + p.green;
temp.blue = blue + p.blue;
```

assign to the local object *temp* the result of adding the function argument to the calling object. The value of temp is returned and assigned to the *pixel p1.* The output generated when *p1* is printed to the screen is

```
110 220 130
```

A memory map is provided in Figure 10.1 to illustrate the passing of information.

The ∗ Operator   The function *pixel operator∗(double v)* `const` has one formal parameter of type `double`. The calling object will provide the first operand for the ∗ operator, and the function argument will provide the second operand. The following is the function definition:

```
/*-----------------------------------------------------------------------*/
/* Multiplication (*) operator.                                          */
/* File name: pixel.cpp                                                  */
```

```
pixel pixel:: operator*(double v) const
{
    pixel temp:
    temp.red = red*v;
    temp.green = green*v;
    temp.blue = blue*v;
    return temp;
}
/*------------------      -----  ---      --------------------------*/
```

We can call this function as follows:

```
pixel p1, p2(100,200,100);
double factor(1.2);
p1 = p2*factor;
cout << p1;
...
```

In this example, *p2* is the calling object and *factor* is the function argument. When the function *
is called, the formal parameter *v* receives the value of the argument, *factor*. The local object
temp is assigned the result of multiplying each data member of the calling object by the floating-
point value *v*. The value of *temp* is returned and assigned to the *pixel p1*. The output generated
when *p1* is printed to the screen is

```
120 240 120
```

A memory map is provided in Figure 10.2 to illustrate the passing of information.

Note that this function does not define multiplication of two pixels, but rather defines
multiplication of a *pixel* by a double. If we want to define multiplication of two pixels, we
can include a function with the following prototype in our *pixel* class definition:

```
pixel operator*(pixel p) const;
```

The / Operator   The function *pixel operator/(int v)* const has one formal parameter
of type int. The calling object will provide the first operand for the / operator, and the function

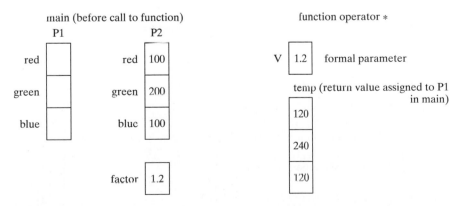

Figure 10.2

argument will provide the second operand. The function definition is the following:

```
/*---------------------------------------------------------------------*/
/* Division (/) operator.                                              */
/* File name: pixel.cpp                                                */

pixel pixel:: operator/(int v) const
{
   pixel temp;
   temp.red = red/v;
   temp.green = green/v;
   temp.blue = blue/v;
   return temp;
}
/*---------------------------------------------------------------------*/
```

We can call this function as illustrated below:

```
pixel p1, p2(100,200,100);
p1 = p2/2;
cout << p1;
...
```

In this example, *p2* is the calling object, and the integer 2 is the function argument. When the function is called, the formal parameter *v* receives the value of the argument. The local object *temp* is assigned the result of dividing the calling object by an integer value. The value of *temp* is returned and assigned to the *pixel p1*. The output generated when *p1* is printed to the screen is

```
50 100 50
```

Note that this function does not define division of two pixels, but rather defines division of a *pixel* by an `int`. If we want to define division of two pixels, we can include a function with the following prototype to our pixel class definition:

```
pixel operator/(pixel p) const;
```

The overloaded operator functions defined above are member functions of the *pixel* `class`. Thus, each function must be called by a *pixel* object. This creates a limitation in the use of these operators; the first operand must be a pixel object. Consider the following code segment that uses the + operator:

```
pixel p1, p2(100,200,100), p3(10,20,30);
p1 = p2 + p3; // Valid.
p1 = p2 + 100; // Valid.
p1 = 100 + p2; // Invalid!
```

The first assignment statement

```
p1 = p2 + p3; // Valid.
```

is valid, since both operands of the + operator are *pixel* objects. The second assignment statement

```
p1 = p2 + 100; // Valid.
```

is also valid, since the first operand, the calling object, is a *pixel* object. The second operand is an integer, not a *pixel*. However, since our *pixel* class includes a constructor function with one integer argument, this constructor is used to promote the integer 100 to a *pixel* object with the value (100,100,100) and the function call is successful. The third statement

```
p1 = 100 + p2; // Invalid!
```

is not valid, since the first operand, the calling object, is an integer object, rather than a *pixel* object. This statement will generate an error at compile time. This limitation can be removed by defining operators as `friend` functions instead of member functions. We will discuss `friend` functions in the next section.

Practice!

Assume the following function prototypes have been added to the pixel class declaration. Write function definitions for each of the following functions.

1. `pixel operator/(pixel p1);` //divide a pixel by a pixel

2. `bool operator==(pixel p1);` //return true if p1 is
                               //equivalent to calling object

---

friend Functions

A `friend` function is not a member function; however, a `friend` function does have access to the private data members of the `class` in which it is included. To declare a function as a `friend` function, the function prototype in the `class` declaration must begin with the keyword `friend`. Since a `friend` function is not a member function, the function is not affected by the `public` or `private` keywords. In our *pixel* `class`, we include the `friend` functions in the `public` section, along with the other operator functions.

If we wanted to define the + operator as a `friend` function rather than as a member function, the prototype would be:

```
friend pixel operator+(pixel p1, pixel p2);
```

Notice that this function prototype requires two formal parameters. Because `friend` functions are not member functions, there is no calling object. Instead, we must include both operands as formal parameters in the function prototype and the function header. The following code segment illustrates the use of this function:

```
pixel p1, p2(100,200,100), p3(10,20,30);
p1 = p2 + p3; // Valid.
p1 = p2 + 100; // Valid.
p1 = 100 + p2; // Valid!
```

The third assignment statement

```
p1 = 100 + p2; // Valid!
```

is now a valid statement. The integer 100 provides the first argument of the + function, and p2 provides the second argument. Since the function is expecting *pixel* objects as arguments, a constructor is used to promote the integer 100 to the *pixel* object (100,100,100), and the function call is successful. The definition of the function is as follows:

```
/*------------------------------------------------------------------*/
/* Addition (+) operator as friend function.                        */
/* File name: pixel.cpp                                             */

pixel operator+(pixel p1, pixel p2)
{
   pixel temp;
   temp.red = p1.red + p2.red;
   temp.green = p1.green + p2.green;
   temp.blue = p1.blue + p2.blue;
   return temp;
}
/*------------------------------------------------------------------*/
```

Notice that the keyword `friend` is not included in the function definition. `Friend` status can only be granted in the `class` declaration. Compare this function definition with the member function definition. Since this function is not a member function, there is no calling object, and the references to *red, green,* and *blue* in the member function definition have been replaced by references to *p1.red, p1.green,* and *p1.blue* in the definition of the `friend` function.

Practice!

Assume that the following function prototypes have been added to the pixel class declaration. Write function definitions for each of the functions.

1. `friend pixel operator*(pixel p1, pixel p2);`

2. `friend pixel operator/(pixel p1, pixel p2);`

3. `friend pixel operator-(pixel p1, pixel p2);`

The ≪ Operator Our pixel class declaration includes a function to overload the ≪ operator. The function has the following prototype:

```
friend ostream& operator<<(ostream& out, const pixel& p);
```

This function is defined as a friend function with two formal parameters, and the function returns an *ostream* reference. The ≪ operator cannot be defined as a member function of the *pixel* class because the first argument of the function must be an *ostream* reference. However, the function needs to access the private data members of the *pixel* argument, so we declare it to be a friend function of the *pixel* class. *For efficiency, we have chosen to make the second formal parameter a* const *pass by reference instead of a pass by value.* This allows a reference to be passed, but prevents modification of the argument pointed to by the reference. The function definition is as follows:

Style

```
/*- - - - - - - - - - - - - - - - - - - - - - -  - - - - - - -  - - - - - - - - - - - - - - - - - - - -*/
/* Output << operator.                                                                    */
/* File name: pixel.cpp                                                                   */

ostream& operator<<(ostream& out, const pixel& p)
{
    out << p.red << ' ';
    out << p.green << ' ';
    out << p.blue;
    return out;
}
/*- - - - - - - - - - - - - - - - - - - - - - - - - - - - - - - - - - - - - - - - - - - - - - - - - - -*/
```

The function must return an *ostream* reference, thus the statement

```
return out;
```

is required. Our function outputs the *red, green,* and *blue* values of the *pixel p,* separated by whitespace. We can use the function as follows:

```
pixel p1, p2(100,200,100);
cout << "P1: " << p1 <<"  P2: " << p2 << endl;
...
```

The output printed to the screen is

```
P1: 0 0 0   P2: 100 200 100
```

We can also use our ≪ function to send output to a file. Recall that the *ofstream* class is derived from the *ostream* class. Thus, all *ostream* operations can also be applied to *ofstream* objects. The following code segment uses our ≪ function to write to the file *pixel.dat*:

```
...
pixel p1, p2(255);
ofstream outfile("pixel.dat");
outfile << "P1: " << p1 <<"  P2: " << p2 << endl;
...
```

The output written to the file *pixel.dat* is

```
P1: 0 0 0   P2: 255 255 255
```

Style

Notice that our ≪ function does not output a newline following the value of the pixel. This allows us to output multiple pixel values on the same line and is consistent with the performance of output operators defined for the built-in data types.

The ≫ Operator   Our *pixel* class declaration includes a function to overload the ≫ operator. The function has the following prototype:

```
friend istream& operator>>(istream& in, pixel& p);
```

This function is defined as a friend function with two formal parameters, and the function returns an *istream* reference. The ≫ operator cannot be defined as a member function of the pixel class because the first argument must be an *istream* reference. However, the function needs access to the private data members of the *pixel* argument, so we have declared it to be a friend function of the *pixel* class.

Since the function is defined to input a *pixel* value, the function must modify the object referenced by the formal parameter, *p*. Therefore, this formal parameter must be a pass by reference. The function definition follows:

```
/*--------------------------------------------------------------------*/
/* Input (>>) operator.                                               */
/* File name: pixel.cpp                                               */

istream& operator>>(istream& in, pixel& p)
{
   in >> p.red >> p.green >> p.blue;
   return in;
}
/*--------------------------------------------------------------------*/
```

This function must return an *istream* reference.

Overloading the ≫ operator is similar to overloading the ≪ operator, except that the potential for encountering errors on input is greater. The function attempts to input three integer values to be assigned to the *red, green,* and *blue* data members of *p*. This function looks to the input stream for three integer values, separated by whitespace. Any unexpected character in the input stream, such as a comma or a colon, will place the *istream* in a fail state.

If our *pixel* class required a special format for input, our ≫ function would need to check for the required format. If the required format was not encountered, the function would need to place the *istream* in a fail state. For illustration, assume that the format for entering a pixel value required the integer values to be separated by a colon, as in

```
100:150:100
```

Our function can be modified to check for this format and place the *istream* in a fail state if the format is not correct:

```
/*---------------------------------------------------------------------        */
/* Input (>>) operator.                                                        */
/* Expected pixel format is 100:150:100                                        */
/* File name: pixel.cpp                                                        */

istream& operator>>(istream& in, pixel& p)
{
// Declare local objects.
   char ch;

// Input integer value for red data member.
   in >> p.red;

// Input colon.   If colon not encountered,
// set error state and return.
   in >> ch;
   if(ch != ':')
   {
      in.setstate(ios::failbit);
      return in;
   }

// Input integer value for green data member.
   in >> p.green;

// Input colon.   If colon not encountered,
// set error state and return.
   in >> ch;
   if(ch != ':')
   {
      in.setstate(ios::failbit);
      return in;
   }

// Input integer value for blue data member.
   in >> p.blue;

   return in;
}
/*---------------------------------------------------------------------------*/
```

In this function definition, the function *setstate()* is used to place the *istream* in a fail state. The function *setstate()* is a member function of the *istream* `class`. In the statement

```
in.setstate(ios::failbit);
```

the *istream* object referenced by *in* calls the setstate function, and the failbit is set to true.

Modify!

1. Complete the definition of the *pixel* `class` and test it with a simple program that tests each of the functions provided in the function declaration.

2. Modify the output function

   ```
   friend ostream& operator<<(ostream& out, const pixel& p)
   ```

   so that the value of a pixel is output using colons, instead of whitespace, to separate the red green and blue values.

3. Modify the input function

   ```
   /*------------------------------------------------------------*/
   /* Input >> operator. Expected pixel format is 100:150:100*/

   friend istream& operator>>(istream& in, pixel& p)
   ```

   to handle incorrect format by alerting the user and requesting new input. (*Hint:* Refer to error handling discussed in Chapter 4.)

10.2 Problem Solving Applied: Color Image Processing

The following is a picture of Io, one of Jupiter's moons, taken by the Galileo spacecraft:

This jpg image was downloaded off the Web from

http://www.jpl.nasa.gov/galileo/io/

bitmap

The image was converted to an ASCII file format, using the unix utility *xv*. The following is a sampling of the underlying pixel values, called a **bitmap,** taken from the ASCII file:

```
 43   56 100 147 160 204 148 160 208 147 159 207 146 158 210
149 161 213 146 159 212 145 158 211 143 158 213 143 158 213
143 159 211 143 159 211 142 160 210 142 160 210 142 160 208
140 161 208 136 158 208 135 158 208 136 156 207 138 155 207
139 155 207 140 153 206 142 151 206 142 151 206 148 155 210
149 156 211 148 157 212 148 159 213 147 158 212 143 159 211
142 158 210 141 156 211 142 154 212 142 152 213 141 151 212
140 150 211 139 149 210 139 149 210 140 150 211 140 150 211
142 152 213 142 152 213 143 153 214 144 154 215 144 154 215
143 153 214 142 152 213 142 152 211 145 154 211 144 153 208
143 152 207 143 152 207 144 153 208 145 154 209 147 156 211
148 157 212 146 155 210 147 156 211 148 157 212 148 157 212
149 158 213 150 159 214 151 160 215 151 161 214 152 162 215
152 162 213 152 162 213 152 162 213 152 162 213 152 162 213
```

ppm file format

The first pixel in the bitmap is represented by the triple 43 56 100. Each row of the bitmap holds five pixel values. The complete image is stored as an ASCII file, using a ***ppm* file format.** A *ppm* file contains a header that must be preserved in order to view or convert the image. The header contains a "magic number" (P3 for ppm files), possible comment lines (comment lines begin with a # in column 1), the width and height of the image, and the maximum color value. The header for this image is

```
P3
# CREATOR: XV Version 3.10a  Rev: 12/29/94
259 256
255
```

Once the image has been modified, the ASCII file can be viewed using the xv utility, or converted back to a jpg or gif file for viewing on other platforms. The "smoothed" image of Io is shown in the following:

Write a program that inputs an image from an ASCII ppm file and performs a smoothing operation on the image. The smoothed image is written to a new ppm file.

1. PROBLEM STATEMENT

Modify a color digital image by performing a smoothing process on the image.

2. INPUT/OUTPUT DESCRIPTION

The input to this program is the data in the image file Io.ppm. The output is the modified image. We must first read the header information to determine the size of the image. We can then use the information in the header to allocate memory and input the pixel values.

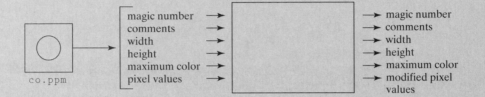

3. HAND EXAMPLE

To perform the smoothing process on the image, we will take an average of the current pixel and the four adjacent pixels; the pixel to the left, the pixel above, the pixel to the right, and the pixel below. We will replace the original pixel value with the smoothed pixel value as we perform the calculations. For our hand example, we will determine the smoothed value for one pixel from the image of Io.

Original image:

```
143  159  211  142  160  210  142  160  210
136  158  208  135  158  208  136  156  207
140  153  206  142  151  206  142  151  206
```

The current pixel has a red value of 135, a green value of 158, and a blue value of 208. The smoothed value for this pixel is calculated as follows:

```
red value -> (135 + 136 + 142 +136 +142)/5 = 138
green value -> (158 +158 + 160 + 156 +151)/5 = 156
blue value -> (208 + 208 + 210 + 207 + 206)/5 = 207
```

Modified image:

```
143  159  211  142  160  210  142  160  210
136  158  208  138  156  207  136  156  207
140  153  206  142  151  206  142  151  206
```

This process is repeated for every interior pixel in the image. Pixels on the boundaries are missing one of the four adjacent pixels just described (corner pixels are missing two) and will not be modified in this application.

4. ALGORITHM DEVELOPMENT

We first develop the decomposition outline because it breaks the solution into a series of sequential steps.

Decomposition Outline

    (1) Read the header information.

    (2) Write header information to the new file.

    (3) Read the pixel values.

    (4) Perform smoothing on each interior pixel.

    (5) Write smoothed pixel values to the new file.

Steps 1 and 2 involve reading the header information from the data file and preserving this information by writing it to a new file. We will write a function to perform this task. Step 3 requires reading the pixel values into a two dimensional array. The array size depends on the information in the header, so we will use the *vector* class to define a two-dimensional array type pixel. Step 4 involves performing a smoothing modification on the image. We will write a second function to perform this task. To easily store and modify the pixel elements in the image, we will use the *pixel* class developed in Section 10.1. The refinement in pseudocode can now be developed:

Refinement in Pseudocode

```
main():
    open data files
    read_header(fin, fout, width, height, max_color)
    read image
    smooth(image,width, height)
    write image
read_header(fin, fout, width, height, max_color):
        read magic_num
        while(next_ch == '#')
            read comment_line
            write comment_line to new file
        read width, height, max_color
        write width, height, max_color
smooth(image, width, height):
    set i to 0
    set j to 0
```

```
        while(i<height)
          while(j<width)
            image[i][j] = (image[i][j] + image[i][j-1] + image[i-1][j]
                          + image[i][j+1] + image[i+1][j])/5
```

We are now ready to convert the pseudocode to C++:

```cpp
/*-----------------------------------------------------------------*/
/* Program chapter10_1                                             */
/*                                                                 */
/* This program reads an ASCII digital image and perform a        */
/* smoothing operation on the on the image. The smoothed image    */
/* is written to a new file.                                      */

#include "Pixel.h"
#include <fstream>
#include <string>
#include <vector>
using namespace std;

//Function prototypes.
void read_header(istream& fin, ostream& fout,
                 int& width, int& height, int& max);
void smooth(vector <vector<Pixel> >& , int w, int h);

int main()
{
   // Declare objects.
   int height, width, max, i, j;
   string filename;
   ifstream fin;
   ofstream fout;

   // Prompt user for file name and open file for input.
   cout << "enter name of input file ";
   cin >> filename;
   fin.open(filename.c_str());
   if(fin.fail())
   {
      cerr << "Error opening input file\n";
   }
   else
   {
   // Open new file for output.
      filename = "smoothed_"+filename;
      fout.open(filename.c_str());

   // Read and write header information.
      read_header(fin,fout, width, height, max);
```

```
      // Declare image array.
        vector< vector<Pixel> > image(height, width);

      // Read the image.
        for(i=0; i<height; i++)
          for(j=0; j<width; j++)
          {
            fin >> image[i][j];
          }
      // Smooth the image.
        smooth(image, width, height);

      // Write modified image to new file.
        for(i=0; i<height; i++)
          for(j=0; j<width; j++)
          {
            fout << image[i][j] << ' ';
            if((j+1)%5 == 0) fout<<endl;
          }
      }

      // Exit program.
      return 0;
}
void read_header(istream& fin, ostream& fout, int& width,
                 int& height, int& max)
{
  char header[100];
  char ch;
// Get magic number.
  fin.getline(header, 100);
// Write magic number.
  fout << header << endl;
  cout << header << endl;

// Get all comment lines and write to new file.
  fin >> ch;
  while(ch == '#')
  {
    fin.getline(header, 100);
    fout <<ch << header << endl;
    cout << ch <<header << endl;
    fin >> ch;
  }
  fin.putback(ch);
// Input width and height of image.
  fin >> width >> height;
  cout << width <<" " <<  height << endl;
  fout << width << " " << height << endl;
// Input maximum color value.
```

```
        fin >> max;
        cout << max << endl;
        fout << max << endl;
        return;
}
void smooth(vector< vector<Pixel> > &image, int w, int h)
{
    for(int i=1; i<h-1; i++)
      for(int j=1; j<w-1; j++)
        image[i][j] = (image[i][j] + image[i+1][j] + image[i-1][j]
                      + image[i][j+1] + image[i][j-1])/5;
}
```

5. TESTING

The following is the smoothed image of Io along side the original to illustrate the effect:

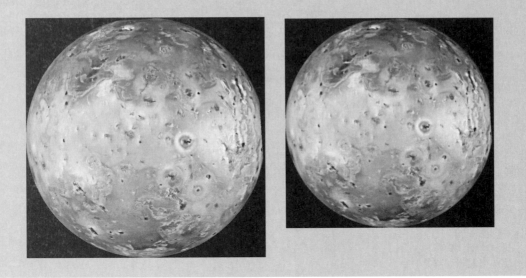

1. Modify the smooth function in program chapter10_1 to include eight adjacent pixels in the average, instead of four.

2. Modify the smooth function in program chapter10_1 to include the pixels on the boundrys, including the corners, in smoothing process. Be careful not to include references to pixels that are outside the bounds of the image.

Inheritance

In Chapter 4, we discussed the use of inheritance in the definition of the *ifstream* class and the *ofstream* class. In this section, we will introduce features of the C++ programming language that support inheritance, and we will illustrate the use of inheritance in programmer defined classes. We will limit our discussion to **public inheritance** from a single base class. In general, most uses of inheritance are implemented using single inheritance. However, a more complete discussion of inheritance, including multiple and virtual inheritance can be found in *C++ Primer,* Third Edition, Addison Wesley, Copyright 1998 by Stanley B. Lippman and Josee Lajoie.

public inheritance

base class
derived class

Inheritance is one of the most important aspects of object oriented programming. Inheritance allows a new class to be **derived** from an existing class. The existing class is referred to as the **base class.** A **derived class** inherits the data and functionality of its base class. In addition, the derived class can override and enhance the capabilities of the base class for specialized use. A derived class needs to provide code only for those capabilites that override or enhance its base class. This provides an effective mechanism for complex software design and also provides for efficient use and reuse of code.

To illustrate the use of inheritance, we will use our *rectangle* class, developed in Chapter 8, as a base class for developing two new classes; a *square* class and a *cube* class. Figure 10.3 illustrates the geometric representation of these objects.

The square Class   The internal representation of a square can be represented by four data members: the x-coordinate, the y-coordinate, the width and the height. These are the same

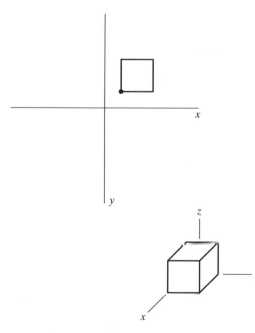

Figure 10.3 Square and cube objects.

data members required for representing a rectangle. In fact, a square is a rectangle with four equal sides. Thus, the width and the height must be equal.

is a relationship

Since a square *is a* rectangle, all functions that can be applied to a rectangle can also be applied to a square. This *is a* **relationship** between a rectangle and a square suggests that we can use our *rectangle* class as a base class for the definition of a *square* class. Using the *rectangle* class as a base class will eliminate the need to rewrite functions such as *area, translate, print, input,* and the accessor functions. These functions will be inherited by the *square* class. A new definition for the *set_value* function will be included in the the *square* class and will override the definition of the *set_value* function provided by the *rectangle* class.

In the original declaration of the *rectangle* class, we used the keywords public and private to control access to the members. Recall that members declared under the keyword private can be accessed only by member functions and friend functions of the class. Members of a class that are private cannot be accessed, and will not be inherited, by any derived class. Thus, to effectively use the *rectangle* class as a base class, we need to replace the keyword private with the keyword **protected.**

protected

Members declared under the keyword protected can be accessed by all member functions and friend functions of the class, as well as member and friend functions of any class derived from the class. The modified *rectangle* class declaration is as follows:

```
/*------------------------------------------------------------------*/
/*  Class declaration for the rectangle class.                      */
/*  File name: rectangle.h                                          */
/*                                                                  */
#ifndef RECTANGLE_H
#define RECTANGLE_H
#include <iostream>
using namespace std;

class rectangle
{
public:
// Default constructor
rectangle();

// Constructor with four formal parameters
rectangle(double x, double y, double w, double h);

// Accessor functions
double get_x_coord() const;
double get_y_coord() const;
double get_width() const;
double get_height() const;

// Functions for input and output.
void input(istream& in);
void print(ostream& out) const;
```

```
// Additional member function prototypes
void set_value(double x, double y, double w, double h);
void translate(double dx, double dy);
double area() const;

protected:
// Declaration of data members:
double x_coord, y_coord, width, height;
};
#endif
/*-------------------------------------------------------------*/
```

All member functions of the *rectangle* class are public, and all data members are now protected, rather than private. We will now illustrate the use of public inheritance to define a *square* class using the *rectangle* class as a base class. The class declaration of the derived *square* class is as follows:

```
/*-------------------------------------------------------------*/
/* Declaration of the square class.                          */
/* File name: square.h                                       */

#ifndef SQUARE_H
#define SQUARE_H
#include "rectangle.h"
using namespace std;

class square : public rectangle
{
public:
// Default constructor
square();

// Constructor with three formal parameters
square(double x, double y, double side);

// Input function
void input(istream& in);

// Additional member function prototypes
void set_value(double x, double y, double side);
};
#endif
/*-------------------------------------------------------------*/
```

Notice the first line of the class declaration:

```
class square : public rectangle
```

The : operator is required to specify inheritance. The keyword public specifies the type of inheritance and is followed by the name of the base class.

When `public` inheritance is specified, the derived `class` inherits all of the `public` and `protected` members of the base `class`, and the access type of the inherited members remains the same as in the base `class`. Thus, the derived `class` *square* inherits all of the `public` accessor functions, functions for input and output, and additional member functions of the rectangle class, as well as the four `protected` data members.

The declaration of the *square* `class` includes four function prototypes: two constructor functions, the *set_value()* function and the *input()* function. The *set_value()* function and the *input()* function override the corresponding functions defined in the *rectangle* `class`. It is important to understand the difference between overriding and overloading a function. When a function is overloaded, each new definition of the function has the same name, but it must have an unique formal parameter list, or **function signature.** The function signature is used to determine which version of the function to execute when an overloaded function is called. When a derived class overrides a function, the function may have the same signature or a different signature than the function it overrides. When an overridden function is referenced, the data type of the calling object determines which function will be called.

We will now write the implementation of the *square* `class` and discuss the required syntax:

```
/*------------------------------------------------------------*/
/* Implementation of the square class.                        */
/* File name: square.cpp                                      */

#include "square.h"

//Constructor functions.
square::square()
{
   // Implicit call of the rectangle default constructor.
   // Nothing added.
}
square::square(double x, double y, double side)
 : rectangle(x,y,side,side)
{
  // Explicit call of rectangle constructor
  // in the member initialization list.
  // Width and height will be equal.
}

//Input function
void square::input(istream& in)
{
  double x, y, side;
  in >> x >> y >> side;
  rectangle::set_value(x,y,side,side);
}
```

```
void square::set_value(double x, double y, double side)
{
  // Explicit call of rectangle set_value function.
  // width and height will be equal.
  rectangle::set_value(x,y,side,side);
}
/*-------------------------------------------------------------*/
```

We will look first at the constructor functions of the *square* class. A constructor function of a derived class must call a constructor function of the base class to initialize inherited data members of the base class. Notice the definition of the default constructor for the square class. There are no statements in the body of the function definition. Since no constructor function of the *rectangle* class is referenced, the default constructor from the *rectangle* class will automatically be called when an object of type *square* is defined as

```
square s;
```

Values provided by the default *rectangle* constructor will be used to initialize the data members as follows:

```
s.x <- 0
s.y <- 0
s.width <- 1
s.height <- 1
```

A derived class should include its own set of constructor functions. A derived class does not inherit the constructor functions of its base class.

The header of the second constructor function in the *square* class

```
square::square(double x, double y, double side)
  : rectangle(x,y,side,side)
```

includes an explicit call to a constructor function of the *rectangle* class in the member initialization list. The value of *side* is passed for both *width* and *height*.

In the definition of the *set value()* function, the scope resolution operator is used in the call to the *set_value()* function defined the *rectangle* class. The value of *side* is passed for both the *width* and *height*. If the scope resolution operator is omitted, errors will occur.

In the definition of the *input()* function, we require only three values to be input, since it would be redundant to require both the *width* and the *height* of a square to be entered. After the three value are input, the *set_value()* function is called to set the values of the data members. Since the *square* class is derived from the *rectangle* class, it has access to the private data members of the *rectangle* class. Thus, we could have assigned values to the data members directly. However, this would make our *square* class dependent on the implementation of the base class. It is preferable to use the *set_value()* function provided by the base class for this task. In the event that changes are made to the implementation of the base class, the *square* class will not be affected, since it does not directly reference any of the data

Style

members. *A well-designed class should always include functions for support of the data members, and avoid direct references to data members of its base class.*

We will now write a main() function to illustrate the use of the *square* class:

```
/*************************************************************************/
/*  Program chapter10_3                                                  */
/*                                                                       */
/*  This program illustrates the use of the square class.               */
/*  The square class is derived from the rectangle class.               */
/*                                                                       */
#include <iostream>
#include "square.h"
using namespace std;

int main()
{
   // Declare objects.
   square s1;                      // Default constructor.
   square s2(1,1,5);               // Constructor with 3 arguments.

   // Output value of s1 and s2.
   // print function inherited from rectangle class.
   cout << "s1: ";
   s1.print(cout);
   cout << endl << "s2: ";
   s2.print(cout);

   // Set the value of s1.
   s1.set_value(0,0,4);

   // Output new value of s1
   cout << endl << "s1: ";
   s1.print(cout);

   // Input a new value for s1
   cout << "\nEnter value of square: x y side ";
   s1.input(cin);

   // Output the area of s1 and s2.
   // the area function is inherited from rectangle class.
   cout << endl << "Area of s1 is " << s1.area() << endl;
   cout << "Area of s2 is " << s2.area() << endl;

   return 0;
}
```

The output generated by this program is as follows:

```
s1: Fixed point at: (0,0)
Width:1
Height:1

s2: Fixed point at: (1,1)
Width:5
Height:5
```

```
s1: Fixed point at: (0,0)
Width:4
Height:4

Enter value of square: x y side 2 3 7

Area of s1 is 49
Area of s2 is 25
```

The cube Class   A cube is a three-dimensional representation of a square. This relationship suggests that we can use the *square* class as the base class for the definition of a *cube* class. The *cube* class will override the *print()* function. A new function to calculate the volume of a cube will be added to enhance the functionality of the class. The complete definition of the cube class is the following:

```cpp
#ifndef CUBE_H
#define CUBE_H
/*---------- --------------------------------------------------------*/
/* Declaration of the cube class.                                    */
/* File name: cube.h                                                 */

#include "square.h"
class cube : public square
{
  public:
  //Constructor functions.
    cube();
    cube(double x, double y, double s);

 //Output function
    void print(ostream&) const;

    double volume() const;
};
#endif
/*-------------------------- -------------------- -----------------------*/
/* Implementation of the cube class.                                 */
/* File name: cube.cpp                                               */

#include "cube.h"

// Constructor functions.
   cube::cube()
    : square()
    {
    }
```

```
cube::cube(double x, double y, double s)
  : square(x,y,s)
{
}

double cube::volume() const
{
    return(width*width*width);
}

void cube::print(ostream& out) const
{
    square::print(out);
    out << "Depth: " << width << endl;
}
```

 Omitting the square:: in the call to the *print()* function will result in recursive calls and generate an execution error. We will now write a `main()` function to test the *cube* `class`:

```
/**************************************************************************/
/*   Program chapter 10_4                                              */
/*                                                                    */
/*   This program tests the functionality of the cube class.          */
/*   The cube class is derived from the square class.                 */
/*                                                                    */
#include <iostream>
#include "cube.h"
using namespace std;

int main()
{
// Define objects.
   cube c1;

  // Test input and output functions.
   cout << "Enter value for cube: x y and length of side ";
   c1.input(cin);
   cout << "Value of cube: ";
   c1.print(cout);

  // Output area and volume.
   cout << "Area " << c1.area() << endl;
   cout << "Volume " << c1.volume() << endl;

  // Translate cube.
   c1.translate(5,3);
   cout << endl << "Value of cube after translation: ";
   c1.print(cout);
   return 0;
}
```

Output from a sample run of the program is given below.

```
Enter value for cube: x y and length of side 1 1 3
Value of cube: Fixed point at: (1,1)
Width: 3
Height: 3
Depth: 3

Area 9
Volume 27

Value of cube after translation: Fixed point at: (6,4)
Width: 3
Height: 3
Depth: 3
```

10.4   virtual **Functions**

static objects

All member functions defined in our *rectangle, square,* and *cube* classes are, by default, nonvirtual. When a nonvirtual member function is called, the function executed is the member function defined by the static class type of the calling object. In C++, **static objects** are named objects that we manipulate directly. Consider the following example:

```
cube c1(1,1,3);
rectangle r1(5,5,2,4);
r1 = c1;
r1.print(cout);
```

In this example, *r1* is a static object of type *rectangle* and *c1* is a static object of type *cube*. An assignment is made from *c1* to *r1*. Since the *cube* class is derived from the *rectangle* class, this assignment is valid, and the data members of *r1* are assigned the values of the corresponding data members of *c1*. However, the data type of *r1* is still *rectangle*. Thus, when *r1* calls the *print()* function, it calls the *print()* function defined by the *rectangle* class. The output generated by the foregoing lines of code is

```
Fixed point at: (1,1)
Width: 3
Height: 3
```

This output may surprise us. Since the assignment statement is valid, we may be expecting to see the value of a cube printed to the screen, but this is not the case. Consider the next example:

```
cube c1(1,1,3);
rectangle *rptr;
rptr = &c1;
rptr->print(cout);
```

In this example, the static type of *rptr* is *rectangle** (pointer to rectangle). However, the dynamic type of *rptr,* at the time the print function is called, is *cube**, because *rptr* is pointing to an object of type *cube*. Since the *print( )* function is a nonvirtual member function, *rptr* will again call the function defined by the *rectangle* class (the `static` data type of *rptr*), and the output will be as follows:

```
Fixed point at: (1,1)
Width: 3
Height: 3
```

Again, since *rptr* is pointing to a *cube,* the output may not be what we were expecting.

virtual member function dynamic data type

A `virtual` **member function** is called based on the **dynamic data type** of the calling object. Dynamic objects are objects that we manipulate through pointers. If the *print( )* function was defined as a `virtual` function in the *rectangle* class, the function called by *rptr* in the preceding example would be the function defined in the *cube* class, since the dynamic data type of *rptr* is *cube** at the time the *print( )* function is referenced. The output would be as follows:

```
Fixed point at: (1,1)
Width: 3
Height: 3
Depth: 3
```

Notice that the depth of the cube is printed, indicating that the *print( )* function defined in the cube class was called.

Member functions are defined to be `virtual` by specifying the keyword `virtual` at the beginning of the function prototype. The keyword `virtual` is not used again in the function definition. To define the *print( )* function as a `virtual` member function of the *rectangle* class, we will modify the *rectangle* class declaration to include the following function prototype:

```
/*-----------------------------------------------------------------*/
/*  Class declaration for the rectangle class.                     */
/*  File: rectangle.h                                              */
...
virtual void print(ostream& out) const;
...
```

The function definition is not changed, and no modification to the definitions of the *square* class or *cube* class is required. The significance of `virtual` functions, when working with dynamic objects, is illustrated in the next section.

Practice!

Assume that the *print( )* function defined in the *rectangle* class is a **virtual** function. Given the declaration statements:

```
cube *cptr, c1(1,2,4);
square *sptr, s1(0,0,5);
rectangle *rptr, r1(2,2,7,9);
```

show the output generated by the following code segments: Use the cube class and the square class defined in this section.

```
1. cptr = &c1;
   c1.print(cout);
   cptr >print(cout);

2. r1 = c1;
   r1.print(cout);

3. sptr = &s1;
   r1 = s1;
   rptr = sptr;
   r1.print(cout);
   cout << endl;
   rptr->print(cout);
```

10.5   Problem Solving Applied: Iterated Prisoner's Dilemma

The iterated prisoner's dilemma (IPD) is a popular game from game theory. The traditional form of the prisoner's dilemma game has two players. Each player must choose between one of two possible *moves:* defect or cooperate. The combination of your *move* and your opponent's *move* determines some form of payoff, usually represented as a score.

The name "prisoner's dilemma" is derived from the following situation: Two prisoners are serving time for a minor offense. However, both are suspected of having committed a far more serious crime. The police approach each prisoner, privately, with the same deal. Each is given the choice between

1. implicating the other prisoner (i.e., defect, relative to the other prisoner) and thereby getting paroled

2. not implicating the other prisoner (i.e., cooperate, relative to the other prisoner) and thereby continuing to serve time for the minor offense.

In this example, each suspect has only one move and one payoff. If both cooperate, each continues to serve their remaining time in prison. If both defect, each gets paroled; however, each is then convicted of the more serious crime and must serve a new, longer jail sentence. If one defects and the other cooperates, the defector goes free, and the cooperator spends a lot of time behind bars. What would you do in this situation? What do you hope your fellow prisoner does? How will you behave towards your fellow prisoner in the future if he or she implicates you in the crime? This situation is the basis for interesting research in many areas, including political science, biology, and economics.

In the implementation of the IPD game, you will have repeated interactions with your opponent, rather than just one, thus the name *iterated* prisoners dilemma. Your first move in the game, cooperate or defect, will be decided with no knowledge of how your opponent will move. However, on all subsequent moves you can decide whether to cooperate or defect based on your opponent's last move. This is when the strategy becomes interesting.

You will be competing with your opponent, and you will also be competing with other players who will be playing against you and your opponents. The goal of the game is to accumulate the maximum number of points in a given number of moves. The payoff table for the prisoner's dilemma is as follows:

IPD Payoff Table

	cooperate	defect
cooperate	3,3	0,5
defect	5,0	1,1

If you look at the table carefully, you will notice that the highest payoff occurs when your opponent cooperates and you defect. However, if both players cooperate, each player will receive a higher payoff than if both had defected.

If the game consisted of only one move, then you could argue that it is rational to defect on the first move to give yourself the best chance of winning the game, since you will not encounter your opponent again. However, since you will encounter your opponent multiple times, and your opponent will know your behavior, you may have a better chance of accumulating points if you attempt to form a cooperative relationship with your opponent. Developing a cooperative strategy, while protecting oneself from defectors, is what makes this game an interesting behavior model, and a challenging programming assignment. The Web is a good source for information on the IPD. Good strategies incorporate AI algorithms that attempt to learn their opponents strategy and optimize their own. One very simple and effective strategy is called "tit for tat." With this strategy, your next move is always your opponents last move. "Tit for Tat" is one of the strategies we will develop.

To implement the iterated prisoner's dilemma game in C++, we will define a player class to be used as the base class. The virtual member functions of the player class will define the play of the game. However, the actual moves of the individual players will be defined by classes derived from the player class. The derived classes will override the functions defined in the player class. The definition of the base *player* class is

```
/*------------------------------------------------------------*/
/* The Player class declaration.                          */
/* File Player.h                                          */

#ifndef PLAYER_H
#define PLAYER_H
#include <iostream>
class Player
{
public:
// Constructor
  Player();
```

```cpp
// Accessor Function
  virtual int get_score() const;

// Print player's name.
  virtual void print_name();

// Print name of the player's algorithm.
  virtual void print_algorithm();

// Player's first move.
  virtual bool play();

// Player's subsequent moves.
  virtual bool play(bool opponents_last_play);

// Cumulative score.
  virtual void accumulate(int);
protected:
int score;
};
#endif
/*-------------------------------------------------------------*/
/*-------------------------------------------------------------*/
/*                                                             */
/* The Player class implementation.                            */
/* This implements the always cooperate strategy.              */
/* File Player.cpp                                             */

#include "Player.h"

// Constructor
  Player::Player() : score(0)
  {
  }

// Accessor function
  int Player::get_score() const
  {
      return score;
  }

// Print player's name.
  void Player::print_name()
  {
   cout << "Base Class Player";
  }

// Print name of the player's algorithm.
  void Player::print_algorithm()
```

```
    {
     cout << "Always Cooperate\n";
    }

// Implement player's first move.
    bool Player::play()
    {
     return true;
    }

// Implements player's subsequent moves.
    bool Player::play(bool opponents_last_play)
    {
     return true;
    }

// Keep a cumulative score.
    void Player::accumulate(int s)
    {
        score+=s;
    }
```

1. PROBLEM STATEMENT

Write a program to implement the iterated prisoner's dilemma for two players. Using the *player* class as a base class, derive a new class that implements the "Tit for Tat" strategy. Play this strategy against the default strategy of the player class.

2. INPUT/OUTPUT DESCRIPTION

The input to this program is the number of iterations in a game. The output is the total score of each player and the winner of the game.

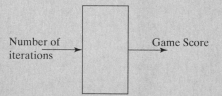

Number of iterations → [ ] → Game Score

3. HAND EXAMPLE

If both players cooperate at each play and the game runs for 10 iterations, the score for each player will be 30. The program will output the following results:

```
Player1 and Player 2 tied at 30 points each.
```

4. ALGORITHM DEVELOPMENT

We first develop the decomposition outline to break the problem into a sequence of steps:

Decomposition Outline

(1) Define a player object for each player, and setup the game.

(2) Input the number of iterations.

(3) Player1 first move

(4) Player2 first move

(5) Determine payoff

(6) Additional moves and payoffs for the specified number of iteration.

(7) Report the score.

Step 1 requires that each player develop a strategy for playing the game and define a `class`, derived from the base *player* `class`, to implement their strategy. Objects of each player `class` are then defined, and the game reports on the players. We will write a function to set up the game. Steps 2–6 form the heart of the game. We will write a function to perform these steps for the desired number of iterations. We will also write a function to determine the payoff of each move. This function will be used in steps 5 and 6. Step 7 reports the final scores. This will also be done in a function. We will now develop the refinement in pseudo code:

Refinement in Pseudocode

```
main():
    setup(player*, player*)
    play_game(player1* ,player2*)
    report(player1*, player2*)
end main
play_game(player* player1, player* player2):
    input number of iterations.
    p1move = player1->play()
    p2move = player2->play()
    player1->accumulate(payoff(p1move, p2move))
    player2->accumulate(payoff(p2move, p1move))
    for(count =1, count < iterations, count++)
        p1save = p1move
        p1move = player1->play(p2move)
        p2move = player2->play(p1save)
        player1->accumulate(payoff(p1move, p2move))
        player2->accumulate(payoff(p2move, p1move))
end play_game
payoff(p1move, p2move):
    if(p1move)
        if(p2move)
            return 3
```

```
            else
                return 0
        else
            if(p2move)
                return 5
            else
                return 1
end payoff
report(player* player1, player* player2):
    if(player1->score > player2->score)
        output player 1 wins
    elseif(player1->score < player2->score)
        output player 2 wins
    else
        output tie
end report
```

Our `main` function calls three functions to implement the game. Each functions has formal parameters of type *player**. Since the *player* `class` uses the keyword `virtual` in its class declaration, the dynamic objects referenced by the formal parameters in the functions will call the overriding functions defined by the dynamic data type of the object, and the game will function properly for multiple players. We are now ready to convert the pseudocode to C++ code:

```cpp
#include <iostream>
using namespace std;

#include "player.h"      //base class player
#include "TitforTat.h"   //TitforTat player

//Function prototypes
void setup(player*, player*);
void play_game(player*, player*);
void report(player*, player*);
int payoff(bool move, bool opponent_move);

int main()
{
// Declare objects.
    player p1;
    TitforTat p2;
    player* ptr1 = &p1;
    player* ptr2 = &p2;

// Notify players.
    setup(ptr1, ptr2);
    play_game(ptr1, ptr2);
    cout << endl;
```

```cpp
      report(ptr1, ptr2);

      return 0;
}
void setup(player* p1, player* p2)
{
   // Announce players.
   p1->print_name();
   cout << " is playing ";
   p1->print_algorithm();
   cout << endl;
   p2->print_name();
   cout << " is playing ";
   p2->print_algorithm();
   cout << endl;
}
int payoff(bool move, bool opponent_move)
{
   if (move)
   {
      if (opponent_move)
      {
         return 3; // Both cooperate.
      }
      else
      {
         return 0; // I cooperate, opponent defects.
      }
   }
   else
   {
      if (opponent_move)
      {
         return 5; // I defect, opponent cooperates.
      }
      else
      {
         return 1; // Both defect.
      }
   }
}
   /* Play a single game of the iterated
    * prisoner's dilemma between two players.
    */
void play_game(player* p1, player* p2)
{
// Declare objects.
   int max_iterations;
   bool p1_move, p2_move, old_p1_move;
```

```
        cout << "Enter the number of iterations for the game: ";
        cin >> max_iterations;

        p1_move = p1->play();  // get the first move.
        p2_move = p2->play();  // get the first move.
        for(int i=1; i<max_iterations; i++)
        {
            old_p1_move = p1_move;
            p1_move = p1->play(p2_move);          // get the next move
            p2_move = p2->play(old_p1_move);  // get the next move

            // Update the scores for this round of play.
            p1->accumulate(payoff(p1_move, p2_move));
            p2->accumulate(payoff(p2_move, p1_move));
        }
}
void report(player *p1, player *p2)
{
  if (p1->get_score() > p2->get_score())  // Player 1 won.
  {
    p1->print_name();
    cout << " (" << p1->get_score() << ") beat ";
    p2->print_name();
    cout << " (" << p2->get_score() << ").\n";
  }
  else if (p2->get_score() > p1->get_score()) // Player 2 won.
  {
    p2->print_name();
    cout << " (" << p2->get_score() << ") beat ";
    p1->print_name();
    cout << " (" << p1->get_score() << ").\n";
  }
  else // The players tied.
  {
    p1->print_name();
    cout << " and ";
    p2->print_name();
    cout << " tied at " << p1->get_score() << " each.\n";
  }
}
```

The class TitforTat is derived from the *player* class. The complete definition of the
TitforTat class is

```
#ifndef TITFORTAT_H
#define TITFORTAT_H

#include "player.h"
/*---------------------------------------------------------------*/
/*                                                               */
```

```cpp
/* This implements the Tit for Tat strategy.              */
/* filename TitforTat.h                                    */
class TitforTat : public Player
{
public:

// Print player's name.
  void print_name();

// Print name of the player's algorithm.
  void print_algorithm();

// Implement player's first move.
  bool play();

// Implements player's subsequent moves.
  bool play(bool opponents_last_play);

};
#endif

/* This implements the Tit for Tat strategy with initial defect. */
#include <iostream>
using namespace std;

#include "TitforTat.h"

  void TitforTat::print_name()
  {
    cout << "Jeanine ";
  }

// Print name of the player's algorithm.
  void TitforTat::print_algorithm()
  {
    cout << "Tit for Tat";
  }

// Implement player's first move.
  bool TitforTat::play()
  {
    return false;
  }

// Implements player's subsequent moves.
  bool TitforTat::play(bool opponents_last_play)
  {
    return opponents_last_play;
  }
```

5. TESTING

A sample run of the program is as follows, with Jeanine playing the base class player:

```
Base Class Player is playing Always Cooperate.

Jeanine is playing Tit for Tat.

Enter the number of iterations for the game: 10

Jeanine (32) beat Base Class Player (27).
```

The difference in the score is the result of the first move, when player Jeanine defected and Base Class Player cooperated. On the remaining plays, both players cooperated.

Modify!

Define a player class, derived from the base class, to implement an always-defect algorithm.

1. Run program **chapter10_2** playing always defect against always cooperate. What are the results after 25 iterations.

2. Run program **chapter10_2** playing always defect against tit for tat. What are the results after 25 iterations.

3. Remove the keyword `virtual` from the player `class` declaration. Run program chapter10_2. What is the output?

SUMMARY

In C++ the `class` mechanism supports object-based programming. Classes are used to define new abstract data types, and overloading of operators allows these new data types to provide definitions for the existing, built in operators. Friend functions and overloading of operators provides for easy, convenient use of these new data types. The use of inheritance and `virtual` functions form the basis for object-oriented design of large programs. The utilization of these advanced topics are illustrated with the development of a *pixel* `class` and the development of two new classes derived from the *rectangle* `class`. The power of inheritance and `virtual` functions is demonstrated in a program to implement the iterated prisoner's dilemma.

Key Terms

base `class`	overloading operators
derived class	pixel
dynamic data type	`protected`
`friend` function	public inheritance
image processing	`static` data type
inheritance	`virtual` function
iterated prisoner's dilemma	

C++ Statement Summary

Prototype for member function of overloaded + operator:

return data type operator +(*data type*);

Example:

```
Pixel operator +(Pixel) const;
```

Prototype for `friend` function of overloaded + operator:

`friend` *return data type* operator +(*data type, data type*);

Example:

```
friend Pixel operator +(Pixel, Pixel);
```

Prototype for `friend` function of overloaded ≪ operator:

friend ostream& operator ≪(ostream&, data type);

Example:

```
friend ostream& operator <<(ostream&, Pixel);
```

Prototype for `friend` function of overloaded ≫ operator:

friend istream& operator ≫(istream&, data type&);

Example:

```
friend istream& operator >>(istream&, Pixel&);
```

Class definition for public inheritance

`class` *classname* : `public` *base class name*

Example:

```
class square : public rectangle
{
public:
...
protected:
...
};
```

Specification of virtual functions

Prototype: `virtual` *return data type function name* (*parameter list*);

Example:

```
virtual void print(ostream&);
```

Style **Notes**

1. Use constructors and member functions of the base class to assign values to inherited data members.

Debugging Notes

1. Function to overload ≪ operator must return an ostream reference.
2. Function to overload ≫ operator must return an istream reference.
3. Derived class must include a set of constructor functions.
4. Derived classes do not inherit constructor functions from their base class.

Problems

Exam Practice!

True or False
Indicate whether each of the following is true (T) or false (F).

1. A derived class inherits the constructor functions of the base class.
2. Overloaded functions must have unique function signatures.
3. The function signature of an overridden function must be unique.
4. A `virtual` function is called based on the dynamic data type of the calling object?
5. A `friend` function of a class has access to all of the public, protected, and private members of the class.

Multiple Choice

6. Assume that the following function prototype is provided in the declaration of a class named Myclass:

```
friend void input(istream&, Myclass&);
```

Which of the following is a valid function header for this prototype?
1. friend void input(istream& in, Myclass C)
2. friend void Myclass::input(istream& in, Myclass C)
3. Myclass::input(istream& in, Myclass C)
4. void input(istream& in, Myclass)
5. Myclass::friend input(istream& in)

7. Assume that the following function prototype is provided in the declaration of a class named Myclass:

```
virtual void input(istream&);
```

Which of the following is a valid function header for this prototype?
1. virtual void input(istream& in)
2. virtual void Myclass::input(istream& in)
3. void Myclass::input(istream& in)

4. void input(istream& in)

5. void Myclass::virtual input(istream& in)

Jaime Browne, an undergraduate student in computer science at the University of New Mexico, maintains a Web page that illustrates many creative modifications of digital images that he has programmed using the pixel class developed in this chapter.

8. Visit Jaime's Web page at http://www.cs.unm.edu/~thorax, download an image, and implement the function to dither an image.

9. Visit Jaime's Web page at http://www.cs.unm.edu/~thorax, download an image, and implement the function to fade an image.

10. Download an image from the Web and implement a function to perform your own creative modification.

11. Define a rational number class. A rational number is a number composed of two integers with division indicated, as in 1/2, 2/3, 4/5. A rational number is defined using two integer objects; numerator and denominator. Overload the $\ll$ and $\gg$ operators and arithmetic operators to perform the following operations:

```
a/b + c/d = (a*d + b*c) / (b*d) (addition)
a/b - c/d = (a*d - b*c) / (b*d) (subtraction)
(a/b) * (c/d) = (a*c)/(b*d) (multiplication)
(a/b) / (c/d) = (a*d) /(c*b) (division)
```

12. The game of WAR is a simple card game for two players. Each player receives a deck of 52 cards. Each deck is shuffled and placed face down in front of the player. Play then proceeds as a series of rounds. During each round, both players draw the top card from their deck and place it face up. The player with the highest-ranking card wins both cards. If the two cards have the same rank, there is WAR. In the case of WAR, both players draw six cards from their deck and place them face down. A seventh card is drawn and turned face up. The player with the highest-ranking card wins all the cards that have been played. If the two cards have the same rank, there is WAR. The traditional game ends when one player runs out of cards, but you may wish to simplify the game by ending the game when all 52 cards have been played once. The player with the most cards at the end then wins the game. Write a program to simulate the game of WAR. Define and implement a Card class and a Player class. You may find the following class declarations useful:

```
class Card
{
public:
Card(); //default constructor
Card(char, int); //constructor
char evaluate_suit(); //accessor function
int evaluate_rank(); //accessor function
void display_card(); //display the rank and suit
protected:
char suit;
int rank;
};
```

```
class Player
{
public:
        Player();              //default constructor
        void Shuffle_Deck();   //shuffles a player's deck
        Card Draw();           //returns the top card from a
                               //player's deck
        void Add_Points(int n); //adds n points to a player's
                               //score
        int Display_Score();   //displays a player's score
        int Deck_Empty();      //returns a value of 1 if
                               //player's deck is empty.
private:
        Card mydeck[52];
        int score;
        int next_card;
};
```

13. Write a simulation for a high-tech vending machine. After an initial state is established for the machine (i.e., the items for sale, their costs, and the initial inventory counts), the user can have an interactive dialog with the simulation. In this dialog, the user can view the current state of the machine, deposit money (cents) into the machine, purchase an item in the machine, get the item and any change due in return, and execute a coin return function to get back all deposited money. For simplicity, assume that the vending machine has exactly nine types of item for sale. An item can be defined using three objects:

string, represent the name of the item
The cost (in cents) of the item
The quantity of the item initially available for sale

The following data can be used to establish the initial state of the machine:

Tortilla_Chips 60 3
Pretzels 60 10
Popcorn 60 5
Cheese_Crackers 40 2
Creme_Cookies 65 1
Mint_Gum 25 5
Chocolate_Bar 55 3
Licorice 85 9
Fruit_Chews 55 7

Conceptually, the items can be organized as a 3-by-3 matrix as follows:

```
A1   A2   A3
B1   B2   B3
C1   C2   C3
```

Define two classes, an item class and a machine class to implement this simulation.

14. Modify the program chapter10_2 to allow more than two players to play IPD. This can be considered an IPD tournament, where every player plays every other player in an IPD game. In this case you may want your strategy to vary from opponent to opponent. The winner is the player who accumulates the most points during the tournament.

15. Modify the IPD tournament program to allow players to meet each other more than once during a tournament. In this game you can improve your strategy by "remembering" your opponents strategy for the next time you meet.

APPENDIX A ■ C++ Standard Library

This appendix presents a short discussion on the information defined in a few of the many header files in the Standard C++ Library. These brief discussions are not intended to provide all the details necessary to use the functions, but to provide enough information so that you can determine whether the functions may be of use in a particular application; you can then obtain more details from the Web. A good Web resource is http://www.cplusplus.com/ref/.

`<cassert>`

The header file `<cassert>` provides a definition of the assert function that can be used to provide diagnostic information when testing a program. This system-dependent diagnostic information is stored in the standard error file, which can be accessed after a program is completed.

`<cctype>`

The header file `<cctype>` defines several functions for testing and converting characters. The function prototype statements and corresponding discussions use the following definitions:

digit	one of the characters 0123456789
hexadecimal digit	a digit or one of the characters ABCDEFabcdef
uppercase letter	one of the characters ABCDEFGHIJKLMNOPQRSTUVWXYZ
lowercase letter	one of the characters abcdefghijklmnopqrstuvwxyz
alphabetic character	an uppercase or a lowercase letter
alphanumeric character	a digit or an alphabetic character
punctuation character	one of the characters ! "#%&'();<=>?[\]*+,-./:^
graph character	an alphanumeric character or a punctuation character
print character	a graph character or the space character
motion control character	one of the control characters form feed (FF), new line (NL), carriage return (CR), horizontal tab (HT), vertical tab (VT)
whitespace	the space character or one of the motion control characters
control character	one of the motion control characters or bell (BEL) or backspace (BS)

We now list each function prototype and give a brief definition for the corresponding function:

```
int  isalnum(int c);
```
returns a nonzero (true) value if and only if the input character is a digit or an uppercase or lowercase letter
```
int  isalpha(int c);
```
returns a nonzero (true) value if and only if the input character is an uppercase or lowercase letter

```
int   iscntrl(int c);
```
returns a nonzero (true) value if and only if the input character is one of the control characters
```
int   isdigit(int c);
```
returns a nonzero (true) value if and only if the input character is a digit
```
int   isgraph(int c);
```
returns a nonzero (true) value if and only if the input character is a graph character
```
int   islower(int c);
```
returns a nonzero (true) value if and only if the input character is a lowercase letter
```
int   isprint(int c);
```
returns a nonzero (true) value if and only if the input character is a printing character
```
int   ispunct(int c);
```
returns a nonzero (true) value if and only if the input character is a punctuation character
```
int   isspace(int c);
```
returns a nonzero (true) value if and only if the input character is a whitespace character
```
int   isupper(int c);
```
returns a nonzero (true) value if and only if the input character is an uppercase character
```
int   isxdigit(int c);
```
returns a nonzero (true) value if and only if the input character is a hexadecimal character
```
int   tolower(int c);
```
converts an uppercase letter to a lowercase letter
```
int   toupper(int c);
```
converts a lowercase letter to an uppercase letter

⟨climits⟩

The header file ⟨climits⟩ provides several macros that give various limits and characteristics for integer values. These macros and their definitions are as follows:

```
int   CHAR_BIT;
```
number of bits for the smallest nonbit value
```
int   CHAR_MIN;
int   CHAR_MAX;
```
minimum and maximum values for type char
```
int   INT_MIN;
int   INT_MAX;
```
minimum and maximum values for type int
```
int   LONG_MIN;
int   LONG_MAX;
```
minimum and maximum values for type long int

```
int   MB_LEN_MAX;
      maximum number of bytes in a multibyte character
int   SCHAR_MIN;
int   SCHAR_MAX;
      minimum and maximum values for type signed char
int   SHRT_MIN;
int   SHRT_MAX;
      minimum and maximum values for type short int
int   UCHAR_MAX;
      maximum values for type unsigned char
int   UINT_MAX;
      maximum value for type unsigned int
int   ULONG_MAX;
      maximum value for type unsigned long int
int   USHRT_MAX;
      maximum value for type unsigned short int
```

<cmath>

The header file <cmath> defines many useful functions for scientific programming.

```
double   acos(double x);
         computes the arccosine or inverse cosine of x, where x must be in the range
         [−1, 1]; returns an angle in radians in the range [0, π]
double   asin(double x);
         computes the arcsine or inverse sine of x, where x must be in the range
         [−1, 1], returns an angle in radians in the range [ −π/2 , π/2 ]
double   atan(double x);
         computes the arctangent or inverse tangent of x; returns an angle in radians
         in the range [ −π/2 , π/2 ]
double   atan2(double y, double x);
         computes the arctangent or inverse tangent of the value y/x returns an angle in
         radians in the range [−π, π]
   int   ceil(double x);
         rounds x to the nearest integer towards ∞ (infinity)
double   cos(double x);
         computes the cosine of x, where x is in radians
double   cosh(double x);
         computes the hyperbolic cosine of x, which is equal to (e^x+e^{−x})/2
double   exp(double x);
         computes the value of e^x, where e is the base for natural logarithms, or ap-
         proximately 2.718282
double   fabs(double x);
         computes the absolute value of x
   int   floor(double x);
         rounds x to the nearest integer towards −∞ (negative infinity)
```

```
double   log(double x);
```
computes ln x, the natural logarithm of x to the base e; errors occur if $x \leq 0$
```
double   log10(double x);
```
computes $\log_{10}x$, the common logarithm of x to the base 10; errors occur if $x \leq 0$
```
double   pow(double x, double y);
```
computes the value of x to the y power, or x^y; errors occur if $x = 0$ and $y \leq 0$, or if $x < 0$ and y is not an integer
```
double   sin(double x);
```
computes the sine of x, where x is in radians
```
double   sinh(double x);
```
computes the hyperbolic sine of x, which is equal to $\frac{e^x - e^{-x}}{2}$
```
double   sqrt(double x);
```
computes the square root of x where $x \geq 0$
```
double   tan(double x);
```
computes the tangent of x, where x is in radians
```
double   tanh(double x);
```
computes the hyperbolic tangent of x, which is equal to $\frac{\sinh x}{\cosh x}$

```
<cstdlib>
```

The header file `<cstdlib>` defines types, macros, and functions that did not fit in any of the other header files. The types `div_t` and `ldiv_t` are structures for storing a quotient and a remainder. The macros are the following:

```
NULL
```
an integer value of binary zero
```
EXIT_FAILURE
EXIT_SUCCESS
```
integral expressions used to return unsuccessful or successful termination status, respectively, to the host
```
RAND_MAX
```
an integral expression that is the maximum value returned by the RAND function
```
MB_CUR_MAX
```
a positive integer expression whose value is the maximum number of bytes in a multibyte character

The functions that are most likely to be used in engineering application are as follows, with the function prototype statement and a brief description:

```
void   abort(void);
```
causes an abnormal program termination of the program
```
int   abs(int k);
long int   labs(long int k);
```
computes the absolute value of the integer k
```
int   atexit(void (*func)(void));
```
registers the function pointed to by func to be called without arguments at normal program termination

```
   double   atof(const char *s);
      int   atoi(const char *s);
 long int   atol(const char *s);
   double   strtod(const char *s, char **endptr);
 long int   strtol(const char *s, char **endptr, int base);
 unsigned
 long int   strtoul(const char *s, char **endptr, int base);
```
converts the initial portion of the string pointed to by s to a numerical representation

```
     void   *bsearch(const void *key, const void *base, size_t n,
                        size_t
    size,   int(*compar)(const void *,const void *));
```
searches an array of n objects searching for the value pointed to by key

```
     void   *calloc(size_t n, size_t size);
```
allocates space for an array of n objects, each of size size

```
    div_t   div(int numer, int denom);
   ldiv_t   ldiv(long int numer, long int denom);
```
computes the quotient and remainder of the division of numer by denom

```
     void   exit(int status);
```
causes normal program termination to occur

```
     void   free(void *ptr);
```
deallocates the space pointed to by ptr

```
     void   *malloc(size_t size);
```
allocates space for an object of size size

```
     void   qsort(void *base, size_t nmemb, size_t size,
                       int (*compar)(const void*, const void *));
```
sorts an object of n objects into ascending order

```
      int   rand(void);
```
returns a pseudorandom integer in the range of 0 to RAND_MAX

```
     void   *realloc(void *ptr, size_t size);
```
changes the size of the object pointed to by ptr

```
     void   srand(unsigned int seed);
```
uses the seed to initialize a new sequence of values from the RAND function

<cstring>

The header file <cstring> defines the type size_t, which is an unsigned integer, and the macro NULL, which has the value of binary zero. In addition, the header file defines a number of functions for handling strings.

```
     void   *memchr(const void *s, int c, size_t n);
```
returns a pointer to the first occurrence of c in the initial n characters of the object pointed to by s

```
      int   memcmp(const void *s, const void *t, size_t n);
```
returns an integer greater than, equal to, or less than zero, accordingly, as the string pointed to by s is greater than, equal to, or less than the string pointed to by t

```
void    *memcpy(void *s, const void *t, size_t n);
```
copies n characters from the object pointed to by t into the object pointed to by s

```
void    *memmove(void *s, const void *t, size_t n);
```
copies n characters from the object pointed to by t into the object pointed to by s, using a temporary area

```
void    *memset(void *s, int c, size_t n);
```
copies the value of c into the first n characters of the object pointed to by s

```
char    *strcat(char *s, const char *t);
```
concatenates string pointed to by t to the end of string pointed to by s; returns a pointer to string pointed to by s

```
char    *strchr(const char *s, int c);
```
returns a pointer to the first occurrence of the character c in the string pointed to by s

```
int     strcmp(const char *s, const char *t);
```
compares string s to string t in an element-by-element comparison; returns an integer greater than, equal to, or less than zero, depending on whether the string pointed to by s is greater than, equal to, or less than, respectively, the string pointed to by t

```
int     strcoll(const char *s, const char *t);
```
returns an integer greater than, equal to, or less than zero, depending on whether the string pointed to by s is greater than, equal to, or less than, respectively, the string pointed to by t

```
char    *strcpy(char *s, const char *t);
```
copies string pointed to by t to string pointed to by s; returns a pointer to string pointed to by s

```
size_t  strcspn(const char *s, const char *t);
```
returns the length of the initial segment of the string pointed to by s that consists entirely of characters not in the string pointed to by t

```
size_t  strlen(const char *s);
```
returns the length of the string pointed to by s

```
char    *strncat(char *s, const char *t, size_t n);
```
concatenates at most n characters of string t to string s; returns a pointer to string pointed to by s

```
int     strncmp(const char *s, const char *t, size_t n);
```
compares at most n characters of string s to string t in an element-by-element comparison; returns an integer greater than, equal to, or less than zero, depending on whether the string pointed to by s is greater than, equal to, or less than, respectively, the string pointed to by t

```
char    *strncpy(char *s, const char *t, size_t n);
```
copies at most n characters from string pointed to by t to string pointed to by s; if t has fewer characters than s, then s is padded with null characters; returns a pointer to s

```
char    *strpbrk(const char *s, const char *t);
```
returns a pointer to the first occurrence in string pointed to by s of any character of string pointed to by t

```
char    *strrchr(const char *s, int c);
```
returns a pointer to the last occurrence of the character c in the string pointed to by s
```
size_t  strspn(const char *s, const char *t);
```
returns the length of the initial segment of the string pointed to by s that consists entirely of characters in the string pointed to by t
```
char    *strstr(const char *s, const char *t);
```
returns a pointer to the start of the string pointed to by t within the string pointed to by s

\<ctime\>

The header file \<ctime\> defines two macros, four types, and several functions for representing and manipulating calendar time and local time. The types clock_t and time_t are arithmetic types capable of representing times, and the structure tm contains a calendar time broken into seconds (tm_sec), minutes (tm_min), hours (tm_hour), day of the month (tm_mday), months since January (tm_mon), years since 1900 (tm_year), days since Sunday (tm_wday), days since January 1 (tm_yday), and a daylight saving time flag (tm_isdst); the order of the values in the structure is system dependent. The related macros are the following:

```
CLOCKS_PER_SEC
```
number per second of the value returned by the clock function
```
NULL
```
an integer representing binary zero

Function prototypes and brief descriptions of their related computations follow:

```
char    *asctime(const struct tm *timeptr);
```
returns a pointer to the string containing a converted time
```
clock_t clock(void);
```
returns the current processor time
```
char    *ctime(const time_t *timer);
```
returns a pointer to a string containing a converted time
```
double  difftime(time_t time1, time_t time0);
```
computes the difference between two calendar times
```
struct  tm *gmtime(const time_t *timer);
```
returns a pointer to a time expressed in Coordinated Universal Time
```
struct  tm *localtime(const time_t *timer);
```
returns a pointer to a time converted from calendar time
```
time_t  mktime(struct tm *timeptr);
```
converts the broken-down time to a calendar time value
```
time_t  time(time_t *timer)
```
returns the current calendar time
```
size_t  strftime(char *s, size_t maxsize, const char
                     *format, const struct tm *timeptr);
```
converts time into a formatted multibyte character sequence

`<iostream>`

The header `<iostream>` contains many functions used for standard input and output. We now list a few of them in their most general form:

`istream functions:`

```
istream& operator >>
```
Input (extraction) operation
```
int gcount();
```
Returns the number of characters extracted by last input operation
```
int get(char ch);
```
Extract one character from input stream
```
getline(C_string Var, int Max, [char delimiter]);
```
read Max-1 characters or until delimiter is found. \n is the default delimiter
```
ignore();
```
Extract and discard a character from the input stream
```
char peek();
```
Returns the value of next character on the input stream
Leaves the character on the input stream (does not extract)
```
putback(ch);
```
Put the last character back on the input stream

`ostream functions:`

```
ostream& operator<<
```
Output (insertion) operator
```
flush();
```
Flush output buffer
```
put(ch char);
```
Put char in the output stream

APPENDIX B ■ ASCII Character Codes

The following table contains the 128 ASCII characters and their equivalent integer values and binary values. The characters that correspond to the integers 1 through 31 have special significance to the computer system. For example, the character BEL is represented by the integer 7 and causes the bell to sound on the keyboard.

The order of the characters from low to high is the collating sequence and has several interesting characteristics. Note that the digits are less than uppercase letters and that uppercase letters are less than lowercase letters. Also, note that special characters are not grouped together: Some are before digits, some are after digits, and some are between uppercase and lowercase characters.

Character		Integer Equivalent	Binary Equivalent
NUL	(Binary Zero)	0	0000000
SOH	(Start of Header)	1	0000001
STX	(Start of Text)	2	0000010
ETX	(End of Text)	3	0000011
EOT	(End of Transmission)	4	0000100
ENQ	(Enquiry)	5	0000101
ACK	(Acknowledge)	6	0000110
BEL	(Bell)	7	0000111
BS	(Backspace)	8	0001000
HT	(Horizontal Tab)	9	0001001
LF	(Line Feed or New Line)	10	0001010
VT	(Vertical Tabulation)	11	0001011
FF	(Form Feed)	12	0001100
CR	(Carriage Return)	13	0001101
SO	(Shift Out)	14	0001110
SI	(Shift In)	15	0001111
DLE	(Data Link Escape)	16	0010000
DC1	(Device Control 1)	17	0010001
DC2	(Device Control 2)	18	0010010
DC3	(Device Control 3)	19	0010011
DC4	(Device Control 4-Stop)	20	0010100
NAK	(Negative Acknowledge)	21	0010101
SYN	(Synchronization)	22	0010110
ETB	(End of Text Block)	23	0010111
CAN	(Cancel)	24	0011000
EM	(End of Medium)	25	0011001
SUB	(Substitute)	26	0011010

(continued)

Character		Integer Equivalent	Binary Equivalent
ESC	(Escape)	27	0011011
FS	(File Separator)	28	0011100
GS	(Group Separator)	29	0011101
RS	(Record Separator)	30	0011110
US	(Unit Separator)	31	0011111
SP	(Space)	32	0100000
!		33	0100001
"		34	0100010
#		35	0100011
$		36	0100100
%		37	0100101
&		38	0100110
'	(Closing Single Quote)	39	0100111
(		40	0101000
)		41	0101001
*		42	0101010
+		43	0101011
,	(Comma)	44	0101100
-	(Hyphen)	45	0101101
.	(Period)	46	0101110
/		47	0101111
0		48	0110000
1		49	0110001
2		50	0110010
3		51	0110011
4		52	0110100
5		53	0110101
6		54	0110110
7		55	0110111
8		56	0111000
9		57	0111001
:		58	0111010
;		59	0111011
<		60	0111100
=		61	0111101
>		62	0111110
?		63	0111111
@		64	1000000
A		65	1000001
B		66	1000010
C		67	1000011
D		68	1000100
E		69	1000101
F		70	1000110

(continued)

G		71	1000111
H		72	1001000
I		73	1001001
J		74	1001010
K		75	1001011
L		76	1001100
M		77	1001101
N		78	1001110
O		79	1001111
P		80	1010000
Q		81	1010001
R		82	1010010
S		83	1010011
T		84	1010100
U		85	1010101
V		86	1010110
W		87	1010111
X		88	1011000
Y		89	1011001
Z		90	1011010
[		91	1011011
\		92	1011100
]		93	1011101
^	(Circumflex)	94	1011110
_	(Underscore)	95	1011111
`	(Opening Single Quote)	96	1100000
a		97	1100001
b		98	1100010
c		99	1100011
d		100	1100100
e		101	1100101
f		102	1100110
g		103	1100111
h		104	1101000
i		105	1101001
j		106	1101010
k		107	1101011
l		108	1101100
m		109	1101101
n		110	1101110
o		111	1101111
p		112	1110000
q		113	1110001
r		114	1110010
s		115	1110011

(continued)

Character	Integer Equivalent	Binary Equivalent
t	116	1110100
u	117	1110101
v	118	1110110
w	119	1110111
x	120	1111000
y	121	1111001
z	122	1111010
{	123	1111011
Ω	124	1111100
}	125	1111101
,	126	1111110
DEL (Delete/Rubout)	127	1111111

APPENDIX C ■ Using MATLAB to Plot Data from ASCII Files

To understand engineering problems and engineering solutions to problems, it is important to be able to visualize the numerical information that is involved. Therefore, the ability to easily obtain simple xy-plots from data files is an important capability in solving engineering problems.

In this appendix, we present a simple C++ program that generates a data file, and we then show how to use MATLAB to obtain a plot of the data. We chose MATLAB (MATrix LABoratory) to generate the plots in this appendix and also in the text chapters because it is an extremely powerful software environment for interactive numeric computations, data analysis, and graphics. An extensive discussion on generating different types of plots and on additional options that can be specified within the plots is included in Chapter 7 of *Engineering Problem Solving with MATLAB*, by D. M. Etter, Prentice Hall, 1993.

In the following example, we use a C++ program to generate an ASCII (American Standard Code for Information Interchange) data file, and we then plot the information using MATLAB. An ASCII data file can also be generated using a word processor, and then the same steps can be used to plot the information using MATLAB. If the data file is generated with a word processor, it is important to select the options for saving the file such that it is saved as a text file instead of as a word processor file.

The program that follows generates a data file containing 100 lines of information. Each line contains the corresponding time and function value from the equation for a damped sine function, namely,

$$f(t) = e^{-t} \sin(2\pi t),$$

where $t = 0.0, 0.1, 0.2, \ldots, 9.9$ seconds.

C++ Program to Generate a Data File

```
/*------------------------------------------------------------*/
/*  Program app_c                                          */
/*                                                         */
/*  This program generates a data file of values          */
/*  from a damped sine function.                           */

#include<iostream>
#include <fstream>
#include <cmath>
using namespace std;
const double PI = 3.141593;
```

```cpp
int main()
{
   /*  Define objects.  */
   double t, f;
   ifstream dsine;

   /*  Generate data file.  */
   dsine.open("dsine.dat");
   for (int k=1; k<=100; k++)
   {
      t = 0.1*(k-1);
      f = exp(-t)*sin(2*PI*t);
      dsine << t << f << endl;
   }

   /*  Close data file and exit program. */
   dsine.close();
   return 0;
}
/*-----------------------------------------------------*/
```

ASCII Data File Generated by the C++ Program

The data file generated by this program is an ASCII file that contains two numbers per line. The first few lines of information and the last line of information are

```
0.0  0.000
0.1  0.532
0.2  0.779
...
9.9  0.000
```

Generating a Plot with MATLAB

To generate a plot of this information with MATLAB, we only need two statements. The first statement loads the file into the MATLAB workarea, and the second statement generates the xy-plot:

```
>>load dsine.dat
>>plot(dsine(:,1),dsine(:,2))
```

These steps generate the plot shown in Figure C.1.

Since it is important to label the information in a plot, we could also add the statements to give the plot a title, to label the axes, and to add a background grid:

```
>>load dsine.dat
>>plot(dsine(:,1),dsine(:,2)),
>>title('Damped Sine Function'),
>>xlabel('Time, s'), ylabel('f(t)'), grid
```

The plot with these labels is shown in Figure C.2.

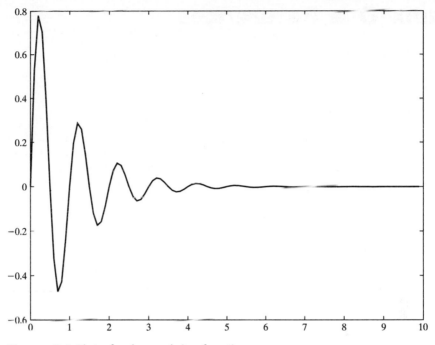

Figure C.1 Plot of a damped sine function.

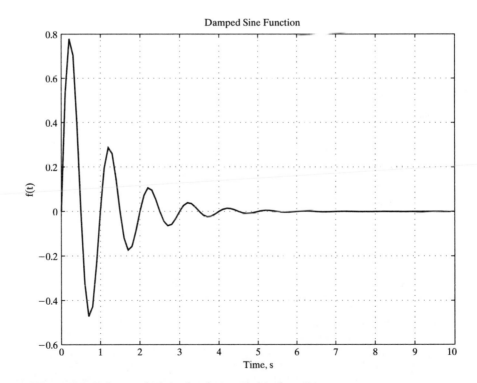

Figure C.2 Enhanced plot of a damped sine function.

APPENDIX D ■ References

[1] "10 Outstanding Achievements, 1964–1989." National Academy of Engineering, Washington, DC, 1989.

[2] Etter, D. M. *Structured FORTRAN 77 for Engineers and Scientists,* 4th ed. Benjamin/Cummings, Redwood City, CA, 1993.

[3] "The Federal High Performance Computing Program." Executive Office of the President, Office of Science and Technology Policy, Washington, DC, September 8, 1989.

[4] Etter, D. M., and J. Bordogna. "Engineering Education for the 21st Century." IEEE International Conference on Acoustics, Speech, and Signal Processing, April 1994.

[5] Fairley, R. *Software Engineering Concepts.* McGraw-Hill, New York, 1985.

[6] Etter, D. M. *Engineering Problem Solving with MATLAB.* Prentice Hall, Englewood Cliffs, NJ, 1993.

[7] Plauger, P. J. *The Standard C Library.* Prentice Hall, Englewood Cliffs, NJ, 1992.

[8] Jones, E. R., and R. L. Childers. *Contemporary College Physics.* Addison-Wesley, Reading, MA, 1990.

[9] Etter, D. M. *FORTRAN 77 with Numerical Methods for Engineers and Scientists.* Benjamin/Cummings, Redwood City, CA, 1992.

[10] Spanier, Jerome and Keith B. Oldham. *An Atlas of Functions.* Hemisphere Publishing Corporation, 1987.

[11] Edwards, Jr., C. H., and D. E. Penney. *Calculus and Analytic Geometry.* 3d ed. Prentice Hall, Englewood Cliffs, NJ, 1990.

[12] Master, G. M. *Introduction to Environmental Engineering and Science.* Prentice Hall, Englewood Cliffs, NJ, 1991.

[13] Gille, J. C., and J. M. Russell, III. "The Limb Infrared Monitor of the Stratosphere; Experiment Description, Performance, and Results," Journal of Geophysical Research, Vol. 89, No. D4, pp. 5125–5140, June 30, 1984.

[14] Roberts, Richard A. *An Introduction to Applied Probability.* Addison-Wesley, Reading, MA, 1992.

[15] Richardson, M. *College Algebra,* 3d ed. Prentice Hall, Englewood Cliffs, NJ, 1966.

[16] Kahaner, D., Cleve Moler, and Stephen Nash. *Numerical Methods and Software.* Prentice Hall, Englewood Cliffs, NJ, 1989.

[17] Rallston Anthony and Edwin D. Reilly, eds. *Encyclopedia of Computer Science,* 3d ed. Van Nostrand Reinhold Publishing Company, New York, NY, 1993.

[18] Kreyszig, E. *Advanced Engineering Mathematics.* John Wiley & Sons, New York, 1979.

[19] Wirth, Niklaus. *Algorithms + Data Structures = Programs.* Prentice Hall, Englewood Cliffs, NJ, 1976.

Solutions

Chapter 2

PRACTICE! PAGE 30

1. valid

2. valid

3. valid

4. valid

5. valid

6. invalid, (special character -)

7. valid

8. invalid, (special character *)

9. valid

10. invalid, (keyword)

11. invalid, (special character #)

12. invalid, (special character $)

13. valid

14. invalid, (keyword)

15. invalid, (special characters (and))

16. valid

17. valid

18. invalid, (special character .)

19. valid

20. valid

21. invalid, (special character /)

PRACTICE! PAGE 31

1. 3.5004×10^1 4 digits

2. 4.2×10^{-4} 1 digit

3. -5.0×10^4 0 digits

4. 3.15723×10^0 5 digits

5. -9.997×10^{-2} 3 digits

6. 1.0000028×10^7 7 digits

7. 0.0000103

8. -105000

9. -3552000

10. 0.000667

11. 0.09

12. -0.022

PRACTICE! PAGE 36

1. const double LightSpeed = 2.99792e08;

2. const double ChargeE = 1.602177e-19;

3. const double N_A = 6.022e23;

4. const double G_mss = 9.8;

5. const double G_ftss = 32;

6. const double EarthMass = 5.98e24;

7. const double MoonRadius = 1.74e6;

8. const char UnitLength = 'm';

9. const char UnitTime = 's';

PRACTICE! PAGE 40

1. 6

2. 4.5

3. 3.1 is computed value, 3 is assigned to integer a

4. 3.0 is computed value

PRACTICE! PAGE 42

```
const double G_mss = 9.80665;
```

1. `distance = x + v*t + a*t*t;`

2. `tension = (2*m1*m2)/(m1 + m2)*G_mss;`

3. `p2 = p1 + (p*v*(a2*a2 - a1*a1))/(2*a1*a1);`

4. $centripetal = \frac{4\pi^2 r}{T^2}$

5. $potential\ energy = \frac{-GM_E m}{r}$

6. $change = GM_E m(\frac{1}{R_E} - \frac{1}{R_E + h})$

PRACTICE! PAGE 46

1. z $\boxed{8}$ x $\boxed{3}$ y $\boxed{4}$

2. z $\boxed{12}$ x $\boxed{3}$ y $\boxed{4}$

3. x $\boxed{6}$ y $\boxed{4}$ z $\boxed{?}$

4. y $\boxed{0}$ x $\boxed{2}$ z $\boxed{?}$

PRACTICE! PAGE 49

1. Output:
   150 12.368

2. Output:
   15012.368

3. Output:
   150
   12

4. Output:
   150
   12.37

5. Output:
   150,12.4

6. Output:
   150,12.368

7. Output:
   150
   12

8. Output:
   ----12.368
   ------150

PRACTICE! PAGE 55

1. 75.92   89.35   111.25   109.92

2. 0.69   1.6   1.71   1.87

3. There are five time values that correspond to 110 degrees, as can be seen from Figure 2.5. These values can be computed to be the following:
1.71   2.84   3.39   4.42   5.33

PRACTICE! PAGE 62

1. -3

2. -2

3. 0.125

4. 3.16

5. 25

6. 11

7. -1

8. 32

PRACTICE! PAGE 63

1. velocity = sqrt(pow(v0,2) + 2*a*(x − x0));

2. length = pow(len − pow(v/c,2),1.0/k);

3. center = (38.1972*(pow(r,3) − pow(s,3))*sin(a))/((pow(r,2) − pow(s,2))*a);

4. $Frequency = \dfrac{1}{\sqrt{2*\pi*\frac{c}{l}}}$

5. $Range = \dfrac{v_0^2}{g} * \sin(2\theta)$

6. $V = \sqrt{\dfrac{2gh}{1+\frac{I}{mr^2}}}$

Chapter 3

PRACTICE! PAGE 88

1. true

2. true

3. true

4. false

5. true

6. true

7. true

8. false

PRACTICE! PAGE 93

1. ```cpp
   if(time > 15.0)
      time++;
   ```

2. ```cpp
   if(sqrt(poly) < 0.5)
      cout << poly;
   ```

3. ```cpp
   if(abs(volt1 - volt2) > 10.0)
      cout << volt1 << ' ' << volt2;
   ```

4. ```cpp
   if(den < 0.05)
   {
      result=0;
   }
   else
   {
      result = num/den;
   }
   ```

5. ```cpp
   if(log(x) >= 3)
   {
      time=0;
      count--;
   }
   ```

6. ```cpp
   if(dist < 50.0 && time > 10.0)
   {
      time+=2;
   }
   else
   {
      time+=2.5;
   }
   ```

7. ```cpp
   if(dist >= 100.0)
   {
      time+=2;
   }
   else if(dist >=50)
   {
      time++;
   }
   else
   {
      time+=0.5;
   }
   ```

PRACTICE! PAGE 96

1. ```cpp
   switch(rank)
   {
      case 1:
      case 2:
   ```

```
          cout << "Lower division" << endl;
          break;
        case 3:
        case 4:
          cout << "Upper division" << endl;
          break;
        case 5:
          cout << "Graduate student" << endl;
          break;
        default:
          cout << "Invalid rank" << endl;
      }
```

PRACTICE! PAGE 102

1. 18

2. 18

3. 17

4. 0

5. infinite loop

6. 15

Chapter 4

PRACTICE! PAGE 142

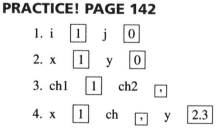

1. i ⬚1 j ⬚0

2. x ⬚1 y ⬚0

3. ch1 ⬚1 ch2 ⬚,

4. x ⬚1 ch ⬚, y ⬚2.3

Chapter 5

PRACTICE! PAGE 171

1. **Formal Parameters**	a	b	c
	25	5	−5
Function Arguments	x	sqrt(x)	x−30
	25	5	−5

2. total = 2

PRACTICE! PAGE 175

1. valid
   before: x ☐1☐   y ☐3☐
   after: x ☐3☐   y ☐1☐

2. invalid: cannot pass constant to reference parameter

3. invalid: cannot pass expression $(y + 5)$ to reference parameter

4. warning: parameter type mismatch, *double* to *int*. Test this on your system.

5. output:
   0
   2

Chapter 6

PRACTICE! PAGE 230

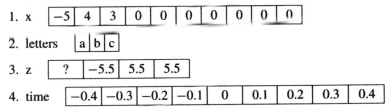

1. x | −5 | 4 | 3 | 0 | 0 | 0 | 0 | 0 | 0 | 0 |

2. letters | a | b | c |

3. z | ? | −5.5 | 5.5 | 5.5 |

4. time | −0.4 | −0.3 | −0.2 | −0.1 | 0 | 0.1 | 0.2 | 0.3 | 0.4 |

PRACTICE! PAGE 233

1. output:
   3 8
   15 21
   30 41

2. output:
   8 30

PRACTICE! PAGE 238

1. 9.8

2. 9.8

3. 3.2

4. 1.5

PRACTICE! PAGE 243

1. 9.0

2. 6.0

3. 5.36

4. 2.32

5. 2.5

6. 5.75

PRACTICE! PAGE 264

1. The Cheese

2. The mice, Cheese

3. The mice, Sniff and Scurry, had only simple brains.

Chapter 7

PRACTICE! PAGE 286

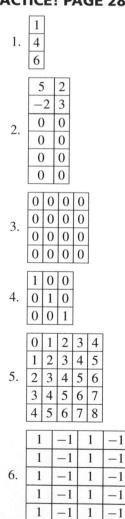

1.

1
4
6

2.

5	2
−2	3
0	0
0	0
0	0
0	0

3.

0	0	0	0
0	0	0	0
0	0	0	0
0	0	0	0

4.

1	0	0
0	1	0
0	0	1

5.

0	1	2	3	4
1	2	3	4	5
2	3	4	5	6
3	4	5	6	7
4	5	6	7	8

6.

1	−1	1	−1	1
1	−1	1	−1	1
1	−1	1	−1	1
1	−1	1	−1	1
1	−1	1	−1	1

PRACTICE! PAGE 289

1. 9

2. 4

3. −6

4. 3

PRACTICE! PAGE 292

1. 13

2. 2

3. 18

4. 22

PRACTICE! PAGE 303

1. −8

2.
5	−1	3
3	−3	2

3.
−5	9
1	−5
−6	6

4.
−2	−2	4
7	−9	10

5.
8	−24	32
−12	20	−24
14	−18	20

PRACTICE! PAGE 310

1. $x = 2, y = 1$

2. $x = 3, y = -1, z = 2$

Chapter 8

PRACTICE! PAGE 330

1. void rectangle::resize(double dw, double dh)

2. class implementation file (rectangle.cpp)

PRACTICE! PAGE 336

1. valid

2. valid

3. invalid (( ) not used with default constructor)

4. invalid (no constructor with two arguments)

5. invalid (input operator not defined for rectangle class)

6. invalid (ouput operator not defined for rectangle class)

7. valid

8. valid

9. invalid (print function is not a value returning function)

10. invalid (print function is not a value returning function)

11. valid

12. invalid (addition operator is not defined for rectangle class)

Chapter 9

PRACTICE! PAGE 364

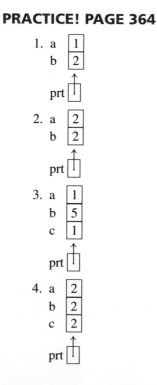

PRACTICE! PAGE 368

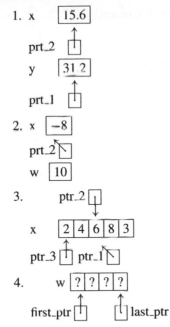

1. x 15.6
   prt_2
   y 31 2
   prt_1

2. x −8
   prt_2
   w 10

3. ptr_2
   x 2 4 6 8 3
   ptr_3 ptr_1

4. w ? ? ? ?
   first_ptr   last_ptr

PRACTICE! PAGE 370

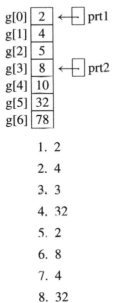

g[0] 2 ← prt1
g[1] 4
g[2] 5
g[3] 8 ← prt2
g[4] 10
g[5] 32
g[6] 78

1. 2
2. 4
3. 3
4. 32
5. 2
6. 8
7. 4
8. 32

PRACTICE! PAGE 377

1. valid
2. not valid (jptr is const)

3. not valid (can't use cptr to modify object)

4. not valid (can't use cptr to modify object)

5. valid

6. valid

PRACTICE! PAGE 388

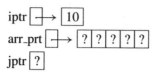

1. 10 10
   two hex address
   two garbage values

2. hex address
   0 1 2 3 4
   hex address plus 20 (assuming 4-byte integers)
   five garbage values (why?)

3. two hex addresses
   0 2
   garbage value
   invalid address
   invalid reference

Chapter 10

PRACTICE! PAGE 417

```
1. pixel pixel::operator/(pixel p1)
   {
     pixel temp;
     temp.red = red/p1.red;
     temp.green = green/p1.green;
     temp.blue = blue/p1.blue;
     return temp;
   }

2. bool pixel::operator==(pixel p1)
   {
     if( red==p1.red &&
         green==p1.green&&
         blue==p1.blue )
       return true;
     return false;
   }
```

PRACTICE! PAGE 418

1.
```
pixel operator*(pixel p1, pixel p2)
{
    pixel temp;
    temp.red = p1.red*p2.red;
    temp.green = p1.green*p2.green;
    temp.blue =p1.blue*p2.blue;
    return temp;
}
```

2.
```
pixel operator/(pixel p1, pixel p2)
{
    pixel temp;
    temp.red = p1.red/p2.red;
    temp.green = p1.green/p2.green;
    temp.blue =p1.blue/p2.blue;
    return temp;
}
```

3.
```
pixel operator-(pixel p1, pixel p2)
{
    pixel temp;
    temp.red = p1.red-p2.red;
    temp.green = p1.green-p2.green;
    temp.blue =p1.blue-p2.blue;
    return temp;
}
```

PRACTICE! PAGE 438

1. Fixed point at: (1,2)
   Width: 4
   Height: 4
   Depth: 4 Fixed point at: (1,2)
   Width: 4
   Height: 4
   Depth: 4

2. Fixed point at: (1,2)
   Width: 4
   Height: 4

3. Fixed point at: (0,0)
   Width: 5
   Height: 5
   Fixed point at: (0,0)
   Width: 5
   Height: 5

Index